Pacific Asia in the Global System

An Introduction

P. W. Preston

BLACKWELL
Publishers

Copyright © P. W. Preston 1998

The right of P. W. Preston to be identified as the author of this work has been asserted in accordance with the Copyright, Designs and Patents Act 1988.

First published 1998

2 4 6 8 10 9 7 5 3 1

Blackwell Publishers Ltd
108 Cowley Road
Oxford OX4 1JF
UK

Blackwell Publishers Inc.
350 Main Street
Malden, Massachusetts 02148
USA

British Library Cataloguing in Publication Data

A CIP catalogue record for this book is available from the British Library.

Library of Congress Cataloging-in-Publication Data

Preston, P. W.
    Pacific Asia in the global system: an introduction/P. W. Preston.
       p. cm.
    Includes bibliographical reference and index.
    ISBN 0–631–20237–4. — 0–631–20238–2
       1. East Asia—Civilization.   2. Asia. Southeastern—Civilization.
    3. East Asia—Social conditions.   4. Asia, Southeastern—Social conditions.
    5. East Asia—Economic conditions.   6. Asia, Southeastern—Social conditions.
    I. Title
    DS509.3.P74   1998
    950.4'29—dc21   97–43338
                                                                              CIP

Printed in Great Britain by T.J. International Limited, Padstow, Cornwall

This book is printed on acid-free paper

Pacific Asia in the Global System

Contents

Contents   v

Preface   vii

Acknowledgements   viii

Part I: The Shift to the Modern World   1

1   Classical Social Theory   3

Part II: The Shift to the Modern World in Pacific Asia   15

2   Analysing the Process of the Shift to the Modern World in
     Pacific Asia   17

3   From Ancient Empires to Nineteenth-century Industrial-
     capitalism   32

4   The Shift to the Modern World: Reactions, Resistance and
     Empire   54

5   After the Pacific War: Decolonization, Nation-building and the
     Cold War   87

6   The Emergence of Pacific Asia   110

Part III: Changing Relationships in Contemporary Pacific Asia   135

7   The Region and the Global System   137

8   Changing Patterns of Relations between Japan, the USA and
     China   154

9 Contemporary Pacific Asia in the 1990s   169

Part IV: The Development Experience of Pacific Asia   **185**

10 The Particularity of the Historical Development Experience of
    Pacific Asia   187

11 The Pacific Asian Model I: Political-economic and Social-
    institutional Processes   199

12 The Pacific Asian Model II: Cultural and Political-cultural
    Processes   224

Part V: Pacific Asia in the New Global System   **249**

13 Pacific Asia in the Twenty-first Century Global System   251

Bibliography   **260**

Index   **267**

Preface

It sometimes seems that one cannot enter a bookshop these days without finding another probably rather alarmingly titled business-economics book dealing with the development of Pacific Asia. The rapid rise and sometimes equally rapid projected decline of the Pacific Asian region has been advertised frequently in the many pages of the books comprising this distinctive genre. Ordinarily one might disregard these texts and move on. However, notwithstanding the fashionable froth of comment it is true that there is something special about the Pacific Asia region.

The rise of the Pacific Asian region within the tripolar global industrial-capitalist system is of extraordinary interest. It is clear that the Pacific Asian region is undergoing extensive change but the logic of these processes, their likely end-point and the implications of these matters for analysts in other parts of the world, are not well understood and remain questions of intense interest for a wide community of enquiry. It is likely that the task of deciphering the interplay of the divergent cultural logics of the three regions of Pacific Asia, North America and the European Union will occupy scholars, policy analysts and political actors for some considerable time.

In preparing this text I was concerned to review the social scientific debates away from the enthusiasms and anxieties of the commentators. The text will consider the historical development experience of the countries and peoples of the region in terms of the intellectual resources of the classical European tradition of social theorizing which has long been concerned with elucidating the dynamics of complex change in the process of the ongoing shift to the modern world. I hope that the book will help those who are new to the study of Pacific Asia and offer a useful overview for those specialists who are more routinely concerned with the details of particular cases.

Acknowledgements

I began work on the essays from which this manuscript developed in the early months of 1994 in the course of visits to the Asia Research Centre at Murdoch University, Australia, the Institute of Southeast Asian Studies, Singapore, and the Department of Anthropology and Sociology of the National University of Malaysia. The material was revised further whilst I was Canon Foundation Research Fellow in the Faculty for Comparative Culture of Sophia University, Japan, and the early drafts of this manuscript were made in the Department of Political Science and International Studies of the University of Birmingham in the United Kingdom. I have benefited enormously from conversations with friends, colleagues and students in these and other institutions in Asia and Europe and I am happy to record my debt to their generous intellectual criticism and to the hospitable ways in which they have made me welcome within their several communities of scholarship.

Part I
The Shift to the Modern World

1

Classical Social Theory

The classical European tradition of social theorizing is concerned with the political economic, social institutional and culture critical analysis of broad patterns of complex change. The origins of this particular intellectual tradition lie in the responses of scholars, political actors and governments in the period of the shift to the modern industrial capitalist world which took place first in Europe over the long period from the sixteenth to the nineteenth century and which was thereafter reproduced in a variety of contexts around the world.

The experience of European theorists has produced a broad body of work which may be turned to the analysis of other regions within the global system. The historical development experience of the countries of Pacific Asia can be analysed in terms of the ways in which particular agent groups have read and reacted to the demands and opportunities presented by changing structural circumstances. In this way it is possible to speak of a variety of 'routes to the modern world' amongst the countries of the area. It is the contemporary pattern of structural forces and associated agent reactions which is grasped in terms of the notion of the Pacific Asian region.

It should be noted, therefore, at the outset, that the text analyses Pacific Asia in an intellectually self-conscious fashion with reference to materials generated within the context of the European experience of the shift to the modern world. This orientation amounts to a sceptical affirmation of the intellectual and ethical core of the received classical European tradition. The formal implications of these remarks are as follows: (i) there are no theoretically innocent social science descriptions because any description of the facts is made on the basis of an elaborate set of intellectual commitments; (ii) the sets of commitments which theorists affirm are very largely received from the culture which they inhabit and are not to be seen as an extensive and freely chosen set of methodological precepts; (iii) the modernist project stands at the core of the classical tradition of social theorizing; and (iv) as a matter of simple report, there are both critics of this project proposing alternate analytical strategies and other forms-of-life carrying their own cultural and intellectual resources.

In this text I will attempt to tell an intellectually self-conscious version of the tale of the shift to the modern world of the countries of Pacific Asia and to note the ways in which they have moved towards the status of an integrated bloc within the global system. I hope that the material will be of interest to all those analysts who are concerned with elucidating the dynamics of complex change and who are working within or with reference to the classical European tradition. It is the tradition which the author inhabits. It is the basis upon which interpretive analyses are made and in turn these are understood to be the basis for dialogic exchanges with scholars and commentators working within or with reference to other traditions.[1]

The theme of the shift to the modern world as it is appears within the classical tradition can be addressed in terms of three aspects: (i) the formal character of the arguments for the shift to the modern world; (ii) the substantive characterizations of the process; and (iii) the character of contemporary debate in respect of the argument strategies and substantive processes at issue in respect of the (ongoing) shift to the modern world.

The Shift to the Modern World as a Formal Element of the Classical Tradition

The classical tradition of social theorizing is concerned with the elucidation of the dynamics of complex change in the shift to the modern world. It is an interpretive, critical and engaged task because the process is indeterminate, open-ended and enfolds those theorists, policy analysts and political agents who undertake to pursue particular courses of action.

Interpreting patterns of historical change

Within the classical tradition there is a long established concern with analysing complex change.[2] The notion of complex change points to those periods when inter-related change takes place in the political economy, social-institutions, and culture of a people. Such periods are often somewhat traumatic as clarity in regard to sequences and endpoints is not readily available to those caught up in the processes. The material of the classical tradition was deployed in order to read changing structural patterns in order to identify ways in which agent groups might progressively respond.

Illuminating the process from the inside

Gellner[3] has addressed the problem of theorizing the modern world by looking at established social scientific work in order to fashion an approach to the problem of complex change. The analysis which he made is highly instructive. He begins by arguing that any society needs a legitimating ideology (which explains what sort of society it is, and why it is legitimate), and notes that in the contemporary world any society must be industrial (or

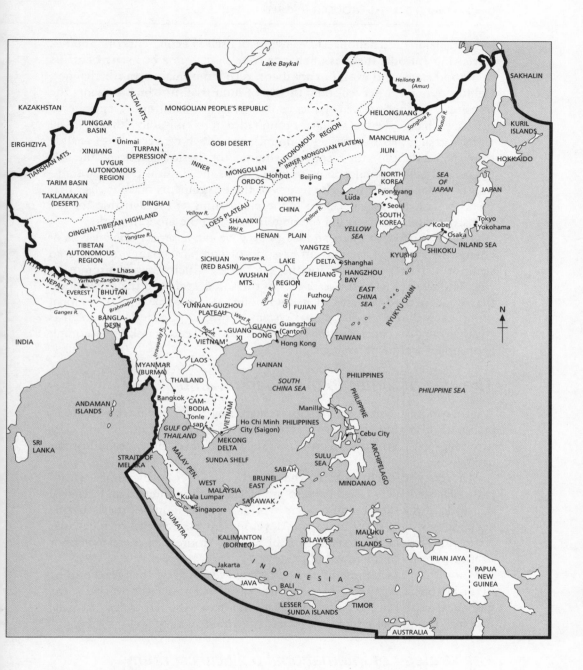

Map 1.1   Pacific Asia region

industrializing) and national (have a sense of itself as a coherent community). Reviewing episodic theories of change (one shift from a bad state of affairs to a good state) and evolutionary theories (of continual pervasive change), Gellner opts for a neo-episodic theory of industrialism which presents the transition to the modern world as one presently continuing episode of pervasive change, where we have a rough idea of its end-point (that is, it will be industrial rather than say agricultural), and which we needs must analyse from the inside using the sceptical techniques of classical sociology (the heir to classical political philosophy, or in my terms the classical European tradition of social theorizing). The results of these arguments make it clear that the core task for social science is the elucidation of the dynamics of the industrial-capitalist system in the ongoing shift to the modern world.

Gellner's approach offers an idea of how we can approach the analysis of change in Pacific Asia: it is an episode of complex change to received structures, patterns of activity and discourses which we can attempt to elucidate by deploying the resources of the social science in the expectation that we have a rough idea of its end point, that is some sort of regional grouping within a tripolar global system. However, Gellner's treatment is clearly formal and his reflections centre on the intellectual task of fashioning appropriate argument strategies.

The idea of routes to the modern world

A rather more substantive strategy is offered by Moore[4] who constructs an elaborate historical sociology centred on the exchanges of shifting class groupings within the overall process of the global development of industrial-capitalism.

Moore's approach looks to the patterns of internal dynamics within particular territories as groups respond to the shifting internal and external demands of the developing modern world. It is the nature of these specific exchanges which determines the development trajectories of particular territories. It is possible to take from the work of Moore the general metaphor of 'routes to the modern world'.

Moore's approach presents an idea of how we can grasp the broad outline of the historical experience of the territories of Pacific Asia: the process of the global expansion of industrial-capitalism has drawn the territories of Pacific Asia into this global system in a variety of particular ways.

The strategy of international political economy

The analytical core of the classical tradition comprises the political-economic analysis of structures, the social-institutional analysis of social forms and the culture-critical elucidation of patterns of meaning. In the nineteenth century these analytical machineries were turned to the analysis of the expansion of industrial-capitalism. It is a rich and subtle tradition which has found recent representation in the work of structural and critical international political economy.

Strange[5] argues that the global system must be thought of as a network of structures of power within which agents (usually states) manoeuvre for position. Strange distinguishes between structural power (which sets the broad agendas within which agents operate), relational power (which focuses on specific exchanges between agents), and bargains (which are the compromises agents make within a given situation).

Strange identifies four key structures of power in the global system: the security structure (which embraces matters relating to the deployment of force, plus attendant bi-lateral and multi-lateral regulatory linkages); the productive structure (which embraces matters relating to the extent to which any country is effective in the production of goods and services); the financial structure (which embraces matters relating to the ability of countries or other organizations to create or obtain credit, the necessary condition of development); and the knowledge structure (which indicates where new ideas and technologies are generated). It is with reference to these four basic power structures that agents manoeuvre as they endeavour to assert their interests in exchanges with other agents.

At the present time the global industrial-capitalist system is becoming both more integrated and tripolar and the strategy of international political economy lets us grasp the ensemble of changes. In the case of Pacific Asia we can posit: (i) the continuing development of the expansionary dynamic of capitalism which is drawing the region ever more deeply into the global industrial-capitalist system – here the business of complex change proceeds at the slow but inexorable pace that it manifests in other parts of the system; (ii) the break/shift within the region from the phase of the post-war pursuit of effective nation statehood within a US-dominated cold war context to the phase of the integration of the region around the core economy of Japan which is expressed in terms of the idea of Pacific Asia – here the business of complex change proceeds more rapidly than in the system as a whole; and (iii) the future of the region in terms of the implied end point of present patterns of complex change seems to be some sort of Pacific Asian region having a distinctive variant of industrial-capitalism.

The Shift to the Modern World as a Substantive Element of the Classical Tradition

The major theorists of the classical tradition, Smith, Marx, Durkheim, Weber and so on, offered a range of analyses which revolved around the exchanges between changing structures and variously powerful agent groups. The substantive tales which they told, their general theories, had different emphases but all revolved around the exchanges of various social groups in the process of the production of material life.

In the case of Europe we can point to a series of broad phases: (i) the rise of mercantile-capitalism in the Renaissance city states of Northern Italy and the Low Countries; (ii) the subsequent slow demise of feudal Europe along with the development of mercantile capitalism in the towns; (iii) the phases of the long drawn out European enlightenment of the seventeenth to nineteenth centuries which culminated in the shift from mercantilism to industrial and democratic patterns of life; (iv) the nineteenth-century development of industrial-capitalism; (v) the twentieth-century development of mass production industrial-capitalism with mass consumption and welfarism. The high point of European industrial-capitalist dominance of the global system was in the years before the Great War.

The industrial-capitalist form of life developed in Europe and has slowly expanded to embrace and remake a series of other cultures. In schematic terms the expansion took this form: (i) by 1550 precious metals traded, or seized; (ii) by 1700 spices and other luxury goods traded; (iii) by 1800 agricultural goods produced for developing industrial capitalist system; and (iv) by 1900 plantation agricultural goods and minerals produced for developing industrial-scientific capitalist system. As the economic concerns of the Europeans shifted and their demands on the territories with which they were engaged deepened, then there was a related political expansion, which roughly took this form: (i) by 1550 there were occasional trade visits; (ii) by 1700 there was routine trading plus local agents (factory); (iii) by 1800 there was extensive trading plus growing political influence; and (iv) by 1900 trade was conducted within the frame of imposed colonial rule. Overall, geographically, the expansion of European industrial-capitalism took this form: (i) 1550-1800 Latin America (Portugal, Spain); (ii) 1550–1800 North America (France, UK); (iii) 1700–1900 Asia (France, Netherlands, UK, Russia, USA); and (iv) 1800–1935 Africa (France, Portugal, Spain, Belgium, UK, Italy).

Overall, the materials of these theorists and the traditions upon which they draw offer a way of analysing the historical experience of Pacific Asia. In this region we have witnessed a series of routes to the modern world and at the present time the region offers a particular model of modernity. However, we should note that these matters are not straightforward and the debate in respect of the nature of the modern world continues within contemporary social theorizing.

The Shift to the Modern World as an Element of Contemporary Social Theory

The nature of the ongoing shift to the modern world is addressed within contemporary social theory and two broad positions can be identified: (i) those who argue for the imminent global triumph of Western-style liberal democratic market systems; and (ii) those who urge that the continuing development of the global industrial-capitalist system is much more problematical and differentiated.

Globalization, the end of history and the emergence of postmodernity

The ideas of globalization, the end of history and postmodernity were presented in the late 1980s. One set of ideas points to a series of changes within the global economy and on this basis argues that the world system has attained an entirely novel pattern where economic life is dominated by transnational productive, trading and financial flows. The related set of ethico-political ideas points to an alleged decline of overt public ideological debate and argues that this evidences the general global acceptance of the claims of liberal democracy. Thereafter the general ideas of postmodernity subsume all particular changes within a postulated shift to a new global consumption centred market-based world of lifestyle choice.

The 1980s have seen an emphatic representation by the celebrants of metropolitan capital of the intellectual machineries of liberalism. The central role within the social world of the marketplace has been reaffirmed. It has been argued that the dynamism of the market system was leading to the rapid absorption of all economic activity within one integrated global system within which an enormous variety of business enterprises were increasingly able to service the needs of their customers free from the interference of the machineries of the nation state. Clearly, this was not simply a change in intellectual fashion but was the ideological counterpart to a sustained reassertion within the Anglo-Saxon metropolitan world of the material interests of capital over and against the concerns of other social groups, which had found partial expression in the social democratic Keynesian regimes of the post-Second World War period, and more broadly, against the interests of other forms-of-life lodged within the global system.

In the same way the explicit celebration of the ethico-political end of history announced by Fukuyama[6] collapses all available political philosophical debate within a manichean frame of liberal democracy versus communism in order to celebrate the victory of the former. The liberal-democratic ethical and institutional pattern is taken to provide for the maximization of individual human liberties within the context of broadly progressive polities. Yet, against these arguments it can be pointed out that both the political ethic of liberal democracy is widely challenged within the West itself and that as a matter of report there are a diversity of extant political cultures which cannot simply be dismissed.

In a more general way the theory of postmodernity details the transformation of industrial capitalism such that the system is now knowledge-based, geared to consumption in the marketplace and global in its reach. The power of the marketplace in the First World is taken to be self-evident whilst the Second and Third Worlds are assimilated to the overall perspective via the notion of emerging markets. The key figure in this work Lyotard[7] who argues that the two great nineteenth-century European metanarratives of progress which were constructed alongside the rise of science-based industrial society, the French-inspired ideas of the Enlightenment and the German-inspired systems of speculative idealism, have undergone a dual process of decline: intellectually they have undermined themselves in shifts towards either state-linked bureaucratic control, or abstract, formalized, and finally empty disciplines of learning (especially philosophy); and in practical terms the political-economic systems in which they operate have become dominated by the pragmatics of the power of technical means, and the ethical points of orientation of the metanarratives are no longer of any great concern. This dual process of decline has allowed the expression of a new political economy and culture where the global political economy of the present is dominated by flows of knowledge or information, produced via a natural science oriented to the production of novelties rather than the old modernist task of the display of a coherent body of truth, and within these flows individuals and groups move within the global consumer marketplace.

One important aspect of the postmodernist material is its insistence that received patterns of social theoretical argument are now in need of radical renewal. In place of the experience of continuous intelligible progress, the experienced world of postmodernity has become one of partial truths and relativistic subjective perspectives. In our ordinary lives we are invited to select from proffered consumer alternatives in order to construct a life-style, and in the realm of social theorising we are similarly enjoined to reject received traditions aspiring to universal knowledge in favour of the local, the partial and the contingent. In the work of the theorists of postmodernity, the concerns of the theorists of the classical tradition with the emancipatory analysis of complex change are now redundant, as the era of the meta-discourses of progress is passed.

In reply, Bauman[8] distinguishes the roles of legislator and interpreter and suggests that the former is the familiar positivistic expression of the classical European tradition (and is unsatisfactory by virtue of its positivistic aspiration to legislate for others) whereas the latter represents a less routinely invoked aspect of social science which looks to the interpretive and critical elucidation of social circumstances; a sceptical restatement of the modernist project.

Overall, it can be argued that it is possible to reply to postmodernists with a reaffirmation of the ethic of the modernist project together with an acknowledgement of the cultural context-dependency of the epistemology of the project. The celebration of reason is particular to our received culture and may be taken to constitute its core. In the social sciences the central task of scholarship is emancipatory critique and around this other modes of engagement can be ranged. In other words our received cultural traditions are particular and diverse, thus legislation must give way to interpretation, critique and dialogue if we are to advance the original modernist project. The universalist impulse of modernity has to be curbed in an acknowledgement of the other. The key epistemic idea becomes dialogue (coupled to interpretation and maybe thereafter involving critique). It is clear that we can accomplish the reworking of the modernist project. Bauman's reaffirmation of the modernist project acknowledges both the criticisms of the postmodernists in respect of the culture-boundedness and contingency of the modernist pattern of life and thought (which it should be noted have been made by many others) and the related claims that the world system has altered to become a global system encompassing diverse cultures (which have also be made by others) by looking to the sceptical, piecemeal and dialogic pursuit of emancipation.

The processes of internationalization and regionalization

In respect of the economic claims of the liberal globalization theorists Hirst and Thompson[9] argue that the recently influential discussion of globalization is mistaken. In its strong form the thesis suggests that economic activity (and thereafter cultural and political actions) is now conducted at the level of an integrated self-sustaining global system. Hirst and Thompson argue that this is simply false and that the occasion for this theorizing (when it was more than simple free-market rhetoric) was the decline of the Bretton Woods system and the recent reconfigurations of the world economy (where there has been some financial globalization and some changes in familiar manufacturing patterns – the influence of MNCs and the rise of East Asia). It is better, argue Hirst and Thompson, to plot the shifts and collapses of the old Bretton Woods system in order to correctly appreciate the extent of the internationalization of hitherto national economic spaces and thereafter to identify accurately the political networks which control these economic flows (and which might better control them when the misleading notion of globalization is set aside). Against the claims of the strong globalization thesis Hirst and Thompson suggest that the world economy is more likely to develop as a series of large trading blocs in Europe, America and Pacific Asia.

In detail, against the theorists of globalization Hirst and Thompson argue that 'The present highly internationalized economy is not unprecedented: it is one of a number of distinct conjunctures or states of the international economy . . . In some respects, the current international economy is less open and integrated than the regime that prevailed from 1870 to 1914'.[10] Hirst and Thompson[11] then record that 'Genuinely transnational companies (TNCs) appear to be relatively rare. Most companies are nationally based and trade multinationally on the strength of a major national location of production and sales'. Hirst and Thompson note that 'Capital mobility is not producing a massive shift of investment and employment from the advanced to the developing countries. Rather, foreign direct investment (FDI) is highly concentrated among the advanced industrial economies'.[12] Then, fourthly, they note that '. . . the world economy is far from being genuinely "global". Rather, trade, investment and financial flows are concentrated in the Triad of Europe, Japan and North America and this dominance seems set to continue'.[13] And they draw the important conclusion that 'These major economic powers, the G3, thus have the capacity, especially if they coordinate policy, to exert powerful governance pressures over financial markets and other economic tendencies'.[14]

Hirst and Thompson look to changes within the international economy which offer a context in which the claims to globalization can attain a modest initial plausibility. The authors note, firstly, 'The effects of the collapse of the Bretton Woods system and the OPEC oil crisis in producing turbulence and volatility in all the major economies through the 1970s and into the early 1980s. Significant in generating such turbulence and undermining previous policy regimes was the rapid rise in inflation in the advanced countries brought about by domestic policy failures, the international impact of US involvement in the Vietnam War, and the oil price hikes of 1973 and 1979'.[15] Then, secondly, 'The efforts by financial institutions and manufacturers, in this period of turbulence and inflationary pressure, to compensate for domestic uncertainty by seeking wider outlets for investments and additional markets. The results were widespread bank lending to the Third World during the inflationary 1970s, the growth of the Eurodollar market, and the increasing foreign trade to GDP ratios in the advanced countries'.[16] And, thirdly, 'The public policy acceleration of the internationalization of financial markets by the widespread abandonment of exchange controls and other market deregulation in the late 1970s and early 1980s, even as the more extreme forms of volatility in currency markets were being brought under control by, for example, the development of the European monetary system (EMS) in 1979 and the Louvre and Plaza accords in the 1980s'.[17] The authors go on to add, fourthly, 'The tendency towards "de-industrialization" in Britain and the United States and the growth of long term unemployment in Europe, promoting fears of foreign competition especially from Japan'.[18] Then, fifthly, 'The relatively rapid development of a number of newly industrializing countries (NICs) in the Third World and their penetration of First World markets'.[19] And, finally, sixthly, 'The shift from standardized mass production to more flexible production methods, and the change from the perception of the large nationally rooted oligopolistic corporation as the unchallengeably dominant economic agent towards a more complex world of multinational enterprises (MNCs), less rigidly structured major firms, and the increased salience of smaller firms – summed up in the widespread and popular concept of "post-Fordism"'.[20]

Overall, these changes were read as creating a new situation. They came as a shock to thinkers used to Keynesian optimism and when monetarist nostrums also failed the international economy was perceived as ungovernable. At this point the notion of globalization seemed both accurate and more pointedly reassuring – political agents were excused their inactivity and loss of imagination. Hirst and Thompson suggest that 'One can only call the political impact of "globalization" the pathology of over-diminished expectations'.[21]

Hirst and Thompson review these debates with reference to explicit models. First, an inter-national economy in which the principal entities are national economies. There is national specialization and an international division of labour. Domestic and international spheres are kept relatively separate. This can be a result of government ordering decisions or an automatic mechanism. In the latter case we have a liberal international system which operates according to specified rules and with an agreed monetary system. The classic case of such an international economy was the UK sponsored liberal trading regime of the late nineteenth and early twentieth century ordered around fixed exchange rates and the gold standard. The Great War wrecked this system and it was not replaced by an analogous system until the post-Second World War Bretton Woods system. Against those who argue that globalization is new, it is enough to point to the period of the gold standard. Against those who argue that globalization means a permanently and irreversibly unregulated economy it is enough to point to the inter-war period of regulation and national blocs.[22] And second, a globalized economy, which sees distinctive national economies subsumed within international flows of economic and financial power. The new system has certain characteristics: it is less subject to governance, which may set entrepreneurs free or just invite conflict; MNCs will become genuine TNCs; the bargaining power of labour would fall; and in the system there would be a multipolarity of political power with a range of institutions involved alongside the old familiar state.[23]

Hirst and Thompson argue that there is no globalized economy and the talk obscures the task of detailing how the international economy has actually changed in recent years. On this the authors note: (i) the key players are the major developed economies; (ii) there has been an internationalization of financial markets in the wake of the end of the Bretton Woods system, but it is neither unprecedented nor irreversible and uncontrollable; (iii) there has been an increase in trade of semi-manufactured and manufactured goods and this restricts power of states but the patterns of trade do tend to fall into blocs; (iv) there is more international trade and internationally ordered manufacturing but MNCs predominate; and (v) perhaps the key novel feature of the international system at present is the growth of regionalism, the three big blocs of the Americas, Europe and Pacific Asia.

In sum, the theorists working within the classical tradition see a new pattern of industrial-capitalism with new forms of production, social-institutional novelties, shifting cultural linkages and new political cultures and all these changes are assimilated to a continuing, dynamic and expanding industrial-capitalist system. The new situation is novel precisely because it evidences an intriguing and important regional variation upon the continuing common theme of industrial-capitalism.

Conclusion

The theme of the shift to the modern world as it is appears within the classical European tradition of social theory has three aspects: (i) the formal character of the arguments; (ii) the substantive characterizations; and (iii) the contemporary debate in respect of the argument strategies and substantive processes at issue in respect of the (ongoing) shift to the modern world.

In the light of these sets of ideas it is possible to read events in the world as evidencing the continuing working out of the modernist project. The resources of the classical European tradition of social theorizing allow the detail of the patterns of life of people within the global system to be characterized in a way that historically locates forms-of-life and identifies their inherent dynamics. As Moore[24] might have it, there are a series of still unfolding routes to the modern world. In the next section we will consider the dynamics of complex change within Pacific Asia.

Notes

1   P. W. Preston 1996: *Development Theory: An Introduction*, Oxford: Blackwell.
2   A. Giddens 1971: *Capitalism and Modern Social Theory*, Cambridge: Cambridge University Press.
3   E. Gellner 1964: *Thought and Change*, London: Weidenfeld.
4   B. Moore 1966: *The Social Origins of Dictatorship and Democracy*, Boston: Beacon.
5   S. Strange 1988: *States and Markets*, London: Pinter.
6   F. Fukuyama 1992: *The End of History and the Last Man*, London: Hamish Hamilton.
7   J.-F. Lyotard 1979: *The Postmodern Condition*, Manchester: Manchester University Press.
8   Z. Bauman 1987: *Legislators and Interpreters*, Cambridge: Polity.
9   P. Hirst and G. Thompson 1996: *Globalization in Question*, Cambridge: Polity.
10   Ibid., p. 2.
11   Ibid.
12   Ibid.
13   Ibid.
14   Ibid., p. 3.
15   Ibid., p. 5.
16   Ibid.
17   Ibid.
18   Ibid.
19   Ibid.
20   Ibid., p. 6.
21   Ibid.
22   Ibid., pp. 8–10.
23   Ibid., pp. 10–13.
24   Moore 1966.

Part II

The Shift to the Modern World in Pacific Asia

2

Analysing the Process of the Shift to the Modern World in Pacific Asia

The classical tradition of social theorizing is concerned with elucidating the dynamics of complex change in the ongoing shift to the modern world, in brief, the historical development of industrial capitalism. In the case of the historical development of Europe the shift to the modern world was accomplished in a discontinuous, episodic and uneven fashion. In a similar way, in substantive terms, the expansion and deepening of the industrial-capitalist form-of-life in the Pacific Asian region took place in a discontinuous, episodic and uneven fashion.

The historical development experience of Pacific Asia can be grasped in terms of the phases in the development experiences of the parts of the region, the breaks in the development trajectories of particular parts of the region, the shifts in patterns of development within the region and shifts in the patterns of relationships between the region and the wider developing global system. At the same time a series of reactions can be identified on the part of the various agent groups lodged within these shifting structural patterns. Overall, in this chapter we will supplement the materials of the introductory chapter with further strategies of argument which are suitable for the more specific historical development experience of Pacific Asia.

Reading Patterns of Change

In the period of the high tide of European expansion the available notions of social science tended to be positivistic, unreflexive and disposed to 'legislation'.[1] The multiple confidences of the period in respect of the civilization of the Europeans, the power of their science and the progressive nature of their vigorous commerce combined to produce an approach to the analysis of the social world which was deeply Euro-centric. The experiences of the denizens of other forms-of-life were measured according to the standards of Europeans. It is clear that this opens up a series of problems for contemporary scholarship: first, we have to acknowledge that the contemporary world, for all its increasing inter-connectedness, is home to diverse voices, to different ways of reading the intermingled common history of humanity; and relatedly we have to acknowledge that theorists working within or with reference to the classical tradition face similar problems in reconstructing a plausible narrative of the intermingled history of the development of the modern world. We can no longer take the historical experience of the West as a model of the historical experience of all peoples, or as a universal model to which all peoples must necessarily defer. In sum, what must be accomplished is a reflexive analysis of complex change.

Reflexive criticism, other voices and the multiple nature of history

The classical tradition of social theorizing represents the materials which commentators in Europe deployed in formulating, ordering and responding to the shift to the modern world. It is a practical intellectual tradition.

The modern global system is dominated by industrial-capitalism, which originated in Europe and slowly spread to cover much of the world. This form-of-life comprises the general celebration of the power of human reason, the extensive development of natural science, and a political-economic, social-institutional and political-cultural system dedicated to material progress via science-based industry. In the perspective of the classical European tradition the expansion of the global industrial-capitalist system has been discontinuous, episodic and uneven. In substantive terms, the expansion and deepening of the industrial-capitalist form-of-life in the Pacific Asian region took place in a similar fashion.

The process of the shift to the modern world within the territory of Pacific Asia took place via the establishment of trading links, the imposition of colonial territories and the reordering attendant upon the post-colonial pursuit of independent effective nation statehood. It is clear that there are a number of perspectives from which the overall tale could be told. In respect of the process of expansion and colonization we can note the various perspectives of the indigenous elites, the indigenous masses, the traders, missionaries and soldiers who vehicled the expansion, and the people in power in the metropoles who orchestrated the process. In Long's terms there was a 'battlefield of knowledges' which was intimately linked to the real military and trade battlefields of imperial expansion.[2] And similarly, in respect of the pursuit of effective nation statehood, we can note the divergent perspectives of modernizing elites, the masses of the new nation states, the concerns of international capital and the concerns and activities of metropolitan centres.

It is clear that the classical tradition of social theorizing offers one way of reading the ongoing shift to the modern world, yet there are other ways of reading events: for example, great religious traditions; or little local traditions; or more interestingly for adherents of the classical tradition the presentation of alternative models of industrial-capitalist modernity (such as talk about a Pacific Asian model of development).

In sum, in analysing the process of expansion, we need to be aware of the various versions of events, and routes to the future (political-cultural projects), which were in play at the time. And in respect of debates about the present, we need to be aware of the culture-boundedness of social scientific analyses. It is clear that reflexive scepticism in respect of claims to knowledge is a necessary condition of scholarship.[3] Overall, the story has been one of the initial dominance of the tales told by the West, but in the post-war period of decolonization and the pursuit of development this was reworked and with the talk of the rise of Pacific Asia it looks as though it is being reworked again.

Phases, Breaks, Shifts and Agents

The analytical approach of structural international political economy offers a way of accommodating within a coherent overall scheme the changes typically found in the historical development experiences of particular regions of the global system. In substantive terms the expansion of the industrial-capitalist form-of-life within the Pacific Asian region was discontinuous, episodic and uneven.

Phases in the historical development experiences

The idea of phases points to the discontinuous nature of development for any particular area. The historical development experience of any particular region will involve both periods of relative stability and episodes of more or less rapid complex change. It is clear that there have been discrete phases in the development experiences of the various parts of the Pacific Asia region. Within the frame of any one phase we would expect to find a specific and continuing pattern of economic, social and cultural life. A more or less settled way of doing things. The settled form-of-life could be characterized both in terms of its internal dynamics and the linkages which it had with the relevant wider system.

In the case of the broad territory now identified as Pacific Asia it is clear that it has experienced relatively long periods of relative stability as extant patterns of life continued down the years. In this fashion we can point to the period before the arrival of the West when the region saw the rise and fall of a succession of dynasties within the frame of an enduring primarily agrarian political economy. Thereafter the various territories of the region were drawn into the Western colonial system and as their polities were reordered so were their political economies extensively reconstructed in line with the demands of the expanding global industrial-capitalist economy and the region took on its characteristic colonial era pattern. The post-colonial pursuit of effective nation statehood saw a similar period of reordering and a new pattern of relative stability. In recent years the post-colonial phase has modulated gently into a new regionally ordered phase.

What we should note in all this, is that within the parameters of a particular historical developmental phase there is a specific political-economic, social-institutional and cultural pattern within the territory and definite patterns of linkages with the wider global system. It is within the confines of these broad frameworks that the people of the territory make their ordinary lives, pursue their several projects and elaborate their cultural self-understandings. It is also true that when these settled patterns are disturbed, either as a result of the logics of internally secured advance or as the result of shifts in the enfolding global structural pattern, then the business of orchestrating coherent responses is very difficult, and the resultant period of complex change can be traumatic for elite and mass alike.

Breaks in the historical development experiences

It is clear that there have been breaks in the historical development trajectories of particular parts of the Pacific Asian region either as a result of internal developments or as the enfolding global or regional system reconfigured and offered the particular territory a new route to the future.

The original historical occasion of industrial-capitalism has been widely debated and Brenner[4] has pointed to the pattern of circumstances which linked the early development of scientific knowledge, and thus the possibility of increasing absolute levels of production, with a pattern of class alliances which allowed existing merchants within agrarian societies to advance their own interests against the established power holders of monarchy and church. It was out of this fortuitous pattern of circumstances that a system developed which required enterprise level innovation and the system as a whole prospered.

The innovative dynamic of capitalism was not restricted to the immediate domestic sphere but similarly encouraged geographical expansion. In the sixteenth, seventeenth, eighteenth and nineteenth centuries the capitalist system which had been initiated within Europe spread to encompass large areas of the globe. It is clear that for many cultures the impetus to radical change came with shifting patterns within the global system. Change has been impressed upon many cultures. The routes to the modern world have depended upon the ways in which local elites have read and reacted to shifting patterns within the enfolding global capitalist system.

As the global system reconfigures the extant patterns of structural power will change. These patterns of structural power flow through the territory of any extant community. In the modern period the rise of the state system has offered a way of curbing global structures and the drive towards regionalization offers a contemporary elite-sponsored response to current structural patterns. As global and regional structural patterns reconfigure the patterns of economic, social and cultural activity within any particular territory will adapt. A new pattern of structural circumstances implies a new spread of possible lines of activity (and it implies that previous practices may become untenable).

In this way it is possible to conceive of relatively rapid and widespread changes within the structural circumstances encompassing the form-of-life of a particular territory. It is usual to look first for changes in the material conditions of life of a territory and to read thereafter related changes to society and culture.

The process of the expansion of global industrial-capitalism can be taken to have made a series of shifting demands on the particular territory whose history therefore will be recorded as a series of discrete phases. The movement from one phase to the next will be discontinuous. It will not be an evolutionary movement but a break as one pattern is set aside and another developed. It is clear that discontinuous change can place a considerable strain upon existing patterns of social order. An episode of more of less complex change implies that there will be groups who are 'winners' and some who are 'losers'. It is at this point that we might begin to speak of political responses within territories: (i) the shifts and changes initiated by elite groups which might include resistance, accommodation, or supercession;[5] (ii) the responses of the masses within a territory which again might involve a range of responses;[6] and (iii) the patterns of action of a spread of minority groups such as ethnic, religious or economic.[7] It is clear that the ways in which the internal dynamics of response to shifting enfolding patterns are resolved and local political projects inaugurated will effect the overall trajectory of the shift to the modern world achieved by the territory.

Pacific Asia has experienced a series of fairly abrupt breaks within its overall historical development experience, in broad terms, the process of the expansion through the region of industrial-capitalism. The earliest contacts were made in Southeast Asia where the demands of the incoming Western traders were initially supportable within the confines of extant patterns of life. However, as the pace of economic advance within the metropolitan core accelerated the demands made upon the territories of Southeast Asia increased, and in the absence of any coherent overall response by local elites these areas eventually came to experience a process of absorption within colonial systems, and consequent extensive economic, social and cultural reconstruction. A little later the ruling elites of China made the mistake of underestimating the dynamism of the capitalist system which supported the Western traders coming to Chinese ports, and over the latter part of the nineteenth century China was absorbed as a quasi-colony. It was only at the high water mark of Western expansion in the islands of Japan that an indigenous Asian elite managed to contrive a coherent response to the novel demands placed upon them and by the end of the century, after a rapid modernization self-consciously ordered by the elite, the Japanese had joined the ranks of the Western powers as an industrial society.

Intra-regional and extra-regional shifts in patterns of historical development experience

It is clear that there will be shifts in patterns of development within a region as particular areas advance relative to others. The historical development experience of a particular territory can be described directly, that is, as a history of that territory, but of course these individual patterns of development are always lodged within the contexts offered by the wider system. The dynamics of change within territories will not be equivalent. Against the modernization theory inspired expectations of a single logic of modernization repeating itself in diverse contexts, such that all territories might expect equal advance in the absence of accidental inhibitions to progress, structural international political economy recognizes the fundamentally uneven nature of progress. Global structures of power are not regular and different territories will advance, or retreat, at different rates.

In a similar way it is clear that there will be shifts in the patterns of relationships between the region and the wider developing global system as patterns of development advance unevenly at the global system level.

In the case of Pacific Asia it is clear both that the region has undergone a recent period of rapid relative advance within the global system and that within this general pattern of advance particular countries within the region have advanced more rapidly than others. At the present time the region has a core economy in Japan, a series of vibrant peripheral territories and a rapidly developing Chinese sphere.

Agent's projects in historical development experience

If we turn to the agent level, we can analyse the strategies of the various actors who animate the overall tale. The key players will be state-regimes, multinational corporations and other commercial operations, international organizations and the groups of peoples involved in the region (the weak, the newly prosperous, the marginals and so on).

In the long process of the shift to the modern world of the territories of Pacific Asia it is clear that the key players were the incoming Western traders, manufacturers, financiers and thereafter the whole extensive apparatus of colonial rule. The place of indigenous elites was marginal, except for the case of Japan, and everywhere, as Worsley[8] has noted, the ordinary people saw their lives remade over the generations. However, the expansion of the Western industrial-capitalist system generated the intellectual and political means whereby local agents could resist the formal colonial system, and in the confusions attendant upon the Pacific War indigenous nationalist groups attained a measure of influence and eventually secured independence for their countries. The replacement elites have thereafter acted as state-regimes and have reacted to shifting structural circumstances in order to plot an overall route to the future, order their populations accordingly and disseminate legitimating explanations and ideologies.

In contemporary Pacific Asia it is clear that the key players in recent years have been the state-regimes of the various countries, certain international organizations and the region's MNCs. At the present time the role of international organizations is attaining a more prominent role, in particular the formal institutions, such as ASEAN, which are oriented to the concerns of the region itself. Overall, it is clear that elite groups within the region are becoming more conscious of the region's identity, power and future.[9]

Discontinuities, episodes and conflict in the shift to the modern world

Overall, we can speak of the particular pattern of development within the global system and the regions which comprise that system. The overall shift to the modern world has been achieved in a discontinuous and episodic fashion. The breaks marking the transition of a particular territory from one broad configuration of economy, society and culture to another have often been accompanied by conflict, either simply internal as domestic groups manoeuvre for advantage, or also involving the incoming forces of global industrial-capitalism. In the long process of the shift to the modern world in Pacific Asia the lines of social discontinuity have been diverse and the patterns of conflict correspondingly complex.

Identifying the region of Pacific Asia

In the long period prior to the invasive spread of industrial-capitalism the region was Sino-centric. Subsequently the expansion and deepening of the demands of industrial-capitalism led to the absorption of the region within the system of colonial empires. In the period of the Pacific War the region formed a part of the Greater East Asian Co-Prosperity Sphere which was centred upon Japan. Thereafter, most recently, it has been divided by cold war alliances into a western sphere lodged within the US centred Bretton Woods system and an inward looking socialist sphere. The Western-focused group have been subject to the political-economic, political and cultural hegemony of the USA. However, the Western-focused group is undergoing considerable change and in brief this may be summarized as the beginnings of a political-economic and cultural emancipation from the hegemony of the USA. At the same time the countries of the socialist bloc which had spent decades following autarchic development trajectories are now opening up to the Western-focused group.

The recent end of the cold war system, even though the process of winding down conflict had begun in Asia with the Sino-American rapprochement of the early 1970s, has opened up the issue of the delimitation and future shape of the region.[10] In the post-cold war period the identity of the region as a whole is contested. The regional project in Asia is contested and a series of variants can be identified, in particular those affirmed by Chinese, Japanese and American commentators.

The US view is still shaped by cold war security thinking with a significant relocation of anxieties from geo-strategy to geo-economics. The region is economically threatening and needs must be ordered according to US agendas, hence APEC. In contrast the Japanese view is ordered around the image/programme of flying geese. The NICs slot in just behind the leader with their economies growing along with that of Japan, and ASEAN brings up the rear of the formation. And finally the Chinese view the regional arena within the frame of Greater China, or the China Circle. The growing economic power of China is taken to be expanding and drawing in the other powerful economies of the region. Overall, it can be said that regionalism within East Asia is only developing slowly and it will develop in its own fashion, with slow networking rather than decisive formal institutional shifts.

In this text we will consider a series of phases in the development experience of the territories of the region where each represents a particular way in which the region was configured and lodged within the wider system. It will be argued that the discussion of the Pacific Asian region addresses the latest of what has been a series of phases. In this text these phases with their intervening shifts/breaks are read as intrinsic to the developmental logic of capitalist modernity and talk of postmodernity,[11] or a new global era[12] is unnecessary. The present phase can be understood in terms of the notions of internationalization and regionalization[13] and can be readily accommodated within the received classical European tradition with its concern for elucidation of the dynamics of complex change in pursuit of the project of modernity.

An Outline of the Shift to the Modern World in Pacific Asia

In respect of the long process of the shift to the modern world in Pacific Asia it is possible to identify a series of substantive phases: (i) the long period prior to the invasive development of industrial-capitalism when a series of civilizations flourished; (ii) the empire phase; (iii) the post-war phase o ،ew nations and cold war; and (iv) the Pacific Asia phase.

In the period of Asian civilizations – a multipolar non-global system

The long phase of Asian civilizations can be taken to have comprised four main areas having long established forms-of-life and patterns of interaction: China, the Japanese islands, Indo-China, and the islands of the archipelago.

In China the polity was ordered by an elaborate centralized bureaucratic state with an emperor as the political core. The centre established law and a mechanism of rational administration, where office holders were recruited by examination, and the economic base of the system revolved around peasant agriculture. The society was ordered around family, kin network, clan group and language group. The culture celebrated family and ancestors and had religious expression in the traditions of Confucianism, Buddhism and Islam. The Chinese state established itself as the central power within a wide circle of tributary states including Korea and Taiwan. The empire system was established in the second century BC and endured with a succession of emperors. The system had wide influence within the region and until the mid-sixteenth century decision to withdraw from trade and turn inwards it was involved in extensive trade networks. The decision to turn inwards co-incided with the start of the expansion of Europe so that when the traders arrived in Asia they found the region without major established competitors. Thereafter, the incursion of traders, missionaries and adventurers slowly overturned the extant forms-of-life and drew China into a severely dis-advantaged position within the developing global industrial-capitalist system.

In the Japanese islands a similar pattern of life developed. The Japanese were influenced extensively by Chinese models of civilization. The Japanese polity developed around a series of regional lords who owed a nominal allegiance to the Japanese emperor. However, the Japanese system developed in a less centralized fashion and it was not until the feudal Tokugawa Shogunate was established in the early 1600s that the country attained a measure of coherence. The key economic nexus was the land and the peasants who worked it and control of these means of material produc-tion were the basis of secular power. The society was rigidly hierarchical and individuals were subsumed within the family unit, village and the domain of their lord. The culture of the Japanese celebrated family and routines of duties to superiors and found religious expression in Buddhism and Shinto. The Tokugawa Shogunate closed the country to the outside world in the early seventeenth century and a sophisticated culture developed within the confines of the Japanese islands. However, as with the Chinese court, the decision to turn inwards left the region to the control of the traders of a rapidly expanding Europe. The Japanese exchange with the expanding empires of the West in the late nineteenth century proved to be a fatal shock to the extant formal polity and as the old order was overthrown the new elite moved quickly to learn the lessons of the West.

In Indo-China the influence of the Chinese Empire had considerable influence. Vietnam eventually emerged from the shifting kingdoms of the region, and the suzerainty of the Chinese around AD 1000, and an agrarian bureaucratic system similar to that of China was developed and sustained until the nineteenth-century incursions of the French. Elsewhere in the sub-region the pattern of life more resembled that of the wide Malay sphere with a shifting pattern of empires centred on the charismatic and material success of a leading royal family. These empires had very fluid structures and succeeded one another as local centres of power ran through the sequence of advance and retreat. There were major civilizations in Cambodia, Thailand and Burma, and the history of the region recalls a series of shifting alliances and wars. Again the region was economically based on peasant agriculture with the family as core and with religious cultural expression in Buddhism and Islam. The region was ethnographically diverse. The arrival of the Europeans saw the entire area formally colonized with the exception of Thailand whose rulers exploited their status as a buffer between competing colonial powers to order their own shift to the modern world.

In the islands of Southeast Asia the Malay sultanate pattern is evident throughout the region. A shifting series of maritime trading empires grew up typically around a key trade port controlled by a royal family. The family and the trading port would attract followers and traders from the region and these empires could grow quickly. However, they were shifting and fluid and the patterns of trade within the region could easily reconfigure leaving one empire in decline whilst a new one grew quickly in replacement. The empires traded across great distances within the archipelago and the economy revolved around small-scale agriculture and trade. The region was ethnograpically very diverse. The area received merchants from Arabia and the Indian subcontinent and along with them Islam and the extensive culture influences of the Hindu world. The earliest European contacts were in the sixteenth century and by the end of the nineteenth the area had been largely absorbed into European and American colonial systems.

Overall, what we need to note is that within each of these broad areas there were well established forms-of-life. It is clear that the pre-contact region contained advanced and sophisticated cultures, in particular China. In the fifteenth to seventeenth centuries the trading linkages within the region were particularly well developed. However, the linkages of these areas to the wider global system were minimal with the key country China having turned away from long distance trade in the mid-sixteenth century. More generally we can say that there was no developed global system and long distance links were via trading routes carrying specialist and luxury goods. It is also true to say that the technological level of the region had fallen behind that of the countries of the metropolitan capitalist core and this was to prove decisive in the period of the rapid expansion of the global system.

In the empire phase – a multipolar global system

The colonial phase of the development experience of Pacific Asia comprised six main interrelated areas: a British sphere, a French sphere, a Dutch sphere, an American sphere, and a Japanese sphere, with China divided between all these powers. The European, American and Japanese empires in Asia expanded rapidly in the late nineteenth and early twentieth centuries. In each of these empire spheres we find a distinctive form-of-life as the metropolitan core orders the systemic demands of industrial-capitalism in the light of its domestic political agendas. Overall, the period saw the systematic reconstruction of the subject territories in line with the demands of the industrial-capitalist system.

The British sphere comprised Singapore, the Malay peninsula, the northern coast of the island of Borneo, a scatter of islands in the South Pacific and a series of trading concessions in China. The British expansion was conducted under the aegis of the ideology of liberal free trade and having taken control of territories there was an adherence to a colonial policy of eventual independence. Within these territories the impact of the arrival of the British was considerable. The traditional Malay form of life was pushed to one side as the colonial power moved to develop the territory by opening up mines and plantations and facilitating significant inward migration. One aspect of colonial expansion was the routine conflict with other European, and later American and Japanese, powers. The process of expansion and thereafter rule in the colonial peripheries was shaped very significantly by the shifts and changes of policy in the metropolitan centres. As the structure of the colonial system took shape, with industry, commerce and administration, the outlines of contemporary Malaysia, Singapore and Brunei also took shape. The experience of colonial rule is not one of straightforward exploitation but can be read in this instance as a particular route to the modern world and political independence, which followed the Pacific War.

The French sphere comprised Vietnam, Laos, Cambodia, some islands in the Pacific and trading concessions in China. The expansion of the overseas French empire in Asia had involved a series of conflicts with the British and the territory of Indo-China was acquired in the nineteenth century. The French had to overcome in a rather direct fashion the established bureaucratic emperor system within Vietnam and did so through a series of local wars. And towards the end of the nineteenth century they had established their colonial territory of Indo-China. Thereafter French colonial policy vacillated between commercial exploitation and discharge of the mission to civilize. The economic reordering of the country was extensive with light industries, commercial undertakings and the infrastructure of a modern society being slowly put in place. In the rural areas there was land reclamation and the development of commercial rice farming and rubber plantations. The territories were transferred by the Vichy regime to the Japanese in 1940 and notwithstanding the post-Second World War attempts of the French to restore the status quo they were ejected in 1956 leaving a divided Vietnam to the cold war attentions of the USA.

The Dutch sphere comprised most of the islands of archipelagic Southeast Asia along with trading concessions in China. The Dutch began their slow expansion through the islands in the seventeenth century and took control through a series of wars against local sultanates. The colonial policy was for many years seen to be highly exploitative of the local population who were drawn into a brutal system of tropical agricultural production. However, in the years after the Great War the Dutch moved to revise the style and intention of their rule even though real change was only provoked, as elsewhere in the region, by the Japanese occupation during the Pacific War; and the Dutch thereafter withdrew.

The American sphere comprised the territory of the Philippines, a series of islands in the Pacific, and trading concessions in China. The Americans came relatively late to the business of overseas colonial expansion having pursued the task of moving westwards across the continental USA (a process of internal colonization as the native Indians were pushed aside) and having had the issue of the appropriate route to the future for the USA collapse into civil war. In the late nineteenth century the USA seized territory from the Spanish and established a colony in the Philippines and looked to secure a wider influence in East Asia. The American colony secured the power of large landholders who operated commercial plantation agricultural holdings. After the interregnum of the Pacific War where the local elite collaborated with the Japanese, the returning Americans confirmed the power of the local elites, suppressed a local land-reform movement and left the Filipinos a legacy of misdevelopment which persists to the present day.

The Meiji Restoration of 1868 brought to power a modernizing oligarchy who proceeded over the next thirty years to turn Japan into an industrial economy. On the basis of the newly acquired economic and military power the Japanese moved to expand their influence within East Asia by military means, and wars against China and Russia left Japan in control of a significant empire in the region. The Japanese sphere comprised Korea, Taiwan, the Ryujuku Islands, the Kurile Islands, and after the Great War a further series of islands in the Pacific. The nature of the Japanese colonial period involves a mixture of industrial and agricultural development coupled to repressive exploitation as the occupied territories were managed with a view to their role within the Japanese sphere. It was only the military defeat of the Imperial Japanese armed forces in the Pacific War that led to the independence of the colonized territories.

In China the foreign powers extended their influence from the time of the two Opium Wars in the mid-nineteenth century. The Qing emperor was slow to respond and by the late nineteenth century central authority was disintegrating. The country became a quasi-colony of the Europeans and Americans and was divided into a series of spheres of influence. The revolution of 1911 ushered in a nominal republic but the country was ruled by a series of warlords through to the outbreak of the open war against the Japanese in 1933. The war against the Japanese was simultaneously a civil war between nationalists and communists and the country only recovered a measure of coherence in 1949 with the victory of the Chinese Communist Party led by Mao Tse-tung.

In this period within Pacific Asia the impacts of the expanding colonial ordered industrial-capitalist system were extensive. The extant forms-of-life were all more or less extensively reconfigured to meet the demands of the metropolitan capital[14] with the key link of local area and global system being provided by colonial primate cities.[15] It is also the case that the linkages of these areas to each other were extensive, as elements within the one expansive system, but controlled, as the empires were mercantilist, liberal and then protectionist before finally being swept away.[16]

In the nation-building plus cold war phase – a bipolar global system

In the period of nation-building and cold war we can see that the region comprised five main areas, divided into two interlinked groups: Japan, the NICs, and Southeast Asia, on the one hand; and China with Indo-China on the other. It was the episode of the Pacific War which saw the empire system swept away. The confusion of war meant both that the pattern of relationships of the territories within the region were radically remade and that the pattern of linkages between region and global system were also reordered. The process of decolonization and the subsequent extension of the cold war to Asia all contributed to the present configuration of Pacific Asia.

Japan was partially reformed by the American occupation authorities and thereafter pursued a strategy of domestic recovery centred on economic progress. The cold-war bipolar system provided a satisfactory environment for the pursuit of economic progress. The post-war development experience of Japan has run through a series of phases from an initial concern to rebuild war damage, through the careful bureaucratically directed rebuilding of an export effective economy, through to present-day influence throughout the region.

The NICs were for many years the frontline in the cold war in Asia. A series of authoritarian rulers established economic advance as the overriding national goal. It was within the framework of US defence and open markets that these economies grew. There have been significant links with Japan in terms of trade and investment. Overall, these economies have grown rapidly in recent years.

In Southeast Asia the process of decolonization was not simple. A confusion of objectives on the part of the returning colonial powers, coupled with a series of ethnic tensions, with the whole business being overlain by the cold war concerns of the Americans, meant that routes to the future for the various territories were not easy to identify. The upshot was the formation of a series of new countries: Malaysia, Singapore, Indonesia, Brunei, Papua New Guinea and the Philippines. The long period of bipolarity has seen the influence of the West decline relative to that of Japan which is now the regional core economy to which the countries of Southeast Asia look.

In China the revolution of 1911 had lead to a period of warlordism, invasion and civil war. It was not until the victory of the Chinese Communist Party in 1949 that the country attained any stability. The inward looking phase of revolutionary development had mixed results until the reforms of 1978 inaugurated a period of rapid economic growth.

And in Indo-China the countries suffered first from the necessity of waging a long war against the returning colonial power and thereafter against the Americans. It was not until 1975 that the sub-region was free of outside interference and with the complications of a war in Cambodia the territory did not resume a normal pattern of relationships with the wider regional and global systems until 1993 when President Clinton discontinued American embargoes.

The linkages of the free world group to the US dominated global system were extensive. On the other hand the linkages of the socialist bloc to the global system were minimal. However, the bipolar organization of the region began to break down after 1978 when Deng Xiao Ping inaugurated economic reforms in China and in 1985 the Plaza Accords revalued the yen leading to a flood of Japanese FDI within the region. When the cold war ended in 1991 there were already significant regional linkages amongst the countries within the area of Pacific Asia.

In the Pacific Asia phase – a tripolar global system

The Pacific Asia phase of the development of the region comprises an increasingly interrelated grouping around a core Japanese economy of five main areas: Japan, inner periphery, outer periphery, reforming socialist bloc, and Australasia.

The Japanese economy is now the region's core economy. It is the world's second most powerful economy and has developed extensive linkages throughout the region. In the inner periphery, the territory of the NICs, there is burgeoning growth. In the outer periphery, the countries of ASEAN, there is extensive growth as investment flows into the area. In the reforming socialist bloc there is rapid growth and China is becoming a major economic and political power. And in Australasia there is an uneven concern to be a part of Pacific Asia.

The linkages of the region to the global system are very extensive and becoming more extensive. The linkages between the various parts of the region are also becoming extensive and deepening. The region has a core economy, extensive economic linkages, new political/trade mechanisms and a measure of cultural coherence. An integrated regional grouping can be taken to be in process of formation (although the end point is most unclear and the extent of integration should not be overstated).

In the wake of the collapse of the bipolar system it has become clear that the global industrial-capitalist system has developed into three broad regions. The regions trade amongst themselves and evidence distinct varieties of industrial-capitalism. The current situation within the world system thus displays a mixture of global internationalization and regionalization. The three regions can be seen to have political-economic cores and a spread of peripheral territories. The regions comprise the Americas, the European Union and Pacific Asia. It is the recognition of this new global pattern that makes the developing region of Pacific Asia interesting to scholars, political actors and policy makers in countries within the region and within the territories of the other regions.

Conclusion

The approach adopted in this text derives from the classical tradition of social theorizing with its central concern for elucidating the dynamics of complex change in respect of the historical development of industrial-capitalism. It is clear that the path of development is not smooth but is marked by discontinuities and reconfigurations. All these features are intrinsic to the process of industrial-capitalist intensification and expansion. It is clear that there have been a series of discrete phases in the development experience of the Pacific Asian region. One might speak of a series of interlinked routes to the modern world. In this text the particular substantive focus will be the expansion and deepening of the industrial-capitalist form-of-life in the Pacific Asian region.

Notes

1   Z. Bauman 1987: *Legislators and Interpreters*, Cambridge: Polity.
2   N. Long, ed., 1992: *Battlefields of Knowledge*, London: Routledge.
3   P. W. Preston 1985: *New Trends in Development Theory*, London: Routledge.
4   R. Brenner 1977: The Origins of Capitalist Development: A Critique of Neo-Smithian Marxism in *New Left Review* 104.
5   E. Gellner 1983: *Nations and Nationalism*, Cambridge: Cambridge University Press.
6   J. C. Scott 1985: *Weapons of the Weak*, New Haven, CT: Yale University Press.
7   H. D. Evers and H. Schrader, eds, 1994: *The Moral Economy of Trade*, London: Routledge.
8   P. Worsley 1984: *The Three Worlds: Culture and World Development*, London: Weidenfeld.
9   R. Higgot 1996: Ideas and Identity in the International Political Economy of Regionalism in *ISI-JAIR Joint Convention*, Makuhari: Japan.
10 A. Gamble and T. Payne 1996: *Regionalism and World Order*, London: Macmillan; M. Shibusawa et al. 1992: *Pacific Asia in the 1990s*, London: Routledge; C. Mackerras, ed., 1995: *Eastern Asia*, London: Longman.
11 R. Robertson 1992: *Globalization: Social Theory and Global Culture*, London: Sage.
12 M. Albrow 1996: *The Global Age*, Cambridge: Polity.
13 P. Hirst and G. Thompson 1996: *Globalization in Question*, Cambridge: Polity.
14 P. Worsley 1984: *The Three Worlds*.
15 A. D. King 1990: *Urbanism, Colonialism and the World Economy*, London: Routledge.
16 E. Hobsbawm 1994: *The Age of Extremes: The Short Twentieth Century*, London: Michael Joseph.

3

From Ancient Empires to Nineteenth-century Industrial-capitalism

In the period prior to the invasive development of industrial-capitalism within the region there were a series of discrete forms-of-life, each having distinctive political economies, social-institutional structures and cultures. These societies were long established and can be seen to fall into four spheres: (i) China and Northeast Asia; (ii) the Japanese islands; (iii) the lands making up the territory of Indo-China; and (iv) the broad spread of mainland and island Southeast Asia.

In China the polity was ordered around an emperor ruling a centralized bureaucratic state which established law, a mechanism of rational administration, and oversaw the operation of the economic base of the system which revolved around peasant agriculture. The Chinese state established itself as the central power within a wide circle of tributary states, and had wide influence within the region.

Thus it is clear that Japan was influenced extensively by Chinese cultural models. However, the Japanese polity developed in a less centralized fashion around a series of regional lords. As in China the key economic resource was the land. The society was hierarchical and individuals were subsumed within the family unit, village and the domain of their lord. A sophisticated culture developed within the confines of the Japanese islands.

It is also clear that the influence of the Chinese Empire in Indo-China was extensive. Vietnam eventually emerged from the shifting kingdoms of the region and the suzerainty of the Chinese around AD 1000. In Vietnam an agrarian bureaucratic system similar to that of China was developed. However, elsewhere in the ethnographically diverse sub-region the pattern of life more resembled that of the wide Malay sphere with a fluid shifting pattern of empires based on agriculture and centred on the charismatic and material success of a leading royal family. There were significant civilizations in Cambodia, Thailand and Burma.

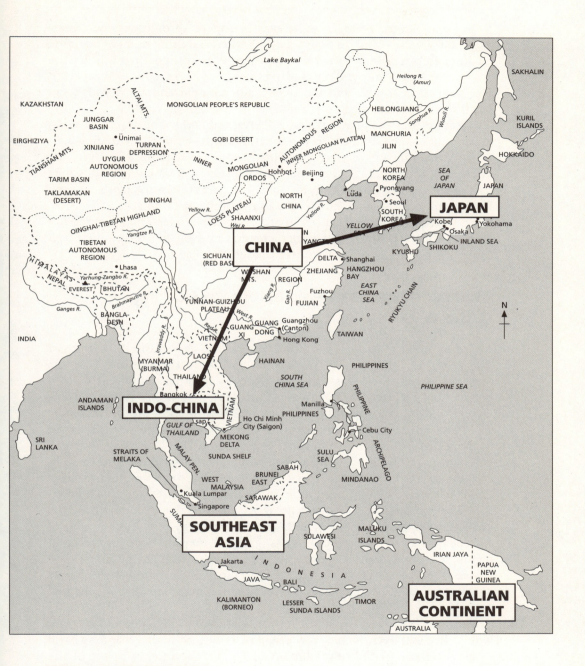

Map 3.1   The civilizations of Asia

And the pattern of Malay sultanates is evident throughout the ethnograpically diverse islands of Southeast Asia where a shifting series of maritime trading empires rose and fell. These empires traded throughout the archipelago and beyond, including China. The region also received merchants from Arabia and the Indian subcontinent and along with them Islam and the extensive culture influences of the Hindu world.

It is clear that the region contained advanced and sophisticated cultures, in particular China. In the fifteenth to seventeenth centuries the trading linkages within the region were particularly well developed.[1] However, the linkages of these areas to the wider global system were minimal with China having turned away from long distance trade in the mid-sixteenth century. In this period we speak of indigenous forms-of-life, yet when these forms-of-life are contacted by the European and American traders, missionaries and soldiers they are slowly put under pressure and by the early nineteenth century they have been brought to the edge of collapse.

China and Northeast Asia Before the Coming of the West

Moise comments: 'Most of the world has changed very drastically in the past 100 years, but few areas have been altered more than China. First the imperial government was brought down by internal decay and foreign pressure, and replaced by a republic. Then central authority collapsed completely, and the country was divided amongst provincial warlords. Incapable of organised defence, China became the prey of foreign powers whose "spheres of influence" sometimes approached the status of outright colonies. Corrupt officials, marauding armies, and natural disasters periodically ravaged the peasantry'.[2] It is clear that the shift to the modern world in China has seen extensive economic, social and political dislocation and conflict. The contemporary Chinese elite were simply unable to comprehend the challenge which the modern industrial-capitalist system in the guise of European traders represented. It was not until the final years of the nineteenth century that the Chinese elite tried to engineer change but by then it was far too late. Over the years of the nineteenth century the Chinese empire was reduced to a semi-colonial situation and thereafter it collapsed entirely.

The overall story of the shift to the modern world in China will be dealt with in this text over the next few chapters. However, in this chapter we will recall the story of the development of China, the establishment of the emperor system, the rise to pre-eminence in East Asia and the deep reluctance to acknowledge the wider non-Chinese world.

The form-of-life of China: geography, economy, society and culture

The Han Chinese originated in the Yellow River region. The recorded history details rulers from about 2700 BC and archaeological evidence can confirm these materials to 1300 BC. At this time a typical state was a city with some surrounding agricultural land. The period experienced shifting patterns of power, war and cultural advance. The Han Chinese slowly expanded and drew into their society the peoples of the surrounding areas. The core areas of China have for centuries been the valleys of the Yellow River, Yangtze River and Pearl River. There are peripheral areas including Manchuria, Mongolia, Sinkiang and Tibet where central control has waxed and waned.[3]

The regional geography of the country consequently has three main areas: (i) north China, around the Yellow River, the original home of the Chinese people; (ii) central China, around the Yangtze River, which is the most populous area; and (iii) south China, which has a mild climate. In each of the three main regions there are central areas of productive agriculture which have supported large populations, have developed infrastructural facilities (irrigation, roads, villages and towns) and which have in more recent years provided the cores of expanding urban industrial-commerical towns and cities. Indeed, one noticeable feature of the countries of the Pacific Asia region is that populations still tend to be concentrated where food production is most effective.

Over most of its history China has been predominantly agricultural. The Chinese system is also bureaucratic and centralized, and in this way the local area was integrated within wider economic and political structures. As Moore[4] has it, the political centre provided law and administration in an hierarchical fashion which rested upon the labour of a vast number of poor peasant farmers. The pre-contact history of China can be noted here in terms of a series of aspects: (i) economy; (ii) society; (iii) culture; and (iv) politics. Overall, the Chinese empires and the Sino-Centric system prospered until the demands of the unwanted representatives of the modern world proved unsustainable.

In pre-contact China the economy was agrarian and the keys to prosperity were land and the peasantry which could farm the land. The characteristics of peasant agriculture have been detailed by the anthropologist Worsley[5] who points to a general model which centres on the collective production and consumption of the necessities of human life with surpluses used for exchange, taxes and tithes. Worsley also details the impact of the shift to the modern world upon traditional patterns of agraian life and details two processes of destruction whereby rural life is made a subordinate element of the modern industrial world: first, the shift to commercial farming and then second, the establishment over this century of communes in the USSR and PRC. At the present time China is still a predominantly rural country, the land is central and farming is the key activity. The basic unit of farming is the household and in this way economic and social relations are inextricably intertwined.

In Chinese society the household is the basic unit around which kinship networks revolve. The structure of the family is hierarchical with the father and sons central. The family has an ideal form in the extended family where 'parents live with their sons and their wives and their male descendants and their families under one roof'.[6] However the impacts of high mortality rates and the personal clashes familiar within families meant that 'the most commonly observed household types in traditional China were the nuclear-family household and the stem-family household.[7] The household was central. In peasant communities the household will be a site for production, consumption and welfare. In China it is clear that the 'primary goals of a Chinese family are continuity and prosperity. Only male children can continue the family line, and transmit family property to succeeding generations. Accordingly, a Chinese family must have a son who continues the family line, performs rituals for the ancestors and provides for the parents in their old age.[8] One implication of this pattern of life is that marriage is ordered in line with the needs of the collectivity, rather than individuals, and in China the priority of the man left only a secondary role to women. Within the collectivity, in the Chinese village, 'lineage was a way of organising a village community'.[9] The various members of the lineage group all lived within one settlement and the life of that settlement revolved around the internal organisation of the lineage group. Atsumi notes: 'A lineage consisted of sub-lineages, each of them represented by a head, and further segmented into branches and smaller units . . . A lineage collectively owned land . . . and this corporate landowning played an important role in the economy of the village and in keeping lineage members together in the close vicinity . . . The lineage protected the members from other lineages, and walls and moats guarded the lineage property from thieves and bandits. In this way, the identity and solidarity of the members were strengthened'.[10] Overall, as Atsumi notes, 'the basis of the society is not the individual, but the household'.[11] The centre of social life was the group and individuals found their existence within its confines, and moreover family membership included ancestors, whose status required ritual acknowledgement, so the group both extended over time and found support in religious practice.

Howell notes that 'most of the religious behaviour that one sees amongst Chinese is most accurately described . . . as Chinese folk religion . . . Followers of Chinese folk religion believe that nature and society are unified rather than dichotomized, which means in practice that what is done in society, especially by the sovereign, affects happenings in nature. They also believe that the dual forces, yin and yang [female and male], permeate the entire universe'.[12] Howell goes on to note that: 'The most basic ritual of Chinese folk religion is sacrifice to the ancestors . . . Worship takes place at various shrines, temples, graves and altars. It is most commonly found at what is called the domestic altar . . . Ancestors are worshipped only by their descendants; thus this activity emphasises the separateness of family and descent groups. Worship of gods, however, is done on a wider basis at the community temple, thus integrating disparate kinship units'.[13] It is only thereafter that one confronts the organized religions or philosophies of great traditions. In China these would include, first, the philosophical system of Confucianism, a secular humanism oriented to securing order in society through the cultivation of proper actions, and Legalism which was a more pessimistic version of the tradition stressing the need for rules and authority. The doctrines were conservative prescriptions for hierarchical enlightened order in society. Confucius presents his materials in the fifth century BC and the doctrines are elaborated by later scholars, in particular Mencius. Then secondly, there is Taoism (or Daoism) which originates around the third century BC and offers a mixture of occult sciences and physical regimes designed to alert adherents to the flows of natural power within them and their environment. The religion never developed an elaborate institutional form. And finally there is the imported religion of Buddhism in its more popular and less individualistic Mahayana tradition (the other is Theravada, which is influential in Sri Lanka, Burma and Thailand). The influence of Buddhism seems to date from the third century AD when it offered a way of dealing with the conflicts and violence of the period.

Overall, it is clear that the patterns of agricultural life, society, administration and culture formed an integrated functioning whole. The great tradition of Confucianism came to serve as a legitimating philosophy for the empire system. The Confucian scholar became the rational bureaucrat of the empire, appointed to his post by the emperor as a result of open examination. The bureaucratic system was firmly established by the time of the Tang Dynasty (AD 600–900) and was subsequently strengthened as imperial absolutism advanced. Mackerras notes that 'The period from the time the Mongols reunified China in 1280 to the fall of the Manchu dynasty in 1911 was one of absolutism in China'.[14] The bureaucratic system was very elaborate. Mackerras records that the Ming and Qing Dynasties 'developed a three-sided administration . . . The three were a civil bureaucracy under six ministries, a centralised and hierarchical military bureacracy, and the censorate [which had investigative oversight of the system] . . .The bureaucracy existed at regional, provincial, district and county levels, as well as centrally'.[15] The system drew in a large number of officials. Mackerras reports that an 'estimate for 1469 suggests that there were altogether more than 100,000 civil and over 80,000 military officials in the Chinese bureaucracy'.[16]

The sequence of empires, and the collapse of the final Qing Dynasty

The first unified Chinese empire was established in 221 BC and although the Qing Dynasty lasted only twenty years, the empire system lasted for the next 2000. Moise[17] presents a cyclical description/theory of the sequence of political empires which are taken to move from vigorous youth, with power ordered around a strong centre, through slow loss of control, as regional centres secure more power, through to collapse and renewal. However, against the temptations of the stereotypes of modernization theory (with its schema of static traditionalism and dynamic modernity) we should note that China as a whole was neither static nor unchanging and overall the society did advance.

The first major dynasty to run through the cycle was the Han Dynasty, from 206 BC through to AD 220. There was then a collapse of nearly 400 years. The Sui Dynasty restored the situation of the Han Dynasty in the period 581–618. The Tang Dynasty carried on the advance over the period 618–907. Further advance was evident in the Song Dynasty 960–1279. At this time a successful urban culture was evident, with government dominated by an educated civil service, and with extensive trading networks within China and to Southeast Asia. In 1279 the Mongols under Kublai Khan conquered China and ruled as the Yaun Dynasty. In 1368 they were expelled and the Ming Dynasty was established.

The Ming Dynasty had a series of despotic emperors who ensured that no regional powers arose and who kept control of their crucial scholar-bureaucrat civil servants. The Ming Dynasty came to turn inwards and did not stress trade. The culture stagnated. And the Sino-centric view of the world, which placed China at the core of a series of circles with Northeast Asia and Indo-China as tributory states and the rest of the world as outer-barbarians, placed the Chinese ruling class at a disadvantage when the Europeans began to arrive in the sixteenth century. The dynasty declined and was replaced by the final Manchu-led Qing Dynasty in 1681. Again, power was centralized and the regions of the country were ruled via scholar-bureaucrats. The rational central intention was as ever in tension with local level kin and family networks. The tension between centre and region which is characteristic of Chinese political history found expression in the later decades of the nineteenth century as the Qing Dynasty weakened. A set of interlocking internal and external problems mounted for the Qing Dynasty until it was finally overcome by the intrusive demands of the Western trading powers and collapsed in 1911.

The internal problems were severe. Moise notes that the 'population had increased dramatically under the Qing; it probably reached 400 million some time between 1800 and 1850. Traditional forms of technology were not capable of providing a decent living for so many people. At the same time the government was growing lax . . . Wealthy individuals acquired greater influence over local administrators and thus became increasingly able to evade taxation, throwing the burden onto the poor. The peasants, short of land, paid increasingly heavy taxes . . . Poverty drove thousands into banditry'.[18] Moise goes on to note that the ability of the state to assert its power declined because the Manchu army 'had deteriorated badly . . . As the government's ability to maintain order declined, local leaders began raising their own militias to protect their villages'.[19] At this point the extent of systemic decay was very advanced. Moise notes that there was 'a serious rebellion by the "White Lotus" Buddhist sect in Central China at the end of the eighteenth century. The outbreak of the Taiping Rebellion in the mid nineteenth century led to an even greater crisis . . . The Manchus then turned to regional militias formed by the local gentry, and allowed some of these militias to develop into real armies'.[20] Moise notes that the militias 'put down the Taiping Rebellion . . . [however] The leaders of these regional armies acquired tremendous power'.[21]

At the same time external problems mounted for the Qing Dynasty. The European traders had been a growing presence in the eighteenth century but had been restricted to a few ports. The trade had been primarily Chinese agricultural exports (tea) in exchange for silver (the currency of trade in Southeast Asia). The results of this pattern of trade saw silver currency moving into China and remaining there in the absence of significant Chinese imports from the West. However, this imbalance of trade was a problem for the Europeans and the British finally forced the issue when in response to the 1839 suppression of the country traders' opium business in Canton by the Chinese administrator Lin Zexu, the British launched the Opium Wars of 1840–2 which obliged the Chinese government to acquiesce in opening China to trade.[22] The Chinese ceded Hong Kong to the British and a series of other 'treaty ports' were established. In the following years the Chinese government was obliged to cede control of a number of other ports. Moise[23] notes that by 1917 there were 92 treaty ports.

The combination of internal decay and external conflicts led to a vigorous debate amongst the Chinese ruling class in respect of the business of learning from the foreigners in order to modernize the country. The proponents of the status quo proved the more influential and the drift of the country towards semi-colonial occupation continued. The country avoided outright colonization only by accident when the Europeans and Americans came to the view that as no one country could be allowed pre-eminence in China then all should be allowed in principle to trade wherever they wished. In practice, a series of spheres of influence grew up and these had a more or less quasi-colonial character. The dynasty thereafter moved inexorably towards final collapse in the revolution of 1911.

The tributary regions of Northeast Asia: Korea and Taiwan

In the pre-contact period the territories of Northeast Asia, Korea and Taiwan, fell within the sphere of the Chinese empire and as that empire disintegrated over the period of the nineteenth century these areas came to fall within the sphere of the Japanese empire. It is only in the post-Second World War period that the countries have operated with difficulty as modern nation states.

The early history of Korea blends into legend, where it is claimed that 'the first ruler of Korea, Tankoon, was the son of the creator. Tankoon chose Pyongyang . . . as the capital of his new country, to which he gave the name "Chosun", meaning "the Land of Morning Freshness"'.[24] However, the social scientific tale begins with the confusions of many small tribes in the territory around the Yalu River at the time of the end of the Bronze Age in the fourth century BC. Around this time there was an incursion from northern China and the kingdom of Chosun was founded in 194 BC.[25] However, the territory was fairly quickly absorbed by the Han Dynasty and the Chinese established colonies some of which survived beyond the collapse of the Han Dyansty. Thereafter, in the third and fourth centuries invaders overran northern China and the colonies 'sank into oblivion'.[26] However, it is clear that the influence of China upon Korea began very early and consequently we can track the experience of a further bureaucratically ordered agrarian society.

A little later, three small, native Korean kingdoms grew into the power vacuum: Koguryo in the north, Paeckche in the southwest, and Silla in the southeast.[27] These kingdoms engaged in a series of conflicts and whilst Koguryo was the largest power it never secured overall control. Eventually in the seventh century the peninsula was unified by Silla. The establishment of Silla was achieved in the context of conflict with the recently established Chinese Tang Dynasty. Borthwick comments: 'The importance of a major Silla victory over the Tang in 676 can hardly be exaggerated. Not only did it result in Tang recognition of Silla's claim to control the peninsula, it enabled Korean society and culture to develop relatively unhindered by outside aggression during a critical, formative stage. It also set the tone for Korea's "tribute" relationship to China'.[28] It was the most enduring tribute relationship and the dynamic was fluid so that as Chinese power waxed so did the sphere of operation of Korean leaders wane.

The country was successful but never stable. The elite could not resolve the contradiction between acknowledging the role of warrior aristocrats in establishing the kingdom and celebrating the Confucian model of rational bureaucracy. As the elites feuded amongst themselves the country saw a mixture of merchant and scholarly success co-existing with peasant exploitation. Out of the confusion one local power eventually prevailed, and established a reunified state in 918 called Koryo. The regime borrowed from the Tang dynasty models of administration and became conservative. At this time most economic and political acitivity took place in the capital city with the rural areas left as merely sources of agricultural supply, and again conflicts occured in the rural areas. The Koryo dynasty was drawn within the Mongol sphere in the early thirteenth century.

It was not until 1392 that the Korean general Yi Sung-Kae seized power and established the Yi dynasty which had tributory relations with the Chinese Ming dynasty. The country continued as before, the influence of China was strong and the elite continued to foster an aristocratic lifestyle and to neglect the development of the peasant economy which operated at a relatively low level. The Yi dynasty survived in this form until the Manchus replaced the Ming as the central power within the Sino-Centric sphere. The dynasty continued in the eighteenth and nineteenth centuries as an inward looking sphere within the Chinese area. And as the Qing Dynasty moved towards collapse the Chinese government was obliged to contest influence within the territory with a strongly expansionist Japan which formally annexed the territory in 1910 thereby absorbing Korea within the contemporary colonial enterprise.

Finally, the history of the island territory of Taiwan can be noted. Taiwan lies approximately one hundred miles off the coast of China. It had an indigenous Malayo-Polynesian population which established an agricultural and trading economy. In the thirteenth century some mainlanders fled to the island when the Mongols invaded China but the island was not brought under mainland control. After the Mongols withdrew from China the island was not brought under Ming Dynasty administration. The territory remained a backwater. It began to attract mainland immigration in the seventeenth century when the Dutch established a trading base in the southern part of the island and was a base for traders in the area. The territory was finally absorbed within the Chinese sphere by the Qing Dynasty in 1683. Yet the involvement of the mainland remained slight. Taiwan only began to effect a shift to the modern world when it was transferred to the control of the Japanese Empire in 1895.

Pre-modern Japan to the Fall of Tokugawa

It is likely that the Japanese archipelago was populated whilst it was a part of the mainland some 30,000 to 50,000 years ago but the timing is disputed and archaeological evidence of occupation is slight prior to 30,000 years ago.[29] The geography of Japan has shaped settlement patterns and agriculture. Crisman notes that '"Old Japan" was centered on the . . . plains in the Kansai region of west-central Honshu at the eastern end of the Inland Sea, the southern and western shores of which consist of the main islands of Shikoku and Kyushu respectively'.[30] Crisman adds that 'although Japanese society has been transformed since the Meiji restoration of the mid-nineteenth century . . . the distribution of the Japanese population has not been radically altered from what it was when Japan was a feudal agrarian society'.[31]

The pre-contact history of Japan can be noted here in terms of three aspects: (i) the very early and medieval history of Japan when the country first established a stable agrarian feudal system whose stability was thereafter disturbed by division and warfare; (ii) the following ordered hierarchical feudal period of the Tokugawa Shogunate when the country was closed to the outside world and attained a high level of material and cultural development; and (iii) the pattern of exchanges with the outside world over the later periods which were to culminate in the collapse of the shogunate.

The early and medieval history of Japan

The earliest clearly demarcated period of history is called the Jomon period (10,000 to 300 BC) and the people seem to have been hunters and gatherers who, unusually, had settled sites and left pottery and tools. The culturally significant shift to agriculture was begun in the Yayoi period (300 BC to AD 300). The Yayoi people undertook wet rice cultivation with other grains on higher drier ground, and bronze and iron were in use. The earliest reliable history deals with the agrarian societies of the sixth century AD.[32]

In the period from AD 300 to AD 710 the Yamato state was formed. Borthwick comments: 'The history of Japan during the first few centuries AD is clouded in myth, but from the late sixth century on a picture emerges of tribal groups (uji) unified under the state of Yamato on the islands of Honshu, Kyushu and Shikoku and on the southern tip of Korea'.[33] Borthwick adds that 'the interchange culturally and politically with Korea was probably heavy through the eighth century as migrations and alliances continued to take place between the Yamato people of Japan on the one hand and the Silla and Paekche peoples on the other'.[34]

The archaeological evidence shows a rich agricultural community, and there is evidence of much trade and cultural links with kingdoms in the Korean peninsula. They had writing and the court histories of Yamato are the earliest Japanese literature. The period also saw urbanization with a series of capital cities in the Nara region. Towards the end of the period there was a shift of attention towards China as a new source of models of government and civilization. In the seventh century following the visit of a large delegation to China the governmental system was overhauled in the Taika reform which initiated a legal system embodied in the Taisho Code of 701. Subsequently, the Nara period from AD 710 to AD 794 saw further administrative advances, new capitals and denser patterns of communication. Nara came to rule most of Honshu and Kyushu. The period saw a rise in independence for temples and a dual authority, secular and divine, develops. In both cases it is possession of land which serves as the economic base.

The medieval age encompasses three periods: (i) late Heian from AD 794 to AD 1185 when Japan had a population of five million and a capital city with 100,000; (ii) Kamakura from AD 1185 to AD 1336; and (iii) Muromachi from AD 1336 to AD 1573 with capitals in Kyoto and Kamakura.

The Heian period is regarded as the flowering of early Japan: government, religious orders, economy and cultural activities all prospered for most of the period. However rivalries continued between powerful families and in the Heian period the Fujiwara family established the system of dual secular power with the emperor as nominal leader but with real power with the most powerful of the lords. The religious groups also grew in power. In the capital city the court and lords ruled via an elaborate Chinese inspired bureaucracy. At the end of the Heian period the stability inaugurated in the Yamato state fell away. The prosperity and slow advance of earlier epochs were slowly lost in the devevloping confusions of warfare in the Kamakura and Muromachi periods.

The Kamakura bafuku took the capital to the town of Kamakura and the period saw a series of wars. In this period there was also an attempted invasion from the Korean peninsula by the Mongols in 1274 and 1281. In this period power began to drift from the centre to the regional lords. Borthwick comments: 'Following the rise in Japan of the Minamoto faction in 1192 and a new shogun, Minamoto Yoritomo, the era of warrior rule over Japan began'.[35] Borthwick records that its 'central administrative structure was called the bakufu. Although it began as a rather simple governmental structure . . . the bakufu eventually transformed itself into an elaborate, sophisticated bureaucracy. The shogun, formally appointed by the Emperor, became in effect the principal administrator over the domain of his family, that of his vassals, and to a lesser extent of the vassals allied to the emperor'.[36] Yet the Kamakura bakufu period was relatively stable. Borthwick notes that: 'Art and culture were no longer the exclusive domain of the elegant courtiers in Kyoto. The samurai, with their new power and affluence, became new patrons of the arts . . . Buddhism also spread from the temples and became a more popular religion'.[37]

In the fourteenth century the Muromachi bafuku returned to Kyoto and the shogunate became more embroiled in court politics whilst the regional lords increased their power. There were about two hundred and fifty important regional lords. It was a period of decentralization, ruling group disaggregation and warfare. Borthwick comments that: 'the status and power of the shoguns began to decline when their provincial governors became more wealthy and independent. By the fifteenth century open conflict broke out between rival alliances over the succession to the position of shogun. Entering the sixteenth century, Japan had become fragmented into small domains and was mired in civil war among powerful regional lords'.[38] It is interesting to note that in this period of confusion new patterns of economic activity were undertaken. Borthwick notes: 'local merchants and entrepreneurs [were able] to increase their economic activities . . . stimulating overall economic growth during the Muromachi period'.[39]

Overall the medieval age saw: (i) the disintegration of the ordered polity of Yamato; (ii) a continuing slow population rise along with economic advance; and (iii) the rise of important competing land-owning lords as the key players in the increasingly fractious polity. The period of confusion and war was finally ended at the Battle of Sekigahara in 1600 when Tokugawa Ieyasu defeated the other regional lords and assumed power, taking the title of Shogun in 1603.

Tokugawa and the end of pre-modern Japan

The Edo Period lasted between 1603 and 1867 when Japan was ruled by the Tokugawa Shogunate. The founder of this dynasty was Tokugawa Ieyasu (1542–1616) who gradually defeated and brought under control all other warlords, the temples and the peasantry. It was the first period of peace for some three hundred years. Beasley[40] notes that the polity was feudal with a ruling group around the shogun, who nominally followed the rule of the emperor, plus a series of regional lords and a wide spread of nobles, the samurai, and thereafter farmers, artisans and merchants. The Shogun's people dominated court life in Kyoto which was ceremonial, without real power, and strictly regulated down to dress, marriages, behaviour and pastimes. The emperor was in effect a pensioner of the Shogun who ruled in Edo. The Shogun and his immediate samuarai had vast landholdings which funded their government. Many thousands of officials and administrators lived in Edo. The office of the Shogun was in principle absolute and heredi-tary but in practice more flexible. The core group was the Tokugawa clan.

The feudal lords, the daimyo, ruled landed territories. They were appointed to these territories by the Shogun and could be moved around. The lords were ranked in terms of their families' relation to the Shogun. Each domain had its local bureaucracy and derived its wealth from the land. The feudal lords were controlled by the alternate attendance system whereby the lords had to reside in Edo for alternate years and leave family in Edo when they were in their home areas. In addition there were pledges of allegiance, dynastic marriages, restrictions on local forces and required public works. The system controlled the behaviour and wealth of the regional lords.

The economy was agricultural, and in the early years was mainly sub-sistence as a result of the upheavals of decades of civil wars. Beasley[41] notes that the period saw: (i) a growing population, rising from eighteen million in 1600 to thirty million in 1850; (ii) urbanization, such that Edo had a population of one million in the early 1700s; and (iii) commercial develop-ment as production began to rise above subsistence levels and farmers produced for the market, and as basic transport systems, distribution systems and credit facilities were developed.

The overall social system was clearly hierarchical. In Tokugawa Japan each person in his place owed a duty of allegiance and obedience to their superior. The caste system of Tokugawa Japan derived from Confucian models and was quite rigid: lord, samurai, farmer, artisan, merchant. The society of the common people centred on the continuing family, and thereafter the village. In the continuing family, patterns of life were tightly controlled. The family owned property (rather than individuals) and worked as a group within which the rights and duties of individual members were specified. Atsumi notes the links between family and economy, and reports that: 'The economy of the Japanese village at the time was primarily based on paddy-rice agriculture which required corporate management of waterways and intensive labour at the time of transplanting and harvesting. A household contained five or six members on average and was too small to fulfill all the necessary agricultural and life needs in the village . . . To meet the various needs of villagers, several were organised into a fairly constant corporate unit. These formed a community, and cooperated with one another through labour exchanges, mutual aid and assistance, and participation in festivals and other religious activities'.[42]

As the Tokugawa period wore on the rise in agricultural production and the rise in the power of the towns began to weaken established patterns of production and power. An important element of urbanization was the new class of merchants. It was also where the samurai warrior-bureaucrats resided. However, the samurai warrior-bureaucrats were losing track of events in a confusion of maladministration and debt (addressed via forced loans, taxes and the granting of monopolies). As new classes began to emerge – merchants, richer farmers and artisan craft producers – the class make up of the urban economies began to shift and the samurai turned out to be a key group as elements eventually became progressive reformers.

The Shogun controlled both the distribution of land, which was the key resource along with its people in an agricultural society, and force of arms in particular via the bureaucrat-warriors known as the samurai. It is clear that the system brought peace but it had its drawbacks: the shogun's economic power was limited in relation to the extensive demands of a state; the daimyo often prioritized local interests; and the samurai warrior-bureaucrats were inefficient. The shogun's power began to decline fairly early on due to internal problems and changes and it was wholly unable to cope with the arrival of the West. In sum, Tokugawa Japan began as an inward-looking feudal country which prospered within the limits of this framework, which was clearly pre-modern, and which began to develop towards the end of the period without however coming to the point of making that shift to the modern world which had been contrived over roughly the same period in Europe. The Tokugawa shogunate had become moribund and could deal neither with internal problems occasioned by growing populations and modest economic prosperity and advance nor with the demands of the European and American colonial traders.

Yet, overall, Sheridan[43] suggests that the period did contribute to later post-Meiji success by establishing: (i) low birth and death rates; (ii) urban growth and commercialization in villages; (iii) ethnic uniformity; (iv) irrigation systems; (v) commercial and financial systems; and (vi) systems of land tenure and taxation. Sheridan notes that prosperity grew steadily if slowly over the whole period. However, people were still poor and lived hard lives. Sheridan also notes what the period did not produce: no capital for industrialization; no technology for industrialization; and no entrepreneurs to run the system. In sum, a stable and growing agricultural and craft-based economy that had by pre-Meiji days developed just about as far as it could go.

The exchanges with the outside world

After Japan adopted the closed country policy in 1633 all trade and links with the outside were tightly controlled and Nagasaki was the only point of access for Chinese junks and Dutch traders. Over this long period some ideas did enter Japan, known as the 'Dutch learning', and included natural science, medicine and military equipment. The spread of this Dutch learning was slow and was also resisted by patriots who saw it as implicated in the moral decline of the country.

In the seventeenth and eighteenth centuries trading vessels from America and Europe became frequent visitors to Pacific Asia. The Russian empire also made overtures. The European and American movement into the region gathered pace and reached its imperial apogee in the mid-nineteenth century when the Western powers forced the Chinese government to open up a series of trading ports. A mixture of technological advantage, commercial advantage and military force drew China into the developing global economic system.

All this was watched by the Japanese elites with some anxiety. Eventually the traders began to look to Japan. The Tokugawa shogunate had become moribund by the late nineteenth century and could deal neither with internal problems occasioned by growing populations and modest economic prosperity, nor with the demands of the American and European colonial traders.

After a series of rebuffs Commodore Perry forced the Shogunate to sign a treaty in 1854 which allowed trade. The period from 1854 to 1867 sees the slow increase in influence of the West with its traders moving into Japan to a very uncertain welcome. The political elite in Japan were split and there was pressure for resistance. Indeed there was small scale violent conflict on several occasions. Eventually the Western powers bombarded the Choshu town of Kagoshima in 1863 and the Shimonoseki Straits forts in 1864. The European powers secured treaties which allowed trade and extra-territorial rights for foreign nationals; the Japanese called them unequal treaties and regarded them as a national disgrace. The episode precipitated a political crisis in Japan which led to the collapse of the Shogunate. The Meiji restoration saw power seized by a group of dissident regional lords determined to reconstruct the country so as to resist the encroachment of the colonial powers.

The Peoples of Indo-China

The region is geographically and culturally complex. For present purposes we may take it to include the territories of Vietnam, Laos and Cambodia (as is usual today) plus the neighbouring territory of Thailand. In the premodern period the economic base of the cultures of the region was wet-rice production. The social organisation was usually some mixture of peasant farming and religiously sanctioned figures of authority. The great religious traditions included Confucianism and Buddhism. The Confucian influence was felt strongly in Vietnam which had a rather centralized system of organization. In the Buddhist-influenced areas such as Thailand patterns of authority could be much more dispersed. Overall, the political pattern was one of small shifting fluid states which occasionally generated larger empires.

In the early modern period, from the fifteenth to the seventeenth century, as the Europeans and Americans moved in it was the contemporary variants of these fluid and shifting 'statelets' and empires with which the incomers had to deal. It is, therefore, only in the modern period, in particular in the nineteenth and twentieth centuries, via the episode of colonial rule, that these territories have made the shift to the modern world. It is only in the modern period that relatively fixed territorial nation states have been established. And it is only in the modern period that Western ideas of nationalism have been taken into the cultural resources of these territories.[44]

In the area of modern day Vietnam, an early empire was Funan which existed from approximately AD 0 to AD 400 and which was centred on the Mekong Delta. The later Champa Dynasty which existed from approximately AD 400 to AD 700 was centred on the coast of the South China Sea. Later from approximately AD 900 the Vietnamese broke away from China and established themselves at the expense of Champa. In Vietnam the Red River valley provided the core of the territory of Tonkin. This was the major sphere of Chinese influence. In the centre of the country along the coast lay Annam, which was 'the locus of the traditional Vietnamese state'.[45] The Vietnamese spread southwards, displaced the local Chams and occupied the delta of the Mekong River. The result was that a marked bipolar distribution of the Vietnamese population developed with major concentrations of population in the Red River and Mekong Deltas.[46] A sophisticated economy and society developed. Yet in the late nineteenth century the French were to draw the area within the ambit of their colonial control.

The Khmer kingdom which existed from approximately AD 1000 to AD 1200 was centred on the settlement at Angkor. The area has long been a centre for the Khmer people whose economy revolved around agriculture. The great civilization of Angkor had its economic base in an elaborate system of water control and a centralized pattern of political order whereby local rulers acknowledged the centre. The system was sophisticated, successful and fragile and eventually came under pressure from the neighbouring Thais. The territory of Cambodia was subsequently of modest political and economical importance within the region and was absorbed by the expanding French Indo-China colony in the late nineteenth century.

And finally we can note that the Laotian people are 'closely related in language, culture and religion to the northeastern Thais'.[47] The country of Laos as it is today only came into being when the French detached a portion of the northeastern Thai-speaking region in the late nineteenth century.

The Sukhothai kingdom existed from approximately AD 1200 to AD 1400 and was located in the central part of modern Thailand. The agricultural economy supported a ruling elite centred on the person of a warrior chief who would be presented as the father of his people. The kingdom engaged in a series of conflicts with its Burmese, Lao, Khmer and Vietnamese neighbours. In 1431 the Thais overran Angkor. The Sukhothai dynasty lost its pre-eminence in the late fifteenth century and was succeeded by the Ayuthya dynasty. The economy continued to be agrarian but the polity was significantly revised and the new rulers established a codified body of law and an elaborate system of status distinctions amongst its ruling elites and related bureaucracy. In 1767 the Burmese defeated the Thais and the dynasty fell. The capital was moved to Bangkok and in 1782 the present Chakri dynasty was founded. It was this dynasty which was approached by the British in the mid-nineteenth century and the reforming ruler King Chulalongkorn (1868–1910) established a pattern of rule modelled on the neighbouring colonial pattern in British Malaya and proceeded to begin the modernization of Thailand.[48]

The period between approximately AD 1600 and AD 1800 saw warfare between these indigenous kingdoms. In contemporary terminology, between both (i) the Thai, Burmese and Lao; and (ii) the Thai, Khmer and Vietnamese. After 1800 the Europeans began to move into the area. The British moved into Burma and the southern Malay peninsula. The French moved into Vietnam, Laos and Cambodia (together called Indo-China). The Thai kingdom escaped colonization as it served as a buffer between the British and French colonial spheres. Over the period of colonial rule the traditional forms-of-life slowly retreated and over time declined and faded away.

The Peoples of the Archipelago of Southeast Asia

There is a broad distinction to be drawn in respect of the economic livelihoods of the people of the region between land powers, with economies based on rice, and maritime trading powers working networks over relatively long distances in the archipelago.

In the pre-contact period the region was ethnographically diverse. The diversity in the long pre-contact period can be expressed in racial terms: there was a mongoloid migration from the north into the islands. Approximately twenty per cent of the population are aboriginal non-mongoloid peoples. The cultural and ethnic pattern is very diverse. There are two main formal religious traditions: Islam and Hinduism.

In general the political economy of the region comprised numerous petty states which occupied small shifting territories. It was from this context that a series of maritime empires grew and these were based around a royal family and a key port. The extent of the territories could be large. It might also be noted that a series of distinctive kingdoms developed and flourished prior to the full establishment of the influence of the Europeans on the island of Java.

Overall, the patterns of loyalty were personal and familial and the trading networks were extensive and wealthy.

The sequence of empires includes Srivijaya, centred on eastern Sumatra and the Malay peninsula, which existed over the period AD 450 to AD 1000. It seems that Srivijaya enjoyed a tributory relationship with China and was thus a major trading empire. In the thirteenth century the empire of Mahapahit was founded on Java and eventually gave way to the Javanese kindgom of Mataram. The empire of Malacca is sometimes regarded as the successor to Srivijaya and it survived until the Portuguese conquered the key port in 1511. Thereafter, the successor kindgom was Johor-Riau, itself absorbed within British and Dutch colonial holdings, as were a series of similar fluid empires in the whole spread of the archipelago: Acheh, Bantam, Brunai, Celebes, Ternate and Tidore.

The political forms in the region were various. Tate comments: 'Given the vastness of the region, the variety of peoples in it and the widely differing geographical circumstances which prevail, the absence of any political cohesion prior to modern times should not be at all surprising. Although . . . it is possible to speak of a basic Malaysian/Indonesian culture, nearly every conceivable form of political and social organization has developed amongst the peoples of the region. With the Menangkabau of West Sumatra, for instance, we find a matriarchal society based on the family, clan and village, while in Bali the social organization is patriarchal and patterned on the irrigation system. In Java, society was hierarchical and bureaucratic, based on a closely worked out system of land tenure; in Ceram it was based on tribal groupings and in Timor simply on class. Monarchy was the traditional political form in the Malay states, oligarchy was the rule amongst the Bugis of South Celebes and republican forms were reflected in the government systems of the Menangkabau. This wealth of political and social forms is matched by the incoherent nature of the region's political history'.[49]

Tate argues that modern Southeast Asia is a product of the last hundred years or so – a mix of industrialism and imperialism – and that the contemporary pattern of nation states is therefore relatively new.

Up to the beginning of the nineteenth century the impact of the Europeans had been slight. The Europeans were simply one more group within a very diverse area. However, as the industrial revolution gathered strength in Europe the schedule of demands for trading goods changed from exotic indigenous products to the products of plantation agriculture. The new schedule of demands, coupled to technological advances in communications, plus the military-technological superiority of the West, all provided the basis for greater involvement on the part of the West in the affairs of these petty states and empires. In time, the involvement was expressed in the form of colonial empires, and traditional forms-of-life declined and disappeared.

Australia and the Pacific Islands

The pre-modern period of history in Australia is difficult to access as it is over-lain with myth and is usually read in terms of the debates of the present day. Hughes recalls the myth: 'A static culture, frozen by its immemorial primi-tivism, unchanged in an unchanging landscape – such until quite recently was, and for many people still is, the common idea of the Australian Aborigines'.[50] Hughes goes on to argue that the myth grows from a series of key ideas centred on the image of the noble savage untamed by civilization and its conceits; a related series of simple errors about the level of aboriginal technology which underestimate its development; and the broad influence of the pervasive racism of early Australian society. Hughes goes on to add that 'one of the chief myths of early colonial history as understood and taught up to about 1960 . . . was the idea . . . that the First Fleet sailed into an "empty" continent, speckled with primitive animals and hardly less primitive men, so that the "fittest" inevitably triumphed'.[51] It is on the basis of this deconstructive reading that Hughes pursues his attempt to see matters clearly.

Hughes makes a broad summary of a history shorn of myth: 'At the time of the white invasion, men had been living in Australia for at least 30,000 years. They had moved into the continent during the Pleistocene epoch. This migration happened at about the same time as the first wave of human migrations from Asia into the unpeopled expanse of North America . . . The first Australians also came from Asia . . . Apart from their northern origin, no one knows who these Pleistocene colonists were or whence they emerged'.[52] Hughes goes on to describe the slow process of dispersal across the huge continent. It took very many years and the result was that whilst the territory was occupied it was at a very low population density. Hughes remarks that: 'When the First Fleet arrived, there were perhaps 300,000 Aborigines in the whole of Australia – a continental average of one person to ten square miles'.[53]

Hughes notes: 'The Australians divided themselves into tribes. They had no notion of private property, but they were intensely territorial, linked to the ancestral area by hunting customs and totemism. . . . The tribe . . . was linked together by a common religion, by language and by an intricate web of family relationships; it had no writing, but instead a complex structure of spoken and sung myth whose arcana were gradually passed on by elders to the younger men'.[54]

Hughes points out that at the time of the arrival of the whites there were maybe up to nine hundred tribal groups. The means of livelihood was hunting and gathering. Thereafter, the anthropology of the aboriginals is as complex as that of other similar 'primitive peoples'.

A similar tale could be told for the islands of the Pacific: (i) Micronesia, lying to the east of the Philippine islands; (ii) Melanesia, lying to the east of Papua New Guinea; and (iii) Polynesia, lying to the south of the Hawaiian islands. These small isolated communites were settled by Malay travellers in the years before recorded history and developed a spread of distinctive cultural forms before being drawn into the modern world by the demands of European colonialism. [55]

The Impact of the West up to the Early Nineteenth Century

The impact of the West up to the early nineteenth century was relatively slight. The European and American traders had a series of problems to confront: vast distances to travel; primitive technology; and small numbers. The European expansion in Pacific Asia did not begin in any significant way until the later years of the eighteenth century and the early years of the nineteenth. The concerns of the Western traders shifted as the political economy of the West developed. The demands of industrial-capitalism were different from those of mercantile-capitalism. The new schedule of demands flowed from the requirements of new technologies, expanding home populations and newly constructed cultural ideas of the superiority of the West. The impact of the West in the subsequent years was to remake the patterns of lives of the peoples of Pacific Asia.

Conclusion

In the pre-contact period the region can be seen to fall into separate spheres: (i) China and Northeast Asia; (ii) the Japanese islands; (iii) Indo-China; and (iv) Southeast Asia. The related contiguous territories of Australia and the Pacific Islands played relatively slight roles until the period of colonization. In the region there were pre-contact forms-of-life having political economies, social-institutional structures and distinctive cultures. The impact of the West up to the early nineteenth century slowly drew these areas into the developing global industrial-capitalist system. The existing patterns of life were slowly overborne and recast.

It can be argued that up until the threshold of the nineteenth century the demands of the West were sustainable by indigenous forms-of-life. The demands of the mercantile-capitalist traders were for exotic goods and these could be supplied with relatively minimal disturbance to existing patterns of political-economic, social-institutional and cultural life. However, the industrial revolution in Europe in the late eighteenth and early nineteenth centuries radically altered the schedule of demands of the capitalist West. As the pattern of demands altered in line with the development of industrial-capitalism the depth of penetration of the West within indigenous cultures grew much deeper. It is in the late eighteenth and early nineteenth century that the broad reconstruction of non-Western forms-of-life begins. It finds juridical expression in the formal colonial empires of the Europeans and Americans. In this period indigenous forms-of-life are slowly absorbed within the various empire structures of the developing global industrial-capitalist system, and this process we turn to in the next chapter.

Notes

1   A. Reid 1988/93: *Southeast Asia in the Age of Commerce*, New Haven, CT: Yale University Press.
2   E. Moise 1994: *Modern China*, London: Longman.
3   Ibid., pp. 4–5.
4   B. Moore 1966: *Social Origins of Dictatorship and Democracy*, Boston: Beacon.
5   P. Worsley 1984: *The Three Worlds: Culture and World Development*, London: Weidenfeld.
6   R. Atsumi 1995: Basic Social Structures and Family Systems in C. Mackerras, ed., *Eastern Asia*, London: Longman, p. 51.
7   Ibid.
8   Ibid.
9   Ibid., p. 53.
10   Ibid., pp. 53–5.
11   Ibid., p. 59.
12   J. Howell 1995: Religious Traditions in Asia in Mackerras, ed., 1995, p. 63.
13   Ibid., p. 64.
14   C. Mackerras 1995: Administration and Rebellion in East Asia in Mackerras ed. 1995, p. 93.
15   Ibid., p. 94.
16   Ibid.
17   Moise 1994, p. 17.
18   Ibid., p. 32.
19   Ibid., p. 33.
20   Ibid.
21   Ibid., p. 34.
22   B. Inglis 1979: *The Opium War*, London: Coronet.
23   Moise 1994, p. 32.
24   M. S. Dobbs-Higginson 1995: *Asia Pacific: Its Role in the New World Disorder*, London: Mandarin, p. 267.
25   M. Borthwick 1992: *Pacific Century: The Emergence of Modern Pacific Asia*, Boulder, CO: Westview, p. 27.
26   Dobbs-Higginson 1995, p. 267.
27   B. Cummings 1997: *Korea's Place in the Sun: A Modern History*.
28   Borthwick 1992, p. 29.
29   R. Bowring and P. Kornicki, eds, 1993: *The Cambridge Encyclopedia of Japan*, Cambridge: Cambridge University Press.
30   L. Crisman 1995: The Physical and Ethnic Geography of East and Southeast Asia in Mackerras, ed., 1995, p. 19.
31   Ibid., p. 21.
32   Bowring and Kornicki, eds, 1993.
33   Borthwick 1992, p. 28.

34 Ibid.
35 Ibid., p. 41.
36 Ibid.
37 Ibid.
38 Ibid.
39 Ibid.
40 W. G. Beasley 1990: *The Rise of Modern Japan*, Tokyo: Tuttle, pp. 2–8.
41 Ibid., pp. 9–15.
42 Atsumi 1995, pp. 57–8.
43 K. Sheridan 1993: *Governing the Japanese Economy*, Cambridge: Polity.
44 M. Osborne 1995: *Southeast Asia*, St Leonards: Allen and Unwin.
45 Crisman 1995, p. 36.
46 Ibid.
47 Ibid., p. 38.
48 J. L. S. Girling 1981: *Thailand: Society and Politics*, Ithaca, NY: Cornell University Press.
49 D. J. M. Tate 1971/9: *The Making of Southeast Asia*, Oxford: Oxford University Press, p. 28.
50 R. Hughes 1988: *The Fatal Shore*, London: Pan, p. 7.
51 Ibid.
52 Ibid., p. 8.
53 Ibid., p. 9.
54 Ibid.
55 H. C. Brookfield 1972: *Colonialism, Development and Independence: The Case of the Melanesian Islands in the South Pacific*, Cambridge: Cambridge University Press.

4

The Shift to the Modern World: Reactions, Resistance and Empire

The broad historical development experience of the region can be grasped in terms of a series of interrelated processes whereby extant forms-of-life were remade in line with the demands of the expanding form of life of industrial-capitalism. In the late nineteenth century and through into the twentieth century the demand of the industrial-capitalist countries simply overwhelmed extant forms-of-life. The period of empire saw the construction of distinctive colonial forms-of-life and by the 1930s most of the region was controlled by groups originating outside the area.

The empire of China was divided amongst the Europeans and Americans and was reduced to the status of a quasi-colony. The elite of Japan engineered successful resistance in the authoritarian reform from above of the Meiji Restoration and quickly moved to establish their own colonial holdings in Asia. The territories of Northeast Asia were overwhelmed by the structural changes flowing through the region, removed from the Chinese sphere and lodged as Japanese colonial territories within the modern industrial world. The Dutch occupied a huge territory in the archipelago of Southeast Asia, the British opened a sphere in Malaya, and the French secured territory in Indo-China, and the Americans established a sphere in the Philippines. In addition, in the more remote Pacific Island areas of the region there were British, French, German, Japanese and American holdings. Finally, modern Australia and New Zealand developed, along with a scatter of islands in the Pacific.

In the region the impact of the expanding colonial ordered industrial-capitalist system were severe. The extant forms-of-life were all more or less extensively reconfigured to meet the demands of metropolitan capital with the key link of local area and global system being provided by colonial cities.[1] The colonial expansion drew the peoples of the region into the industrial-capitalist system and the pattern of colonial rule survived without significant challenge until the violent upheavals of the Pacific War.

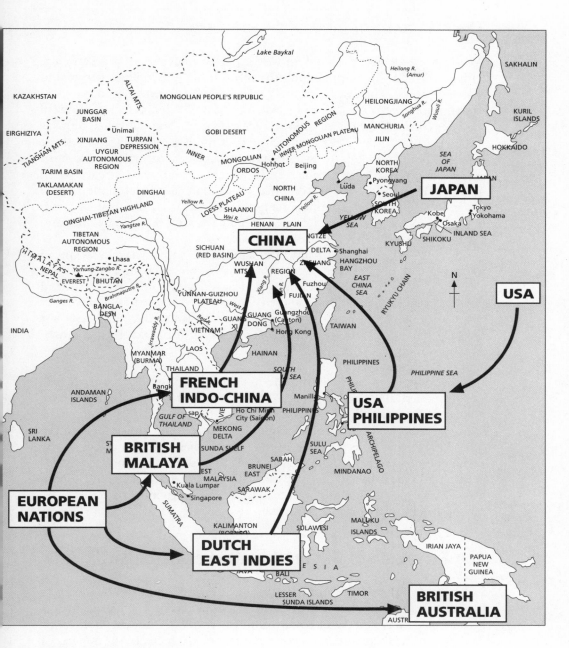

Map 4.1   Colonial period spheres

The Demands of Industrial-capitalism

Worsley[2] argues that the modern world can be understood as a particular cultural form, a way of organising the relationship of people to nature and to other people. The essence of this particular cultural form is its disposition to philosophical materialism and social liberalism. The inhabitants of modern societies construe their lives and societies in material and individual terms.

The cultural form of modernity comprises the general celebration of the power of human reason, the extensive development of natural science, and a political-economic system dedicated to material progress via science-based industry. The modern world is dominated by industrial-capitalism. It is a very dynamic system which routinely refines itself internally, that is it becomes better organized and penetrates more deeply through the social world, and expands externally, that is it grows geographically.

The cultural form of modernity originated in Europe and has slowly spread to cover much of the world. In this long drawn out and continuing process existing local cultures have been slowly drawn into the modern system and their patterns of life variously altered. It can be described as a process of absorption and reconstruction as existing cultural resources are more or less radically remade in line with the expectations and demands of modernity. The expansion has taken place as a series of waves embracing in turn the Americas, Asia and Africa.

The Congress of Berlin in the late nineteenth century divided the world amongst the rival Western powers. Worsley remarks that Asia 'seemed to have gone under for good'[3] but adds that what in retrospect is surprising in the light of its technological and scientific superiority is the brevity of Western rule. An explanation is available in the social upheaval which attended the entire episode. As the peoples of Asia made their shift to the modern world, in the context of colonial rule, they learned how to operate within the system, how to become autonomous agents in the shifting structural patterns of the now global industrial-capitalist system.

The Expansion of the West in the Region of Pacific Asia

In Pacific Asia the European traders had little impact on existing societies in the early years of contact. In the mid-sixteenth century when these traders first arrived they did so in small numbers and with trade expectations confined to small quantities of exotic and luxury products. In the context of regional trading patterns, they were merely one more group of traders. Yet the extent of the European involvement grew over the seventeenth and eighteenth centuries, and in the nineteenth century the involvement of Europeans and Americans in the territories of Pacific Asia deepened significantly. As a result of the dynamics of industrial-capitalism the schedule of demands for trade goods in the region expanded sharply and at the same time the increasing technological superiority of the West in respect of the ruling regimes of the region allowed them to insist that their requirements be acknowledged. The upshot was a slow but steady movement to take control of areas within the region in order to facilitate their integration within the industrial-capitalist system. The final stage of this process was the imposition of formal colonial regimes. It was against this system that the nationalists of the colonized territories were to organize their resistance as the political-cultural resources of the colonizers were turned back against themselves.[4]

Mercantile traders in Pacific Asia

The European involvement with the region of Pacific Asia began before the industrial revolution transformed metropolitan capital into industrial-capitalism. The concern of the first Europeans in the region was with trade in pre-industrial goods and this was pursued within the frame of the mercantilist concern for monopoly. There were three major commercial areas: (i) the India trade; (ii) the Spice trade; and (iii) the China trade, and within each of these areas Europeans manoeuvred against each other in concert with local country powers (as the Westerners called the local polities) for position and advantage.[5]

The major vehicles of early European expansion within the region were the great trading companies.[6] The first company voyage sponsored by the Amsterdam Company travelled to Bantam in 1596–7. A few years later in 1602 the Dutch East Indies Company (VOC) was formed and sought a monopoly of trade beyond the Cape of Good Hope. It was authorized by the Dutch government to wage war, make treaties and build fortresses. In 1611 the Dutch opened a factory at Jakarta which lay within the Bantam Sultanate and in 1619 the Dutch annexed the area so laying claim to the spice trade and blocking their rivals the British. The British established their own East India Company in 1657 and they competed vigorously with the Dutch but were forced back to India whilst the Dutch kept the archipelago. Over the seventeenth century the Europeans manoeuvred for advantage on the Indian coast. The Dutch seized Sri Lanka in 1658 and Malacca in 1641. The French also looked for advantage but were not generally successful.[7]

In the eighteenth century the British extended their power in India and from this base the trade with China began to grow, where the East India Company traded piece goods (cottons, calicos and silk), teas and spices. At the same time the Dutch East Indies Company continued its successful trade in the archipelago. However, the trade entered a slow decline which, in part, was occasioned by the very restrictive monopoly trading practices adopted by the Dutch which had the effect of redirecting trade to the more liberal British. In the late eighteenth and early nineteenth centuries there were wars in Europe and these had a spill-over effect in the trading patterns within the East Indies, where local country powers were drawn into the conflicts and manoeuvring. The upshot, in brief, was that the French were defeated in

Europe at the end of the Napoleonic Wars and the British and Dutch split between themselves the regions of Southeast Asia and India.[8]

The two companies which ran the trade had a quite particular status. They were both founded in the late sixteenth century and they prospered through the seventeenth and into the eighteenth century. However, by the end of the century they were beginning to be overtaken by events, in particular, the rise of competition from independent country traders and the demands of their quasi-governmental role. The older company, the Dutch East Indies Company, was a major business organization with links to the government. The company had a federal structure, reflecting the make up of federal Holland, with a secretariat in The Hague, and the autocratic ruling board were know as the Seventeen. The key overseas base was in Batavia and the resident Governor-General controlled the territory via the strategy of indirect rule. And in a similar way the East India Company had a court of twenty-four directors who managed the overall business whilst the company's administration overseas was divided into the three residencies of Bengal, Madras and Bombay, each with an army and an administration. In all, the number of Europeans involved was fairly small compared to the local populations, maybe 75,000 towards the end of the pre-industrial mercantile period. Indeed, Barraclough argues that one reason for the collapse of the empires in the wake of the Pacific War was the simple demographics of the relationship.[9]

The Dutch presence in the region developed steadily from their base in Batavia, annexed in 1619. The contiguous territory of Bantam was brought under Dutch control in 1664, neighbouring Krawang and Priangan in 1677. The Dutch then moved along the rest of the island of Java securing overall control by 1777 (except for the important kingdoms of Jogjakarta and Surakarta which maintained their independence until 1830). In the archipelago generally, Malacca was Dutch in 1641, Macassar by 1667, Tidore by 1667, Ternate by 1683, Palembang by 1825, Bali by 1854, Banjarmasin by 1860, Acheh by 1899, Flores by 1907, and western New Guinea in the late 1920s.[10] Beyond the archipelago the Dutch had trading interests in Japan, where they had enjoyed trading rights at the port of Nagasaki from the early 1600s. Similarly, they had trading rights in Canton in 1762.[11]

The British presence in the region was more restricted, with Penang occupied in 1786, Singapore in 1819, Malacca in 1824 and the peninsula proper slowly occupied from 1874 through to the turn of the century. Beyond the archipelago the British came to have extensive interests in China and an early trading base became active at Canton around 1715.[12] The trade with China became important, yet as a result of an imbalance of trade the region's silver came to slowly drain into China. The British eventually insisted that the Chinese authorities relax their trade restrictions, in particular on opium, and following the Opium Wars of 1839–42 and 1856–60 a series of treaty ports were opened up. In particular Hong Kong, which was in part ceded to the British in the 1842 Treaty of Nanjing, with the Kowloon Peninsula and the New Territories added later. In the later years of the nineteenth century the British, following Commodore Perry's lead, gained trading rights in Japan.

The expansion of industrial-capitalism

The nineteenth century saw a change in the demands placed upon the region by the Western traders as a result of changes within the sphere of metropolitan capital. The industrial revolution created new schedules of demands for raw materials and the requirement that new markets for the products be opened. The upshot was that the depth of European involvement increased rapidly. The region was thereby brought into the ambit of the industrial-capitalist system as an extensive peripheral area: China became a quasi-colony; Japan a participant in colonial expansion; and the other areas within the region became formal colonies lodged within the sphere of one or other of the great powers.

China Divided Amongst Western Powers and Japan

The Chinese conducted trade on their own terms from the earliest Portuguese contacts, and this continued successfully for several hundred years.[13] However, the situation changed radically in the nineteenth century as Western powers began to demand trading rights. Inside the Chinese ruling class there was considerable debate about the appropriate strategy of response. The established Chinese world view placed the Imperial Court at the centre and ranged all other peoples in circles of descending importance around this core. The culture was inward looking and disinclined to begin the business of learning from outsiders. However, the military defeats of the Opium Wars and the routine evidence of European and American commercial vigour did encourage the pursuit of modernization by some groups within China. Yet, they received no support from the Imperial centre, indeed they were discouraged. Overall, reports Moise,[14] there was little real grasp of the extent of changes required within China if the country was to respond positively to the arrival and demands of the Europeans and Americans.

The slow decline of the Qing Dynasty as a result of internal decay and European and American incursions accelerated over the second half of the nineteenth century in the wake of the Opium Wars and the resultant treaty port system which acknowledged and firmly established the European and American trading presence. In 1899 the Boxer Rebellion, which had the tacit support of the Empress, began to attack foreigners and laid siege to the foreign legations in Beijing. The rebellion was quickly suppressed by a combined expedition of European, American and Japanese forces. The Japanese, it might be noted, had confirmed their status as a major power a little earlier when they defeated the Chinese in the course of the Sino-Japanese War 1894–5. The Europeans and Americans now had additional reason to feel approval for this newest colonial power operating within China.

In the wake of the failed Boxer Rebellion the Qing Dynasty finally began a serious programme of modernization. Systems of education were modified to acknowledge Western skills and techniques. There were reforms to the military. There were also attempts to renegotiate the terms of the treaty ports and tariff systems in order to reassert Chinese control. The structures of administration were reformed and constitutional reform was begun. In 1909 Provincial assemblies were elected. In 1910 a National Assembly was convened – half elected and half appointed by the imperial court. Moore comments that the 'pattern of her [the empress dowager'] actions strongly suggests that her real goal was the establishment of a strong centralized bureaucratic government over which she would be able to exercise direct personal control, roughly along the lines of a Germany or a Japan'.[15] However, the reforms were too modest and the imperial system was swept away.

The 1911 revolution was inspired by Sun Yat Sen who looked to establish a Chinese republic on Western lines. Sun built up a revolutionary organization, the Revolutionary Alliance, and between 1906–11 staged a series of failed armed uprisings. In 1911 the Qing Dynasty central government experienced one more crisis (over railway construction) and there was a widespread revolt amongst provincial gentry and two-thirds of the country quickly fell into the hands of Sun Yat Sen's revolutionaries who declared him President in the provincial city of Nanjing. However, the Qing authorities asked General Yaun to suppress the rebels and in the ensuing confusion both the Dynasty and the newly established republic gave way first to the brief rule of General Yuan, and thereafter a series of regional warlords.

In 1921 the CCP was formed and came to have influence in the rural areas. Sun Yat Sen's Nationalist Party, the Kuomintang, was inherited on Sun's death in 1925 by Chiang Kai-shek who moved to establish a military authoritarian government and this was set up in Nanjing in 1927. Up until 1937 there was a battle for power between the KMT, CCP and regional warlords, and Chiang Kai-shek slowly broadened his power and established a unified Chinese state. Moore[16] characterizes the KMT government with its landlordism, gangsterism and opportunistic commercial factions, its backward-looking nationalism and its militarism as a variant of the familiar European model of fascism. And in addition to these confusions the effective collapse of central authority in China and the political and social chaos which followed left the country open to the demands of foreign powers. The Western colonial powers expanded their spheres of influence. And the Japanese became involved. In 1937 the Japanese began open warfare against the Chinese. Yet for the Chinese the war against the Japanese was simultaneously a civil war between nationalists and communists and the country only recovered a measure of coherence in 1949. In general, it would be reasonable to say that prior to the outbreak of the Pacific War the country was a quasi-colony of the various contending powers.

China's shift to the modern world considered

The Qing Dynasty was incapable of formulating a response to the incursions of the expanding industrial-capitalist system. Moore argues that the incapacity lay in the balance of social forces. The Qing Dynasty system comprised five key groupings: (i) the central authorities, who dispensed laws of property, but whose power was relatively weak; (ii) the powerful scholar-bureaucrats who administered the regions of the country; (iii) the powerful local gentry who were landowners; (iv) the peasantry, who had little scope for independent action; and (v) merchant groups whose activities were not encouraged. The system worked in a quite particular way. The scholar-bureaucrats administered the dynastic system of law, tax gathering and public works. They were recruited by merit in examination but their activities over-lapped with the family and clan-based networks of the landowning gentry. The country was very large and central control was always relatively weak so that local scholar-bureaucrats could establish mutually beneficial relation-ships with local powerful landowners. The system was designed to extract resources from the peasantry. However, the merchant, manufacturing and trading groups were not directly involved in this political-economic system. They existed, so to say, off to one side. The scholar-bureaucrats acted to keep them in check and they did not establish themselves as an independent socio-economic grouping (as had been the case in Europe).

The equilibrium of the system was fatally disturbed by the arrival of Western traders. The hitherto weak Chinese traders now had access to a powerful trading partner in the European and American trading companies. After the Opium Wars of 1842 the Chinese merchant groups began to prosper, in particular along the coasts where they traded as compradores with the Europeans and Americans.

Moore argues that the initial reaction of the dynastic centre to the incursions of the West was wholly inappropriate to the threat which they posed. There was no centrally sponsored attempt to learn the lessons of the West and modernize. There was little attempt to improve agriculture as there was no landlord interest in pursuing such development. The system stagnated and was unable to respond. There was some regionally-based attempt at modern-ization, and this typically centred on armaments technologies. Overall, the dynasty was unable to read and react to the developing demands of the global system in the nineteenth century – and slowly it decayed as regional authori-ties became more powerful and as the European and American presence (and later, the Japanese) coupled to the rise of Chinese compradore traders shifted the economy away from the quasi-feudal agrarian system towards an indus-trial-capitalist system. In the early years of the twentieth century the dynastic centre did attempt to establish the institutional machineries of a develop-mental state, but Moore notes that 'the social basis for such a regime was lacking'.[17] In 1911 the regime collapsed and China thereafter drifted into the chaos of warlordism, civil war and world war.

Japan's Successful Resistance – the Meiji Restoration

As the Western powers extended their influence in China through the nine-teenth century, the attention of traders began to turn towards Japan. The islands of Japan can be taken to have represented the very high watermark of Western imperial advance, however the Japanese were not simply lucky, they responded actively and effectively to shifting patterns of global structural power.

The inability of the old Tokugawa Shogunate to formulate a coherent response to the demands of the Western powers led directly to the Meiji restoration in 1868 which saw political power shift to an oligarchic ruling group. The Meiji state borrowed from the model of the West and in a short period restructured Japanese political-economic, social-institutional and cultural patterns. However, the changes in received cultural ideas and patterns of authority were held to a minimum in a state-sponsored authoritarian modernization from above.[18]

In the political sphere, a new state was constructed by an oligarchic group based on the Choshu and Satsuma daimios which had made the revolution in the name of the emperor. It included a series of elements: (i) a modern pattern of central and local government was instituted and the domains were transformed into prefectures within a modern state centred on Tokyo; (ii) the caste system was abolished; (iii) the daimio and samurai retainers were paid-off; (iv) landownership and taxation were reformed to provide state revenues; (v) a centralized bureaucracy was formed; (vi) the state theory of Germany and the constitutional law of France were studied in order to write and promulgate in the name of the emperor a new constitution in 1889; (vii) a political structure involving emperor, parliament and cabinet was formed, and the oligarchy or genro remained outside as a group of 'elder statesmen advising the emperor' although in practice they both held all the power and held the system together; (viii) political parties formed; and (ix) the system of State-Shinto which stressed the role of the emperor was inaugurated and Buddhism repressed. Thereafter, under the slogan 'rich country – strong army' the Meiji government adopted an industrialization programme in parallel with its political reforms. The key to the industrialization drive was the state sponsored construction of modern industry. A Ministry of Industrial Development was set up to oversee heavy industry. In the agricultural sphere, which was important as a foreign exchange earner with silk, the Ministry of Home Affairs was established. In addition to direct state involvement the Meiji government coopted persons whom it thought could become successful industrialists. And in the social sphere, the Meiji oligarchy looked to draw on the legacies of the Tokugawa period in order to fashion a mobilized corporate society. The key institution was the continuing family which was reworked and enshrined in the new civil code as the principal agent of development. Thereafter the role of education was crucial in inducting citizens into the 'family-state', oriented to the pursuit of development.

In the late nineteenth and early twentieth centuries the political-economic development of Japan was very rapid. The pursuit of economic development drew heavily on the available model of the West. The Meiji pursuit of development came to involve early diplomatic conflict with the great powers in Europe and the USA particularly in respect of Japanese colonial activities. At this time the European powers and the USA were extensively involved in China. It was the period of spheres of influence and trading ports. And in the nineteenth century nation states still had routine recourse to war in order to settle disputes and so Japan pursued its concern for security using an available strategy. As the Meiji state secured a measure of industrial modernization they sought further security in the form of the establishment of a sphere of influence in East Asia.

The Meiji Restoration of 1868 brought to power a committed modernizing oligarchy who proceeded over the next thirty years to turn Japan into an industrial economy. On the basis of the newly acquired economic and military power the Japanese moved to expand their influence within East Asia. In the process of expansion the Japanese simply took the available model in respect of the behaviour of states. There was early Japanese activity in the area of the Russian Far East, in the Korean peninsula, and in China. All these areas were geographically contiguous with Japan and thus, given contemporary notions of empire and inter-state relations, obvious places for the expansion of Japanese interests. The Sino-Japanese war of 1894–5 lasted nine months in which time the Japanese armed forces expelled the Chinese from Korea, captured Port Arthur and the Liaotung peninsula. In the peace treaty additionally Taiwan was ceded to Japan. The conflict with Russia in respect of spheres of influence in Manchuria and Korea led to the Russo-Japanese war of 1904–5 which saw success for the Japanese, who attained influence in Manchuria and Korea, which was made a protectorate in 1905 and formally annexed in 1910. In general all this seems to have attracted at least the passive sympathy of the Europeans, and it is said, particularly with regard to the naval victory over the Russian navy, a strong measure of approval from Asians.[19] However, when Japan began to make demands on China a few years later in 1915 Western sympathy rather tended to fade away and Japan came to be categorized as aggressive. Subsequently, in the 1930s, the Japanese invaded China. A general war was being waged in China by 1937. It would seem that the various elements of the Japanese military could never make up their minds just what their war aims in China were and the upshot was a long, drawn out war. It turned out to be fatal to Japanese military expansion as it was Japanese involvement in China which drew the criticism of the USA and Europeans, and led in due course to the outbreak of the Pacific War.

Northeast Asia

The territories of Northeast Asia comprising Korea, Taiwan and Manchuria had traditionally fallen within the tributary sphere of the Chinese empire.

However, as that empire disintegrated over the period of the nineteenth century control of these areas came into question. There was a three-cornered conflict with the Chinese, Russians and Japanese seeking to assert their interests.

The Japanese movement into Korea began in the late nineteenth century as an attempt to prize the territory away from the influence of China whilst at the same time blocking the advance of Russian influence. These concerns issued in war against China in 1894–5, which saw the annexation of Taiwan. The colonial-style expansion pursued by Japan also involved conflict with Russia in respect of spheres of influence in Manchuria and Korea. The Russo-Japanese war of 1904–5 saw military success for the Japanese, and Korea was made a protectorate in 1905 and formally annexed in 1910. At this time the Japanese also enhanced their position in Manchuria. Overall the Sino-Japanese war of 1894–5 and the Russo-Japanese war of 1904–5 resolved the general situation in favour of Japan.

The competition for influence in Korea

The Koryo Dynasty emerged in 918 from the confusion which followed the fall of the kingdom of Silla but was drawn within the Mongol sphere in the early thirteenth century. As the power of the Mongols declined indigenous rulers sought power, but it was not until 1392 that the Korean general Yi Sung-Kae seized power and established the Yi dynasty which had tributary relations with the Chinese Ming dynasty. The Yi dynasty survived in this form until the Manchus replaced the Ming as the central power within the Sino-centric sphere. The Yi Dynasty saw an elaborate court life supported by an exploited peasantry.[20] In the arts and letters there was advance and the distinctive Korean writing script was developed. In the eighteenth century there was some concern to learn the lessons of the West, however the Practical Learning movement was without great effect and thereafter the people of Korea spent the eighteenth and nineteenth centuries within an inward-looking form of life. The feudal system stagnated within its Chinese tributary sphere and the elite eschewed contact with the outside world.[21]

In the late nineteenth century Korea was caught up in the twin processes of Western expansion and Qing Dynasty decline and the Yi Dynasty slowly collapsed into a series of rival groups. The consequence of this internal confusion was that the government was unable to resist outside pressures. As the Japanese and Chinese contended for influence in the peninsula the Koreans became pawns in the manoeuvres of their neighbours.

The first area of concern of the Japanese was Korea which was nominally independent but lodged within the Chinese sphere of influence. However, with the situation in China unstable the Japanese government feared a Western encroachment into the area to their eventual detriment. Japan imposed 'unequal treaties' on Korea in 1876 which allowed the Japanese significant trading rights in the country and proceeded to struggle with the

Chinese for dominance in the area. Both governments stationed troops in the country from 1882 onwards. The Sino-Japanese war of 1894–5 saw the Japanese defeat the Chinese on the basis of their superior Western military technology. After the war the Japanese promoted a pro-reform Korean government. Borthwick[22] reports that the Japanese tried to draw a local reform movement into government in order to pursue a modernization programme on the model of the Meiji Restoration. The Kabo reform movement lasted from July 1894 to February 1896 before strong opposition from conservative forces within Korea caused it to be abandoned.

The peace accord between China and Japan was made with the Treaty of Shimonoseki. Japan received an indemnity and acquired Taiwan and areas of influence in Korea and Manchuria. However Russia, Germany and France then intervened diplomatically and the Japanese government was obliged to relinquish its gains in Manchuria. This caused public dismay in Japan where the view was that the great powers had deprived Japan of gains legitimately secured. The governments' reaction, having acquiesced, was to reaffirm the ideas of 'strong economy, strong army' and to increase armaments spending the better to resist any future impositions. The Anglo-Japanese Treaty was signed in 1902 and this signalled the Japanese governments' preference for involvement with the British and US notions of the Open Door in respect of China trade such that all were to have access. Over the next few years the Japanese became involved in the great power manoeuvring in East Asia and slowly drifted into conflict with Russia over Korea and Manchuria.

In the Russo-Japanese war of 1904–5 the military exchanges resulted in a decisive naval victory for the Japanese but there was a costly stalemate in the ground war in Manchuria. A mediation effort by the USA achieved a peace with the Treaty of Portsmouth. The peace treaty which ended the war left Korea to the Japanese who also consolidated their influence in Manchuria and received half of Sakhalin island. The Japanese now proceeded to bring the peninsula under their control and direction. Korea was made a protectorate in 1905. The Korean army was disbanded in 1907 and the last Yi Dynasty emperor was forced to abdicate. The Japanese formally annexed Korea in 1910 and the peninsula became a Japanese colony.

The subsequent development of Korea can be analysed in terms of shifting patterns of class-based production as industry slowly emerged. Hamilton comments: 'In Korea the Japanese took much greater direct control of agricultural production by acquiring large tracts of land . . . The traditional Korean landed aristocracy was seriously weakened . . . The twin actions of pre-colonial feudalism and Japanese colonialism caused widespread agricultural pauperisation . . . While the Japanese were diligent in pursuing improved agricultural productivity, they were equally diligent in siphoning off the rural surplus, and more, through high rents and taxes'.[23] There was some industrialization, particularly in the north, to support this colonial economic pattern but it was not until the 1930s that the production demands of rearmament generated significant industrial development.

Borthwick comments: 'The Japanese colonial policy vastly strengthened Korea's transportation and communication infrastructure, but Koreans were pressed into labour gangs to build the roads and telegraph lines that spread rapidly across their country'.[24] Thereafter, at 'the end of the colonial period Korea could boast one of the most advanced transportation and communications systems in Pacific Asia'.[25] However, the occupation also acted to undermine established Korean culture as Japanese models of education, language and family names were imposed.

The colonial regime drew protests. In Korea in 1919 the March First Movement which began with a group of patriots meeting in a restaurant and reading a declaration of independence, only to be promptly arrested by the Japanese police, and thereafter a series of demonstrations were begun in cities across Korea. Borthwick comments: 'Stunned by the massiveness and boldness of the protests, the Japanese responded with brutal violence . . . Schools, churches and houses were burned . . . From this nation-wide slaughter there emerged a more organized Korean resistance movement directed mainly by those who fled the country after the March First Movement'.[26] After the March First Movement was suppressed the Japanese colonial authorities tightened their grip on the country. The economy of the territory grew quickly. However, as the military gained power in Japan the pressure of foreign rule in Korea increased. The outbreak of the Pacific War led to Korea being used as a part of the Japanese war economy and the exploitation of the population reached new levels.

Settling the case of Taiwan

Taiwan was a remote territory of the Chinese empire for centuries. It began to attract mainland immigration in the seventeenth century when the Dutch established a trading base in the southern part of the island and was a base for traders in the area. The territory was absorbed within the Chinese sphere in 1683 by the Qing Dynasty but the involvement of the mainland remained slight and the island remained a backwater. As the Chinese empire declined in the nineteenth century the territory became an objective of the expanding Japanese empire and following the Sino-Japanese war of 1894–5 the island was ceded to the Japanese.

The Japanese inaugurated a development programme in Taiwan with a view to making the island an agricultural supplier for Japan. The Japanese built infrastructure, undertook a land reform which reduced sub-tenancy and eliminated some absentee landlordism, and introduced agricultural extension services. In due course agricultural production for the market and export to Japan rose. A little later in the 1930s as the Japanese economy began to shift towards the production of war materials there was a significant measure of industrialization in Taiwan. The pattern of agricultural and industrial development had the effect of weakening established landed groups without allowing the emergence of independent industrial or working-class groupings. The territory developed firmly within the orbit of the colonial system. Hamilton comments that: 'During the period of intense colonial rule there was no potential indigenous leadership stratum to speak of, except perhaps for scattered cabals of intimidated nationalists'.[27] Indeed, it is reported that the colonial period was relatively benign and whilst the 'people were required to speak Japanese and to trade their Chinese names for Japanese names . . . the Chinese on Formosa never resented the Japanese with the fervour of other peoples later colonized by Japan'.[28]

The competition for influence in Manchuria

The northern part of China bordering on Russia and adjacent to the Sea of Japan was relatively remote from the Han Chinese heartlands to the south and had the character of a borderland. The territory was poor and relatively sparsely populated. It became an area of concern for three powerful groups in the latter part of the nineteenth century.

In the first place it was the heartland of the Manchu Dynasty which had displaced the Ming Dynasty in an invasion which began in 1618 and was finally completed after two generations of warfare. Borthwick notes: '[that] a thin layer of Manchu military elite and civilian government officials were able to maintain control . . . but they also were careful to preserve their own cultural identity'.[29] Thereafter, in the second place, the territory abutted the lands of the Russian Czarist empire which had expanded eastwards over the nineteenth century and looked to the territory of Manchuria as a route to the warmer more southern seas. And then, thirdly, the Japanese looked to Manchuria as an element of a sphere of control and stability surrounding the Japanese home islands. As the Japanese industrialized in the latter years of the nineteenth century they noted the slow collapse of the Qing Dynasty and the developing interests of Czarist Russia with disquiet.

After the Japanese victory over the Czarist empire in 1904–5 the Japanese increased their involvement in Manchuria. A key agent of the extension of their power was the South Manchurian Railway Company. The Japanese slowly displaced the influence of the Chinese and Russians. The area became a major centre of influence and concern for the Japanese army. The area was extensively developed and eventually was given a nominal independence in 1932 as the state of Manchuko.

The drift towards military rule in Japan

After these successes the Japanese continued to press the Chinese. It was also the case that these imperialist moves met with displeasure from the Western powers and this in turn provoked a negative reaction amongst the Japanese political elite whose view of the West became yet more sceptical.

There was intermittent war in China from the late nineteenth century through to the military invasions of the 1930s which sparked warfare that ran on until 1945. The Japanese motivation for these exchanges combined geo-strategy, as they searched for security within the unstable area of Northeast Asia, and geo-economics as they looked to secure supplies of raw materials and access to markets in order to sell their manufactured goods. It was in pursuit of these objectives that the Japanese looked to secure from China the same sorts of trading rights as those enjoyed by the Western powers. The Chinese resisted these demands and only granted concessions slowly as a result of pressure.

The Sino-Japanese war of 1894–5, as noted earlier, lasted nine months in which time the Japanese armed forces expelled the Chinese from Korea, captured Port Arthur and the Liaotung peninsula. Beasley notes that in the negotiations leading to the Treaty of Shimonoseki the Japanese aims included 'demands for an indemnity; for the handing over to Japan of Taiwan (which she had not even occupied) and Liaotung; and for a commercial treaty which would put Japanese privileges in China on a par with those of the Western powers'.[30] The Chinese government conceded all these points, however the Triple Intervention, by Russia, France and Germany obliged the Japanese to withdraw from Liaotung and Port Arthur. As the Europeans and Americans had at that time very extensive colonial holdings this generated some irritation amongst Japanese ruling circles and fed into popular complaint and thereafter into nationalist sentiment. Overall, the Western powers looked at early Japanese advance with tolerance. However, when a few years later in 1915 Japan began to make further demands on China, Western sympathy rather tended to fade away and Japan came to be categorized as aggressive. It is argued that this early rebuff by the Western powers to Japanese borrowings of the notion of empire had the effect of encouraging an aggressive Japanese nationalism which subsequently modulated into the fascism of the inter-war period.

A Dutch Sphere in the Archipelago

The Portuguese began trading in the archipelago in the sixteenth century but they were displaced by the Dutch who slowly took control of most of the archipelago from the seventeenth century onwards. The Dutch expansion involved a series of wars with local Malay maritime sultanates.

In general the Dutch ran their colony for profit. In the early years this centred on controlling the trade in archipelago products such as spices. The Dutch controlled the trade by controlling the key ports. As new schedules of demands emerged in the course of the development of industrial-capitalism and mass markets the pressure on colonies increased. In the period 1830–70 the Cultivation System required villages to produce cash crops which went to government monopolies. The culture system was abolished in 1870 and a nominally free labour system introduced. In this period the agricultural activities in the colonial territory came to centre around plantation agriculture dealing in sugar and rubber. It effectively destroyed the local-level indigenous agricultural economy.

The general pattern of Dutch rule was indirect, they ruled with and through local rulers. Pluvier notes that 'The government in The Hague and the Dutch parliament were empowered to legislate for the colony but the bulk of the legislation relating to the internal affairs of the Indies was usually enacted by the colonial authorities themselves'.[31] And Reid notes 'The genius of Dutch colonialism was always its indirectness, making use of traditional authorities wherever these would serve the economic monopoly the Dutch had at heart'.[32] Yet on this Pluvier is less complimentary noting that the local ruler with nominal spheres of responsibility remained subject to final Dutch control. And it remains the case that the Dutch ruled the territory with the principle concern of securing economic advantage.

Pluvier notes: 'In 1901 they introduced the so-called Ethical Policy . . . a curious compromise between humanitarian and progressive ideas on the one hand and the requirements of powerful economic pressure groups on the other'.[33] Pluvier adds that the colonial authorities pursued the 'Ethical Policy . . . for slightly more than two decades, after which it fell into complete oblivion in the 1930s'.[34] Pluvier goes on to report that the 'major factor responsible for this failure to carry out in practice what had been agreed to in principle was the unexpected emergence of an Indonesian political movement'.[35] In the early years of the twentieth century a measure of political opposition began to be directed against the Dutch. The ideas of the West were turned back against the colonizers and ideas of Indonesian nationalism were advanced.

The first experience of nationalism with a mass base was Serekat Islam, which was active in the period 1912–26 but which thereafter declined. The leaders of Serekat Islam invited anyone to join and some communists did and eventually split away to form the Indonesian communist party (PKI) which then launched a rapidly crushed revolt in 1923. Reid comments: 'Nevertheless the national ideal continued to develop rapidly among the nearly two million urban or educated Indonesians. Taking from Marxism the opposition to capitalism, from Serekat Islam the solidarity of "us" against "them", and from European scholarship the name of Indonesia and the rediscovery of a glorious pre-European past, secular nationalism became the predominant political force after 1926'.[36] The Dutch colonial authorities responded broadly with repression and 'alienation from the colonial regime was universal by 1942, and the Japanese were welcomed as liberators'.[37]

A British Sphere in Malaya

The Malay world prior to the arrival of the West was characterized by the rise and fall of a succession of maritime trading empires.[38] Such empires being geographically loose in their extent; expanding and contracting with the ebb and flow of the power of the central sultanate *vis-à-vis* both more local sources of power, and the activities of competing sultanates. In all, a fluid political system ordered around the person of the sultan with patterns of loyalty personalized rather than formalized. The internal politics of these sultanates seems to have been beset with intra-familial manoeuvrings for power. The economies of these maritime empires were, in the main, based on seaborne trade, and extensive networks of trade were established. The crucial key to political power and authority was possession and control of a regularly used nexus in the pattern of trade within the archipelago. The goods traded involved agricultural products such as spices, rice in places, (thus Java supplied the Moluccan-based trade empires of Ternate and Tidore), and craft goods such as silks and porcelain. In respect of the area encompassing Singapore island, Trocki[39] argues that the key concerns of the rulers of the Riau Sultantate were the trade routes which passed through the Straits of Malacca. Trocki reports that the 'Riau entrepot of 1784 was but the last in a succession of similar "urban" centres whose history stretches back to Srivijaya in the seventh century'.[40]

The island of Singapore was selected within the context of Anglo-Dutch manoeuvring as a likely base for the projection of British mercantile power.[41] This required the political extraction of the island itself from the Johor-Riau sultanate's grasp. This involved a period of intense political manoeuvring which centred locally on inventing a Sultan of Singapore by promoting a weak member of the ruling family. The upshot of all this being that the newly invented Sultan of Singapore signs an agreement with Raffles that gives the British a claim against both the indigenous ruler in Riau, and the Dutch.[42] The Sultan and his Temmengong then expected to rule in concert with the British over an economy and polity which they took, not unreasonably, to be a variation on the long-established notion of a maritime trade centre. The British however had longer term ideas, even if they were none too clear what these were. In 1823 the power struggle between British and Malay rulers came to a head, and this local conflict was resolved in favour of the British, but there then followed an uncomfortable period during which the British confronted a now rather hostile Malay world. In particular the Temmengong's followers continued with their traditional practice of exacting tribute from passing shipping.

In 1835 the Temmengong's successor, Ibrahim, agreed to throw in his lot with the British and assist in the 'suppression of piracy'. Trocki sees this decision as marking the reorientation of Malay economy and society. The traditional pattern had been focused on seaborne trade and rested upon control of a key nexus and the availability of seafarers. Now the focus of activity for the Temmengong was on the land of Johor which at that time was seemingly unpeopled save for Chinese agriculturalists who had been progressively displaced from Singapore island. The shift of focus is crucial: the old maritime pattern declines, and the seafarers disappear. In its stead is the Malay ordered expansion of a polity based on Chinese agriculture. The exchange with the British is also important, and Trocki sees an important mechanism for the later projection of British power into the peninsula.

The early period of Singapore is thus a Malay–British condominium, from 1819 to mid-1840: and this date is when pre-eminent power shifted away from the British–Malays and towards the British–Malays–Chinese. The shift to tripartite rule was driven by demography because by mid-century the Chinese population was the largest single group. They serviced the manpower needs of the trading centre, and through the tax farm on opium they furnished the larger part of the settlement's revenue. And Trocki[43] has argued that the opium farm was also the major social structural institution for the Chinese population. In this early period it seems that what had happened is that the old Johor trade-based empire had been recreated, after spending most of the eighteenth century in disarray, with a key nexus on Singapore island and with the key ruling group no longer Malay but British. Trocki[44] is adamant that in this early period the British did nothing but recreate a traditional trading empire – it was successful because it was familiar.

The period from 1819 to the early 1870s can be taken as the phase of the projection and establishment of British mercantile-capitalist power on Singapore island and within the surrounding archipelago. This power was projected in the context of much manoeuvring with and against both the Dutch and the various indigenous groupings. Within this broad structural context the extension of effective colonial power involved the slow extension of the usual machineries of administration and government within the area of Singapore itself and within the Malay peninsula. The business of the construction of the formal colony was a mixture of cooperation and control and the base was the economic interests of the Europeans, Chinese and Malays.

The new international political concern with formal colonies was accompanied by a movement on the part of the British into the Malay peninsula. As open mercantile trade contracted in terms of the area served by the port the newly opened-up peninsula compensated. Broadly we have a more ordered and extensive colonial capitalist exploitation. The new economic relationship of metropole and peripheral area was mediated by the related establishment of new political arrangements both in the peninsula and in Singapore island itself. The formal shift to colonial status for Singapore was in 1867 and the major British advance into the Malay peninsula began with the 1874 Pangkor Engagement.

In Singapore itself the cooption of the general Malay population seems to have been easily accomplished via the influence of Temmengong and Sultan. And with the Chinese, there is a similar pattern. The basis of the whole edifice was a coincidence of economic interests between European and Chinese merchant classes. In the early years of the nineteenth century the key institution around which the political and economic life of the Chinese population revolved, was the opium tax farm coupled to clan and secret society groups. Throughout the nineteenth century the opium tax farm contributed the major proportion of the territories' tax revenues. The relationship between the British and the Chinese come to be governmentally formalized through first, the 1877 establishment of the Chinese Protectorate which was formed to regulate coolie traffic, then brothels, and then in 1889 with control of secret societies and in the same year the establishment of the Chinese Advisory Board. In sum, Singapore was now a major nexus in the British centred sphere of the world industrial capitalist system. It was a conduit for the extraction of tropical agricultural, mineral and primary products, and for the introduction of European manufactures. This economic and political role continued until 1942.

In the Malayan peninsula the British traded from a base in Penang established by Francis Light in the last years of the eighteenth century.[45] The British also established their trading base in Singapore and took Malacca from the Dutch. In the latter years of the century after the Pangkor Engagement the British slowly increased their influence with the local sultanates. On Trocki's analysis the Temmengong in Singapore was deeply involved in the creation of modern Johor.[46] It seems also to be the case that this line of influence was a major means for the projection of British colonial power into the peninsula. Initially this took the form of the establishment of agricultural operations in Johor, with Malay control and Chinese business/labour. Thereafter the Temmengong, later the Sultan of Johor, was both the head of a model territory and bound up in the extension of this British-made system of sultanates.

As the colony solidified, so too did the system of sultanates and indirect rule whereby the British concerned themselves with development and the traditional rulers with their peoples. The Malay community existed in relative tranquillity for many years. However, as British-ordered development advanced it drew in many immigrants and the territory slowly became multi-ethnic. It was this situation which encouraged the first expressions of Malay nationalism.

Lee[47] reports that the earliest influence upon the indigenous Malays was vehicled through Islam, both from the Middle East via religious revival and from Indonesia with the influence of Serekat Islam. At the time the Malay community was rural and conservative and the burgeoning colonial economy had rather passed them by as the colonial powers encouraged the inflow of Indian and Chinese immigrants. The beginnings of directly political activity can be dated to the 1920s when immigrant groups also began to consider their situations. In the Chinese communities in the 1920s and 1930s communists and the KMT competed for support. The Indian community also organized, however their internal caste distinctions hindered effective action. Overall, this nascent activity did not crystallize as a coherent nationalism, rather it ran on ethnic lines. Lee comments: 'Thus what was marked in the pre-war period was that the political consciousness of the various races was governed largely by a concern for their own separate identities. Each communal group saw little in common with the others and each sought to protect its own economic and cultural interests'.[48]

Lee notes: 'Thus prior to the outbreak of the Second World War, the British had to face few serious challenges. The elites of the various communities supported the status quo from which they benefited, while anti-British organisations failed to mobilize broad support'.[49] Yet all this was changed by the wartime occupation. The Japanese interlude had the effect of reinforcing the ethnic lines along which politics had begun to run and these concerns flowed into the politics of decolonization in the years following.

British influence in Thailand

The kingdom of Thailand managed to avoid becoming a formal colony by virtue of its position between British and French domains and an energetic reforming political elite. In the mid-nineteenth century as the British and French extended their operations in the area, King Mongkut pursued a delicate course between acceding to the demands of the incomers and pursuing the development of Thailand. In the later nineteenth and early twentieth centuries King Chulalongkorn continued the strategy[50] and whilst the Thais had to cede territory to both the French and the British the Anglo-French agreement of 1896 guaranteed the country's autonomy freeing the leadership to pursue development.[51]

The Thai bureaucracy was reformed. In the provinces local royal rulers were gradually replaced by paid officials. A modern army was built up. These state-building activities began in the central region and were extended slowly over the whole country. At the same time the economy was rapidly modernized. Girling[52] points to three key changes: (i) the establishment of an independent peasantry with a rural economy centred on rice growing, which quickly became a key export commodity, along with rubber, tin and teak; (ii) the rapid development of a Chinese business network within the country and acting as compradores for foreign business; and (iii) the generation of substantial tax revenues which funded the development of the state.

King Chulalongkorn died in 1910 and his successors were neither effective nor popular. The army took over power in 1932 and ended the absolute monarchy. Thereafter the three key institutions have been the army, the bureaucracy and the monarchy and, after a wartime alliance with the Japanese, together they have ordered the pursuit of Thai 'bureaucratic capitalism'.[53]

A French Sphere in Indo-China

The Vietnamese had an historically uneasy relationship with the Chinese empire to their north. In the nineteenth century as Chinese power receded Vietnam was colonized by the French. The expansion of the overseas French empire in Asia had involved a series of conflicts with the British and comprised Vietnam, Cambodia, Laos, some islands in the Pacific and trading concessions in China.

Duiker[54] reports that French commercial interests pressed for a French presence in the area as a way of blocking the expansion of the British and securing a route to Southern China. The French had to overcome the established bureaucratic emperor system within Vietnam and did so through a series of local wars. The French mounted an invasion and after a significant war secured control in 1862 of the southern areas of Vietnam. In 1867 further areas in the south were seized, including Cambodia. In 1873 the French moved into the north and took Hanoi and by 1883 the Vietnamese emperor acceded to all French demands and a protectorate was established. A little later Laos was taken from Thailand and added to the French colonial sphere.

The motive for the colonization had been commercial and the pattern of French rule reflected these concerns. At the same time local administrators stressed the 'mission to civilize'. In the event the French developed the territory and the economic reordering of the country was extensive with light industries, commercial undertakings and the infrastructure of a modern society slowly being put in place. In the rural areas there was land reclamation and the development of commercial rice farming and rubber plantations. The economic legacy is difficult to evaluate where, as is usual in colonial territories, the story is a mixture of advance and exploitation.

In the political sphere Pluvier notes that: 'France followed a policy which was the most inflexible of any colonial nation in Southeast Asia. In the four decades since Governor-General Paul Doumer (1897–1902) established a definite system of colonial administration, this system was applied without a single change'.[55] French colonial theory vacillated between assimilation and association but in practice neither were used as the key remained control. Pluvier records: 'French policy was primarily characterised by the principle that Indochina formed an integral part of a closely-knit empire which was to be completely dominated by France'. Pluvier records that: 'French Indochina was an example of a highly centralised system of government without even a semblance of local autonomy. The French offered no power to local people and the colonial apparatus was dominated and guided by France'.[56] However, the grip of the French on Vietnam was fatally weakened by the wartime occupation of the Japanese who began to occupy the country in 1940.

An American Sphere in the Philippines

The Americans came late to the business of overseas colonial expansion having had the task of moving westwards across the continental USA, a process of internal colonization as the native Indians were disposessed, and having had debates about the appropriate the future for the USA collapse into civil war. The American sphere comprised the territory of the Philippines, a series of islands in the Pacific, and trading concessions in China.

The Philippines became part of the Spanish empire in 1565 and were a colony of Spain for three centuries. The area had dozens of local micro-states. The area attained a modest coherence through the years of colonial rule although Spanish influence amongst the Muslim sultanates in the southern islands was relatively restricted. Osborne reports that: 'The long period of Spanish rule over these islands was vitally important in delineating the boundaries of a state where neither boundaries nor any entity equivalent to the modern Philippines existed previously'.[57] The Spanish exerted their control slowly and eventually they came to dominate the lowland areas in the northern islands. Osborne[58] reports that: 'Spanish rule in the Philippines gave the northern islands a new framework for society', and a key cultural introduction was Catholicism.

In economic terms the colony developed initially around an entrepot trade which linked China, local specialist producers and Spain. The Asian territories produced a series of specialist goods and these were exported via Mexico to Spain which supplied in return a flow of silver coins. In the late eighteenth century a limited plantation agriculture began with tobacco, rice and sugar. On the basis of these activities a limited industrialization was to develop which included a successful textile industry. The outcome of the colonial sponsored shift to the modern world was an agrarian feudal society with deep class and ethnic divisions.

The colonial social and political system discriminated against locally born peoples. An indigenous nationalist movement established itself in the latter part of the nineteenth century on the basis of a local national elite which had developed under Spanish rule and promulgated a notion of a Filipino identity. In the 1890s an open revolt began and was successful. Independence was achieved in 1898, the first country in Asia to win freedom from colonial rule.

However, at the moment of success the Americans invaded and seized the territory. McCoy[59] reports that the interests of the US government were strategic and when it was decided that they could not absorb the local population it was decided that independence would be organized. The economy evidenced a mix of classical colonial forms, with large landed estates (the Spanish model) working to produce plantation agricultural crops (the European model). The territory became an economic adjunct of the USA and colonial rule secured the power of large landholders who operated commercial plantations. A rich Filipino elite developed and along with it an impoverished peasant mass. However, the Filipino elite split and one party favoured union with the USA (Federalistas) and one looked to independence (Nationalistas) and in the meantime the country proceeded with an idea of bi-nationalism (people were both Filipino and American). Pluvier notes that: 'After becoming a colonial power . . . the United States did her utmost not to look like one . . . There was, of course, no substantial departure from the actual colonial situation'.[60] Pluvier goes on to remark that a 'more remarkable ambiguity of the American course was the fact that it prepared the Philippines for independence in a political sense whilst it produced an entirely opposite effect in the economic sphere'.[61] The ambiguous relationship with the USA continued up until the Japanese invasion at the outset of the Pacific War. After the interregnum of the Pacific War where the local elite collaborated with the Japanese the returning Americans confirmed the power of the local elites, suppressed a local land-reform movement, and left the Filipinos a legacy of misdevelopment and cultural confusion.

Australia, New Zealand and the Pacific Islands

The continent was called, by early modern European map-makers, Terra Australis Incognita, or the Unknown South Land. It had an indigenous population of aboriginals whose culture was both sophisticated and technologically primitive. It has been estimated that when the colonists arrived there were perhaps 300,000 Aborigines in the whole of Australia.[62]

The aboriginal peoples lived within loosely organized tribal groups based within a particular ancestral territory. The tribal groups had no formal leadership and maintained their group coherence and identity via common language, religion and myth. The means of livelihood was hunting and gathering. Thereafter, the anthropology of the aboriginals is as complex as that of other similar 'primitives'. The form-of-life did not long survive the arrival of industrial-capitalism.[63]

The continent was slowly settled by the British from 1770 onwards. It began as a penal colony and became a colony of settlement in the nineteenth century. Australia became of federation in 1901. The political economy of the territory was based on primary products and only later did significant industry develop within the context of what had become a very rich country.

The political-cultural development of the territory ran along familiar settler-colonial lines with the inhabitants of the newly occupied territory looking to the metropolitan centre. However as the economy, society and culture advanced the inhabitants came to construe themselves as 'Australian'. The shift is crucial and ran through a series of phases. Walter[64] recalls the invention of a British Australia around the turn of the twentieth century with images of Australian identity being constructed around an idea of the immigrant from British stock taking over the empty bush. Australian identity come to be bound up with men and bush life. Walter identified historians, commentators and journalists as the makers of this tradition which ran until the middle of the century. One notable feature is the way in which the aboriginal population of the continent are simply written out of the history. And as Reynolds[65] points out, colonialism was active as the inhabitants were forcibly pushed aside. Later, in the 1940s the idea of the Australian way of life appears and the references to racial stock fall away. The theme also reflects the anti-communism of the period and is implicitly affirming the racist white Australia policy.

And in general terms a similar story can be told of New Zealand. And more distantly in the broad areas of the South Pacific a series of small island communities were drawn into the colonial territories of the Americans and Europeans.

As the high tide of the colonial era continued through the 1930s there was little sense of any need to reform these comfortable countries. However, the upheavals of the Pacific War were to eventuate in a turn towards both their American wartime allies and a little later to their northern neighbours in Asia.

Japan, the Pacific War and the Decline of the Classical Nineteenth-century Empires

The germ of contemporary Japanese national sentiment can be located in the response to the West made by elite and popular groups in the period of late Tokugawa and Meiji. Morris-Suzuki notes that 'nationalism was . . . associated with efforts to overcome the economic and military gap between Japan and the West. These efforts came to be inextricably connected to the issue of overseas expansion and the creation of Japan's own empire in Asia'.[66] The early expression of these sentiments were rebuffed by the West and a drift into militarism began which was to culminate in the catastrophe of the Pacific War.

The early Japanese exchange with the West

After the country adopted the closed country policy in 1633 all trade and links with the outside were tightly controlled and Nagasaki was the only point of access for Chinese and Dutch traders. Over this long period some Western ideas slowly entered Japan. It was known as the 'Dutch' learning, and included natural science, medicine and military technologies. The spread of this Dutch learning was resisted by patriots who saw it as implicated in a moral decline within the country. However, in the seventeenth and eighteenth centuries trading vessels from America and Europe became frequent visitors to Pacific Asia, and the Russian empire made overtures, and eventually in 1854 Commodore Perry forced the Shogunate to agree to establish regular trade relations.

The Japanese exchange with the West has produced a tangled response, a mix of borrowing, incomprehension, rejection and the arguably defensive insistence upon the particularity of the Japanese. Hunter notes that 'Japan experienced a brief period of European contact in the late sixteenth and early seventeenth centuries, but in 1639 the government of Japan . . . effectively severed all contact with the West'.[67] The Japanese economy and society did

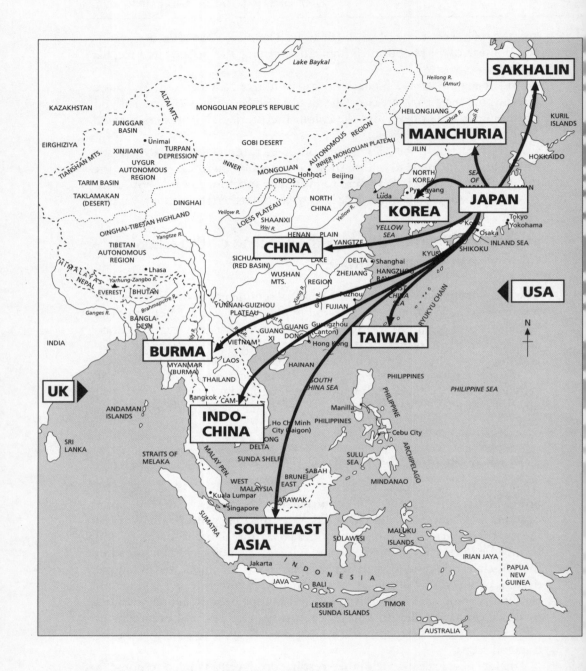

Map 4.2 Japanese colonial sphere 1895–1945

not stand still during the years of the Tokugawa Shogunate, rather they prospered and developed a highly sophisticated culture. It is this pattern of internal advance that produces the basis for an ambiguous reception to Western ideas. Hunter notes that 'the simultaneous existence of both "indigenous" and "Western" modes of thought and behaviour has resulted in acute cultural conflict'.[68] And the manner in which Japan was opened to the West, after Perry's visits, made the issues more acute. Hunter goes on to note that it was clear that 'Japan was both militarily and economically vulnerable and the lack of outside support for her resistance to great power domination reinforced a sense of national isolation'.[69]

The Japanese responded to the West by initiating an elite-ordered drive for development, as the Meiji oligarchy was determined to avoid the fate of China. As the Japanese drive for equality with the West was initiated a related set of concerns grew in respect of the other countries of East Asia. The Japanese elite reasoned that the old tributary relationships with China which had ordered East Asia for centuries were no longer appropriate in the new global system. The Japanese elite therefore assumed a responsibility for the countries of East Asia and began a process of establishing a sphere of influence which was to issue in the construction of a formal colonial sphere in East Asia. In other words, the concern which Japan has shown for its neighbours in East Asia mirrors the concern it has shown for its relations with the Western powers.

The clash with the West

The Great War provided the Japanese government with a further opportunity for expansion in East Asia when, citing obligations under the Anglo-Japanese Alliance of 1902, it moved to take over German interests in China and seize German Pacific island territories. At the same time the various Japanese concerns with China were summarized in the guise of the 1915 'Twenty One Demands' in respect of privileging Japanese interests in China. After the war the Versailles Treaty left the Japanese with their gains, although not with full Western approval. In the 1920s the Japanese joined in the discussions of the great powers and were party to decisions designed to stabilize the situation in East Asia.

At the same time the war years had triggered an economic boom which in turn had shifted population to the urban areas and thereafter fuelled demands for greater democracy in Japan (in line with the optimistic liberalism of President Wilson and the League of Nations). In Japan it was the period of Taisho democracy. In 1925 the government introduced universal male suffrage. Overall the period saw a mix of economic boom and bust (with the power of the zaibatsu rapidly increasing), rapid social change (in particular the growth of the progressive towns at the expense of the more traditional and conservative rural areas), and political confusion as the original Meiji oligarchy slowly left the scene and the state system which they had made slowly came apart as factions within the state machinery vied for control.

In the 1920s and 1930s there were new developments as the Meiji oligarchs and their immediate successors slowly left the political scene. This had the effect of removing an important source of ideas in respect of the appropriate trajectory of development for Japan. There was a measure of democratization in the Taisho period and the beginnings of more extensive party political activity. It should also be noted that an element of unclarity within the Meiji Constitution became evident, namely, the lack of political control over the armed forces. The Great Depression of the late 1920s and early 1930s effectively destroyed the Taisho democracy. There were two areas of problems: firstly, inside the country the polity did not mature into a liberal democracy and instead the nationalistic military gained in strength; and secondly, the country's relationships with the outside world began to decline.

The collapse in world trade effectively extracted the Japanese from the international system within which they had operated and propelled the Japanese into a self-contained East Asian yen bloc. At the same time the economic slump created a mass of unemployed in Japan with strikes in urban areas and widespread poverty in rural areas, and the proponents of ultranationalism found support in these areas. In this environment of political confusion the nationalist and militarist right wing came to the fore.

In the 1930s the military came to exercise great influence in the country, and in some practical respects they became the government. Initially they worked within the 'gaps' in the Meiji constitution which did not precisely specify lines of responsibility and left the military able to claim they were acting on behalf of the emperor, the theoretical core of the system. A series of assassinations took place and from 1932 onwards party politics gave way to rule by non-party cabinets which attempted to reconcile the various interests of the major state-machine players – inevitably the military came to dominate matters.

A military dictatorship might have been established if the army had not been riven by factions. There were two key factions: the Imperial Way Faction (a conservative group stressing martial values, national unity and the centrality of the emperor) and the Control Faction (looking to military modernization within the context of a modernizing economy and society). A failed Imperial Way coup in 1936 led to the dominance of the Control Faction over the whole of Japanese politics. An authoritarian regime then established a 'national defence state' with a controlled polity, and a controlled economy and society.[70] This pattern was reinforced as the decade wore on and the imbroglio in China became ever more demanding. By the late 1930s the Japanese inhabited a mobilized country.

The upheavals of the late 1920s and early 1930s began the slide into war. In China over this period we can note two aspects of the Japanese presence: first, their increasing role in China as their industrialists became more involved and as Japanese troops were deployed to offer them security; and second, the assertion of increasing Japanese control over Manchuria and the effective use of the South Manchurian Railway Company as the vehicle for army sponsored industrial development. In this context it is important to note that the role of the military in China and Manchuria slowly came to escape the control of the politicians in Tokyo. It was locally sponsored military adventurism in China and Manchuria that drew the Japanese into war with China. In the 1930s the Japanese invaded China. Japan left the League of Nations in 1933 and in 1936 signed the Anti-Comintern Pact with Germany. Of course the pattern of events in Europe acted to encourage the militarists in Japan. The Imperial Japanese Army was a key actor in this drama. They had by the 1930s become the dominant force in Japanese politics. The army staged an incident at Mukden on 18 September 1931 and began the seizure of Manchuria. In March 1932 Tokyo officially recognized Manchuko, with Henry Pu-yi as emperor in 1934. Thereafter, an incident in 1937 at the Marco Polo bridge outside Peking proved to be the spark which ignited a general war in China. This war developed and extended in stages until it enveloped a large part of Northeastern and coastal China. It would seem that the Japanese never had a coherent strategy in China and the war simply drifted on. It would seem that the various elements of the Japanese military could never make up their minds just what their war aims were and with whom they might deal at the local level. The prosecution of the war increasingly led to sharp conflict between the Japanese and American governments, and to tension with the governments of the European colonial empires in Asia.

The war in China turned out to be fatal to Japanese military expansion as it was the involvement in China which drew the criticism of the USA and Europeans. The exchanges of the Western powers and the Japanese slowly degenerated. The breakdown in relations with the USA and the European colonial powers lead to the wider war against the West from 1941 to 1945. The whole of Southeast Asia and large areas of the Pacific were drawn into the conflict when the Japanese armed forces launched a series of daring attacks across the northern Pacific area. In the space of six months they drove the Americans out of the Philippines, the Dutch out of the Dutch East Indies, the British out of Hong Kong, Malaya and Burma, and they neutralized the French in Indo-China and found allies in Thailand. All European and American holdings in China were seized.

Altering established balances through the wartime exchanges of Japanese, European, American and Asian peoples

Thorne[71] argues that in the pre-war period two timescales were coming into phase and these were, first, the decline of the European colonial empires as latent nationalism, the growing concern for modernization and the slow acceptance of the case for reform all advanced; and second, the process of the overthrow of white political, economic and social supremacy in Asia. In a rather more mundanely practical sense there were specific areas of tensions between the USA, the UK (the largest colonial power) and the Japanese. In terms of the general positions of the relevant governments, simplifying we can say that the Japanese understood these matters in terms of survival, the Americans saw an opportunity and the Europeans were anxious to defend the status quo. In the event, the episode of the Pacific War sees the European colonies dissolved (with the Japanese interregnum playing an ambiguous role), the Japanese defeated and occupied, and the USA emerging as the key power in the region.

In the period of the war there were a series of shifts in the relationship of the Western allies. The USA very quickly came to be the key partner as it recovered from the opening military reverses of 1942 and began to order a reply. The USA was the key Western power in the military conflict with Japan, and the UK and its empire were unable to contribute until late in the war. As regards the fighting in China, Thorne reports that the USA had illusions about the value of the KMT, whom it actively sought to support, which were only slowly dissipated. In the large swathe of territory within Southeast Asia and Indo-China, which had been the colonial holdings of the Europeans, the US took the position that it was not fighting to re-establish colonies (which is precisely what it did do in respect of the Philippines). The early war years, in other words, saw a shift of power from the UK (and the other European powers) towards the USA which continued as the Americans fought the island-hopping war leading to Okinawa. The final phase of wartime co-operation sees the Americans laying exclusive claim to Japan and leaving their European allies to reoccupy their colonial holdings in Southeast Asia and Indo-China. A variant of the status quo is precariously and provisionally re-established only to be submerged in the twin processes of decolonization and cold war bipolarity.

In all this the Japanese had a quite particular perspective. There were economic conflicts between the Japanese, European and American empires in the Pacific. In particular the war in China was a particular burden and source of tension with the West. Thorne[72] also records that there were racist sentiments overlaying these problems. The Japanese military government came to see war as an opportunity to settle all three matters in favour of Asians. It is clear that this line of argument did command some sympathy from Asian nationalist leaders. It is clear that the region was in flux.

Thorne[73] argues that the Pacific war had its occasion in strategic economic interests and sets of internal politics but nonetheless a belief did persist that the whole business was a revolt of Asia against the West. It is true that nationalist sentiment in Asia did have an anti-Western side. Barraclough[74] notes that the defeat by Japan of the Czarist Russian Empire in 1904–6 was widely read as an Asian defeat of Westerners. In Japan a nationalist stream of thought post-Meiji spoke of Japan leading Asian emancipation from the West and in the period of military fascism these lines of argument found greater expression. It is true that Westerners responded with a taken-for-granted Eurocentrism that was quickly destroyed by the successes of the Japanese in 1941–2. And once the war had begun the East/West, coloured/white, European/Asian distinctions were available to be used by all the combatants – and the terms were used in propaganda during the war by both sides as they dehumanized the other. Yet the conflict did have significant cultural implications. Thorne notes that the Japanese victories of the early war years 'greatly increased the readiness of large number of Asians to discard any remaining loyalty to their European rulers'.[75] Thorne adds that the sense of shock in the West was acute. The Japanese sought to inculcate an idea of 'Asianness' and to advance in an Asian way. They found nationalist sympathizers in Burma, Indonesia, the Philippines and amongst Indian émigrés in Southeast Asia. These nationalists voiced similar ideas and linked the pursuit of independence to the rise of Japan, as in the cases for example of Chandra Bose, Aung San and Sukarno.

In August 1945 the Japanese government surrendered unconditionally. Japan was occupied by the USA. Japan was subject to enforced reform. And the Japanese empire was dismantled. The war also saw the pattern of development of the region radically remade as the pre-war pattern of influence of European and American governments and commercial interests was fatally disturbed. The region came to be divided into an American sphere and an autarchic socialist bloc.

Conclusion

The geographical expansion of industrial-capitalism slowly absorbed and reconstructed extant Asian forms-of-life. The early contacts and exchanges were relatively benign in terms of their impact upon the peoples of the region. However the involvement of the Western powers in the region deepened and their demands grew more onerous. In the later years of the nineteenth century the area was brought into a closely controlled colonial system. It was at this time that the extant forms-of-life were reconstructed along the lines of the demands of the expanding industrial-capitalist system. The Pacific War disturbed the political pattern and in the post-war years a new spread of nation states came into being in the new context of cold war competition between the free world and the communist world.

Notes

1　P. Worsley 1984: *The Three Worlds: Culture and World Development*, London: Weidenfeld; A. D. King 1990: *Urbanism, Colonialism and the World Economy*, London: Routledge.
2　Worsley 1984.
3　Ibid., p. 15.
4　See G. Barraclough 1964: *An Introduction to Contemporary History*, Harmondsworth: Penguin; B. Anderson 1983: *Imagined Communities*, London: Verso.
5　H. Furber 1976: *Rival Empires of Trade in the Orient 1600–1800*, University of Minnesota Press.
6　P. Lawson 1993: *The East India Company: A History*, London: Longman; C. R. Boxer 1990: *The Dutch Seaborne Empire 1600–1800*, Harmondsworth: Penguin.
7　Furber 1976.
8　Ibid.
9　Barraclough 1964, pp. 78–87.
10　D. J. M. Tate 1971/9: *The Making of Southeast Asia*, Oxford: Oxford University Press.
11　M. Borthwick 1992: *Pacific Century: The Emergence of Modern Pacific Asia*, Boulder, CO: Westview, p. 81.
12　Ibid., p. 84.
13　Ibid., p. 90.
14　E. Moise 1994: *Modern China*, London: Longman.
15　B. Moore 1966: *The Social Origins of Dictatorship and Democracy*, Boston: Beacon, p. 184.
16　Ibid., pp. 188–201.
17　Ibid p. 184.
18　Ibid.
19　Barraclough 1967.
20　Borthwick 1992, p. 47.
21　B. Cummings 1997: *Korea's Place in the Sun: A Modern History*.
22　Borthwick 1992, p. 151.
23　C. Hamilton 1983: Capitalist Industrialization in East Asia's Four Little Tigers in *Journal of Contemporary Asia* 13, pp. 38–41.
24　Borthwick 1992, p. 197.
25　Ibid., p. 197.
26　Ibid., p. 194.
27　Hamilton 1983, p. 40.
28　Dobbs-Higginson 1995: *Pacific Asia: Its Role in the New World Disorder*, London: Mandarin, p. 150.
29　Borthwick 1992, p. 52.
30　W. G. Beasley 1990: *The Rise of Modern Japan*, Tokyo: Tuttle, p. 146.
31　J. Pluvier 1977: *Southeast Asia From Colonialism to Independence*, Oxford: Oxford University Press, p. 10.
32　A. Reid 1981: Indonesia: Revolution without Socialism in R. Jeffrey, ed., *Asia: The Winning of Independence*, London: Macmillan, p. 118.
33　Pluvier 1977, p. 9.

34 Ibid.
35 Ibid.
36 Reid 1981, p. 131.
37 Ibid., p. 134.
38 Tate 1971/9.
39 C. Trocki 1979: *Prince of Pirates,* Singapore: Singapore University Press.
40 Ibid., p. xv.
41 For a general history see M. Turnbull 1977: *A History of Singapore 1819–1975,* Oxford: Oxford University Press; S. S. Bedlington 1978: *Malaysia and Singapore: The Building of New Nation States,* Ithaca, NY: Cornell University Press.
42 K. F. Pang 1984: The Malay Royals of Singapore, unpublished dissertation, Department of Sociology, National University of Singapore.
43 C. Trocki 1990: *Opium and Empire,* Ithaca, NY: Cornell University Press.
44 Trocki 1979.
45 K. C. Tregonning 1965: *The British in Malaya: The First Forty Years 1786–1826,* University of Arizona Press.
46 Trocki 1979.
47 K. H. Lee 1981: Malaya: New State and Old Elites in Jeffrey ed. 1981.
48 Ibid., p. 223.
49 Ibid., p. 224.
50 M. Osborne 1995: *Southeast Asia: An Introductory History,* St Leonards: Allen and Unwin, pp. 71–2.
51 J. L. S. Girling 1981: *Thailand: Society and Politics,* Ithaca, NY: Cornell University Press, p. 49.
52 Ibid., p. 62.
53 S. Piriyarangsan 1983: *Thai Bureaucratic Capitalism 1932-1960,* Bangkok: Chulalongkorn University Social Research Centre.
54 W. J. Duiker 1995: *Vietnam: Revolution in Transition,* Boulder, CO: Westview, pp. 27–8.
55 Pluvier 1977, p. 8.
56 Ibid., p. 11.
57 Osborne 1995, p. 77.
58 Ibid., p. 79.
59 A. W. McCoy 1981: The Philippines: Independence without Decolonization in Jeffrey ed. 1981, pp. 28-54.
60 Pluvier 1977, p. 6.
61 Ibid.
62 R. Hughes 1988: *The Fatal Shore,* London: Pan, pp. 8–9.
63 Ibid., p. 9.
64 J. Walter 1992: Defining Australia in G. Whitlock and D. Carter, eds, *Images of Australia,* Queensland: University of Queensland Press.
65 H. Reynolds 1990: *The Other Side of the Frontier,* Ringwood: Penguin.
66 T. Morris-Suzuki 1995: Japanese Nationalism from Meiji to 1937 in C. Mackerras, ed., 1995: *Eastern Asia,* London: Longman, p. 189.
67 J. Hunter 1989: *The Emergence of Modern Japan,* London: Longman, p. 15.
68 Ibid., p. 16.
69 Ibid.
70 Beasley 1990, pp. 184–92.

71   C. Thorne 1978: *Allies of a Kind*, Oxford: Oxford University Press.
72   C. Thorne 1986: *The Far Eastern War*, London: Counterpoint.
73   C. Thorne 1980: Racial Aspects of the Far Eastern War of 1941–45 from *Proceedings of the British Academy*, Oxford University Press.
74   Barraclough 1964.
75   Thorne 1980, p. 343.

5

After the Pacific War: Decolonization, Nation-building and the Cold War

In the years following the Pacific War the countries of the region experienced a series of far-reaching changes associated with the recovery from the chaos of war, the process of decolonization and the new task of nation-building. The region also experienced a schedule of particular difficulties following the extension of the cold war from Europe to Pacific Asia. In order to grasp the underlying structural dynamics of this period we can speak of a series of major phases (or areas of activity): first, the 1945–9 period of the interplay of China, the USA and the Europeans in the context of the disorganized and fluid situation at the end of the Pacific War which finds an unstable contested balance in the machineries and rhetorics of cold war; then second, the 1948–65 period of decolonization which sees a series of new nations engaged in the pursuit of effective nation statehood within the context of the US sponsored Bretton Woods system; and thirdly, the long concern for development on the part of the socialist bloc, initially autarchic and subsequently more outward looking following the 1972 China/USA rapprochement.

Shifting Patterns of Regional Power 1945–49: China, America and the Europeans

In Asia the episode of war and the associated destruction had disrupted long-established economic, social and cultural patterns. The period of the late 1940s was one of great political-economic, social-institutional and cultural change within the region. In the period of immediate and initial recovery from war it was the multiple exchanges of the USA, China and the Europeans which set the broad pattern for the post-war era in Asia.

The European and American colonial empires

The Western allies planned for the immediate post-hostilities period during the later years of the Pacific War. The USA took charge in the Pacific and the Japanese home islands, and responsibility for Southeast Asia was allocated to the British. It was in the areas of Southeast Asia and Indo-China that the European colonial powers moved to re-establish their territories. They did so with the assistance of the British. However, the colonial powers returned to discover opposition from indigenous nationalists. The US government was unsympathetic and took the view that it had not fought the Pacific War in order to see European powers re-establishing colonies. Indeed, the USA professed an emphatic ethical anti-colonialism, however it is clear that the US government was merely asserting its material interests in ordering the region. A little later the French sociologist Raymond Aron was to speak of the misfit between the ethical rhetoric of the USA and its pursuit of an imperial national interest.[1] Overall, the period following the war years saw the first moves towards independence for subject peoples and the removal of the formal colonial empires of the Europeans and Americans.

The UK had held control of India over the war years notwithstanding local pressures for change. And as the war came to an end it re-established control in Burma, the Malay peninsula and Singapore. However, promises of independence had been made to the Indians and the Burmese, and both territories were politically independent nation states within a few years; Burma in 1948, and India in 1949. However, in contrast the situation in the Malay peninsula was more awkward because the population was ethnically divided, there was a strong communist party and the area offered a rich supply of economically valuable primary products. A series of conflicts ensued: first, between local ethnic Malays (whose nascent nationalism the Japanese had encouraged in the war years) and Chinese; second, between the British colonial military and local communist guerrillas (who had grown out of the wartime British supported resistance movement); and relatedly there were further conflicts with neighbouring states where both the Philippines and Indonesia looked unfavourably on the resumption of British influence. It was not until the mid-1960s that the pattern with which we are familiar today was put in place.

At the end of the war the Dutch government sought to re-establish its control over the Dutch East Indies, and did so with the help of the British. The motivation was similar to that of the British in Malaya, as the Dutch East Indies had large resources and the economy of the territory had made significant contributions over the years to the Netherlands' finances. However, during the war years the Japanese authorities had encouraged the expression of nationalist sentiment and as the war came to an end a group of Indonesian

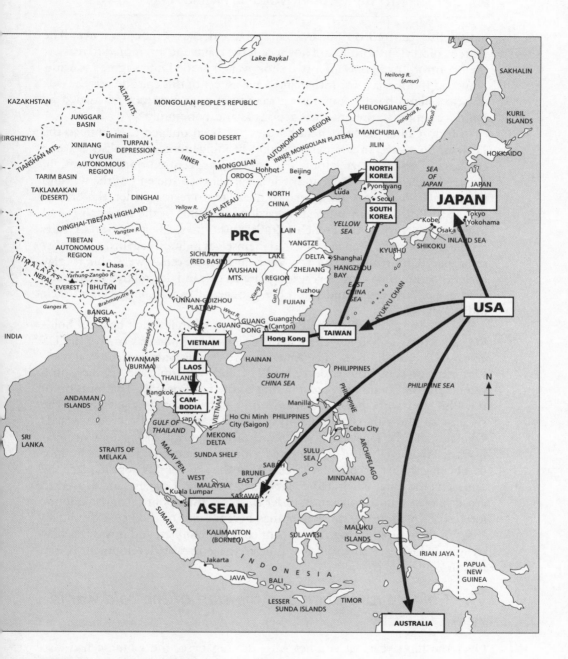

Map 5.1 Cold-war period spheres

nationalists centred on Sukarno and Hatta declared independence. The Dutch colonial authorities did not accept the claim and attempted to reassert their control. It was only after two short wars that the Dutch agreed to withdraw and Indonesia came into being. One aspect of this episode was the lack of help offered by the American government who were not persuaded by Dutch attempts to present their actions as anti-communist.

In Indo-China the French authorities had been obliged to submit to the Japanese in 1940. In Vietnam a group of indigenous nationalists became engaged in resistance activities. The nationalists, centred on the Vietminh, declared their independence in the interval between the end of the war and the arrival of the forces designated by the Allies to restore order, the British. The local British commander disregarded the claims of the nationalists and assisted the return of the French colonial authorities. After a period of fruitless negotiation the French reasserted themselves militarily against nationalist resistance. Unfortunately for the Vietnamese the French were able to play the anti-communist card. A very long, drawn out and destructive war ensued before the Vietnamese and the other peoples of Indo-China secured their independence.

Overall, the attempts of the Europeans to re-establish their colonial holdings after the war had few chances of success. The same was true of the US colony in the Philippines. The Americans re-established their colonial territory after invading the country in 1944 and defeating the Japanese in a campaign which caused great suffering to the local people. The invasion of the Philippines has been characterized as unnecessary in the light of the success of the American's Central Pacific campaign directed towards Okinawa and the Japanese home islands. In the period of Japanese occupation the Filipino elite had collaborated with the Japanese and active resistance had been confined to popular forces. After the war the US kept in place the same Filipino elite which had collaborated with the Japanese and moved to crush reform-minded groups in order to secure their political and economic interests.[2] In addition, the Philippines became one of the key US military bases in the region during the years of cold war conflict, and it was this new struggle which was to strongly influence the post-war development of the region.

The Chinese revolution and the start of the cold war in Asia

Over the long years of conflict with the Japanese, the Chinese had also engaged in an intermittent civil war. The USA had been sympathetic to the nationalist Chinese and in the closing stages of the conflict, following the end of the Pacific War, the USA made available significant financial and military aid.[3] However the KMT forces collapsed in 1949 and the remnants of the nationalist regime withdraw to Taiwan where they were brought under the broad protection of the USA. The armies of the Chinese Communist

Party emerged victorious and secured their revolution. The American right wing responded with hostility to the establishment of the PRC and in Washington politicians spoke of the State Department's experts having 'lost China' and the victory of the CCP was read as one more element of communist expansion.

In a similar way, these perceptions extended to the Korean peninsula where an early US decision not to become involved was reversed. US involvement in Korea was directly informed by anti-communism and the war led to a divided Korea with the north ruled by an old-style Stalinist leader and the south ruled by a long series of military dictatorships. The Korean War became one of the free world's key myths, and it was presented as a partial, heroic victory against communist expansionism. And relatedly, the French colonial war in Vietnam was read by the USA in anti-communist terms which initially tempted them into support and later direct involvement. The Asian region became one of the key areas in the free world's resistance to communism.

A new regional pattern takes shape

In the years following the end of the Pacific War the European powers were concerned with reconstructing a shattered European continent, the Japanese had withdrawn to the territory of the home islands, and the mainland of Asia was lodged within the socialist bloc. In the broad region of Pacific Asia the USA was the dominant power. It was within this context that the territories of the colonial empires secured political independence and began their pursuit of effective nation statehood. The American cold war inspired role in the region, which included wars, associated economic activity, the open domestic US market serving as a destination for Asian exports, and the establishment of a measure of regional stability, offered a quite particular framework for the active state-sponsored pursuit of economic growth.[4] In this period Japan quickly emerged as a key American military base and regional economic centre, and the countries adjacent to the Chinese seaboard began to develop. A little further south, the Philippines were closely linked to the USA, as was South Vietnam up until the 1970s.

Overall, reviewing the period, it might be noted that the European colonial empires had expanded in Asia since the sixteenth century and had drawn the larger part of the territory of the region into an ordered pattern shaped by the demands of metropolitan industrial-capitalism. Yet the system of colonial territories was fatally disturbed by the upheavals of the Pacific War. The years immediately following the end of hostilities were characterized by economic dislocation, social upheaval and political confusion. The period of war and its aftermath were an episode of abrupt complex change. At the end of the period the region had reconfigured and it was within new regional structural patterns that particular state-regimes began to plot a variety of new routes to the future. The discourse of colonialism fell away to be replaced by aspirations to national development and in turn these concerns came to be pursued within a bipolar frame as the region became divided between a US-centred free-market bloc and an autarchic socialist bloc centred on China.

Japan in the Immediate Post-war Years

After the debacle of the Pacific War the Japanese polity was radically remade by the American forces of occupation as the hitherto influential military and nationalist groups were disbanded or removed from the centre of public life. A series of ambitious programmes were inaugurated, but the logic of the cold war curbed reform. Overall, the period of rule by SCAP was instrumental in placing the political centre-right in power in Japan, which in turn lodged the country firmly within the sphere of the free world.

American occupation and the early post-war years

The Allied-Japanese war in Pacific Asia came to an end in August 1945 and the occupation forces arrived in September. The occupation was nominally an allied matter but was in fact almost entirely an American affair. General MacArthur was made Supreme Commander for the Allied Powers, SCAP, the name by which the occupation administration came to be known, and was responsible initially for disarming the Japanese armed forces, and thereafter pursued an ambitious reform programme.

The first task confronting SCAP was the destruction of the Japanese military machine. The armed forces were demobilized, the soldiers returned to their homes, and installations and equipment were destroyed all over Japan. Many civilians from overseas were repatriated as all Japan's territorial gains since Meiji were removed. A war crimes tribunal was held in Tokyo and a number of major war leaders were executed.

Thereafter SCAP undertook an extensive and ambitious programme of political-economic, social-institutional and cultural reform. The objectives of the reform programme were to ensure that the Japanese would not in the future have recourse to war, and that their relations with the international system would be conducted along peaceful lines.[5] A spread of reforms were instituted to secure these related goals, and in brief they amounted to the (partial) liberalization and democratization of the country after the model of the USA. The extent to which the changes were real, as opposed to merely formal, is a matter of some debate, with less orthodox critics pointing to a significant measure of continuity with pre-war days and outright radicals suggesting that the Americans virtually resurrected the pre-war elite in order to secure Japan as an ally in their confrontation with communism.

In the institutional political sphere there was an extensive purge of the machineries of the state to remove potentially anti-democratic personnel. However, the emperor was left in place having first renounced his divinity and embraced a Western-style notion of constitutional monarchy. This was a matter of some debate at the time, and commentators asked why SCAP should leave in place the figure on whose behalf the Japanese had waged war. It was also argued that the emperor carried significant personal responsibility for the war. It has been argued that the US authorities elected to keep the emperor as a figure of authority who would make their occupation of the country easier than it might otherwise have been. It was a contentious decision at the time and remains a matter of debate. However, we can note that the Japanese aristocracy was abolished.

Perhaps more importantly, it can be noted that in the early occupation period the existing political system was used to secure reforms. There was therefore continuity of government activities (although of course power rested with SCAP). Thereafter, in the broader sphere of political life, a new constitution was imposed, and brought into force in May 1947. In general, it was a US-style system, with extensive devolution of powers to regional prefectural governments, but the central government machine was modelled after the British system of a cabinet reporting to parliament (originally the Japanese had borrowed this form). Later, in 1952, a peace treaty was signed, and a part of this was a defence agreement which made Japan, in effect, a military protectorate of the USA.

Finally, in the sphere of social institutions the continuing family was abolished in 1947, and the pre-war stress on nationalism was removed. A spread of general social rights were affirmed, and the suffrage was broadened to include women. There was an important educational reform and a US pattern introduced. The post-war reconstruction lead to significant alterations in patterns of family, social welfare (schools) and work. The broad spread of changes looked to the social liberalization of Japanese society.

The effectiveness of SCAP

In the context of Japan's shift to the modern world, it is clear that from the Meiji restoration to the turn of the century the Japanese economy had made very rapid advances, and these advances continued through the period of the Great War and the 1930s. The destruction wrought by the Pacific War left the Japanese economy in ruins, yet the post-war recovery was rapid, and the success was achieved by a mixture of planning and free market. The iron triangle of bureaucracy, business and politicians was overwhelmingly committed to the pragmatic pursuit of economic growth, as it had been since the days of the Meiji Restoration.

The Japanese resisted the US reform programmes quietly, and all initiatives had to be put into practice through the filtering agency of the Japanese bureaucracy. It is true that in the economic sphere the power of the old urban elites and rural elites was broken. The industrial conglomerates called the zaibatsu which had enjoyed great power in pre-war Japan were broken up and new labour laws were introduced to allow trades unions. There was an important land reform and large agricultural holdings were broken up to create a rural small farmer class. However, after an initial period the reforms were modified, and a conservative-business alliance came to power.

Other than displacing the military, the depth of the changes to Japanese political economy, society and polity accomplished by SCAP have been the subject of much subsequent debate. The political reforms, rural reforms, and education reforms were all taken to have had significant effect, however the familiar criticism of SCAP is that it did far too little. The perceived failure is taken to have flowed from two factors: (i) an initial naïveté in the matter of making reforms; and (ii) a later desire to have Japan become an ally in the American anti-communist crusade.

MacArthur's quite small team was a mixture of New Deal supporters and nascent anti-communist conservatives. As time wore on the latter group came to have more influence with MacArthur, who was the key figure. Buckley[6] comments that one key criticism of MacArthur is that he did far too little and that the task of reform quickly gave way to a preference for Japan as an ally in the containment of communism. In 1949 Mao became leader of China and in 1950 the Korean war began. And the cold war became a fixed part of Western political thinking. A series of elements came together: (i) the limited nature of the SCAP reforms; (ii) the use of Japanese bureaucracy to effect reforms specified by SCAP (iii) the start of the cold war; (iv) the US/Japan defence agreement; and (v) the active US sympathy for the Japanese political right. Together these ushered in a conservative-dominated and US-oriented Japanese ruling group. The outcome was a business-dominated Japanese system firmly lodged within the US sphere of influence.

In total, the reforms undertaken by SCAP were in retrospect arguably rather modest. At the time many of the reforms were viewed unfavourably by the political elite, and aspects of SCAP rule, such as war crimes trials, were resented even at popular level.[7] However the SCAP period did bring Japan firmly into the American sphere of interest. The relationship of Japan and the USA is now the key foreign relations concern of the Japanese state. It dominates all other relationships. At a popular level the influence of America has been strong in the post-war period, in the media, in popular culture and in slowly changing patterns of behaviour attendant upon the development of an insistent consumerism.

Japanese recovery to 1971

In the immediate post-war period the recovery of Japan was rapid. The shift in US policy towards Japan as the cold war developed was significant. The Korean war also offered a boost to the Japanese economy. However, the subsequent rapid economic development owed more to domestic agendas. Waswo comments that: 'The first and arguably most crucial step the Japanese took was to toss aside the model of their economic future bequeathed to them by the Occupation'.[8] The SCAP economists had looked at Japan with liberal eyes and seen cheap labour as the primary Japanese comparative advantage, and plotted a route to a low technology economic future with other industrial nations taking the technological lead. However, the bureaucracy, politicians and industrialists strongly supported the goal of running a first-class economy at the very highest levels of available technology. This policy goal had been in place since Meiji. Waswo notes: 'With the publication of its New Long-Range Economic Plan in December of 1957, the Japanese government made it clear that the static and somewhat self-serving model devised by the Occupation had been replaced by a dynamic development plan that would, if successful, bridge the economic gap between Japan and the leading nations of the world'.[9]

The Japanese miracle was a product of state-regime commitment, the fortuitous circumstances of the post-Second World War 'long boom' and the tolerance of export success within the US market because of cold war alliances. In addition, it is important to note the determination of ordinary Japanese people to redeem themselves, and their country, after the debacle of the war; what has been referred to as 'GNP nationalism'.[10] The early period of post-war growth came to be dominated by heavy industries (steel, ships, chemicals, coal). It is true that by the early 1960s Japan was beginning to emerge as a significant economic power. In the early 1970s their economy was to experience some shocks – the oil price rises and Nixon's decision to float the dollar – but these were made occasions for further success. After internal reconstruction and export orientated growth the economy began to run a trading surplus. Restructuring moved the economy to higher value added goods (cars, consumer appliances, machinery), and the second oil shock of 1979 was weathered fairly easily.[11] It was clear by the middle 1970s that the post-war recovery was a significant success.

The Countries of Northeast Asia

The countries of Northeast Asia have operated over the post-war years within the US sphere. However, the three countries are not identical and the routes which they have taken into the modern world are different. Hong Kong played an important role as a trading centre within the global colonial system of the British. The country has gone on to build on this role in the post-war period. In contrast the territories of South Korea and Taiwan have emerged from the status of adjuncts to the Japanese economy in order to play much wider independent roles.

All three territories were occupied in the war years and experienced the chaos of war. Indeed, there was extensive military activity throughout Asia and some twenty million people died. In the post-war period a new order was established in the wake of the military victory of the USA and the revolution in China. The two spheres were thereafter kept separate.

Japanese occupation, decolonization and the early post-war years

South Korea and Taiwan had been parts of the Japanese empire since the early years of the century. In the wake of the collapse of the Japanese empire they experienced a series of changes including population transfers (Japanese moving out, and in Taiwan mainlanders moving in), the disruption of war (in Taiwan the incoming mainlanders were the defeated KMT and in Korea there was a war from 1950–3), land reform coupled with economic reconstruction and finally absorption within the overarching cold war bloc centred on the USA. The starting point for subsequent success was thus a radically dislocated political and economic situation.

In the case of Korea, Eckert notes that: 'Colonial policies had shattered the foundations of a remarkably stable nineteenth century bureaucratic agrarian society and unleashed new forces in conflict with the old and with each other'.[12] It is clear that Korean society at the end of the war was radically unstable. The population was still predominantly agrarian but there was a spread of other class groups including landlords, factory workers, professionals and capitalists. It was within this context that the Japanese colonial authorities, noting the inevitability of defeat, began in August 1945 to look for a local force to take control.

The political pattern within the fragmented Korean society was very complex. Cummings[13] summarizes the divisions in terms of class position, such that the right comprised propertied and educated groups, who had typically collaborated and who opposed fundamental reform, and the left comprised students, intellectuals, peasants and workers, who were committed to purging collaborators and implementing broad social reforms. The Japanese colonial authorities invited a reputable right-wing figure, Song Chin-U to take over, but he declined, so the Japanese turned to Yo Un-Hyong an equally reputable left-wing figure. Yo accepted the offer and proceeded to establish the Committee for the Preparation of Korean Independence (CPKI) which made contact with a wide spread of popular groups throughout the country, and in a very short time had evolved into a replacement administration. The CPKI then called a representative meeting in Seoul and this declared the establishment of the Korean People's Republic (KPR) and scheduled elections.

However, within the context of the developing cold war the Korean peninsula came to be seen by sections of the American government as a significant territory and agreements made at Yalta and Potsdam, which left the territory to the sphere of the Russians, were redrawn as a result of American proposals to which the Russians agreed. The territory was divided along the 38th parallel. The Americans arrived in southern Korea in September with an army under the command of General Hodge. The Americans declined to acknowledge the KPR or the CPKI and proceeded to install their own occupation administration whose Korean political, administrative and police elements were drawn from the ranks of right-wing nationalists, collaborators and colonial policeman.[14] The American occupation authorities then began the task of suppressing the local committees of the CPKI, and their labour and peasant union allies. This was often a violent business and culminated in a railway strike in Pusan in September 1946 which triggered a general insurrection in the south. The rebellion was suppressed by the local police and American forces. Meanwhile in the northern part of the territory the Soviet occupation had run along with the reformist tenor of the local groups and this allowed the Russian protégé Kim Il Sung to form the 'Interim People's Committee'. In time a communist government emerged from the KPR groups in the north. The US and their local political allies then manoeuvred against the north and the drift towards there being two countries began. The Republic of Korea (ROK) with Syngman Rhee was established on 15 August 1948. The north responded and founded the Democratic People's Republic of Korea (DPRK) on 25 August 1948. The USSR withdrew its forces from the north and a little later the US pulled out of the south.

In the south the right-wing republic was not accepted and between the end of 1948 and June 1950 South Korea was the scene of an indigenous leftist guerrilla war.[15] At the same time the southern regime launched a series of provocative small-scale attacks on the north and Syngman Rhee and his generals spoke openly of reuniting the country by force. On 25 June 1950 the north invaded and the Korean War began. Initially the north had great military success until the USA intervened. The south then had great military success until the PRC intervened and forced them back down the peninsula. The entire country was laid waste and although General MacArthur favoured opening a general war against China, President Truman[16] balked at the idea, and an armistice was eventually signed on 27 July 1953 with the two opposing forces more or less back where they had begun along the 38th parallel.

The war in Korea had two effects, one immediate and the other longer term. In the first place it fixed in place not only the division of Korea but also the bipolar cold war division of Pacific Asia. In the second place, over the longer term, the US commitment to containment in Asia encouraged them to permit free access to their domestic marketplace for the exports of the countries of the region. The Korean economy recovered only slowly in the years following the war, however the dictator Rhee was overthrown in 1960 and in 1961 Park Chun Hee took power. The government of Park was committed to an authoritarian quasi-military development strategy which looked to build up strong industrial conglomerates. In 1965 the Korean government normalized relations with Japan and there was an immediate inflow of investment. In the 1960s the development strategy moved beyond simple import substitution into a new export oriented phase and a long period of strong growth began.

Turning now to the case of Taiwan, which became a Japanese colony in

1895, and which was extensively developed by the Japanese authorities, we find a similar situation. In October 1945 the Japanese handed over power to the nationalist Chinese government, which proceeded to exploit the resources of the island for the benefit of the mainland regime. The nationalist military forces then provoked with their ill-disciplined behaviour a rebellion amongst indigenous Taiwanese. However this was suppressed by the nationalist Chinese troops with many Taiwanese dying in the process. The local population then retreated into an apolitical state similar to that which had obtained in the years of Japanese colonial rule.[17] In 1949 the remnants of the nationalist Chinese army retreated to the island, where the government of the nominally single Chinese state was established as the Republic of China (ROC). The island's assembly was controlled by the KMT, itself dominated by the mainlanders, whose two million people were lodged amongst the nine million Taiwanese. In the context of cold war conflict with the PRC the USA extended generous civilian and military aid to the KMT regime and urged a series of land reforms. The economy of the country prospered within this context at first in terms of import substitution and thereafter in the 1960s as an exporting economy. The country is now a significant economy within the region.[18]

In contrast to the experiences of South Korea and Taiwan, Hong Kong had been a trading port within the British colonial sphere since the early nineteenth century. In the wake of the withdrawal of the Japanese it was reinstated within the British colonial system. However, it was clear that the pre-war status quo belonged to history and could not be recovered. Hong Kong continued as a colonial territory, with a political economy ordered by the non-democratic colonial regime oriented to business activity, but the colony's existence depended upon the tacit consent of the PRC. Over the years it became the key link between mainland China and the global system. The territory received a flow of immigrants from mainland China in the wake of the 1949 success of the Chinese communist party. The economy of Hong Kong was strengthened. The entrepôt trade was supplemented in the fifties and sixties with increasing levels of industrial production, initially low-tech cheap labour but thereafter moving into higher value added areas, and the city is now a major economic centre within the region.

The Countries of Southeast Asia

It can be argued that there are two overall stages in the post-war history of the territories of Southeast Asia: (i) the post-independence phase of the pursuit of effective nation statehood in the context of a cold war divided Asia; and (ii) the later period of rapid success within the growing regional sphere of Pacific Asia. If state-regimes read and react to changing global structural circumstances in formulating political-cultural projects, thereafter ordered and legitimated within their territories, then the broad context for these state-regimes is the withdrawal of the colonial powers, their replacement for a period by the Americans, and most recently the slow emergence of a Japan-centred Pacific Asia. Halliday[19] argues that the countries of Northeast Asia can be referred to as the inner periphery of the new Japanese-dominated sphere of Pacific Asia, and in a similar way Southeast Asia is the outer periphery. The period running up to the early 1970s sees the countries of the region establish themselves as independent nation states displaying significant economic growth.[20]

Malaysia

The withdrawal of the British from their colonial territories in Southeast Asia was not straightforward. The pattern of colonial administration was complex, the area had been disrupted by war and the local population had come to read political action in ethnic terms. In the Malay peninsula British administration had been arranged using three strategies: the Colony of the Straits Settlements, the Federated Malay States and the Unfederated Malay States. This pattern reflected the piecemeal advance of colonial authority in the context of a developing metropolitan industrial-capitalism, a significant flow of immigrants and a local population whose loyalties were directed to a series of local sultanates operating systems of personal rule.

In the 1930s the territory had prospered, however as Osborne notes: 'For all that we may think of the 1920s and 1930s as the heyday of colonialism . . . these were the years when the foundations of colonial rule in Southeast Asia were under very considerable strain'.[21] In the British territories a particular concern was the rising problems associated with the immigration of Indians and Chinese. There was some alarm amongst the Malays. In the years of occupation the local Chinese suffered at the hands of the Japanese and it was primarily from this ethnic group that the local British supported MPAJA resistance was recruited. On the other hand the Malays had been relatively less badly treated and encouraged in their national aspirations, as had the Indian community.

At the end of the war the British re-established control. However, the situation in the colony was thoroughly confused. The various elements of the community had not come together in the war years and they did not come together afterwards, indeed matters drifted towards ethnic violence with MPAJA members summarily executing Malay collaborators, thereby producing a further round of communal tension. The returning British Military Administration (BMA) proved incompetent and the situation deteriorated. The British suggested a new constitution as preparation for independence as the Malayan Union, however this offered citizenship to non-Malays and provoked strong reaction amongst Malays. A new constitution was proposed, the Federation of Malaya, which addressed these problems but in turn provoked a reaction from amongst the Chinese. In May 1948, for reasons never finally clarified, the Malayan Communist Party, mostly Chinese and the key group in the wartime MPAJA, declared an armed struggle and began guerrilla warfare in the rural areas. The British responded with counter-guerrilla tactics and the Malayan Emergency ran on until the late 1950s.

Malaysia became independent in 1957 and its history has to a very significant extent been shaped by the communal division. After independence the government's development strategies looked to evolutionary advance. However, in practice this rather meant giving political power to the Malays and leaving economic power to the Chinese. The strategy broke down in 1969 when race riots occurred in the wake of an election. A new political-cultural project was inaugurated under the title of the New Economic Policy (NEP). The project had the intention of alleviating the ethnic divisions of the country through a strategy of national development designed to assist the circumstances of the rural Malay population. The resultant pattern of development has had many tensions but the balance between the groups has prevented either ethnic group aiming for political closure.[22]

Overall, in Malaysia the imperial Japanese encouraged a nascent Malay nationalist movement. The returning British recognized the need for change and began to look to secure a new settlement. In the post-war period a confused and violent shift to independence left a Malay political elite in power in alliance with a strong Chinese business class. The situation by 1971 sees the eventual establishment of order after some significant ethnic tension and the inauguration of a programme of state-led development.

Singapore

Singapore was brought into the colonial system of the British in the early nineteenth century when the territory was extracted by quasi-legal means from the territory of the Johor-Riau sultanate. The territory was a success economically and its population grew rapidly with Malay and Chinese immigration to the island. As the colonial system in the region developed Singapore came to play a key role linking the Malay peninsula hinterland and the islands of the archipelago (to the extent that the Dutch would allow) to the metropolitan centre in London and thence to the UK's trading networks. The population of the city also became predominantly Chinese. In the colonial period it was never envisaged that Singapore would become independent but when the links with Malaysia failed in 1965 the local political leadership was left with no other choice.

The early years of the island's post-war development were strongly influenced by ethnic tensions. The island's population was predominantly Chinese in 1942 when the British Army surrendered to the Japanese, whose treatment of the Chinese in Singapore was harsh. After the end of the war the British returned and there was some unclarity as to the territory's future. The island's predominantly Chinese population would have made the demographics of an independent Malaya which included them look rather awkward. However, internal self-rule was quickly established in 1959 and the country joined Malaysia in 1963. The marriage was not a happy one. Turnbull comments: 'To bring together the essentially urban, commercial and industrial society of Singapore with the rural, racially divided society of the Federation of Malaya was a most difficult undertaking, given even the most favourable of circumstances. The basic economic needs of the two communities were so fundamentally different that any effective government in the two places must clash on priorities and direction. Constitutional development and nationalism had followed diverse paths'.[23] Singapore became independent in August 1965, an eventuality which had not figured on anyone's agenda, and the new state-regime set about building upon the island's long established trading role. The state moved to exert its control over all sections of society and pursued a vigorous industrialization strategy. The basic spread of activities associated with the trading port were supplemented by manufacturing activity and within a few years the country was recording rapid economic growth.[24]

In sum, in Singapore the Japanese interregnum was difficult for the local predominantly ethnic Chinese population. The return of the British saw a resumption of the established role of regional entrepôt. After unexpected independence in 1965 the country looked to develop as a broad based regional centre and by 1971 had passed a series of local laws which fostered this role.[25]

Indonesia

The Dutch began trading in the archipelago in the sixteenth century and the colonial territory was slowly assembled over many years. The Dutch were preoccupied with profit and ran their colony as a vast agricultural holding, and the impact upon pre-contact forms-of-life was severe. It was the Japanese occupation which destroyed the colonial regime. In the territory the nationalist leaders Sukarno and Hatta advanced their cause with the sympathy of the Japanese. The Japanese also provided the indigenous peoples with experience of administration, and their militaristic youth movement became the basis of the Indonesian Army. As the Japanese occupation ended the nationalists declared a republic on 17 August 1945 and then looked to secure their control over the archipelago. The British and Dutch returned a few weeks later and a period of confused manoeuvring then ensued. The Dutch attempted to resume control of the territory and were supported by the British. The political and military exchanges continued until eventually the Dutch agreed to withdraw and Indonesia became independent formally in 1949, and the new elite had to construct a nation state. Reid points out that: 'Indonesia is a new world for a nation which has taken clear shape only in our own century. Coined by European ethnologists in the late nineteenth century, the world was adopted by nationalism in the 1920s in an extraordinarily rapid discovery of national unity'.[26]

The nationalist movement lead by Hatta and Sukarno (who had first proclaimed the independence of Indonesia after some hesitation in 1945) inaugurated a period of liberal-democratic government which gave way in 1958 to the guided democracy of Sukarno which lasted until 1965. In the period of Sukarno's rule the colonial economy, which the new elite had inherited, drifted and declined as the government were not disposed to deploy the force necessary to keep it running. The situation slowly became untenable and in 1965 Suharto staged a bloody coup and took power. The government thereafter pursued a more rational development strategy based on the country's vast natural wealth and oriented to import substitution. The governing elite of the country comprised the army, the state bureaucracy and business who together ordered what became known as a 'bureaucratic polity'. The country has had a military-bureaucratic rule ever since and the territory's many natural resources have provided the basis for a significant if inequitable pattern of development.

Philippines

The Americans seized the Philippines at the turn of the century just as the indigenous nationalists were on the point of winning their war of independence against the Spanish, and the years to 1942 saw the economy of the islands firmly tied into the American sphere, notwithstanding protestations of their intentions to prepare the islands for independence. When the Japanese arrived in 1942 the Filipino elite collaborated and it was amongst the peasantry that resistance was found. When the USA returned in 1944 they offered their support to that elite and looked to resume the pre-war status quo, with a powerful landed elite in alliance with the commercial interests of the USA, with both disinclined to attend to the rather impoverished situation of the mass of the peasant population.

However, in the post-war period the US miscalculated its response to the resistance movement because the Huks had been active against the Japanese during the war and had established their nationalist credentials. In the 1946 elections to the new independent parliament the Huks won seven seats. This created two major problems for the ruling elite and their US allies: firstly, the Huks were proponents of land reform; and secondly, the seven seats gave the Huks the power to block economic legislation which would have given the commercial interests of the USA a privileged status. The local elite and their US allies took action and excluded the Huks from parliament. The resulting armed guerrilla war reached a peak in the early 1950s but the Americans provided backing for the local elite who eventually prevailed. The economic trajectory of the Philippines was lodged firmly within the parameters set by American commercial interests.

The returning Americans put back in place a landed elite which had collaborated with the imperial Japanese in order to re-establish economic links. The start point for later efforts was one of political/social continuity with war and pre-war years, plus general dislocation and continued conflicts. The situation in the country by the 1970s was that after initial import substituting industrialization success the country declined into the crony capitalism of Marcos. The economy was weak, society unequal and there were regional succession movements.

Thailand

Thailand is historically a special case. It was never colonized, and in the years of colonial expansion it played the role of a buffer state between the British and French holdings. Pluvier[27] notes that the British sought to open trade relations with the Siamese government from the middle of the nineteenth century. In response the Siamese government attempted to modernize in the late nineteenth century so as to avoid the fate of becoming a colony. The reign of King Mongkut (1851–68) and King Chulalongkorn (1868–1910) saw a spread of administrative, financial, judicial and educational reforms put in place.[28] However, the results were a variation upon the theme of a colonial system with rural dislocation and the decline of traditional handicrafts running alongside the development of plantation style agriculture. Pluvier[29] notes that these development efforts produced the economic and social problems similar to those found in the Western colonial territories. In the context of the impact of the global depression in the 1930s the absolute monarchy was abolished in 1932 and an army-led government took over. The country then slid quietly into the ambit of the Japanese. A continuation of army dominated bureaucratic-authoritarian rule was established in the years following the end of the Pacific War.[30]

The Thai elite has typically adjusted to circumstances in a flexible way and came under American influence in the 1960s and 1970s as the wars in Indo-China expanded. In these years a measure of import substituting industrialization was achieved. The situation by 1971 sees a strong American presence and the beginnings of more rapid development although at this time the country was often tagged a bureaucratic capitalist state.

The further development of the countries of ASEAN

The ASEAN countries have subsequently undergone further development. The countries of the region have received large amounts of inward investment and are rapidly shifting from any residual dependence upon primary product exporting as import substituting industrialization increasingly gives way to vigourous export oriented enterprise. It is difficult to summarize their development strategies but various state-regimes have had a strong directing hand. The state-regimes in each country secure order at an elite level (often with close military involvement) and legitimate their rule by reference to national development programmes. The ASEAN countries have ethnically diverse populations with many language groups and traditional patterns of living. However, it is the case that throughout the region the demands of the global industrial-capitalist system are reaching ever deeper into extant forms-of-life and are doing so with the active involvement of local state-regimes.[31]

The Search for Socialist Development: China, North Korea and the Countries of Indo-China

The dynamics of wartime upheaval and political change in the Pacific Asian region had the effect of promoting the influence of the CCP within China. In the long process of the replacement of the centralized emperor system, which had collapsed in 1911, the dynamics of internal conflict complicated by outside invasion and intervention, the radical forces of the rural based communist party came to prevail. The general international situation coupled to the demand within the USA of what Caute[32] has dubbed the 'patriotic imperative' entailed that the USA adopted a hostile position towards the CCP and in due course to the PRC. The cold war division of Asia was thereby inaugurated.

China: the war against Japan, the revolution and the early post-war years

The early part of the modern history of China is one of the collapse of the old emperor system in part through the internal decay of the emperor system and also because of the impact of the incursions of the agents of the expanding industrial-capitalist system.

The emperor system decayed over the latter years of the nineteenth century and in the early twentieth century, in 1911, Sun Yat Sen sought to establish a republic. However this attempt did not wholly succeed and a series of regional warlords emerged. A little while later in 1921 the Chinese communist party was formed and the 1920s and 1930s were marked by the conflicts of Kuomintang (derived from Sun Yat Sen's movement), the CCP and the regional warlords. All were made more complex by the presence of the Western powers.

After the death of Yuan Shikai the first national leader in 1916 the country dissolved into a series of competing warlord holdings. The KMT was militarily successful in the 1920s and in 1924 allied itself with the CCP. The alliance was successful initially in the south around Canton. The KMT leadership launched the Northern Expedition in 1926 and advanced along the coast to Shanghai which was reached in March 1927. In April 1927 the KMT decreed the establishment of a national government and outlawed the CCP. The KMT attacked the CCP and slowly reduced it to a series of base areas which were territories controlled by the communists and out of the effective reach of the KMT armies.

The KMT's core territory lay in the area of Shanghai and Nanjing on the lower Yangtze River. In the period from 1927 to 1937 (when the Japanese invaded) the KMT slowly established a unified territory. There was economic advance and social reform in the sense of new merchant and industrial groups, however the rural landlord and peasant system remained largely untouched. Chiang Kai-shek proclaimed himself and the KMT to be committed to democracy but added that the Chinese were not yet ready. Moise comments that whilst his political thought compounded Confucianism and European fascism, in practice the project was irrelevant to the majority of the people with the elite looking after their own concerns and the masses continuing largely as they had done traditionally. It was clear in this period that the original revolutionary impulse of Sun Yat Sen's movement had largely dissipated.

However, the commitment of the CCP remained intact even as their movement declined under the impact of KMT suppression. The CCP eventually became concentrated in the Jiangxi Soviet in central southern China. The KMT launched a series of pacification drives and eventually succeeded in encircling the territory and cadres of the CCP in Jiangxi. The breakout in October 1934 was the start of the Long March which took the remnants of the CCP to a new base area in northern China near the town of Yanan. In the years running up to 1937 they regrouped under the new leadership of Mao Tse-tung.

The situation became more complex in the years from 1931 to 1937 as Japanese involvement in China became more extensive. In 1937 the Japanese launched an open war against China and the forces of the KMT retreated inland along the valley of the Yangtze River. In early 1937 Chiang Kai-shek was obliged to enter a second alliance with the CCP.

The war against the Japanese proved to be a chaotic period. The KMT, CCP and remaining warlords all manoeuvred against each other and the Japanese. After the defeat of the Japanese by the Allies in late 1945 the putative allies within China moved to seize territory and matériel in order to position themselves advantageously. The USA made significant aid available to the KMT whilst simultaneously presenting itself as an honest broker. After an interval of a year the civil war resumed and, after an initial advance by the forces of the KMT, the CCP replied and in late 1948 the forces of the KMT collapsed and in early 1949 Chiang Kai-shek fled to Taiwan and Mao proclaimed the establishment of the PRC.

China: political-economic, social-institutional and cultural arrangements

The period 1949–71 saw a measure of stability within the country following the success of the communist party in defeating the Kuomintang, local warlords and the Japanese. The European and American quasi-colonial presence has also ceased. At this point, for the first time in many years, China was united under a Chinese government. Thereafter the country saw the pursuit of Maoist inspired socialism; in particular, collectivization, the great leap forward and the cultural revolution.

The early years of communist rule in the 1950s saw the reorganization of rural areas in the form not merely of land reform, but rather the deliberate destruction of long established rural class structures which saw landlords reduced to the status of ordinary peasants and the peasantry politicized. In the urban areas where the cadres of the CCP had less experience the pace of change was slower and a mixed system – combining state ownership and private ownership – was inaugurated. In 1952 the 'Five Anti' campaign looked to suppress bribery, tax evasion, theft of state assets, cheating on contracts and stealing state economic information, and this did restrict further the scope for private activity. The mid-1950s saw further reforms in both rural and urban areas as collectivization and nationalization moved ahead. At the same time the first five-year plan running from 1953–7 was begun.

In 1958 Mao inaugurated a mass rural campaign designed to shorten the period of the transition to socialism. The Great Leap Forward saw large communes formed and a campaign of mass mobilization. The programme ran until late 1960. It was a disaster and levels of agricultural output were severely depressed. Moise[33] estimates that the excess deaths over trend rates for the period comes to some sixteen million.

In the early period of the 1960s the situation of China improved. The economy, society and polity became more ordered and successful. However, the shifting pattern of power within the elite levels of the country had the effect of moving Mao to the sidelines, in particular bureaucrats in the planning departments regarded the Great Leap Forward as a disaster which should not be repeated.

Mao analysed the situation in terms of a new coalescence of interests – bureaucrats with privileged positions, lines of advance for students through schools and into influential positions, and urban workers generally – which were subverting the revolution to their narrowly bourgeois nationalist interests at the expense of revolutionary goals and the interests of peasants and the urban non-privileged. In 1966 Mao launched the Great Proletarian Cultural Revolution with the help of students and allies in the PLA. The campaign against bourgeois ideas developed and drew in factory workers and peasants. It was also turned against the institution of the communist party. The Red Guards appeared in 1966 and a campaign spread throughout the country attacking the 'Four Olds' – old ideas, old culture, old customs and old habits. In the period 1967–8 there was extensive upheaval. The authority of the communist party began to be restored in 1969 and the business of picking up the pieces, with politics balanced between a radical Maoist left and a more pragmatic right, ran on until Mao's death in 1976. At that point, the left were quickly removed and Deng Xiao Ping came to take power.

North Korea: the war against Japan, war with the UN and development policy

In the Pacific War a Korean resistance movement was active against the Japanese. At the end of the war this movement along with popular organizations took control of the country. An American occupation force under a junior officer did not accept this situation. After a period of confusion a divided Korea was the result. A right-wing nationalist, Syngman Rhee, took control in the South and came into confrontation with the North's leader, Kim Il Sung. In 1950 war broke out and the USA, UN and thereafter China became involved. In 1953 an armistice was signed and the country remained divided. In North Korea a centrally planned economy stressing self-reliance was constructed. The country remained lodged within the broad socialist bloc and pursued an autarchic strategy of development.

Indo-China: Vietnam, Cambodia and Laos

The area had been brought under the control of the French in the late nineteenth century. The ancient cultures of Vietnam and Cambodia were seized first and then they were joined by Laos when the French colonial powers took control of what had been a part of Siam. The upheavals of the Pacific War broke the colonial empires but the French attempted to reimpose their control militarily but the entire region became embroiled in a series of wars that were to run for decades.

The Japanese occupied Indo-China in stages in the early war years. The territories were effectively a part of the Japanese empire from 1941–5. At the end of the war in 1945 the British army arrived to occupy the territory. At that time a relatively junior officer declined to accept the claims of the nationalists, led by Ho Chi Minh, and the French colonial power was permitted to return. The situation then grew thoroughly confused until the French turned to the use of force. Thereafter the French attempted to re-establish their colonial authority by military means. However this attempt was ill-conceived and they were defeated militarily by the middle of the 1950s. At that time the French advised the USA not to become involved. However, by the mid-1950s the cold war was raging and this disposed the Americans to become involved. The Americans stepped in and slowly became more deeply involved, eventually committing half a million troops in the late 1960s. The American strategy was to strengthen the south so as to enable them to defeat the north. The southern regime was a corrupt client regime and the policy never worked. The Americans experienced great difficulty in prosecuting their war and by 1971 the financial burdens were such that the convertability of the dollar was suspended, thereby destroying the post-Second World War Bretton Woods system which had been the cornerstone of the US-centred Western liberal trading sphere. A few years later in 1973 the US acknowledged defeat and withdrew. Finally, we should note that over the same period of time the underdeveloped countries of Laos and Cambodia also became peripherally involved in the war with similar catastrophic effects. In the process of these interlinked wars the countries were devastated.

Conclusion

In the early period following the Pacific War it is possible to identify a series of broad phases in the development experiences of the countries of the region. In the first phase the 1945–9 period of the interplay of China, the USA and the Europeans established the broad framework within which local patterns subsequently moved. In the second phase there was a process of decolonization and the pursuit of effective nation statehood within the Western oriented sphere which secured significant prosperity. And at the same time, the inward looking development of the socialist bloc led slowly into relative poverty. It is clear that the patterns of manoeuvre in the earliest years following the war set the pattern for the post-war period in Asia. The European colonial empires were dismantled. The US withdrew from the Philippines. The Chinese secured their revolution and the American reaction divided the region along cold war lines: the free world; and the socialist bloc.

Over many years the USA was the hegemonic power within the free world bloc. It was within the sphere of the USA that the territories of the colonial empires attained independence and began the pursuit of development. The American role in the region offered a framework for the pursuit of economic growth and the establishment of domestic stability. The system continued to advance until the early 1970s when US problems occasioned a further reconfiguring of the region. On the other hand in the socialist sphere the pursuit of development was interrupted by upheavals in China and military engagements sponsored by the USA. The upshot is that the socialist sphere remains largely under-developed. However, Deng Xiao Ping's 1978 reforms inaugurated very extensive reforms which moved economies, societies and polities towards the controlled market model of Pacific Asia. However, overall it was the emergence of Japan over the 1970s as its recovery proceeded, paralleled by a weakening of the economy of the USA (in part as a result of wars in Asia and military spending), which acted to order the integrated development of the region. It is in this later phase that an emergent Pacific Asian region can be identified.

Notes

1   R. Aron 1973: *The Imperial Republic: The USA and the World 1945–1973*, London: Weidenfeld.

2   B. Kerkvliet 1977: *The Huk Rebellion: A Study of Peasant Revolt in the Philippines*, University of California Press.

3   R. C. Thompson 1994: *The Pacific Basin since 1945*, London: Longman, pp. 13–17.
4   C. Hamilton 1983: Capitalist Industrialization in East Asia's Four Little Tigers in *Journal of Contemporary Asia* 13.
5   W. G. Beasley 1990: *The Rise of Modern Japan*, Tokyo: Tuttle, pp. 214–26.
6   R. Buckley 1990: *Japan Today*, Cambridge: Cambridge University Press.
7   S. Tsurumi 1987: *A Cultural History of Postwar Japan 1945–80*, London: Kegan Paul International.
8   A. Waswo 1996: *Modern Japanese Society 1968–1994*, Oxford University Press, p. 107.
9   Ibid., p. 108.
10 Ibid., p. 110.
11 K. Sheridan 1993: *Governing the Japanese Economy*, Cambridge: Polity.
12 C. J. Eckert 1992: Korea: Liberation, Division and War, in M. Borthwick *Pacific Century: The Emergence of Modern Pacific Asia*, Boulder, CO: Westview, p. 374.
13 B. Cummings 1997: *Korea's Place in the Sun: A Modern History*.
14 Ibid.
15 Ibid. See also B. Cummings 1981: *The Origins of the Korean War*, Princeton, NJ: Princeton University Press.
16 Thompson 1994, p. 51.
17 Ibid., p. 56.
18 R. Wade 1990: *Governing the Market: Economic Theory and the Role of Government in East Asian Industrialization*, Princeton, NJ: Princeton University Press.
19 J. Halliday 1980: Capitalism and Socialism in East Asia in *New Left Review* 124.
20 B. N. Pandy 1980: *South and Southeast Asia 1945–1979: Problems and Policies*, London: Macmillan.
21 M. Osborne 1995: *Southeast Asia*, St Leonards: Allen and Unwin, p. 113.
22 K. H. Lee 1981: Malaya: New State and Old Elite, in R. Jeffrey, ed., 1981: *Asia: The Winning of Independence*, London: Macmillan.
23 M. Turnbull 1977: *A History of Singapore 1819–1975*, Oxford University Press, p. 289.
24 G. Rodan 1989: *The Political Economy of Singapore's Industrialization*, London: Macmillan; G. Rodan, ed., 1993: *Singapore Changes Guard*, Melbourne: Longman Cheshire.
25 P. Chen ed. 1983: *Singapore: Development Policies and Trends*, Oxford University Press.
26 A. Reid 1981: Indonesia: Revolution without Socialism, in Jeffrey, ed., 1981, p. 114.
27 J. M. Pluvier 1977: *Southeast Asia From Colonialism to Independence*, Oxford University Press.
28 Ibid., p. 90.
29 Ibid.
30 J. L. S. Girling 1981: *Thailand: Society and Politics*, Ithaca, NY: Cornell University Press.
31 J. Wong 1979: *ASEAN Economies in Perspective*, London: Macmillan.
32 D. Caute 1978: *The Great Fear: The Anti-Communist Purges Under Truman and Eisenhower*, London: Secker.
33 E. Mosie 1994: *Modern China*, London: Longman, p. 142.

6

The Emergence of Pacific Asia

In the 1970s and early 1980s the region underwent significant reconfiguration as the significance of the cold war declined, the hegemony of the USA weakened and the Japanese economy attained a new pre-eminence. Overall the region comes to be read in terms of the notion of Pacific Asia. In this period the increasingly interdependent forms-of-life of the region, with their rapidly changing political economies, social-institutional structures and cultures come to have a clear distinctiveness within the global system.

It has become clear in the wake of the collapse of the bipolar system that the global industrial-capitalist system has developed into the three broad regions of the Americas, the European Union and Pacific Asia. The three regions can be seen to have political-economic cores and a spread of peripheral territories. The regions trade amongst themselves and evidence distinct varieties of industrial-capitalism. The current situation within the global system thus displays a mixture of internationalization and regionalization.

It is the recognition of this new global pattern that makes the developing region of Pacific Asia interesting to scholars, political actors and policy makers in countries within the region and within the territories of the other regions. The linkages between the various parts of the region are becoming extensive and they are deepening. The linkages of the region to the developing global system are also very extensive. The region has a core economy, extensive economic linkages, new political/trade mechanisms and a measure of cultural coherence. An integrated regional grouping can be taken to be in the process of formation, although the end point is most unclear and the extent of integration should not be overstated.

In this period we begin to speak of Pacific Asia as a distinctive region within the global system having an increasingly common form-of-life. By way of an agenda we can consider the following matters: (i) the contemporary patterns of structural changes and the rise of Pacific Asia; (ii) the nature of Japan's relationship with Pacific Asia; (iii) the dynamics of the inner sphere of the NICs; (iv) the relations with the core of the countries of Southeast Asia; (v)

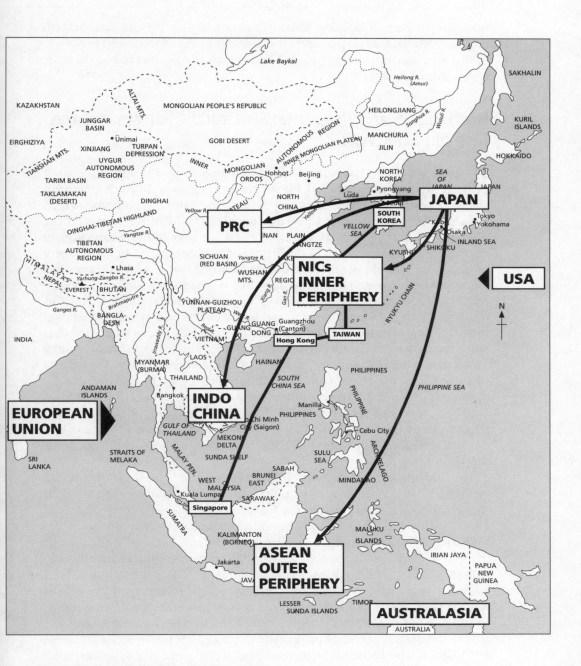

Map 6.1   Post-1991 spheres in tripolar system

the new patterns of development in Australasia; (vi) the dramatic reform processes within China and Indo-China; and (vii) the expectations in respect of the development of an integrated Pacific Asia and the possibilities of leadership from Japan.

Recognition and Response: Structural Changes and the Rise of Pacific Asia

The cold war period saw the wide dissemination of an official ideology centred around the tenets of liberal market capitalism which provided standard truths for elites to deploy within the public sphere and which suffused the private thinking of many people. The ideology expressed the political-cultural project of the post-war USA and found expression in the institutional machineries of the Bretton Wood system, in brief, the sphere of 'the West' (which, of course, embraced a broad spread of peoples around the world). However, behind the rhetoric, economic and political change within the global system continued. The post-war hegemony of the USA owed much to the vagaries of war and as the effects of that massive conflict subsided local creative energies reasserted themselves. It can be argued that when the rhetoric and institutions of the cold war finally slipped into terminal irrelevance in 1991 it was clear that a Pacific Asian region was in the process of formation. All these complex global and regional changes can be summarily presented in terms of three symbolic dates: (i) the US retreat from the Bretton Woods system in 1971; (ii) the inauguration of the economic reform programme within the PRC in 1978; and (iii) the advance of the political-economic power of the Japanese within the region following the 1985 Plaza Accords.

The institutional mechanisms of the 1944 Bretton Woods agreement had been established in order to ensure a regulated liberal trading regime which the designers felt would reduce the likelihood of the occurrence of another 1930s-style Great Depression. The institutional mechanisms included the IMF (which would fund short-term government financial imbalances), the World Bank (which would fund long-term development investment) and the GATT (which would regulate trade). The system ran a fixed exchange rate regime and the key currency which underpinned the system was the US dollar because the country's economy was the world's strongest. In the period from 1945 through to 1971 the western economies enjoyed an unprecedented period of prosperity, the 'long boom'. It is clear that the 1971 decision by President Nixon to suspend the convertibility of the dollar as a result of the financial pressures of the Vietnam War represented a sharp break with the economic policy practices and institutional arrangements which had shaped the overall economic trajectory of the West in the post-Second World War period. The decision of the USA undermined the Bretton Woods system of fixed exchange rates and introduced a period of managed or floating exchange rates. The new system was less amenable to inter-governmental control. In addition in 1973 the oil producers of OPEC raised the price of oil very sharply. The overall result was that the early 1970s saw a less regulated financial sphere suddenly having to deal with an unexpected supply of petro-dollars (the new earnings of the oil-producers). The period saw great confusion within the western world's economic affairs. The Western economies slipped into inflationary recession. In Latin America and Africa large debt burdens were assumed as countries continued to search for development within the context of an inhospitable global system. And the impact within the region of Pacific Asia was at first severe. However, the Japanese response was positive and slowly the countries of the region increased the sophistication of their economies and emerged stronger than they had been at the outset.

The decision by Deng Xiao Ping in 1978 to inaugurate a new economic policy within the People's Republic of China also helped to foster economic growth within the Pacific Asian region. The liberalization of the economy within China and the establishment of a series of SEZs occasioned a rapid increase in economic activity. The new economic activity was located around the coastal regions of China and drew on extensive foreign direct investment, from the region, and from the networks of overseas Chinese. The economic growth within China provided a fillip for the region as a whole. It also marked the beginning of wider reforms within China as the rhetoric and institutions of Maoist socialism retreated.

The Plaza Accords of 1985 addressed US anxieties in respect of its trade deficits with Japan by revaluing the yen in the expectation that this would reduce the trade deficits. However, the Japanese economy proved more than able to deal with the shift in its schedule of costs and prices and, with the help of the windfall rise in the value of its yen holdings, moved to relocate low value added production to cheaper locations within the Pacific Asian region. The Japanese economy emerged after a few years stronger than it had been before the revaluation and with the region more integrated economically than before.

In sum, over a relatively brief period in the 1970s and early 1980s the familiar post-Second World War economic landscape within the region changed quite dramatically. At first the full extent of these changes was not widely recognized, but with the end of the cold war and its associated obfuscatory rhetoric the new structural pattern was available for analysis and action.

In Pacific Asia it would seem that the elite-level response to the sudden withdrawal of long, familiar cold war ways of understanding the world, and the slower softening of China's socialism, has been an interest in the idea of a Pacific Asian region, evident in the plethora of acronyms which now abound. There is a structural occasion for the elite-level discourse in the changing patterns of economic power within the global system, and in this sense it is clear that there is some sort of Pacific Asian region in the process of formation. On this structural basis we can look to the idea of Pacific Asia as an ordering theme for the countries of the region. As elite groups respond to these slowly changing structural circumstances by acknowledging the idea of Pacific Asia one might expect the emergent new identities to find both institutional and popular level expression in new patterns of political linkages, new patterns of economic activity and new patterns of popular understanding. In the future it would seem that a broad commonality in political economy, society and culture will be further deepened around the energetic expansion of the present regional core economy of Japan, coupled, perhaps, to a related expansion of the outward looking elements of the Chinese economy.

Japan and the Development of Pacific Asia

The Japanese economy has grown throughout the post-Second World War period, and betwen 1971 and 1985 became the economic core of the region. The key Japanese trading partner is the USA, yet the Japanese economy has extensive linkages with other regional economies. The development of these links has been a deliberate Japanese policy. At the present time the relationship of Japan and Pacific Asia is bound up with trade, investment and aid networks.

The growth of the Japanese economy after 1971

The post-Second World War history of the Japanese economy can be described in terms of a series of phases where each is marked by a particular policy orientation. These policy stances express the fundamental orientation of the policy makers since the Meiji Restoration, which is to ensure that Japan has a first-class economy operating at the highest technological levels. In the years before the Pacific War this policy was pursued with considerable success, however the economy was overwhelmed as a result of military defeats in 1945.

After the war a new policy was put in place. As we noted earlier the advice of SCAP was that the Japanese economy should be reconstructed as a relatively low-wage, low-technology economy operating in a subordinate position within a global economy effectively dominated by the USA. Waswo remarks that: 'The first and arguably most crucial step the Japanese took was to toss aside the model of their economic future bequeathed to them by the Occupation'.[1] The Japanese planners began from the outset to plan with the objective of establishing a first-class economy. In the immediate aftermath of the war the key task was reconstruction, and this was pursued within the context of American authority and expectations. However, the USA came to change its view of the future of Japan as the cold war developed, and after the establishment of the People's Republic of China in 1949 there was a 'reverse course', and the US began to encourage the development of Japan as an industrialized ally in Asia. The outbreak of the Korean War in 1950 gave a strong fillip not only to the new policy but also to the real economy, and by 1955 real GNP per capita had surpassed pre-war levels.[2] However, in the immediate post-war period available technologies and materials from the war years were used. Sheridan comments: 'In 1955 the economy was still in its semi-industrialized stage, with over 40 per cent of the work force still engaged in farming and other primary sector activities, and 65 per cent of its industrial production consisting of textiles and food processing'.[3] The next period saw a series of policies pursued, oriented to the goal of rapid economic growth.

The pattern of development over the post-Second World War period had been successful in raising the economic level of the country, but had not addressed social welfare issues. In the late 1950s there was social unrest. In 1960 Prime Minister Ikeda addressed these concerns by inaugurating the National Income Doubling Plan which aimed to deploy government resources to provide social capital, raise the standard of living of the population and liberalize trade relations to allow the benefits of trade. The government undertook to foster economic growth and MITI moved to plan key sectors in chemicals, heavy industry and other modern technology sectors. The business community reacted negatively but the plan went ahead. The strategy was pursued explicitly until 1965 when a change of government resulted in revisions to policy, which nonetheless continued along familiar lines. Sheridan records that by 1970 'the demand for workers by the heavy industrial and chemical sectors had led to an exodus of younger workers from villages to factories, thus transforming the economy into a fully industrialised one'.[4] Nonetheless, Sheridan argues that government policy failed to address questions of success (such as high levels of employment, growth and accumulating social problems), and genuinely new thinking had to await the shock of the 1973 oil price hike.[5]

In the early 1970s the Japanese government was obliged by popular opinion to introduce controls on industry to combat pollution. This was the first curb to the otherwise wildly successful policy of rapid growth. In 1973 there was a further curb in the form of the oil shock. The impact upon the Japanese economy was severe and growth rates became negative and did not recover until 1978. The impact of the second oil shock in 1979 was less severe. The response of Japanese policy makers to these events was to argue that the economy had to shift into the lower growth posture of a 'decelerated economy'[6] which could be accomplished by refocusing expectations on creating a knowledge-intensive economy having a higher level of social capital. The new strategy was successful and the broad advance of the Japanese economy continued. However, one issue did cause concern. The economy ran with a persistent trade surplus and friction developed with the USA. In 1985 the Plaza Accords revalued the yen in the expectation that this would curb the economy and thus shrink the trade surplus. The trade surplus did decline for a short period however the response of the Japanese government was to further upgrade the domestic economy and to relocate other activities within the Pacific Asian region.

Japan and the emergent regional pattern

Shibusawa et al.[7] discuss the region's economic growth in terms of trade patterns, investment patterns and development aid patterns. In all three areas they note that the statistics record strong growth, there is more trade, investment and aid. It is also the case that these spheres of activity show complex interdependencies. The authors conclude by arguing that the 'picture of the early and mid-1980s is therefore one of growing global – rather than merely regional – economic integration and interdependence'.[8] However, they also note a regionally integrative element to present patterns and remark that 'the regional changes that began to be seen in the late 1980s, often closely associated with FDI flows, suggest that the 1990s will see an even more complex network of economic interactions. Inevitably, such heightened economic interplay will not be without political repercussions – both domestic and external'.[9] One way in which this new period of reordering has manifested itself is in a concern for ordering the interstate relationships of the Pacific Rim countries. There have been a series of new organizations founded. In contemporary discussions of the development of the Pacific region new acronyms abound – APEC, AFTA, EAEC and so on – and these political manoeuvrings are responses to fundamental changes within the global economy.

The global system is sustained and ordered through a number of institutions and patterns of activity, including: firstly, the formal inter-governmental organizations such as the IMF, World Bank and the GATT/WTO which together provide a regulative framework for economic acitivity; secondly, the inter-state system of treaties which underpin the exchanges of states; thirdly, the presence and activities of global economic organizations (MNCs) and practices (the financial markets) which integrate economies at regional and global levels; and fourthly, there are the surprising capacities of new technologies (communications, via many channels, some outside the control of state governments, thus satellite TV, and relatedly human movement on the basis of long-haul airlines) which underpin new patterns of social activity. At the same time the givens of geography, history and culture, coupled to present economic and political imperatives, are pushing the global system towards a set of regional groupings. In brief, there has been both a measure of globalization in production and exchange (although consumption is still skewed towards the developed countries) and a drift towards regionalization.

The Japanese elite has been concerned with its relations with its Asian neighbours since the period of the Meiji Restoration. Japanese government policy has looked to the creation of a stable regional environment within which the Japanese economy could prosper and advance. In the early phase of the Japanese shift to the modern world this concern came to be exercised in colonial terms within the context of the disintegration of the traditional Sino-centric system in East Asia. However, after the debacle of 1945 this strategy could not be used, and in its place over the post-Second World War period the Japanese government has looked to foster economic linkages.

The earliest expression of this new orientation was the provision of war reparations to countries in the Asian region. These took the form of the provision of credits for Japanese manufactures rather than simple money transfers. In this way an economic linkage was established between Japan and a series of Asian countries. These links have been developed over the succeeding years and presently involve trade, investment and development aid. Rix comments that 'Asian development was more a means of achieving Japanese objectives than a goal in its own right'.[10] A concept of 'comprehensive national security' suggests that national security depends upon regional security, and in turn this is helped by economic growth in the area. Yasutomo[11] argues that the Japanese government pursues five interrelated goals with its aid programmes: (i) 'economic well-being'; (ii) 'national prestige'; (iii) 'domestic support'; (iv) 'peace diplomacy'; and (v) 'national security'. It might be noted that the pattern of Japanese direct investment within the region tends to parallel the pattern of aid. There was an early post-Second World War concentration on primary-product production which has been broadened significantly in recent years to include manufacturing plant. Overall Yasutomo argues that what is crucial in the Japanese aid programme is not the absolute sums of money, rather it is 'the manner of giving' – it is creating an integrated industrial-capitalist region.

The NICs – the Inner Periphery

The expansion of the Japanese state into the area of East Asia began in the late nineteenth century and came to involve large holdings in Manchuria, colonies in Korea and Taiwan, and extensive interests in China. In the early period of successful expansion the Japanese government looked to the formation of a Great East Asia Co-prosperity Sphere – a mutually beneficial economic territory, however, in due course war against China precipitated the Pacific War. In the post-Second World War period the exchange of Japan and East Asia has been cast in economic terms.

The territories of South Korea, Taiwan, Hong Kong and Singapore have all advanced economically in association with Japan. In the post Second World War period the colonies of South Korea and Taiwan were taken from Japanese control and prospered under American protection. Halliday[12] characterizes their extensive economic links with Japan in terms of their constituting an 'inner periphery'. Nonetheless the relationships – at both popular and governmental levels – are somewhat fraught as ever present historical memory continues to haunt otherwise successful economic exchanges.[13] In a similar way the sometime colonial trading bases of Hong Kong and Singapore have grown very rapidly. They are usually associated with South Korea and Taiwan as the NICs. The two territories are similar in that their economies have developed from colonial trading ports to centres of manufacturing, finance and trade within the global system, their populations and societies are predominantly ethnic Chinese and their cultures evidence a mixture of materialism and pragmatic deference to authority.

The record of South Korea

At the end of the Korean War the economy of South Korea was in a parlous state. The USA was underwriting the government budget to the extent of approximately fifty per cent until the late 1950s.[14]

The situation began to improve in 1960 when the nationalist dictator Syngman Rhee was overthrown. After a very brief experiment in democracy General Park Chung Hee staged a military coup. Park had been an officer in the Japanese colonial army and was familiar with the industrial and infra-structural development organized by the Japanese.[15] Park was impressed by the record of a series of late industrializing countries, in particular the Meiji state. It was this model which he copied in his authoritarian modernization-from-above.[16]

Park established in effect a military dictatorship and then turned every attention to growing the economy. The period has been called 'command capitalism' and Bello and Rosenfeld comment that the 'Park period saw not only the consolidation of the military as the nation's political elite but also the emergence of a technocratic elite that assumed command of economic policy'.[17] The government encouraged large conglomerates, chaebol, whose activities recalled those of the Japanese zaibatsu. The industrial base began to grow in the areas of food, textiles, clothing, paper and metals, and by the mid-1970s had begun to deal in steel, electronics and chemicals.

The dictatorship of Park attracted opposition within South Korea, and the opposition was roughly handled. In 1979 the head of the Korean CIA assassinated Park and although the new president, Choi Kyu-Hah, began some reforms, he was quickly deposed in a coup staged by General Chun Doo-Hwan. The coup provoked widespread labour and student protest which came to a head in the southern city of Kwangju. The situation in the city developed into general rebellion, and this in turn was put down by the army with great loss of civilian life. Over this period the economy continued to grow and the chaebol remained powerful although their relationship with government became increasingly corrupt. The authoritarian rule of Chun continued until 1987 when he was forced out of power and his ally Roh Tae Woo took over, winning the presidential election in December 1987. At the same time the liberalization encouraged demands for social reforms, and economic advance slowed as the economy matured and began to face problems of success (in the form of higher expectations and wages). In 1992

President Kim Yong Sam was elected and the period of military dictatorship was finally set aside as the Korean government looked to advance its position within the regional economy.

South Korea constitutes, according to Shibusawa et al.,[18] a 'near-perfect example of a developmental state'. The circumstances of independence plus the dominant role of the military have fed into an authoritarian pattern of development. Yet after some thirty years of post-war success the political economy, society and culture advanced to the point of rejecting the authoritarian aspects of the system. A series of distinct groups can be identified within society, and each has its own interests, and these include the world of business, an educated middle class and an energetic working class. In recent years there has been an extensive political liberalization.

At the same time South Korea has attempted to shift the focus of its development away from Japan and the USA in order to embrace a wider spread of Pacific Asian and OECD partners. The relationship with the USA which was forged in the post-Second World War period of aggressive anti-communism has been crucial to South Korea. It has always been viewed with doubt by sections of the population in Korea and in the USA (with a recent episode of 'Korea-bashing' on economic grounds) and it must be expected that it will change in the wake of the end of the cold war. In contrast the relationship with Japan is both historically long established, deeply difficult, yet close in practical terms.

The record of Taiwan

In the years following the flight of the defeated nationalist Chinese to the island the local economy was heavily dependent upon the USA. The government pursued an ISI strategy which had acknowledged the inherited important role of agriculture. However, by the early 1960s 'planners had to prepare for the end of American aid . . . The government gave less support to the farmers and encouraged aggressive exporters'.[19] The pattern of industrial development revolved around small firms. Dobbs-Higginson records that in the 1970s 'the government linked these constellations of small industries together with a modern infrastructure of roads, telecommunications, and ports'.[20] At the same time the state established capital-intensive industries. And in the early 1980s the pattern of exports to the USA resulted in very rapid local economic growth.

Thereafter the late 1980s saw a relative fall in the price of oil and the revaluation of the yen offered an opportunity for new niche markets to be developed as the overall pattern of industrial production and exporting within the region reconfigured. As the economy matures the rate of growth is expected to fall somewhat, however the economy is now operating in higher value-added spheres and is exporting capital throughout the region. A developing sphere of Taiwanese investment is Fujian Province across the Formosa Strait in China.

One particular issue which bears on Taiwan's future is its relationship with Beijing. It is clear that whilst the Taiwanese polity remained dominated by the authoritarian rule of the Kuomintang, until the death of Chiang Kai-shek in 1975, the aspiration of both Beijing and Taipei to rule over all of the Chinese could be accommodated in a ritualized status quo. However, Chiang was succeeded by his son Chiang Ching-kuo who gradually introduced a measure of democracy. In 1986 Yao Chia-wen formed the Democratic Progressive Party. In 1988 Lee Teng-Hui assumed power on the death of Chiang Ching-kuo and after his re-election in 1990 proceeded to inaugurate a significant democratization process. The prospects of an independent liberal-democratic Taiwan alarms Beijing and the issue of the relationship of the two countries remains to be settled.

In the late 1980s a process of reform-from-above was begun in the political sphere and in recent years attempts have been made to redirect the linkages of the economy with the global system. In this case it is a matter of winding back dependence on the USA and Japan in order to look to the region and the countries of the OECD. However, in the case of Taiwan a major economic linkage is developing with mainland China. In terms of patterns of identity it would seem that as Pacific Asia changes it is the link to China which will dominate Taiwanese thinking for the foreseeable future.

Hong Kong and Singapore

Hong Kong and Singapore are similar in that their economies have developed from colonial trading ports to centres of manufacturing, finance and trade within the global system, their populations and societies are predominantly ethnic Chinese and their cultures evidence a mixture of materialism and pragmatic deference to authority. The two territories have benefited over recent years by both the general growth within the region and the decision of the Beijing authorities to liberalize their economy.

Hong Kong reverted to the control of Beijing in July 1997 and has the status of a Special Administrative Region (SAR). The government of China is committed to maintaining Hong Kong's distinctive pattern of life for fifty years. However, the matter of the future of Hong Kong will be resolved not merely by the high politics of declarations and decisions made in Beijing but also by the practical economics of the relationships of Hong Kong, Guandong Province and the central authorities in Beijing. The headlong pursuit of economic growth which has characterized mainland China since 1978 has strengthened the power of regions against the centre, and the southern area of China around Hong Kong is now one of the richest and fastest growing regions within the country, and it is within this context that the future development trajectory of Hong Kong will be determined.[21]

The economic development of Singapore over the 1970s and early 1980s was very successful. The ruling PAP pursued its goal of industrialization with single-minded dedication and the colonial entrepôt economy which they inherited has slowly been broadened to embrace a significant manufacturing and finanacial role within the region and global system. The essence of the development strategy of the Singaporean government has been to provide an orderly, efficient environment within which regional and global business enterprises can operate.[22]

The debate about the tigers

The debate about the post-war patterns of complex change in the tigers has been very vigorous and seems to have begun amongst development theorists and thereafter to have broadened out to include a spread of social scientists and commentators which culminates in present discussions of the rise of Pacific Asia. In this context, contemporary political-economic arrangements have been widely discussed under the heading of East Asian NIC development. Then contemporary social-institutional arrangements have been widely discussed under the heading of East Asian 'confucianism' – hierarchy, deference and obedience are taken to characterize stable-ordered societies. And finally, contemporary cultural and political-cultural arrangements have been widely discussed under the headings of community and authoritarianism, and in recent debate a notion of 'Asian values' has been advanced.

A significant contribution to the early debate was made by Hamilton[23] who argued that the NICs are to be noted for the state-led establishment of an economic space within the growing post-war global economy. The arguments were echoed by Wade (1990).[24] In a similar fashion significant contributions to the debates was made by Johnson who argued in respect of Japan for the state-directive role of MITI.[25] And Dore,[26] again in respect of Japan, presented a spread of sociological work which argued that the Japanese economy worked in a different way to those of the free market West. A significant contribution to the later debates in respect of learning the available lessons was made by Vogel[27] who argued that the model of state-lead communitarian development evidenced by post-war Japan offers lessons to all developed countries as all can learn from Japan.

It should also be noted that cutting against these materials there has been a significant line of dissent which insists that neither the NICs nor Japan hold any particularly novel lessons because the core of their efforts have been in line with the logic of the free marketplace, that is, a mix of market-friendly policy plus a lot of catching-up. A statement cast in these terms focused on Pacific Asia was made by the World Bank.[28] The Bank offered the argument that the success of the East Asian newly industrialized economies might be due in part to state-leadership, but this was unclear, and in any case unreplicable elsewhere. The Bank suggested that the key lesson of NIC record is that development policies should get the economic fundamentals correct by conforming to market principles.

What is true, is that the success of the countries of the region which began in the 1950s and 1960s has subsequently brought them to the point where the nature of the integration of the Pacific Asian region within the global context is discussed by scholars, political agents and policy analysts.

Overall, at the present time in respect of the East Asian view of the role of Japan within the growing Pacific Asian region we can point to a mixture of historical memory, post-Second World War economic success and a regional situation which is slowly changing in the post-cold war period with the relative eclipse of the USA and the rise of China. As the USA slowly reconfigures its relationship with the countries of the region in the wake of the ending of the cold war, the countries of the inner periphery face the task of maintaining a continuing relationship with Japan where the burgeoning economy and political instability of China constitute a further and developing relevant context.

Southeast Asia – the Outer Periphery

The development of the countries of Southeast Asia in the period since the early 1970s has taken place increasingly within the broad ambit of the economic sphere of Japan. The relationship of Japan with the other Pacific Asian countries is often characterized with reference to the metaphor of 'flying geese' where Japan is the leader with the other countries following stepped down behind. The ideal relationship implied by this metaphor is a regionally complementary division of labour centred on Japan. Cronin[29] points out that the linkages which Japan has with the countries of the region vary significantly and with developing areas such as Southeast Asia (and China) the relationship is one of 'complementary cooperation' skewed in Japan's favour. Overall, Japanese direct investment and development aid are forces for economic growth and regional integration, and as Dobson[30] points out, focusing on the ASEAN case, in recent years host governments have positively welcomed such inward investment.

It can be argued that the recent wave of foreign investment in the ASEAN region was initiated by changes in the circumstances of the Japanese economy.[31] In the 1950s through to the 1970s Japanese foreign direct investment expanded slowly and in the pre-1985 period the focus was on raw materials, cheap labour and market access. There was a distinctive pattern of investment with the East Asian NICs favoured, and thereafter some attention to Singapore, with the rest of ASEAN coming behind. However, after the 1985 Plaza Accords investment in ASEAN increased sharply and focused on export oriented industrialization. Phongpaichit[32] argues that the underlying reason, notwithstanding the issues of the appreciation of the yen and the Japanese government's desire to be seen to be responding to growing US concerns about trade imbalances, was lodged in Japan's shift from an economy centred on labour-intensive heavy industry to one focused on high technology industrial development. This structural change pushed direct investment to offshore production platforms as Japanese capital looked to escape the impact of the high yen, and US restrictions, via a drive to increase markets and production capacity. In the terms of Hamilton,[33] the Japanese economic space expanded within Pacific Asia. Phongpaichit records that this expansion has had a large impact on ASEAN – and she adds that the recipient states have been active participants.

In Malaysia the government instituted an explicit 'look east' policy in the early 1980s which took Japan as the model for Malaysian development.[34] Khoo[35] argues that this was the policy of a group of modernizing technocrats surrounding the Prime Minister Dr Mahathir and that the drive for development has overriden other more traditional groups within Malaysian society. It has been a policy conducive not merely to economic growth but also extensive social conflict which found partial expression in politically charged debates about the nature of 'Malayness'.[36]

In the resource-rich areas of Thailand and Indonesia it has been argued that there are increasing signs that the East Asian NIC model of export-oriented development is being repeated. MacIntyre claims that there have been 'remarkable economic developments'.[37] MacIntyre also comments that there is 'little doubt that their economies have been profoundly influenced by Japan and the four NICs'.[38] It is clear that both countries have benefited from being located in a rapidly growing region. In the future it is likely that the key problems will not be economic, rather they will be political and social as the broader impacts of the recent phase of outward-directed growth work themselves through the societies of Thailand and Indonesia.

In the Philippines, by contrast, the period has seen little advance. On securing independence the country adopted an import substituting industrialization programme and this met with considerable success in the years to the middle 1960s.[39] The country exported sugar to the USA and received a flow of FDI coupled to high US expenditures on their local military bases. However the economy did not effect a shift from ISI to EOI and US interest fell away with the end of the Vietnam War. At the same time the crony capitalism of Marcos deterred other potential investors. The political insecurity of the country has continued, as has the oligarchic crony capitalist system. An obvious source of foreign direct investment and aid is Japan but the Philippines receives low levels of assistance.

In considering the relationship of the countries of the Southeast Asia region to broader Pacific Asian patterns of development, Phongpaichit[40] suggests that we can distinguish between domestic capital, state capital and foreign capital and thereafter we can plot the shifting patterns of interest and how these are expressed in response to incoming direct investment. In ASEAN, broadly, there was an early resistance to foreign direct investment as state and domestic capital prospered. Then in the depression of the early 1980s state capital ran into trouble and began to run up significant debt. At this point foreign direct investment became attractive to ASEAN governments and with the incoming investment the phase of EOI took off. Phongpaichit[41] notes that it is clear that each country has had a particular experience of foreign direct investment-assisted EOI, but in each case insists the acceptance of foreign direct investment must be seen as an expression not of passive acceptance but of agency, as Southeast Asian state-regimes looked to identify routes to the future.

Australia and New Zealand Join Asia

In the 1980s the governments of both Australia and New Zealand had explicit policies which pointed to the future of these countries within the developing Pacific Asian region. In the case of New Zealand the accession of the UK to the EEC caused great damage to the local economy and a process of reorientation began. In the 1980s a series of New Right governments continued the marketization and regionalization of the New Zealand political economy and with it a shift to an Asia-sensitive multiculturalism with regard to identity. Relatedly, in the case of Australia we find a long-running concern with the issue of identity, and indeed many of the terms of debate pre-date the rise of Pacific Asia.[42]

In New Zealand in the long post-Second World War period there was considerable prosperity on the basis of an agricultural exporting trade which was directed in particular towards the UK. The country was conservative minded and ran an elaborate welfare state. However, the accession of the UK to the Common Market in 1973 brought the UK within the ambit of the European Common Agricultural Policy which looked to a controlled agriculture within Europe. The New Zealand economy began to look to Asia as a series of new markets and a little while later the local politicians bought the New Right liberal ideology and proceeded to liberalize the New Zealand economy and caused extensive dislocation. However, the country now trades more extensively with Asia and in recent years has received significant flows of immigration which, along with the belated acknowledgement of the indigenous Maori people, has led the territory to think in terms less of descent from Britain and more in terms of present situationally determined identities and futures.

Walter[43] recalls the invention of a 'British Australia' around the turn of the twentieth century where before there had been only colonies looking to the UK. These ideas of Australia were informed by notions of 'British stock' making up an immigrant community who had, given their pattern of economic life, a particular affinity with 'the bush'. The invention of this tradition can be traced to particular groups of intellectuals and journalists.[44] The native people of the continent, the aboriginals, were simply written out of the story. However, in the post-Second World War period the story itself is revised and a notion of the 'Australian way of life' emerges in the context of a general Western anti-communism, and this view of Australia is implicitly anti-immigrant (in line with ideas of 'White Australia'). The post-war years were a time of great prosperity for Australia which only slowly began to experience problems in the 1970s. Overall, this general record forms the background to the deliberate 1980s turn towards Asia which has seen an explicit 'multiculturalism' in the domestic sphere linked to a concern to locate Australia in its wider geographical context of Asia. Many of the arguments which have been adduced to support this reorientation point to the country's economic linkages to Pacific Asia, yet it has been argued that the economic policies of the 1980s were deeply flawed and that the economic linkages to Asia have been oversold.[45]

The Reform Process in China and Indo-China

The cold war division of Pacific Asia into two blocs began to dissolve in the 1970s and 1980s. A series of factors contributed: (i) the defeat of the Americans in Vietnam and their partial withdrawal from advanced positions in the area; (ii) the rapid advance of the regional economy; (iii) the reforms in China; and then (iv) the collapse of the USSR. In recent years, within the socialist bloc countries of Pacific Asia there has been a significant shift towards decentralized market-based economic systems.

Deng Xiao Ping's reforms

After the death of Zhou En-Lai in 1976 the leftists within the CCP moved to criticize his legacy. There were street demonstrations after which there were purges of rightists, including Deng Xiao Ping. However, the leftist leadership of the CCP was opposed by many intellectuals, bureaucrats and technocrats who took the view that the Cultural Revolution – which had given power under Mao's name to the leftist leadership – had been an unmitigated disaster. The division within the intelligentsia and party was resolved shortly after the 1976 death of Mao, whose presence had protected the leftists, and a new leadership committed to reform was installed. The key figure was Deng Xiao Ping who purged the gang of four and the lower reaches of the communist party and state apparatus. The radical egalitarianism of the Cultural Revolution was repudiated and a modernization programme was begun. Shibusawa et al.[46] report that the 1978 reforms initiated by Deng Xiao Ping looked to secure the 'four modernizations' (agriculture, industry, science and defence) in order to achieve by the turn of the century a modest level of development in China. The story thereafter is one of burgeoning success coupled to internal social and political stress.

In agriculture there was a shift to the 'responsibility system' whereby control over production was shifted away from the centre to more local levels and participants were given incentives in the form of retained profit. The idea was translated into practice in a variety of ways with families, or family groups, or brigades or communes taking the responsibility and ordering their affairs. At the same time the area of private plots was increased. Overall there was a rapid move to a decentralized system which combined broad planning at national and regional level and extensive scope for local level or private initiative on land with long leases. Moise comments: 'By 1984 . . . the government announced that almost all land was to be allocated to the peasants on fifteen-year contracts . . . Collective agriculture was virtually dead'.[47]

In industry the CCP began to relax the central planning in the urban industrial sphere. A measure of freedom of labour was allowed in place of assignment. Some scope for the private employment of workers was allowed. The established socialized enterprises were allowed to contract work in the developing private sphere. On a national scale the CCP established four Special Economic Zones where foreign capitalists were allowed to establish factories, employ local people, export the finished goods and remit profits. Three of these SEZs were in Guandong Province adjoining Hong Kong and the fourth was in Fujian adjacent to Taiwan. The SEZs have been very successful and have made a very significant contribution to the overall reorientation of the Chinese economy.

In education and science the egalitarian stress on mass low-level participation at the expense of more advanced levels was reversed. The pursuit of educational excellence was affirmed and was quickly perceived by the population as a possible route to personal advance. At the same time the Maoist policy of sending youth to the countryside in order to appreciate manual labour was scaled back and eventually abolished. Moise[48] reports that levels of attainment rose rapidly but there were some early problems with unemployed youth and crime. At the most advanced levels Chinese students were sent abroad to study in Western universities in order to raise the scientific base level of the country.

In defence and foreign affairs a new concern was given to upgrading the armed forces. In particular new technology was sought and new patterns of arms procurement were initiated which looked to a modern airforce and deep water navy.

It is clear that the reform process inaugurated by Deng Xiao Ping has led to significant economic advance. There are problems: (i) a drift in population from rural hinterlands to coastal urban areas; (ii) rising inequality between areas and within prosperous regions; (iii) corruption; (iv) regional imbalances as local-level economic development is pursued without adequate central control. The features which commentators now routinely address are two: firstly, the pronounced regional nature of the economic changes with coastal regions experiencing rapid growth, and apparently significantly enhanced regional powers at the expense of Beijing, whilst the inner agricultural regions are rather left behind; and secondly, the increasingly visible and vital linkages of the burgeoning coastal regions of China with the Pacific Asian region in general.

In China these problems have been recognized. The nature of economic growth has occasioned corruption, nepotism and inequality. Moise[49] locates the germ of the Tiananmen Square debacle in the dissatisfaction of university students and ordinary Chinese with the side-effects of the period of rapid market-oriented economic growth. The reaction to the pressure for democratization and reform was repression. Moise characterizes the present situation in pessimistic terms: 'In the early 1990s, a dictatorial party/government apparatus was not supported by any ideology commanding widespread belief, was allowing a great deal of autonomy for local authorities, and a great deal of contact between Chinese and foreigners from countries having democratic systems. This situation seemed inherently unstable'.[50]

Overall, the reforms in the rural areas were initially successful and the farmers launched a variety of industrial activities. Shibusawa et al.[51] note that the impact of these reforms on the images of China held in the region were positive, with China perceived as potentially another 'developmental state'. However, the reform process in the industrial sector turned out to be much more problematical. These industries were long established and closely integrated in the party/state apparatus. The extent of success has been uneven with many state enterprises continuing to operate in a market-inefficient fashion. In this sector reform has been difficult, and indeed the failure of attempts to secure change coupled to the avoidance of political reform to the party/state machinery can be taken to have led to the political tensions which culminated in the Tiananmen Square episode. In the future, commentators anticipate that the outward directed development of China will continue, indeed it is said to be running somewhat out of control, and that social and political change are almost inevitable. A key issue for the future will be the way in which China orders its relationships with the Pacific region in general, and that region's core Japanese economy in particular.

Indo-China

In Indo-China a similar story can be sketched out. The key aspect was the resolution of the Cambodian problem and relatedly the removal of the American veto on multilateral development agency assistance to Vietnam. The region is now reorienting itself to the Pacific Asia region and the global capitalist system.

The struggle of the Vietnamese to establish their own independent nation state began with war against the returning French colonialists and continued against the American-backed South Vietnamese regime. The American involvement was inspired by their own anti-communist cold war rhetoric, however as their military involvement slowly escalated they found that they could not defeat the military and political strategies of guerilla warfare orchestrated by General Giap. In the late 1960s the war in Vietnam came to generate extensive domestic unrest within the USA and the government was obliged to begin to look for a way out of the quagmire. The US government began talks with representatives of North Vietnam, and the Paris Agreements of January 1973 allowed the US to withdraw its forces in March 1973 leaving its South Vietnamese clients to their own devices.[52]

The final North Vietnamese offensive began in March 1975. The southern forces collapsed and the fighting was over by May with the Americans scrambling to leave along with their allies amongst the South Vietnamese elites. In Vietnam the legacy of war left the ruling party the task of reuniting a divided and damaged country. In the first decade of unified government the stress was on state control and direction, and although the country received aid from the USSR it was not very successful. In addition the 1978 invasion of Cambodia placed further burdens upon the economy. In 1986 a reform programme oriented to renovation, or 'doi moi', was launched.[53] The programme looked to decentralization in the polity and economy. It met with some success. However, the crucial turning point was the agreement to end the conflict in Cambodia, and the decision of the Americans to discontinue their policy of 'punishing Vietnam', which led to an inflow of foreign direct investment and a significant upturn in the economy. In 1995 Vietnam became a member of ASEAN.

In Cambodia the confusions of the end of the American war in Vietnam led to the seizure of power by a radical peasant-based Marxist movement, the Khmer Rouge, which pursued an autarchic socialist development strategy that resulted in the deaths of large numbers of the population. In 1978 Vietnam invaded Cambodia and drove out the Pol Pot regime and installed a new government. However, this was never accepted by the regional powers and an unholy alliance of Southeast Asian nations, the Chinese and the Americans set themselves against the Vietnamese-backed government, and for many years the murderous Pol Pot regime was recognized as the legitimate government by the United Nations. The Vietnamese eventually decided to withdraw in 1989 leaving their ally in power. After further negotiations a strategy to secure a settlement was identified, and a new coalition government was elected in a 1993 UN-sponsored election. A limited measure of peace and stability has been restored and development aid and investment is beginning to flow into the country, as it is into the Indo-China region, now perhaps finally at peace after decades of war.[54]

Pacific Asia: Integrated Region and Coherent Model?

On the back of the changes noted here there has been considerable discussion concerning the rise of a coherent regional bloc in Pacific Asia. It is possible to identify broad economic, social, cultural and political similarities amongst the various countries of Pacific Asia. It is also possible to point to recent economic growth – the business of trade, foreign direct investment and development aid – and suggest that available similarities are proving to be the basis for practical exchanges which in due course might be expected to find political expression.

Relatedly there is debate around the arguments to the effect that the pattern of change in the Pacific Asian region is such that we can talk about a

Pacific Asian model of development, where this is taken to be a particular variety of industrial-capitalism distinct from the American or European models. It is all very contentious. However, we can offer a speculative illustration of the political culture of Pacific-Asianness: (i) the economy is state-directed and policy is oriented to the pragmatic pursuit of growth; (ii) state-direction is top-down style and pervasive in its reach; (iii) society is familial and thereafter oriented to the community; (iv) order is secured by pervasive social control machineries and a related hegemonic common culture; (v) political debate and power is typically reserved to an elite sphere; and (vi) culture comprises a mix of officially sanctioned tradition which stresses consensus and eschews open conflict, and market sanctioned consumption.

Overall, it seems clear both that some sort of distinctive 'developmental capitalism' is in process of formation in Pacific Asia, and that its future progress will not be dictated by the USA.[55] However, two points need to be kept in mind: (i) the region is presently dependent on the USA as a market for the consumption of its exports; and (ii) the region is very large and very diverse (in terms of politics, economics, society and culture) and an integrated Pacific Asia could only be taken to exist as a prospective utopian project.[56]

The Region and Questions of Leadership

One theme which runs through the discussions of the role of Japan in Pacific Asia is the matter of leadership. Commentators ask whether Japan wishes to exercise leadership and if so whether Japan is able to exercise leadership. All agree that this implies extensive economic, social and political reforms within Japan and an extensive reworking of Japan's relationships with Pacific Asia. A review of these debates points to a measure of continuity in Japan's relationships with Pacific Asia as the matter of regional coherence, and Japanese leadership has exercised ruling elites in Japan since the Meiji restoration. At the present time, given the historical legacies of the Pacific War it is likely that Japan will remain the core economy but will not move with any speed to assume a leadership role in the region. It is likely that there will be more of a continuing deepening of existing relationships. It is certainly true that the internal reforms needed to underpin a leadership role are extensive – and not obviously in prospect.

A general diagnosis of the problems of Japanese politics is given by Buckley[57] who notes that there are problems with: (i) political and business corruption; (ii) a pork-barrel style of local politics; (iii) a secretive and powerful bureaucracy; and (iv) a general inability of the political system to articulate effectively and thereafter deal with a spread of domestic and international policy problems. In a similar way van Wolferen[58] argues that the political system centred on the bureaucracy is 'results focused' by which he means that it attends not to matters of principle and policy but to the pragmatic resolution of immediate problems. Within a dominating overall commitment to economic expansion, problems are tackled on an ad hoc basis. It means both that the system is hugely successful within its own terms and that it is unable to formulate responses to problems that fall outside its routine frame of expectations. In stronger terms, van Wolferen argues that, strictly speaking, the system is so flexible and pragmatic that it amounts to an absence of a formal state, and instead there are shifting patterns of alliances between the various important players in the bureaucracy, business and politics, and in this it recalls the system established at the time of the Meiji restoration. It is a system running mostly out of the control of its beneficiaries/victims.

The general nature of the criticism of the Japanese economy is that the system is in some way a victim of its own success and that reform is urgently needed to redirect the energies of the system away from production, and the expansion of production, towards consumption, in particular both private and public consumption for the benefit of the ordinary people of Japan. Eccleston[59] notes that the state is routinely interventionist and works in a corporatist fashion. It takes no large equity shares because it does not have to in order to secure control. The state invests in industry and infrastructure. The state holds down social consumption (of schools, hospitals, transfer payments and the like). The state encourages savings and uses them for economic development. The state oversees business activity with MITI offering 'administrative guidance', and in any case the line between administration and business is blurred (thus civil servants retire and shift into the private sector). In all, Japan is a corporatist developmental state.

All this generates a series of issues that are hotly debated and involve: (i) the nature of the role of the state (where debate revolves around the costs/benefits of such interventions;[60] (ii) the nature of the economic structure (where debates revolve around the costs/benefits of the dual structure with a large-firm sector and a small-firm sector); (iii) the nature of employment patterns (where debate revolves around costs/benefits of life-time employment and small-sector employment); (iv) the nature of the costs/benefits accruing to the Japanese consumer of the present system, for example, the controlled retail sector; and (v) the costs/benefits of the production focus of the system to Japan's trading partners.

The schedule of reforms canvassed in respect of polity and economy is large, and their interactions various, and the proposals all have widespread implications for the nature of Japanese society. The problems which are routinely cited include: (i) poor housing; (ii) poor public facilities; (iii) long hours of work (and commuting); (iv) inequality between the sexes; (v) excessive examination-centred schooling; (vi) lack of leisure time for families; (vii) habits of conformity are overstressed; and (viii) the problems of an aged population. In all, the Japanese people are presented as the unwitting victims of the successful corporatist system which they have created and from which they restrictedly benefit.

If we consider the Western commentators, excluding the over-anxious nationalists, then theorists of the right propose the liberalization of the Japanese economy in the expectation that consumer benefits will follow, whilst commentators of the centre-left propose a more consumer-friendly democratic system. In this way one can see a broad similarity in the approaches of the two groups as both are concerned to enhance the position of the Japanese consumer at the expense of current dominant producer interests. Yet if we consider the debate amongst Japanese, Sheridan notes 'there still has been surprisingly little popular public debate in Japan about the future directions of economic development and national purpose'.[61]

After an exhaustive review of the development experience of Japan, Sheridan presents her conclusions. Sheridan argues that it is the case that the Japanese people have become rich and yet there are clear problems: (i) long working hours and long commuting times; (ii) very expensive housing costs; and (iii) lack of adequate social capital (or infrastructure). Sheridan[62] notes that over the 1960s and 1970s there was some improvement both in quality of life (for example with environmental standards) and a reducing inequality in wealth, but the 1985 revaluation of the yen triggered speculation on the back of asset inflation and this has done great damage (especially via land prices which may be expected to feed through into higher housing costs). However, Sheridan does see reasons for hope in the signs that the Japanese people are beginning to shift from a politics of fear to a politics of utopias (that is, away from reactive positions towards prospective stances). And relatedly, the system does allow collective effort in respect of communal goals. Sheridan[63] argues that the system could be shifted away from its pre-occupation with economic expansion towards the provision of the social capital necessary to improve people's lives. It is clear that the Japanese state is an activist state, and it is effective. If the myths of the marketeers are set aside (plus some of the prejudices against social spending of the Japanese government) then a future oriented to quality of life could be envisaged. Sheridan[64] then goes on to unpack this overall proposal in terms of a series of policies: (i) to enhance the position of women (ii) to improve local and neighbourhood life; (iii) to reduce inequalities; (iv) and to reform the land market. All of these goals could be pursued with a 'Japanese strategy' which would draw on the country's established strengths of cooperative collective hard work.

In regard to any leadership role the balance of the argument points to a rational expectation of continued modest advance in respect of the leadership role of the region's core economy. In other words, there will be more continuity than change.[65]

Conclusion

In the 1970s and early 1980s the region underwent significant reconfiguration. The significance of the cold war declined. The hegemony of the USA weakened. The Japanese economy attained a new pre-eminence. A trio of key dates can be mentioned: firstly, the 1971 decision of the USA to float the dollar which effectively brought the pattern of regulation of the global economy established at Bretton Woods in 1944 to an end; secondly, the 1978 decision of the government of the PRC to reorder their economic policy to allow a greater role for the marketplace; and then finally the 1985 Plaza Accord which saw the yen sharply revalued against the dollar.

At this time the region can be seen to fall into five increasingly integrated spheres: Japan; the inner sphere of Northeast Asia; the outer sphere of Southeast Asia; the reforming socialist bloc; and Australasia. The Japanese economy is now the region's core economy. It is the world's second most powerful economy and has developed extensive linkages throughout the region. In the inner periphery, the territory of the NICs, there is burgeoning growth. In the outer periphery, the countries of ASEAN, there is extensive growth as investment flows into the area. In the reforming socialist bloc there is rapid growth. And in Australasia there is an uneven concern to be a part of Pacific Asia. The linkages of the region to the global system are very extensive and becoming more extensive. The linkages between the various parts of the region are also becoming extensive and deepening. The region has a core economy, extensive economic linkages, new political/trade mechanisms and a measure of cultural coherence. An integrated regional grouping can be taken to be in the process of formation.

Notes

1   A. Waswo 1996: *Modern Japanese Society 1968–1994*, Oxford University Press, p. 107.
2   K. Sheridan 1994: *Governing the Japanese Economy*, Cambridge: Polity, p. 136.
3   Ibid., p. 139.
4   Ibid.
5   Ibid pp. 153–7.
6   Ibid., p. 163.
7   M. Shibusawa et al. 1992: *Pacific Asia in the 1990s*, London: Routledge.
8   Ibid., p. 34.
9   Ibid.
10   A. Rix 1993: *Japan's Foreign Aid*, London: Routledge, p. 23.
11   D. Yasutomo 1986: *The Manner of Giving*, Lexington: Heath, pp. 112–14.
12   J. Halliday 1980: Capitalism and Socialism in East Asia in *New Left Review* 124.
13   B. Koppel and R. Orr, eds, 1993: *Japan's Foreign Aid*, Boulder, CO: Westview.
14   B. Cummings 1997: *Korea's Place in the Sun: A Modern History*.
15   Ibid.
16   M. S. Dobbs-Higginson 1995: *Pacific Asia: Its Role in the New World Disorder*, London: Mandarin, p. 273.
17   W. Bello and S. Rosenfeld 1990: *Dragons in Distress: Asia's Miracle Economies in Crisis*, Harmondsworth: Penguin, p. 55.
18   Shibusawa 1992, p. 69.
19   Dobbs-Higginson 1995, p. 155.

20 Ibid.
21 G. Segal 1993: *The Fate of Hong Kong*, London: Simon and Shuster; M. Yahuda 1995: *Hong Kong: China's Challenge*, London: Routledge.
22 P. W. Preston 1994: *Discourses of Development*, Aldershot: Dartmouth.
23 C. Hamilton 1983: Capitalist Industrialization in East Asia's Four Little Tigers in *Journal of Contemporary Asia* 13.
24 R. Wade 1990: *Governing the Market*, Princeton, NJ: Princeton University Press.
25 C. Johnson 1982: *MITI and the Japanese Miracle*, Stanford University Press; C. Johnson 1995: *Japan: Who Governs?*, New York: Norton.
26 R. Dore 1986: *Flexible Rigidities*, Stanford University Press.
27 E. Vogel 1979: *Japan as Number One*, Cambridge, MA: Harvard University Press.
28 World Bank 1993: *The East Asian Miracle*, Oxford University Press.
29 R. P. Cronin 1992: *Japan, the United States and the Prospects for the Asia-Pacific Century*, Singapore: Institute of Southeast Asian Studies, pp. 33–8.
30 W. Dobson 1993: *Japan in East Asia*, Singapore: Institute of Southeast Asian Studies.
31 P. Phongpaichit 1990: *The New Wave of Japanese Investment in ASEAN*, Singapore: Institute of Southeast Asian Studies.
32 Ibid.
33 Hamilton 1983.
34 J. Kahn and L. K. Loh eds 1992: *Fragmented Vision: Culture and Politics in Contemporary Malaysia*, Sydney: Allen and Unwin.
35 K. J. Khoo 1992: The Grand Vision: Mahathir and Modernization in Kahn and Loh 1992.
36 A. B. Shamsul 1996: Nations of Intent in S. Tonneson and H. Antlov eds *Asian Forms of the Nation*, London: Curzon.
37 A. MacIntyre 1993: Indonesia, Thailand and the Northeast Asian Connection in R. Higgot, R. Leaver and J. Ravenhill, eds: *Pacific Economic Relations in the 1990s*, St Leonards: Allen and Unwin, p. 250.
38 Ibid., p. 261.
39 J. Wong 1979: *ASEAN Economies in Perspective*, London: Macmillan.
40 Phongpaichit 1990.
41 Ibid., pp. 69–81, 94–5.
42 G. Whitlock and D. Carter eds 1992: *Images of Australia*, Queensland: University of Queensland Press; H. Reynolds 1982: *The Other Side of the Frontier*, Ringwood: Penguin.
43 J. Walter 1992: Defining Australia in Whitlock and Carter.
44 R. White 1992: Inventing Australia in Whitlock and Carter.
45 M. Byrnes 1994: *Australia and the Asia Game*, St Leonards: Allen and Unwin.
46 Shibusawa 1992.
47 E. Moise 1994: *Modern China*, London: Longman, p. 208.
48 Ibid., p. 196.
49 Ibid., p. 216.
50 Ibid., p. 237.
51 Shibusawa 1992, p. 108.
52 M. Maclear 1982: *Vietnam: Ten Thousand Day War*, London: Thames/Methuen; P. Macdonald 1994: *Giap: The Victor in Vietnam*, London: Warner.

53 W. J. Duiker 1995: *Vietnam: Revolution in Transition*, Boulder, CO: Westview; G. Kolko 1997 *Vietnam: Anatomy of a Peace*, London: Routledge.
54 F. Godement 1997: *The New Asian Renaissance*, London: Routledge.
55 J. Devan ed. 1994: *Southeast Asia: Challenges of the 21st Century*, Singapore: Institute of Southeast Asian Studies; C. Johnson 1993 History Restarted: Japanese-American Relations at the End of the Century in Higgot et al. eds.
56 G. Segal 1991: *Rethinking the Pacific*, Oxford: Clarendon.
57 R. Buckley 1990: *Japan Today*, Cambridge: Cambridge University Press.
58 K. van Wolferen 1989: *The Enigma of Japanese Power*, London: Macmillan
59 B. Eccleston 1989: *State and Society in Post War Japan*, Cambridge: Polity.
60 World Bank 1993; R. Wade 1996: Japan, the World Bank, and the Art of Paradigm Maintenance: The East Asian Miracle in Political Perspective in *New Left Review* 217.
61 K. Sheridan 1993, p. 3.
62 Ibid., pp. 220–2.
63 Ibid., pp. 222–6.
64 Ibid., pp. 228–50.
65 P. W. Preston 1995: Domestic Inhibitions to a Leadership Role for Japan in Pacific Asia in *Contemporary Southeast Asia* 16(4).

Part III

Changing Relationships in Contemporary Pacific Asia

7

The Region and the Global System

Analysing shifting patterns of relationships is an aspect of the general analysis of complex change. In the case of the Pacific Asia region we have two related themes: first, the changing patterns of relationships amongst the territories within the region; and second the changing relations between the region and the wider global system.

In the opening chapter of this text we reviewed the concerns of the classical tradition of European social theorizing with the elucidation of the dynamics of complex change in the shift to the modern world. An element of that tale was the notion of industrial-capitalism as an expansive system which continually deepened its reach within established territory and which continually extended its reach into new territory. The substantive history of industrial-capitalism is one of a global expansion which has seen non-capitalist forms-of-life absorbed and remade so as to fit the demands of the system. In the case of Pacific Asia we can trace the process of the ongoing absorption and remaking of the region in terms of four great phases: pre-contact, empire, nation-building and Pacific Asia. The issue for today is the manner of the internal and external articulation of the region.

The New Situation I: Processes of Recognition

There has been considerable recent debate in respect of the situation of the region within the global system. The debate revolves around the implications, if any, of the rapid economic growth of the last decade, and relatedly the possible role of Japan in the future. This debate has been sharpened in the wake of the ending of the cold war.

In this context the significance of the cold war was multiple: (i) it provided an overarching set of themes which ordered inter-state exchanges both within and between the blocs; (ii) it provided the overarching rationale for a split within the Pacific Asian sphere as between the 'free world' and the 'socialist world'; (iii) it provided an overarching framework for Japanese and American relationships, such that the Japanese adherence to the tenets of the Western bloc overrode any problems with economic exchanges; and (iv) it provided the occasion for US strategic activity which offered opportunities for economic growth to the countries of the region, in particular in East Asia. At the present time, with the end of the cold war, it is clear that ways of reading the political economy of the region which were established in the wake of the Pacific War are called into question. The nature of the relationships between the various countries of Pacific Asia and their relationships with the USA and the wider global system are once again being considered. However, these issues are now raised in a situation radically different from that obtaining in the immediate wake of the Pacific War. In place of a spread of war-damaged economies and polities we have a series of prosperous countries. In other words, where the immediate post-war period of confusion and disorder saw the establishment of the economic, military and political hegemony of the USA – with socialist Asia locking itself away within an inward-looking grouping – the present period of change involves a series of much more equal players.

One way in which this new period of reordering has manifested itself is in a concern for ordering the interstate relationships of the Pacific Asian countries. There have been a series of new organizations founded or old organizations revivified or redirected. In contemporary discussions of the development of the Pacific Asia region new acronyms abound: APEC, AFTA, EAEC and so on. It is clear that these political manoeuvrings are responses to fundamental changes within the global economy.[1]

The global system is ordered through a number of institutions and activities; in particular, the inter-state system of treaties, the activities of global economic organizations (MNCs), and a spread of formal inter-governmental organizations (IMF, World Bank, WTO). In the post-Second World War period these institutional elements were ordered for many years by the USA via its network of economic, military and political links. The resultant global pattern combined a rich Western first world, a partially successful autarchic state-socialist second world and a poor peripheral third world. However, it is now clear that the givens of geography and history coupled to present political-economic, social and cultural imperatives are pushing the global system towards a new set of regional groupings.

It can be noted that as 'a fact of economic geography, the economic world consists of three powerful trading groups: Asia, North America and Europe. These three groups together constitute close to 70 per cent of the global GDP. For each region, the bulk of economic activity and a large part of trade takes place only within the region'.[2] Zysman notes that 'differently structured political economies . . . express different values. Each country, and to some extent each region, is characterized by different market arrangements and social values'.[3] In an increasingly tripolar world the issue of the relationships between the three areas attains a greater significance. In the case of Pacific

Asia the increasing political-economic integration is being mirrored by an increasingly self-conscious elite project of affirming the particularity of Asia.[4] In this context the issues of the nature of the Pacific Asia region – its internal and external articulation – is now high on the agenda of scholars, policy analysts and political actors.

The New Situation II: Recognition, Response and the Logic of Regionalism

The end of the cold war in Pacific Asia was a phased process, rather than the compressed and dramatic collapse which occurred in Europe. A series of dates might be indicated: (i) the decision in 1971 to float the US dollar; (ii) the start of market reforms in China in 1978; (iii) the Plaza Accords of 1985 which revalued the yen; and finally (iv) the dissolution in 1991 of the USSR. As this slow reordering advanced and reached its recent climactic moment, a series of established global structural changes found more explicit acknowledgement in public discourse. As commentators turned to consider the new global situation it was clear that Pacific Asia constituted a nascent regional bloc within a distinctly tripolar global system. In the new context analysts confronted three general issues: (i) the extent of integration within the global system; (ii) the nature of regionalism; and (iii) the linkages between global, regional and local levels of activity.

Globalization versus internationalization

In recent years there has been a strong restatement of some of the central themes of economic liberalism, with its crucial concern for the ordering and expressive roles of free markets, in the guise of a set of claims in respect of the newly global reach of free markets, that is, ideas of globalization. In their narrowly economic liberal guise these claims amount to a delimited-formal ideological celebration of the model of the West in general and the USA in particular.[5] In their broader postmodernist fashion the same claims become an expressive celebration of the power of choice, consumption and life-style.

The theorists of globalization offer market-liberal analyses of the present situation of the global industrial-capitalist system. In these analyses the inherent dynamic logic of the marketplace is taken to be universal, and the process of expansion and its character are taken to be in all essentials fixed. The global industrial-capitalist system is taken to be moving towards a unified open trading marketplace in which goods and services are freely traded. In this perspective the recent expansion of global financial flows, manufacturing activities and trade are evidence of the fundamental dynamism of the system. However, market-liberals acknowledge that the national policy strategies of particular states can cut against the inherent logic of the marketplace, and it is granted that the historical experiences of particular territories can militate against the present expression of the universal market logic. Yet in the liberal perspective, the extent to which the state can usefully involve itself in economic processes, which are essentially systemic and rooted in the givens of human nature, is very limited. In terms of the market-liberal vision all these states should be encouraged to reorganize their economies, societies and cultures so as to permit the dynamism of the marketplace to ensure take-off into sustained growth and high mass consumption.[6]

Against the market-liberal claims, theorists centrally located within the received European tradition offer structural arguments which track the extent and character of globalization. Hirst and Thompson[7] draw a distinction between globalization and internationalization. The former term they read as essentially rhetorical, a matter of the ideological willing of those committed to the market-liberal political project, and they suggest that the latter notion allows a better access to the real-world dynamics of the system. Hirst and Thompson point to a complex pattern. It is clear, firstly, that there has been some globalization of financial markets as a result of the diminution of state regulation coupled to the new possibilities opened up by technological advance. The global financial markets do have significant power, however Hirst and Thompson argue that this power is not fixed once and for all, and the present patterns of financial markets have been different in the past and could be different once again. Thereafter, it is evident that there has also been some extension of multinational production, however this is relatively slight when compared with global production levels. It is also the case that there are no genuinely transnational companies, as the market-liberal position might suggest or anticipate, because multinational firms typically remain rooted in one key country. Finally, it might also be noted that the proponents of globalization cite the development of common cultural pursuits in consumption, tourism and the media, and, looking to the future, the more enthusiastic find an ethico-political end of history in liberal democracy.[8] However, we can suggest that these claims are fanciful in themselves and in any case fall when the economic argument undergirding them is dismissed. Hirst and Thompson,[9] in sum, are not persuaded by the claims about globalization, and they suggest it would be better to track the actual patterns of internationalization within the global system.

Locating the issue of regionalism

Gamble and Payne[10] note that it has been argued that the trend to regionalization is dangerous, and suggest that these anxieties flow from a view of the world system which is essentially market-liberal. The received liberal international relations theory looks to the stabilizing role of a hegemonic power, and if there is no hegemony then there can be no stability. Gamble and Payne affirm an alternative line inspired by Cox[11] who has argued that traditional international relations analysis was positivistic, looked to technical analyses of the status quo and, in its dominant realist form, advanced uncritically the narrow short-term interests of the USA. Cox fashioned an alternative critical international political economy which began with the observation that theory is always for someone and some purpose, and proposed an approach which looked to the process of the historical development of structures which thereafter constrain and enable the actions of relevant actors. Cox suggests that the US-sponsored drive for globalization should be resisted because an ethically defensible post-hegemonic world must acknowledge diversity and look to an ideal of community.

The international political-economy approach has a spread of ideas flowing into it, including elements of world systems analysis, institutional economics, regulation theory, development theory and Gramscian marxism. Overall, the approach looks to the historical development of patterns of structure and agency. In this perspective the modern world order has developed in phases: (i) the rise of the UK-centred liberal world order; (ii) the confused period following the collapse of the position of the UK; (iii) the US-sponsored post-Second World War Bretton Woods period; and (iv) the post-1971 decline of US hegemony. Gamble and Payne argue that a globalized economy constrains the behaviour of states but the desire for local control continues, and the dilemma generates a regional level of governance. Gamble and Payne suggest that this is a key sphere of concern, in particular the extent to which states are promoting regional projects in response to the pressures for globalization.

Overall, it is clear that the debate about regionalism within the global industrial-capitalist system has become more urgent as the incipient tripolarity of the global system has been abruptly acknowledged. The debate in respect of the logic of regionalism points to a series of necessary elements: (i) an economic base in productive activity, intra-regional trade and financial flows; (ii) an institutional structure which acknowledges and orders economic activity; (iii) a common cultural pattern which allows otherwise disparate nations to come together in interdependent economic activities and institutional structures; (iv) a common elite political recognition of the value of interdependence and thereafter a disposition to foster integration; and finally (v) a measure of broad support for integration amongst relevant populations.

In the case of the European Union and North America it is clear that most of these elements exist in some form or other.[12] Yet in the case of Pacific Asia there is much less integration, and the region contains significant diversity. Nonetheless, it is clear that the issue of the internal integration of the discrete regions within the global system is now actively debated. What is at issue is the extent to which economic integration entails social-institutional and cultural integration. A key question, therefore, becomes the extent to which regional elites are pursuing integration and the extent to which they are presenting these arguments to their local populations.

Global, regional and local levels of analysis/practice

It could be said that whilst the idea of globalization points to expanding networks of production, finance and trade, it is not the facts of these new linkages which are in question rather it is their significance.[13] On this, Zysman notes that the 'suddenly pervasive intrusion of the notion of globalism is an effort by governments and companies to apply a label to a diverse package of changes that they do not understand and to devise strategies to adjust to a new economic world they cannot specify'.[14] In order to grasp the dynamics of contemporary patterns of change within the emergent global patterns of production, finance and trade, so far as Zysman is concerned, commentators must deal with three levels of analysis; the global, the regional and the local.

The contemporary global industrial-capitalist system is presently undergoing a broad reconfiguration, and the dynamics of complex change within the system are such that a series of powerful regions are emerging. It is within this new global and regional context that state-regime strategies must be fashioned. As individual state-regimes respond to the demands of their structural locations it is likely that a series of distinct but related routes to the future will be established. Against the claims of the market-liberals it can be suggested that the new regionalized global system has not made the actions of states redundant, but it is reworking their opportunities for action because 'the points of leverage are shifting'.[15]

It is clear that the new global pattern has strong regional foundations. Zysman records: 'As a fact of economic geography, the economic world consists of three powerful trading groups: Asia, North America and Europe'.[16] It is important to note that within each area there is a powerful economy, a strong scientific base and a broadly coherent culture which can generate autonomous growth. In the case of North America and Europe it is evident that there are advanced patterns of regional organization; North America is dominated by the USA and the European Union is advancing its moves towards a similar unification. However, the detail of the dynamics of regionalism within Pacific Asia are much more complex. The shift to the modern world has been made relatively recently in Asia, and the depredations of colonialism, war and civil strife have left a significant negative legacy for present day actors. Zysman notes: 'Of course, we must recognize that there is not a single "Asian" development story'.[17] Indeed there are many. It is the present mix of national state-regime strategies which will shape regional integration.

The new global pattern evidences a strong national persistence. It can be argued that as economies are always lodged within societies then these economies are going to remain national/local in essence. It is likely that we are seeing multiple parallel tracks towards the future as countries respond to the demands of the global system and the regional pattern flows from the interactions of these national/local activities. It is clear that this is not 'convergence' upon a single market-liberal model, and the tales of liberals can be rejected in favour of political economy of change. And in respect of the oft-cited financial sector, Zysman recalls that 'One well-known banker has remarked that "the global financial market is a figment of a Reuter's screen"'.[18] Against the familiar public relations rhetoric of an extant global financial market, Zysman records that the 'vast flows of funds that define the popular image of globalization are wholesale market movements . . . The reality is that, while wholesale global markets are largely international, retail markets and even to a considerable extent commercial lending channels remain national'.[19] Overall, Zysman suggests that it is national developments which have driven changes in global economy. It is clear that national or local bases of economic forms remain, and thereafter regionalism looks to be more important than any talk about an integrated global system.

Patterns of Relationships in Pacific Asia

There are a series of ways of addressing the logic of regionalism. Bernard argues: 'It is important . . . to recognise that the processes that create regional structures must be seen as both historically constituted and located in the context of broader ongoing historical change . . . In other words, there is nothing "natural" or generic about regions'.[20] Within the existing spread of the social sciences there are a number of ways of grasping the logic of regionalism and in brief they include: (i) theories about economic systems; (ii) theories about the necessary logic of inter-state relations; (iii) theories about civilizations and societies; (iv) theories about cultural processes; and (v) structural theories detailing historical patterns of development. All these intellectual resources have been deployed at one time or another to grasp the nature of Pacific Asia.

Bernard[21] reports that the available economic approaches include: (i) an ahistorical neo-liberalism which looks at economic transactions between national economies and argues for freeing up exchanges; (ii) an ahistorical product-cycle theory which looks at a slowly evolving regional divisions of labour where a high tech core slowly offloads outmoded technology which is then passed down to the periphery (flocks of flying geese); and (iii) an apolitical neo-institutionalism which looks at networks of companies within the region. However, Bernard looks to 'region formation in terms of a number of complex interrelationships: the way the region is linked to both the global and the local; the social relationships that exist both between and within states; the relationship between the material and the ideational; and the tensions between forces of integration and disintegration in region formation'.[22]

In the main tradition of international relations there are available theories which look to the necessary logics of inter-state relations, in particular realist analyses which look to the ways in which states pursue their interests within the unregulated inter-state system. This strategy of analysis generates the view that global or regional stability requires a hegemonic power. In Pacific Asia the security system which was in place over the long years of the cold war did see two major powers confronting each other and the USA hegemonic within the richer dynamic market-oriented sphere. Realism also suggests that a group of regional states could come together to establish collective institutions to pursue common problems against an outside power but the plethora of acronyms within Pacific Asia rarely seem to exclude the obvious outside power, namely the USA. If realism looks to states reaching intergovernmental agreements then a related line of analysis which looks to the functional demands of economic activity looks to the slow supranational ordering of otherwise coherent regions. In the case of Pacific Asia it is possible to point to regional organizations, which often include the USA, that do acknowledge the sphere of economic exchange. However, the extent of formal regional integration remains slight.

The territory of theories about civilizations and societies is awkward as it involves making very broad comparisons between cultural spheres and claiming for large areas a received cultural coherence. In the case of Pacific Asia there have been many attempts to distinguish the typically Asian from the typically Western, indeed these attempts date from the nineteenth century when the driving logic of industrial-capitalist expansion brought European and American traders to Asia. In the case of contemporary Pacific Asia it is perhaps worth noting that there is an indigenous line of resistance to Western political ideas expressed via the notion of 'Asian values' which reports that the polities of Asia are more naturally consensual than the individualistic polities of the West and that this finds appropriate expression in disciplined and hierarchical societies and polities. In the same vein, an influential external view of Asia has characterized it as a coherent cultural bloc along with several others, all of which are taken by the author to be potential competitors with the West.

In the related area of cultural analysis, Bernard reports that some commentators 'argue that a region-wide civil society is now emerging . . . [which] constitutes the basis for the region to be a new kind of "imagined community"'.[23] Indeed, it has been suggested that Japanese popular culture is being widely diffused. However, matters are more complex and it is necessary to look at how local areas are located within regional patterns. The movement towards a common civil society could include: (i) regionalized urban spaces, such that the region's cities have increasingly common patterns of production and consumption; (ii) regionalized tourism, for example intra-regional travel and the passion for golf amongst newly affluent elites; and (iii) the networks of Chinese urban bourgeoisie which stretch through much of the region. But all this is tentative and speculative. Bernard concludes by recording both that there has been a growth in interconnectedness within the region and that the prospects for further integration are fraught with difficulties and tensions.

A structural historical analysis which might be pursued in detail using the framework of international political economy offers a strategy which embraces many of the elements noted above in order to grasp the long-term historical dynamics of change within the region in question. It is clear that regions have existed in a myriad historical contexts and taken a variety of forms. It is also clear that regions should be located at the intersection of global processes and more local formations. Bernard states: 'They must be understood precisely as a manifestation of global processes and of the way these processes assume concrete form in a world where power emanates from within historically constituted national social formations. Regions are thus co-determined by processes and social forces that operate transnationally and by the organisation of national communities'.[24]

A structural analysis of Pacific Asia would look to the successive ways in which the region has been configured and to the ways in which the peoples of the region understood themselves and thereafter acted. The idea of an Eastern Asian region has existed since its invention by Japanese theorists in the late nineteenth century. It was constituted in expansionary Japanese military practice in the years up to 1941 but at the end of the war the region was sharply reconfigured. The new patteren owed much to the USA. The US security structure helped to underpin the region whilst the economy of Japan provided the core of a regionalized economy and the USA provided an ever open market. Overall, Bernard argues that the 'regionalized production structure . . . has fostered an awareness of the regional nature of production, particularly through the crystallisation of a region-wide bloc of state and business elites and a cadre of technicians who have been the prime beneficiaries of regionalized manufacturing'.[25] However, the Japan-centred network is not the only one, and there are Chinese networks taking in Hong Kong, Taiwan and Southeast Asia which are establishing 'regional structures built around different kinds of economic activity – such as those related to agribusiness, property development or services – [and] with different spatial contours including a proliferation of ties with state and party elites in coastal China'.[26]

Overall, the Pacific Asian region does evidence an increasingly self-conscious integration. However, in looking at the development of the region it is clear that there are also problems: (i) local production fits into a Japan-centred hierarchy and this creates dependence as Japanese keep control; (ii) regional production has required local political and class patterns be fixed in place and this inevitably creates tensions; (iii) there are ethnic tensions within regional production as some groups are seen to be advantaged relative to others; (iv) in Japan there are the problems of rich country/poor people; (v) there is also the tension created by the region's exports in particular to the USA; and (vi) there is the question of the growing power of China.

The phases of internal relationships

There have been four phases in the development of the region. In each phase there has been a particular pattern of structural power and an associated pattern of agent response. These relatively stable phases are linked with periods of more rapid change as the system reconfigures and is reread by agent groups.

The first pre-contact phase comprised four main areas having long established forms-of-life and patterns of interaction: China, the Japanese islands, Indo-China, and the islands of the archipelago. In each of these broad areas there were well established forms-of-life. It is clear that the pre-contact region contained advanced and sophisticated cultures, in particular China. In the fifteenth to seventeenth centuries the trading linkages within the region were particularly well developed. However, the linkages of these areas to the wider global system were minimal. There was no global system and long-distance links were via trading routes carrying specialist and luxury goods.

The second empire phase comprised six main interrelated areas within the industrial-capitalist colonial global system: a Japanese sphere, an American sphere, a British sphere, a French sphere, a Dutch sphere, with China divided between these powers. The linkages of these areas to the wider global system were extensive – the global expansion of industrial-capitalism drew in new territories, and in the region the impact of the expanding colonial ordered industrial-capitalist system were extensive. The linkage of these areas to each other were extensive – as elements within the one expansive system – but controlled as the empires were mercantile, liberal and then protectionist (after Hobsbawm), before finally being swept away.

The third nation-building/cold war phase comprised five main areas, divided into two interlinked groups: Japan, the NICs, and Southeast Asia, on the one hand, and China with Indo-China on the other. The linkages of the free world group to the US-dominated global system were extensive within the overall framework of the Bretton Woods system. And inside there were increasingly well-developed linkages with each other – however over the period intra-regional and trans-regional trade/integration were controlled. The linkages of the socialist bloc to the global system were minimal. And inside there were some linkages but the economies were at a low level. The bipolar organization of the region began to break down after 1978 when Deng Xiao Ping inaugurated economic reforms in China. And in 1985 the Plaza Accords revalued the yen, leading to a flood of Japanese FDI within the region. When the cold war ended in 1991 there were already significant regional linkages amongst the countries within the area of Pacific Asia.

The fourth Pacific Asia phase comprises an increasingly interrelated grouping around a core Japanese economy of five main areas: Japan, inner periphery, outer periphery, reforming socialist bloc, and Australasia. The linkages of the region to the global system are very extensive and becoming more extensive. The linkages between the various parts of the region are also becoming extensive and deepening. The region has a core economy, extensive economic linkages, new political/trade mechanisms and a measure of cultural coherence. An integrated regional grouping can be taken to be in the process of formation (although the end point is most unclear and the extent of integration should not be overstated). It is in the phase of Pacific Asia that commentary has begun to speak of a tripolar global system.

The Japanese core and the region

After the Meiji restoration Japanese government sought to strengthen the economy as the basis for a strong country able to join the modern world on equal terms with the West. This required both resources from the Asian region and an appropriate framework for securing these resources. In the late nineteenth century these matters were typically construed in terms of spheres of influence and a Japanese empire in Asia was duly constructed. The colonial empire survived until the debacle of 1945 when it was stripped away by the victors.

Thereafter, the ongoing concern of the Japanese government for security and equality has found expression in commerce. The schedule of war reparations was dealt with in terms of the export of goods (rather than the transfer of existing machinery or cash) and this assisted the recovery of Japanese industry and helped secure influence within the region. As the Japanese economy was rebuilt, so too were commercial relationships. A new departure for the Japanese government was economic aid to developing countries. Japanese development aid was disproportionately concentrated in Asia and typically was tied to Japanese suppliers.[27] Over the years a parallel process of aid-financed infrastructural work and private foreign direct investment developed. The Japanese aid strategy within Asia was criticized, however these activities began the process of laying the basis of an integrated regional economy.[28] This process received a further encouragement with the 1985 Plaza Accords which revalued the yen against the US dollar and provoked a wave of Japanese foreign direct investment in the Asian region as manufacturers moved to escape the effects of the revaluation.[29]

It has been argued that the key to understanding the Japanese approach is the metaphor of the flying geese with Japan as the vanguard and the other regional economies strung out behind in formation. The Japanese ideal is of an integrated and complementary regional division of labour. This division of labour should flow from the revealed comparative advantage held by each country (in other words, Japan is the advanced core and the other countries are variously materials suppliers and providers of lower technology manufactures).[30]

A series of quite particular relationships between Japan and the various countries in the region can be identified. In the first place, Japan's relationship with the four tigers (Singapore, Hong Kong, Korea and Taiwan) is complementary-competitive. They are relatively advanced and have trade surpluses with the USA and deficits with Japan. Singapore and Hong Kong are largely production platforms for exports to third countries and have very high deficits with Japan. Taiwan and Korea have a broader trade exchange with Japan. Then in the second place, Japan's relationship with Southeast

Asia and China (the regional LDCs) is skewed but complementary. Japan traditionally had a trade deficit with Southeast Asia as it imported raw materials but in recent years there has been a surplus as Southeast Asia takes more manufactured goods (some of which are components for products to be exported). Relatedly, in the case of China, Japan has a large trade deficit. However, this exchange is at a relatively early stage given cold war problems over many years. And finally, Japan's relationship with Australasia is complex and multifaceted as these are both DCs. Japan takes raw materials from Australia and primary products from New Zealand. Thereafter there are a range of exchanges with tourism, real-estate, and manufactures.

Cronin takes the view that Japanese trade is a force for regional integration. However there is relative movement amongst the component parts of the region. It is not a static relationship. The rise of Japan as a core economy within the region has been complemented by the parallel rise of the Asian tiger economies. These economies are now investing in the countries of the region and intra-regional linkages are growing rapidly. The most recently established destinations for Japanese and tiger economy investments have been the countries of the former socialist bloc in Asia, that is, China and Indo-China. Abegglen[31] speculatively identifies a South China region encompassing Hong Kong, Canton, Fujian and Taiwan. Relatedly, the economic integration of the region has been paralleled by a modest acknowledgement in the form of various institutional mechanisms – the Asian Development Bank, ASEAN, APEC, EAEC and so on. All these are modestly developed institutional vehicles for cooperation. At the present time cooperation within Asia seems to be based on the pragmatic pursuit of material advance rather than the ideological schemes of pan-Asianism which have been mooted in earlier periods of concern for the integration of Asia. Yet it should be noted that the precise extent of regional integration (as a result of aid, investment and trade) is not easy to grasp. There are difficult issues involved in deciding what counts as integration. Nonetheless, so far as can be judged, it does seem to be the case that there is a significant element of regional integration, notwithstanding the continuing wide links of all the regional units to the wider global system.

The relationship of the region to the global system

It has become clear in recent years that the USA, Pacific Asia and the European Union are the three major economic groupings within the global industrial-capitalist system. The rough outline of the tripolar world can be illustrated by comparing the broad economic data for the three regions. A grasp of the simple orders of magnitude involved can be achieved. Wilkinson[32] makes it clear that the European Union, the USA and Japan are the three major economies within the global system.[33]

In a similar fashion Zysman comments that there are now three major regions within the global economy and that these 'three groups together constitute close to 70 per cent of the global GDP. For each region, the bulk of economic activity and a large part of trade takes place only within the region'.[34]

The data points to the following conclusions: (i) the three areas are very roughly the same economic size; (ii) they dominate the global economy; (iii) they are regionalized (which is to say that they trade internally to a significant extent); and (iv) they engage in significant inter-area trade. It is clear that there is some sort of interdependent global industrial-capitalist system and that there is some sort of tripolar inclusionary regionalism within this system.

The Possible Implications of the Premier Role of Japan in the Region

As the region becomes more integrated a series of crucial questions have been raised and these include the possible political leadership role of Japan. Cronin (1992) argues that Japan can constitute the core of the region but that the region's export-dependency on the USA means that the region cannot become a closed bloc.

Cronin[35] has considered the post-1989 phase of the development of the global system in the Pacific region in terms of three distinct scenarios: (i) the constructive globalization of Japan; (ii) a heightened rivalry between the USA and Japan; and (iii) the emergence of an Asia-Pacific region dominated by Japan. Overall, Cronin looks to a period of reordering in the Pacific area, but argues that Japan's room for manoeuvre is constrained by the USA and historical legacies.

Competition and globalization

The first scenario is of the competitive globalization of Japan. In the first scenario Japan builds links with the USA and Pacific Asia so as to further develop an open market Asian region, and the impetus to this flows from reform within Japan as its system comes in line with the underlying logic of economics.

Cronin argues that this 'would have Japan interacting with Asia as an increasingly open economy, partially supplanting the United States as an export market for Asia-Pacific countries, while at the global level using its financial resources to undergird the present system'.[36] A wider spread of concerns in respect of ODA might also be anticipated. Cronin suggests 'greater participation by non-Japanese firms and more emphasis on human resources development . . . investment projects would involve more participation by local subcontractors, transfer more technology, and be more oriented to the Japanese market'.[37] Cronin argues that this scenario is close to the optimistic reform position within Japan and would find support in the

USA. It would mean, reports Cronin, Japan 'using its growing economic power to support the current global trading system'.[38] On optimistic analyses the result would be an expanding global economy and a stable international environment. Cronin notes that an 'important theoretical basis for this scenario is the premise that Japan cannot suspend indefinitely the operation of what many see as universal economic laws'[39] and that liberalization will have to take place. However, he immediately adds that support within Japan for globalization remains weak. In sum, this scenario involves Japan building on established links with the USA and Pacific Asia in order to further develop the open markets of the region as the closed Japanese system bows to economic market logic and opens up to the global system.

Competition and rivalry

The second scenario sees 'Japanese aid and investment in Asia as primarily acting to increase the competitive position of Japanese companies in world markets *vis-à-vis* the fast rising NIEs, while Japan's own markets remain relatively closed'.[40] In the second scenario of heightened rivalry, the Japanese continue to build up their own position thereby fostering conflict as other economies respond to protect themselves. This thesis is affirmed by those who analyse Japan as being neo-mercantile.

Cronin speculates that this is an unstable line of advance as trading partners might react against the lack of reciprocity. And over the longer term the Japanese relationship with the USA could wither away, and such an eventuality would call into question many currently taken-for-granted ideas in respect of order in Pacific Asia. A school of thought has now emerged, reports Cronin, which holds that Japan 'will not significantly abandon its neo-mercantilist policies'[41] and there are many problem areas that could tip the Pacific system towards protectionism (for example, the issue of the US trade deficit). In sum, the second scenario is one of heightened rivalry as Japan continues to build up its own position thereby fostering conflict as other states respond to protect their economies. The implication is one of various patterns of breakdown of the established global order.

Competition and regionalization

The third scenario sees 'Japanese aid and investment, and increasing access to the Japanese market by Asian exporters, as producing a Japan-centred Asia-Pacific economy'.[42] In the third scenario, a Japan-dominated Asia-Pacific, the provision of more ODA and FDI coupled to greater access to the Japanese market for Asian exports, results in the formation of a yen zone. Cronin adds that given that the export success is a matter of the US importing these goods, it is difficult to see such an outcome coming to pass, and he draws a distinction between a core economy and a yen zone.

Cronin comments that this scenario could develop in a beneficial way for most non-US countries or could turn into a second co-prosperity sphere. Cronin suggests that in both versions 'Asia-Pacific countries would become increasingly dependent on Japan for capital flows (both aid and investment) and increasingly tied to Japan by trade links'.[43] One condition required by this scenario is that the Japanese market supplant that of the US as the regional core – able to draw in the region's imports and fuel the region's need for new capital and technology. Cronin notes that there is no agreement at present on how the system is moving, and that there are arguments for and against the notion of an emerging yen zone. However, Cronin takes the role of the US as a market and investment location to be of continuing importance, and thus the emergence of a yen bloc looks unlikely. In sum, the third scenario is a Japan-dominated Pacific Asia where more ODA and FDI plus trade access for Asians to the Japanese market results in the creation of a yen bloc. However, cutting against this possibility is the general extent of global integration and the particular links which Japan has with the USA.

In terms of the arguments presented in this text, Cronin's analysis is very interesting. The crucial issue is the extent to which the present role of the USA – as key market – will be altered or adjusted. Cronin looks to stability in this matter and thereafter consequent wider stability within the global system. However, we have seen that the region is growing very quickly and it is significantly inward-looking. On the analyses of this text, Cronin is too sanguine, and the future does look tri-regional.

Conclusion

Analysing shifting patterns of relationships is an aspect of the general analysis of complex change. In the case of the region we have the two related themes of the changing patterns of relationships amongst the territories within the region, and between the region and the wider global system, over the series of four phases that constitute the region's shift to the modern world. We can trace the process of the ongoing absorption and remaking of the region in terms of these four great phases. It is the contemporary phase that is called 'Pacific Asia'.

We can note that there has been considerable recent debate in respect of the situation of the region within the global system. It has been occasioned by the very rapid growth of the area, in particular in the years following the Plaza Accord revaluation of the yen when commentators began to speak of Pacific Asia.

There are two polar positions identifiable within Western debate: (i) that the integration of the region is virtually guaranteed as the recent economic successes have been the product of a quite distinctive Asian developmental capitalism; and (ii) that the integration of the region within the global economy is virtually guaranteed as a result of the operation of the universal laws of economics.

In the region there are multiple identifiable positions: (i) there are proponents of both the two lines familiar in Western debate; (ii) there is a sub-species of this debate which stresses the particularity of Asian values in order to defend an authoritarian status quo; and (iii) there are nationalisms and anxieties about the intentions of neighbours, in particular the Japanese and Chinese. In general it is clear that the Western free marketeers are wrong. It is probably also true that the Western enthusiasts for reading Pacific Asia as an integrated bloc are overstating their case. There is a measure of economic integration and some institutional order but there is a diversity of cultural, political and historical experience in the region which militates against any rapid movement towards close integration.

Notes

1   The boundaries and character of the region and its future development are all contested and the diverse views find expression in a variety of ways including the acronyms used to label the proliferating institutions. In this text the key distinction is between including (or not) the countries of the Americas, in particular the USA. An inclusive term is 'Asia-Pacific' or 'Pacific Rim' whereas a more exclusive term would be 'East Asia'. My own formulation of 'Pacific Asia' points to the countries of Asia, that is, an 'Asian Asia'.

2   J. Zysman 1996: The Myth of a Global Economy in *New Political Economy* 1.2, pp. 159–60.

3   Ibid., p. 180.

4   R. Higgot 1996: Ideas and Identity in the International Political Economy of Regionalism: The Asia Pacific and Europe Compared in *ISA-JAIR Joint Convention*, Makuhari: Japan.

5   P. W. Preston 1994: *Discourses of Development*, Aldershot: Avebury.

6   W. W. Rostow 1960: *The Stages of Economic Growth: A Non-Communist Manifesto*, Cambridge: Cambridge University Press.

7   P. Hirst and G. Thompson 1996: *Globalization in Question*, Cambridge: Polity.

8   F. Fukuyama 1992: *The End of History and the Last Man*, London: Hamish Hamilton.

9   Hirst and Thompson 1996.

10   A. Gamble and T. Payne 1996: *Regionalism and World Order*, London: Macmillan.

11   R. Cox 1995: Critical Political Economy in B Hettne, ed., *International Political Economy: Understanding Global Disorder*, London: Zed.

12   P. W. Preston 1997: *Political-Cultural Identity: Citizens and Nations in a Global Era*, London: Sage.

13   Zysman 1996, p. 157.

14   Ibid.

15   Ibid., p. 159.

16   Ibid., pp. 159–60.

17   Ibid., p. 162.

18   Ibid., p. 173.

19   Ibid.

20   M. Bernard 1996: Regions in the Global Political Economy in *New Political Economy* 1(3), p. 339.
21   Ibid.
22   Ibid.
23   Ibid., p. 346.
24   Ibid., p. 340.
25   Ibid., p. 343.
26   Ibid.
27   A. Rix 1993: *Japan's Foreign Aid*, London: Routledge.
28   D. Yasutomo 1986: *The Manner of Giving*, Lexington: Heath.
29   P. Phongpaichit 1990: *The New Waves of Japanese Investment in ASEAN*, Singapore: Institute for Southeast Asian Studies.
30   R. P. Cronin 1992: *Japan, the United States and the Prospects for the Asia Pacific Century*, Singapore: Institute for Southeast Asian Studies.
31   J. C. Abegglen 1994: *Sea Change*, New York: Free Press.
32   E. Wilkinson 1990: *Japan Versus the West*, Harmondsworth: Penguin.
33   In 1960 the USA GNP was US$ 500 billion, with a GNP per capita of US$2,500; the EEC GNP was US$ 270 billion, with a GNP per capita of US$ 1,000; and Japan's GNP was US$ 40 billion, with a GNP per capita of US$ 400 (Wilkinson 1990, p. 8). At this time the USA had the world's most powerful economy. However, in 1989 the USA GNP was US$ 5.2 trillion, with a GNP per capita of US$ 21,000; the EU GNP was US$ 4.8 trillion, with a GNP per capita of US$ 15,000; and Japan's GNP was US$ 2.8 trillion, with a GNP per capita of US$ 23,100 (Wilkinson 1990, p. 8). At this time the USA had the world's single strongest economy but was only one of three more or less similarly powerful economies. In the case of Japan the data in respect of a broad sphere of economic activity in Pacific Asia can be added. In this context, the particular strength of the Pacific Asian economies would imply that the three regions are of similar size on conventional economic measures.
34   Zysman 1996, pp. 159–60.
35   Cronin 1992.
36   Ibid., p. 107.
37   Ibid.
38   Ibid.
39   Ibid., p. 109.
40   Ibid., p. 111.
41   Ibid., p. 112.
42   Ibid., p. 115.
43   Ibid.

8

Changing Patterns of Relations between Japan, the USA and China

In the period following the Pacific War the USA exercised military and economic sway over the Western-oriented areas of the region whilst China was the dominant force within the Asian socialist bloc. The two blocs represented themselves as distinct, and to a significant extent developed independently. However, over the years a series of changes to this general pattern occurred as extensive regional economic linkages developed within and between the two blocs. In the wake of the ending of the cold war and the intellectual confusions associated with the assiduous promulgation by engaged state-machines of a series of ritualized official ideologies, these regional patterns of linkages have now been widely acknowledged.

The changes revolve around the shifting relative positions of Japan, the USA and China, within the developing global industrial-capitalist system. This is neither a mechanical nor a unilinear process; on the contrary, the changes in relative position have involved diverse phases, discontinuities and reversals. All these complexities make grasping the logic of change awkward and problematical. However, it can be suggested that over the post-war period in Pacific Asia the key aspects of change have been, firstly, the economic recovery of Japan, its emergence as a regional core economy and the country's growing military and diplomatic presence in the region, and secondly, the shifting contribution of the USA as the early post-Second World War concern with security gives way to a preoccupation with economic linkages (from geo-strategy to geo-economics), and thirdly, the stability and increasing openness of China as the utopian socialism of Mao gives way to the market-centred strategies of Deng Xiao Ping. At the present time the key to the slow reconfiguration of the Pacific Asia region is the continuing economic success of Japan. It is clear that Japan is the core economy of the region and it is around this factor that other patterns of change revolve.

The Emergence of Japan as the Core Economy of the Region

Japan escaped colonization in the late nineteenth century and became the first Asian country to make the shift to the modern world. In the period of Japan's modernization from above, in the late nineteenth and early twentieth centuries, the government routinely looked to its relationships with Asia and came to aspire to a regional leadership role. Japan established a colonial sphere of influence in East Asia. The justification or rationale of this expansionism was twofold: firstly, flowing from contemporary ideas of nation statehood, the argument that Japan as a major power had an interest in securing its position in the region; and secondly, flowing from nationalist ideology, the argument which stressed that the Japanese people inhabited a resource-poor island and had perforce to attend to their economic needs by securing access to resources and markets. If we date the start of Japan's shift into the modern world from the period of the Meiji Restoration in 1868 and its arrival as a major power from the date of its first expansionist war against China in 1894–5, then given its subsequent expansionism it is clear that Japan was preoccupied with security for the whole of its pre-Second World War modern history. Overall it was involved in active expansion from 1894 to 1945, including in total approximately sixteen years of open warfare.[1]

In the period following the Pacific War the Japanese economy has grown very significantly and the country's relationship with its Asian neighbours has come to revolve around economics: trade, investment and aid. In the immediate post-war period Japan began making reparations to the countries of Pacific Asia. There was a preference for transfers of goods (rather than monies) and a stress on subsequent self-reliance on the part of recipients. In other words, resource transfers were controlled and pragmatic. In the early post-war years resource transfers were relatively slight but with economic reconstruction and success these transfers grew. They have taken two main forms: development aid and direct investment. Since the mid-1980s Japanese aid and investment has tended to focus on Pacific Asia and is taken by many commentators to have been both clearly at the service of Japanese interests and a major contributory factor to the region's recent economic growth.

Japan is now the premier economy of Pacific Asia, and is acquiring a greater political role. The question of the relationship of the Japanese economy to the other regional economies has often been answered in a fashion that implies the existence of an ordered grouping. Social theorists have spoken of the Japanese core being surrounded by an inner periphery, the NICs, and an outer periphery, ASEAN, to which a new circle has recently been added in the guise of the reforming socialist bloc. The increasing prominence of Japan within the region creates significant problems as particular countries look to present strengths in the light of memories of earlier conflicts.

The role of Japan within the region: trade, investment and aid

As we noted earlier, it can be argued that the key to understanding the Japanese approach to patterns of trade within the region is the metaphor of the 'flying geese', with Japan in the vanguard and the other economies strung out behind in formation.[2] The Japanese ideal is of an integrated and complimentary regional division of labour. This division of labour should flow from the revealed comparative advantage held by each country (in other words, Japan is the advanced core and the other countries are variously materials suppliers and providers of lower technology manufactures). In the first place, Japan's relationship with the four tigers (Singapore, Hong Kong, South Korea and Taiwan) is complementary-competitive. They are relatively advanced and have trade surpluses with the USA and deficits with Japan. Singapore and Hong Kong are largely production platforms for exports to third countries and have very high deficits with Japan. Taiwan and Korea have a broader trade exchange with Japan. In the second place, Japan's relationship with Southeast Asia and China (the regional LDCs) is skewed but complementary. Japan traditionally had a trade deficit with Southeast Asia as it imported raw materials but in recent years there has been a surplus as Southeast Asia takes more manufactured imports (some of which are components for products to be exported). Relatedly, in the case of China, Japan has a large trade deficit. However, this exchange is at a relatively early stage given cold war problems over many years. And in the third place, Japan's relationship with Australasia is complex and multifaceted, as these are both DCs. Japan takes raw materials from Australia and primary products from New Zealand. Thereafter there are a range of exchanges with tourism, real-estate, and manufactures.

Cronin takes the view that Japanese trade is a force for regional integration. However there is relative movement amongst the component parts of the region. It is not a static relationship, although it is almost impossible to imagine significant change in Japan's core role. However, we should recall once again that the extent of regional integration (as a result of aid, investment and trade) is not easy to grasp. There are difficult issues involved in deciding what counts as integration. At the same time the relationships of the region with the global system continue. However, so far as can be judged it does seem to be the case that there is a significant element of regional integration, notwithstanding the continuing wide links of all the regional units to the wider global system. In the post-1985 period the rapidly deepening integration of the Pacific Asian region has been a matter of considerable interest and concern within the USA.

Japanese direct investment within the region has contributed to the establishment of trading linkages. Cronin[3] remarks that in recent years Japan has overtaken the USA as the premier source of investment in Pacific Asia, and that recent trends suggest that Japan will consolidate its role in the 1990s. Japanese and NIE investment in Asia has been heavy in the 1980s and intra-regional trade has increased to US$ 270 billion so that it now exceeds Asian exports to the US at US$ 206 billion and the EU at US$ 182 billion. Cronin[4] reports that in all this Japan has been the catalyst and America the market. The key event seems to have been the 1985 Plaza Accord which revalued the yen upwards against the dollar such that the resultant pressure on Japanese manufacturers encouraged them to shift production offshore, whilst the rise in the value of the yen meant both that existing yen holdings were upwardly revalued and that continuing flows of exports generated ever greater dollar earnings, which in turn were recycled in the form of development aid and direct investment in Pacific Asia. The result has been a series of what Phongpaichit[5] refers to as production platforms in the countries of Pacific Asia which operate with Japanese investment and are exported to America. Cronin[6] points out that the linkages which Japan has with the countries of the region vary significantly from complementary and competitive with the NICs, through complementary cooperation skewed in Japan's favour with the developing areas, to a complex and multifaceted exchange with Australasia.

Overall, Japanese direct investment is a force for economic growth and regional integration, and as Dobson[7] points out, focusing on the ASEAN case, in recent years host governments have positively welcomed such inward investment. Phongpaichit looks at the ASEAN case and argues three broad points: (i) that the key issue in respect of direct investment is the matter of the host government securing beneficial control; (ii) that the recent wave of direct investment arose from Japan; and (iii) that the ASEAN countries have actively pursued their own agendas in respect of this flow of direct investment.

Phongpaichit notes three areas of debate in respect of direct investment: the work of Western economists focusing on MNCs; the particular arguments of some Japanese scholars; and the view of the ASEAN policy makers.

With regard to the first issue, Phongpaichit notes that work which looked at capital movements within the global system has recently given way to work derived from industrial organization theory and product-cycle theory which focuses on the advantages to MNCs of involving themselves in direct investment: advantages in terms of organization and technology allow high profits. Against this line of work, critics working with non-mainstream economic ideas have spoken of exploitative relationships and of the overweening power of the global MNCs. At the same time, figures such as Streeten[8] have argued that the key issue is how the activities of the MNCs can be ordered to the greater benefit of the host countries. In sum, their role in LDCs is widely regarded as less than self-evidently generally beneficial.

In the case of Japanese work on these matters, Phongpaichit[9] records that critics have tagged this sort of direct investment as oligopolistic and, by implication, exploitative. It is suggested that other forms of foreign direct investment could have more positive effects. It is suggested that Japanese direct investment typically looks to enhanced complementary comparative advantage within an ordered international division of labour. It would seem that non-Japanese commentators are sceptical of this characterization, yet at the same time it is the case that Japanese aid and investment are both intertwined and act to generate an integrated regional bloc, that is, a regional complementary division of labour centred on Japan.[10] The policy makers of ASEAN are reportedly sceptical of Japanese theories and have preferred Western explanations. However, Phongpaichit[11] argues that all these discussions are flawed by a neglect of host country demand. It cannot be assumed that host country governments and capitals are passive, for they have their own agendas. Thus for host governments foreign direct investment generates tax revenues, job creation, and export earnings, whilst for domestic capitals the incoming MNCs are a source of disturbance, opportunity and threat: again, the issue is how to control the impact of the MNCs.

It can be argued that the recent wave of foreign investment in the ASEAN region was initiated by changes in the circumstances of the Japanese economy. In the 1950s through to the 1970s, Japanese direct investment expanded slowly, and in the pre-1985 period the focus was on raw materials, cheap labour and market access. There was a distinctive pattern of investment with the East Asian NICs favoured, and thereafter some attention to Singapore, with the rest of ASEAN coming behind. However, after the 1985 Plaza Accords investment in ASEAN increased sharply and it was now focused on export-oriented industrialization. Phongpaichit[12] argues that the underlying reason, notwithstanding the issues of the appreciation of the yen and the Japanese government's desire to be seen to be responding to growing US concerns about trade imbalances, was lodged in Japan's shift from an economy centred on labour intensive heavy industry to one focused on high-technology industrial development. This structural change pushed out direct investment to offshore production platforms as Japanese capital looked to escape the impact of the high yen, and US restrictions, via a drive to increase markets and production capacity. In the terms of Hamilton,[13] the Japanese economic space was expanded in Pacific Asia. Phongpaichit records that this expansion has had a large impact on ASEAN – and she adds that the recipient states have been active participants.

After the style of the political economists, Phongpaichit suggests that we can distinguish between domestic capital, state capital and foreign capital, and thereafter we can plot the shifting patterns of interest and how these are expressed in response to incoming foreign direct investment. In ASEAN, broadly, there was an early resistance to direct investment as state and domestic capital prospered. Then in the depression of the early 1980s state capital ran into trouble and began to run up significant debt. At this point direct investment became attractive to ASEAN governments and with incoming investment the phase of export-oriented industrialization takes off. It is clear that each country has had a particular experience of direct investment-assisted, export-oriented industrialization but in each case Phongpaichit[14] insists the acceptance of aid must be seen as an expression not of dependent passivity but the active pursuit of locally specified goals.

If we turn finally to development aid programmes, it is worth noting that all aid programmes express a set of assumptions made by the aid-donors in respect of the purpose of the programmes. Such assumptions can be taken to be the product of a mix of factors including, most obviously: historical legacies; contemporary concerns; and projected interests.

The contemporary official rationale for development aid is one of helping the less fortunate. Rix[15] reports that it is possible to discern a continuity in respect of the idea of self-help, rather than simple charity, which runs back to the period of Meiji, but otherwise there is no consistent view of development. Japan's aid programmes are linked to the concerns of the Japanese, and there is thus a stress on Pacific Asia. Rix notes that 'Asian development was more a means of achieving Japanese objectives than a goal in its own right'.[16] Rix goes on to remark that 'The geographical, cultural and racial entity of Asia is a powerful image for the Japanese mind, and at home Japan's role in Asia is widely accepted, even encouraged'.[17]

Rix[18] records that trying to grasp the detail of Japanese development aid motivation is difficult, although one can broadly point to differences in emphasis amongst the various bureaucratic groupings involved; hence MITI stresses trade, resources and markets, whilst MOFA looks to diplomacy and security. In terms of the detailed politics of aid policy Orr[19] argues that this is largely contained within the bureaucracy, with little impact from other sectors of Japanese society. Orr makes clear that aid has been subordinated to concerns for resource security. The oil-shock of the early 1970s did change the pattern of Japanese aid disbursements away from an exclusive focus on Asia but the intention remained constant.

Japanese economic interests in Pacific Asia have clearly shaped development-aid disbursements. The geographical spread of aid, the size of aid-donations, the way in which money was disbursed and with what conditions, have all favoured Japanese interests. Orr reports that the dominant player in the aid game at the Japanese end has been the bureaucracy, rather than politicians or other groups, and the bureaucracy maintains close links with the world of industry. Orr notes that much of the aid has been infrastructural in nature – dams, bridges, ports and the like – with Japanese companies as virtually the sole agents. In a similar fashion Dobson[20] records that the Japanese government has been concerned to strategically foster economic development and that development aid has been one instrument deployed to this end.

In general, it is the case that Japanese aid to the LDCs has been linked directly to the economic interests of Japan and has been focused on the Pacific Asian area.[21] In its earliest form, aid was presented as war reparations. The Japanese distributed goods rather than money and thus the link of aid and Japanese development was made from the outset. In this way, as Rix[22] points out, a measure of continuity with pre-war concerns was maintained, and this concentration on development aid as a way of furthering the interests of Japan has been somewhat modified but in essentials it continues.

The developing Japanese role within the region

The economic success of Japan in the years following the Pacific War has made it the core economy of the region. The Japanese have attained a particular pre-eminence within the region on the basis of their economic activities. The economics provide the basis for the display of further aspirations. The Japanese self-defence forces are now very strong. The Japanese have a modern army, airforce and navy. The military strength of Japan is noted by its neighbours. However, it is in another area that the Japanese have presented themselves as ready to shoulder wider burdens, that is the economic/diplomatic realm. Japan is now the world's largest single donor of foreign aid to developing countries. The Japanese government and people see this as an appropriate and acceptable route to a greater political role within the world community. It is for these reasons that the Japanese government has made it clear that it would like to become a permanent member of the UN Security Council. Overall, it is clear that the burgeoning success of the Japanese economy will require some form of accommodation in the not too distant future.

The USA and the New Pacific Asian Region

The USA began to deal extensively with the Pacific Asian region in the early modern period, although American trade links were weakened by the civil war which left the territories of Asia open to the European powers for a crucial period in the late nineteenth century. The American colonial empire came to include the Philippines and a scatter of islands throughout the Pacific Ocean. In addition they were significant players in the late nineteenth century quasi-colonization of China. It was not until the Pacific War that the USA became a dominant power within the region and it did so in the context of cold war competition with those countries affirming official ideologies of socialism.

The cold war in Asia and the US assumption of leadership

As we noted earlier, the US position during the Pacific War centred upon its military campaign against Japan, sympathy for the cause of nationalist China, a disinclination to support the re-establishment of European colonial territories and a broad determination to order the post-war world in a progressive fashion which would enable countries to move beyond the damaging confines of economic protectionism and narrow nationalism that had typified the inter-war years.[23]

It quickly became clear as the Second World War developed that the USA would emerge from the conflict as the most powerful economy within the global system. In the USA the machineries of the Bretton Woods system were put into place during the later years of the war. The US plan for an open, liberal, trading region provided the general framework for US economic and foreign policy. In Europe the Marshall Plan for the reconstruction of the continent was put in place over the summer months of 1948 and made an immediate contribution to the economic recovery of Europe.[24] At the same time the collapse of the wartime grand alliance continued such that the creation of the US-centred, liberal trading area was paralleled by the creation of a state-socialist pattern in the areas controlled by the Soviet Union, a bifurcation which was to find institutional and rhetorical expression as the cold war. The characteristic mix of US economic and foreign policy concerns also found expression in Asia.

The military defeat and occupation of Japan allowed the Americans the opportunity to impose their will upon the Japanese. The early phase of SCAP was informed by a variation upon the reformist themes of the New Deal, and Japan was significantly remade in line with American notions of liberal democracy. The broad reforming impulse might be taken to have found related expression in the US preference for decolonization within the European colonial territories of Asia; and the US made the Philippines independent. However, if these two areas of concern can be taken to have shown a measure of US success, then failure must be recorded in respect of the third area of concern, China.

The USA had a long relationship with the nationalist Chinese and at the end of the Pacific War when there was a brief pause in the fighting in China, the USA made large shipments of materials to the nationalists. However, when the fighting resumed the nationalists were quickly defeated and in 1949 the remnants of Chiang Kai-shek's armies escaped to Taiwan. The defeat of the nationalists was taken by sections of the Washington political community as a defeat for the USA and they spoke of 'the loss of China'. It was a matter of a few months later that the war in Korea began and the USA became deeply involved on the South Korean side. The cold war was thereafter reprised in the Pacific Asia region and the USA became the dominant power within the broad spread of Western-oriented countries.

The decline of US leadership

The establishment of US leadership within the non-communist countries of the region was accomplished in a series of phases; in Japan, in South Korea and Taiwan; in French Indo-China; in the British spheres; and then in Indonesia. It is clear that by the middle of the 1960s the influence of the USA throughout the region was extensive. In fact it had reached its apogee. The decline began around about the same time when the USA allowed itself to be sucked into the war in Vietnam. The war placed burdens upon the USA which quickly proved to be unsustainable.

The military demands could not be met as the USA was unable to defeat either the South Vietnamese peasant guerrillas or the North Vietnamese regulars. The war quickly became bogged down. At the same time the financial demands of the war led to the collapse of the Bretton Woods system. And finally, the war caused great political conflict within the USA and by the early 1970s the Americans were looking for a way to extricate themselves. In 1973 the Americans withdrew their forces and South Vietnam fell to the forces of the North in early 1975.

The military defeat of the Americans and the collapse of the Bretton Woods system significantly damaged the US economic and political project within the region. A few years later, with market reforms in China, strong economic growth in the Asian Tigers and the strengthening economic miracle in Japan, the Pacific Asia region began to form.

Lines of response to the rise of Pacific Asia

One aspect of the American literature dealing with Pacific Asia, sometimes overt and sometimes covert, is an anxiety in respect of the position of the USA where the point is repeatedly and variously made that the USA may be surrendering its pre-eminence. We can note work which celebrates in positive vein the rise of the Pacific Century,[25] work which looks in more critical vein to the economic competition offered by Pacific Asia,[26] and we can note those who speak pessimistically of the forthcoming clash of civilizations.[27]

The material which speaks of the rise of the Pacific Century is broadly historical in character and offers a sweeping and optimistic view of the development of the Pacific Basin. The situation of the USA is made integral to this story and present conflicts over trade issues which are set to one side as essentially minor blemishes on what is otherwise a marvellous sweep of historical development. On the other hand, there has been a related body of work which followed the Japanese miracle. As the miracle ran its course a literature grew up within the USA which was concerned with 'learning the lessons from Japan'. The economy, society and polity were examined for strategies which might be transferred to the USA. And thereafter as the success of Japan continued, and as the integration of Pacific Asia became more evident, the focus shifted somewhat, away from learning the lessons and towards living within a tripolar system.

Against these relatively optimistic lines of commentary it is now clear that there are voices expressing disquiet at the rise to power within the global system of Japan. It would seem to be the case that a nascent appreciation of the power of the Japanese economy was growing amongst American commentators throughout the 1980s and that doubts expressed then have received a sharp impetus, at least in terms of their public visibility, in the wake of the ending of the cold war. It seems to be the case that this particular conservative anxiety is primarily an American phenomenon. The economic success of Japan and Pacific Asia has been read as indicative of American decline. There seem to be two variants: the business-economic and the international-relations.

The business-economic line of reflection is concerned with the economic, and thereafter strategic, implications for the USA of the continuing expansion of the Japanese economy. A series of themes are routinely present in the texts of this genre: (i) the rapid and continuing rise of the economic power of Japan; (ii) the threat of this power to the position of the USA; (iii) the unfair nature of the competition from Japan (a mix of export drives and closed home markets are often cited); and (iv) the urgent necessity for the US to take action to remedy the situation (from restructuring the US economy to compete more effectively, through to retaliating against the Japanese with trade restrictions).

The related international-relations variant shifts from an economic focus to speak broadly of a clash of civilizations. In a now notorious piece, Huntington spoke of the post-cold war era being likely to be dominated by a clash between East and West as the two regions competed for global dominance. Recalling Wilkinson[28] on the mutual stereotyping of Japan and the West it is not too difficult to see this sort of argument as one more version of the nineteenth-century concern for the 'yellow peril'.

However, against approaches which adopt a strategy of analysing Pacific Asia in terms derived unreflexively from the experience of the West, it can be suggested that a better grasp of the situation can be generated in terms of the exchange between shifting structural patterns within the global system and the ways in which local agent groups read and react to the opportunities/constraints thereby engendered.

The reordering of US links with Pacific Asia

The integration of Pacific Asia is likely to be a slow business. The linkages of the territories of Pacific Asia with the USA are likely to continue. However, it seems clear that the hegemonic position enjoyed by the USA during the period of the cold war is now in relative decline. There are two aspects to this issue: security and economics.

It is certainly the case that US strategic power was pre-eminent within the

Pacific Asian sphere. However, the reorientation of US concerns runs parallel to a regional concern to order security matters. The armed forces of Japan are strong and the armed forces of China are being modernized. At the same time the Asian tigers and the countries of ASEAN are upgrading their armed forces. In this context it would be true to say that the US is playing a more modest role although its key alliance with Japan remains fixed in place.

Thereafter, a new relationship centred on economic concerns is in the process of construction. The pre-eminent concern for strategic defence relationships has been replaced in recent years with a preoccupation with broader trade relations. It may be that the key institutional vehicle for ordering these complex relationships – region to region, and country to country – will be the APEC. It is within the context of a newly prominent concern for trade relations that the US can appear less evidently the premier country, simply because the Japanese economy is large and successful – as are the economies of most of the countries of the region.

The Processes of Reform in China

China was unified under the leadership of Mao Tse-tung in 1949 and there-after pursued a strategy of state-socialist development which had a particular stress on the role of the peasantry. After the death of Mao in 1976, and after a brief interval, Deng Xiao Ping came to power and in 1978 initiated a major economic reform programme. In the years following, the economy of China has grown rapidly within the general context of the Pacific Asia region. The response of various countries to the resurgence of China could be summa-rized around the presentation of a simple dilemma, which is that it is not clear whether Pacific Asia has a new economic tiger or a new China problem. However, it is economic success which is underpinning the growing military and diplomatic importance of China.

The economic reforms

Shibusawa et al.[29] report that the 1978 reforms initiated by Deng Xiao Ping looked to secure the four modernizations (agriculture, industry, science and defence) in order to achieve by the turn of the century a modest level of development in China. However, these efforts were not narrowly economic-technical, and indeed it can be argued that the whole process was driven by political commitment.[30] The story thereafter is one of burgeoning success coupled to internal social and political stress.

The reforms in the rural areas were initially successful. The rural pattern of cooperative farms was quickly abandoned and the farmers launched a variety of agricultural and industrial activities within the context of quite extensive social changes.[31] Shibusawa et al. note that the impact of the reforms on the images of China held in the region were positive, China looked as if it were becoming another developmental state.

The reform process in the industrial sector turned out to be more problematical. These industries were long established and closely integrated in the party/state apparatus. In this sector reform was difficult and slow. At the same time the coastal regions of China, where SEZs were permitted, have grown apace as foreign direct investment has been attracted. The economic reforms have had a mixed effect. There has been very rapid economic growth, but only in some geographical areas. There has been a sharp growth in inequality amongst the population. There has been a sharp growth in inequality across the regions of China with the coastal areas advancing much more rapidly than the rural hinterlands.[32] It is also clear that there have been problems of corruption and maladministration. The failure of attempts to secure change within the state economic sector, coupled to the avoidance of political reform to the party/state machinery, can be taken to have led to the political tensions which culminated in the Tiananmen Square débâcle.

In general it is clear that the reform process inaugurated by Deng Xiao Ping has led to significant economic advance, however in recent years in addition to the tensions noted above there have been three key features which commentators now routinely address: (i) the pronounced regional nature of the economic changes with coastal regions experiencing rapid growth, and significantly enhanced regional powers at the expense of Beijing, whilst the inner agricultural regions are rather left behind; (ii) the increasingly visible and vital linkages of the burgeoning coastal regions of China with the Pacific Asian region in general;[33] and (iii) the Chinese defence build-up in the context of post-cold war US retrenchments. In the future, commentators anticipate that the outward-directed development of China will continue, indeed it is said to be running somewhat out of control, and that social and political change are almost inevitable.

Diplomatic and security issues

It is in the light of these recorded economic successes that commentators suggest that a key issue for the future will be the way in which China orders its relationships with the Pacific region.[34] China has made it clear that it is committed to recovering what it regards as integral elements of China; not merely Hong Kong and Macau, but also Taiwan. The Chinese government has declined to rule out the use of force. At the same time the Chinese have lodged claims to large parts of the South China Seas where there are thought to be significant deposits of oil. It is also appropriate to note that the modernization of the defence forces proceeds apace, indeed the growth of the Chinese military is now a major concern within the region.

In all these cases there is a widespread view amongst Western and regional observers that the Chinese actions are significantly destabilizing. Their anxieties are underscored by a series of judgements in respect of the processes of change presently underway in China. The marketization of the country is taken to have undermined the commitment of elite and mass to the notion of socialism. In the case of the masses it is suggested that there is a return in progress to more traditional Chinese concerns of material security within the context of kin and clan networks. And in the case of the elite it is suggested that the diminution of the utility of the ethic of socialism is being addressed via the promulgation of an aggressive nationalism. At the same time observers add that matters are made much more problematical by the transfer of power in Beijing following the death of Deng Xiao Ping.

Within the region there have been a variety of responses. The countries of Southeast Asia have responded to the more outward-looking stance of the Chinese by upgrading their armed forces. The dispute about ownership of the Paracel and Spratley Islands continues.[35] The regional organization ASEAN is expanding with Vietnam joining in 1996, and Laos, Cambodia and Burma scheduled to join in 1997. Relatedly, the Taiwanese government continues to enjoy the support of the USA and continues to upgrade its military forces.

In the case of Japan, against an historical backdrop which includes both centuries of exchange where Japan was the cultural borrower, and a post-Meiji series of antagonisms culminating in the war of 1937–45, the linkages of the recent decade have been dominated by the pragmatics of economic expansion. At the same time it should be noted that Japan's armed forces are very significant and that although Japan is not a nuclear power it does possess all the requisite technologies and resources to become an independent nuclear power very quickly.

In a slightly wider context, the USA retains a security presence in the region. The USA has a key military alliance with Japan, where there is a major concentration of American forces. The USA continues to support South Korea and Taiwan and has more informal links with a number of Southeast Asian countries. The American presence is taken to be a force for stability although the depth of their commitment and its likely future duration are not perhaps as clear as they once were.

China into the 1990s

As the region reconfigures in the wake of the ending of the cold war the situation of China offers one major source of significant tension. The matter has been presented by Western commentators in terms of the choice between containing China on the one hand and drawing the country into the global system of states on the other. Many commentators take the view that containment is not a practical option. However, it is not clear how the second strategy might be accomplished. At the same time, the economic growth of China continues rapidly. It is too early to say whether or not the region has a new tiger or a new problem.

Conclusion

In the Pacific Asia region in the period following the Pacific War the USA exercised military and economic sway over the Western-oriented areas of the region whilst China was the dominant force within the inward-looking socialist bloc. Over the years a series of significant changes to this general pattern have occurred: first, the economic recovery of Japan; second, the shifting contribution of the USA; and third, the new openness of China. In general it can be asserted that Pacific Asia is becoming a coherent unit within the ever more integrated global system. It is also clear that for the foreseeable future Japan will be the core economy of Pacific Asia. However, these countries are diverse and any idea of regionalism must be handled carefully – the notion points to arrangements within the global system rather than separate from the system (regionalism is not old-style autarchy writ large).

Notes

1   With regard to the episode of war, these years are either ignored or taken as essentially unproblematical in the sense that states are taken to have wars and the Japanese state had one which it happened to lose. The idea that Japan was the aggressor and wrought unparalleled destruction across the area is not widely entertained. See I. Buruma 1994: *Wages of Guilt*, London: Cape.

2   R. P. Cronin 1992: *Japan, the United States and Prospects for the Asia-Pacific Century: Three Scenarios for the Future*, Singapore: Institute for Southeast Asian Studies.

3   Ibid., pp. 1–8.

4   Ibid., p. 8.

5   P. Phongpaichit 1990: *The New Wave of Japanese Investment in ASEAN*, Singapore: Institute for Southeast Asian Studies, p. 38.

6   Cronin 1992, pp. 29–39.

7   W. Dobson 1993: *Japan and East Asia: Trading and Investment Strategies*, Singapore: Institute for Southeast Asian Studies, p. 67.

8   P. Streeten 1994: The Role of Direct Foreign Investment in Developing Countries, in Sophia University, Tokyo, ADMP Series.

9   Phongpaichit 1990, pp. 10–19.

10   Dobson 1993.

11   Phongpaichit 1990, p. 23.

12   Ibid., pp. 33–8.

13   C. Hamilton 1983: Capitalist Industrialization in East Asia's Four Little Tigers in *Journal of Contemporary Asia* 13.

14   Phongpaichit 1990, pp. 69–81, 94–5.

15   A. Rix 1993: *Japan's Foreign Aid*, London: Routledge.

16   Ibid., p. 23.

17   Ibid., p. 140.

18   Ibid., p. 20.

19   R. M. Orr 1990: *The Emergence of Japan's Foreign Aid Power*, New York: Colombia University Press.

20 Dobson 1993.
21 B. M. Koppel and R. J. Orr, eds, 1993: *Japan's Foreign Aid: Power and Policy in a New Era*, Boulder, CO: Westview.
22 Rix 1993.
23 G. Kolko 1968: *The Politics of War: US Foreign Policy 1943–45*, New York: Vintage.
24 S. Pollard 1983: *The Development of the British Economy 1914-1980*, London: Arnold, pp. 238–9; E. A. Brett 1985: *The World Economy Since The War: The Politics of Uneven Development*, London: Macmillan.
25 W. McCord 1991: *The Dawn of the Pacific Century: Implications for Three Worlds of Development*, New Brunswick: Transaction.
26 E. Vogel 1980: *Japan as Number One*, Tokyo: Tuttle; L. Thurow 1994: *Head to Head: The Coming Economic Battle Among Japan, Europe and America*, New York: Morrow; J. C. Abegglen 1994: *Sea Change*, New York: Free Press.
27 S. P. Huntington 1993: The Clash of Civilizations in *Foreign Affairs*.
28 E. Wilkinson 1990: *Japan versus the West*, Harmondsworth: Penguin.
29 M. Shibusawa et al. 1992: *Pacific Asia in the 1990s*, London: Routledge.
30 J. Howell 1993: *China Opens Its Doors*, Hemel Hempstead: Harvester.
31 E. Croll 1994: *From Heaven to Earth: Images and Experiences of Development in China*, London: Routledge.
32 D. Goodman and G. Segal, eds, 1994: *China Deconstructs*, London: Routledge; G. Segal 1994 *China Changes Shape: Regionalism and Foreign Policy* (Adelphi Paper 287), London: International Institute for Strategic Studies.
33 J. Wong 1995: China in the Dynamic Pacific Asia Region in *The Pacific Review* 8(4); S. Breslin 1996: China in East Asia: The Process and Implications of Regionalisation in *The Pacific Review* 9(4).
34 For a brief overview see M. Yahuda 1996: *The International Politics of the Asia Pacific, 1945–1995*, London: Routledge, chapter 6.
35 L. T. Lee 1995: ASEAN and the South China Sea Conflict in *The Pacific Review* 8(3); J. N. Mak 1995: The ASEAN Naval Build-Up: Implications for Regional Order in *The Pacific*.

9

Contemporary Pacific Asia in the 1990s

Pacific Asia has emerged in a series of phases which can be noted in a series of key dates, including 1971, 1978, 1985 and 1991, and now constitutes one of the three major areas within the global industrial-capitalist system. In the years following the Plaza Accords the region has experienced rapid economic growth, a measure of social-institutional integration and a dawning sense of cultural coherence all of which were directly acknowledged following the end of the cold war and the related shift of policy attention away from geo-strategy towards geo-economics. Nonetheless, at the present time the region evidences certain disintegrative features. In all, there is a mix of progressive integrative economic success conjoined to both inherited and novel political disintegrative conflicts.

The Phases of Regional Dynamics

An historical structural analysis of the region which might be pursued in detail using the framework of international political economy offers a strategy to grasp the long-term historical dynamics of change. Regions are embedded within historical processes and analysis must deploy abstract ideas in specific contexts. It is clear that regions should be located at the intersection of global processes and more local formations. As Bernard states, regions 'must be understood precisely as a manifestation of global processes and of the way these processes assume concrete form in a world where power emanates from within historically constituted national social formations. Regions are thus co-determined by processes and social forces that operate transnationally and by the organisation of national communities'.[1] An historical structural analysis of Pacific Asia would look to the successive ways in which the region has been configured, and to the ways in which the peoples of the region have understood themselves and thereafter acted.

There have been four phases in the development of the region, and in each there has been a particular pattern of structural power, and an associated pattern of agent response. These relatively stable phases have been linked with periods of more rapid change as the system has reconfigured: (i) the first phase comprised four main areas having long established civilizations and patterns of interaction, including China, the Japanese islands, Indo-China and the islands of the archipelago; (ii) the second phase comprised six main interrelated areas within the industrial-capitalist colonial global system, including a Japanese sphere, an American sphere, a British sphere, a French sphere, a Dutch sphere, with China divided between these powers; (iii) the third phase comprised five main areas, divided into two interlinked groups, including Japan, the NICs, and Southeast Asia on the one hand, and China with Indo-China on the other; and finally (iv) the contemporary phase, the Pacific Asian region.

The Pacific Asia phase comprises an increasingly interrelated grouping of five main areas: Japan, the inner periphery of the NICs, the outer periphery of ASEAN, the reforming socialist bloc, and the linkages to Australia, New Zealand and the islands of the Pacific. The linkages between the various parts of the region are becoming extensive and deepening. The region has a core economy, extensive economic linkages, new political/trade mechanisms and a measure of cultural coherence. An integrated regional grouping can be taken to be in the process of formation, although the end point is unclear and the extent of integration should not be overstated.

Contemporary Regional Dynamics

The present regional Pacific Asian pattern owes much to the role of the USA in ordering the post-war world. The American security structure helped to shape the region such that regionalism was 'underpinned by a US security structure of bilateral alliances and region-wide military bases designed to prevent the spread of communism'.[2] The economy of Japan provided the core of a regionalized economy and the USA provided an open market for the region's export goods. The post-war period also allowed a distinctive form of production to become established as initially the Japanese economy was reconstructed as a state/business-dominated system oriented to dynamic growth and thereafter the pattern was reproduced throughout the region; in brief, 'developmental states' ordering 'developmental capitalisms'. Pacific Asia has seen the development of a series of economic networks, the rise of a new middle class and the continuing presence of significant numbers of rural and urban poor throughout the region.

Economic patterns

The regionalization was accomplished in the context of bipolarity and the post-colonial pursuit of development of a series of new countries. Various forms-of-life emerged as the ex-colonies looked to pursue effective nation statehood within the cold war divided region. The countries had different historical legacies, development dynamics or trajectories, and different links to regional neighbours and the USA. The result is a very diverse pattern:

'In Japan's former colonies, South Korea and Taiwan, the withdrawal of Japanese interests following its defeat in 1945, along with export promotion and state-allocated credit, created respective indigenous industrial capitalist classes that, although structurally different from one another, were protected by the state from the presence of foreign capital. The large scale vertically integrated conglomerates (chaebol) in Korea and the smaller-scale firms in Taiwan became linked to Japanese industry, often on the basis of personal relationships dating back to the colonial period, in production networks tied to Japanese supplies of key components, machinery, materials, marketing channels and technological trajectory. By comparison, in Southeast Asia post-colonial states, in most cases, coexisted with an ethnic Chinese commercial and financial bourgeoisie and the continued presence of capital from the former metropolis. Indigenous industrialization was weaker and state-imposed constraints on foreign capital, such as high tariffs, were intended more for the purpose of extracting rents than fostering local industry'.[3]

It is clear that within each of these broad spheres the mixture of local capital, state capital and foreign capital was different. In each sphere it was the precise mixture of economic interests which determined the initial limits of state-regime projects for development. Thereafter the broader international context further shaped the limits within which state-sponsored action could work. In due course these initial trajectories provided the context within which moves towards regional integration were to take place. It is clear, firstly, that the Northeast Asian NICs were encouraged by a mixture of established nascent industrial development, a legacy of colonial days, the presence of the USA, and the beginnings of Japanese recovery, and that they embarked upon industrialization programmes that had a significant measure of local capital participation. Then, secondly, in the sometime colonial territories of Southeast Asia local capital was less significant as the economies had developed, in general, as primary product exporters, often controlled by metropolitan trading companies. At the same time, the networks of commercial capital were extensively controlled by minority groups, in particular the overseas Chinese, whose concerns were with trade. In the case of the countries of Southeast Asia, and the 'southern' NICs of Hong Kong and Singapore, industrial and commercial development were to come later and to have significantly different characteristics. With the exception of Hong Kong where migrant Chinese capital was to play a central role, along with long established colonial trading companies, industrial and commercial economic growth was to be ordered by foreign MNCs, from the USA and in particular Northeast Asia, indeed critics have spoken of 'ersatz capitalism'.[4]

The region presently evidences a diversity of economic forms. In the advanced industrial areas large hi-tech firms supplied by local specialist companies and often supported by local states operate competitively within the global industrial-capitalist system. From this perspective the region presents itself as a network of sub-regional urban areas stretching from the islands of Japan, down the Chinese seaboard and into Southeast Asia. At the same time, a parallel line of development can be discerned as the great urban areas of China and Southeast Asia draw in migrant populations from their underdeveloped rural hinterlands, who find low-paid unskilled employment in low-tech manufacturing, services and the burgeoning informal sectors. Thereafter, much of the population of the region remains within the rural areas where long established agricultural economies continue.[5]

One aspect of the recent economic growth in the region has been the process of the dispersal of economic power throughout the societies. At the end of the Pacific War political and economic power were redistributed. The post-colonial political elites were clearly new, yet perforce operating within existing domestic, regional and global structural configurations. In the economic sphere the situation was more complex as state-regimes looked to manage the divergent concerns of foreign and domestic capital along with the demands and aspirations of their own peoples. The pursuit of economic growth in the region was routinely sponsored by the state and intimate relations developed between the state and the various economic groups represented within their domestic arenas. In the post-war period state capital, domestic capital and foreign capital looked to the state machine for assistance and the policy strategies were generally corporatist, and economic advance was oriented to building nations rather than allowing free markets to flourish spontaneously. In recent years domestic economic success has issued in shifting class patterns; in particular, there is a new Asian middle class.[6]

The new middle classes can be taken to comprise a series of streams, but in broad terms there is a new bourgeoisie owning property and a new middle class with intellectual skills which can be deployed in the employment market. In both cases there are new schedules of consumption and new patterns of politics. It would be wrong to say that new economic prosperity entails new more liberal political action, but the emergent new middle classes must now be taken into account by established state-regimes.

It is clear that the extent of regional advance should be carefully specified. The pattern of regional production which emerged in Northeast Asia in the 1970s as the Japanese economy began its expansion only came to include some parts of Southeast Asia after the 1985 Plaza Accords revalued the yen. In other words, the regional pattern is a recent and restricted achievement in terms of the extent of its development and the range of its participants. Nonetheless, recent economic advance 'has fostered an awareness of the regional nature of production, particularly through the crystallisation of a region-wide bloc of state and business elites and a cadre of technicians who have been the prime beneficiaries of regionalized manufacturing'.[7]

However the Japan-centred industrial production network is not the only one. As we noted earlier, in the long period before the eruption of industrial-capitalism into the region there were a series of trading networks taking in Arab, Indian, Malay and Chinese traders. In the colonial period these networks were submerged within the new structural configuration, however the economic practice of indigenous peoples intersected effectively with the industrial-capitalist networks in a number of ways as local people responded to new opportunities. One particular role linked the local economic trading networks with those of the incoming representatives of industrial-capitalism, and in China and Southeast Asia the role of middleman was played by Chinese merchants. In contemporary Pacific Asia 'networks of Chinese commercial capital initially originating in Hong Kong and Taiwan but increasingly spreading throughout Southeast Asia are now forging regional structures built around different kinds of economic activity – such as those related to agribusiness, property development or services – with different spatial contours including a proliferation of ties with state and party elites in coastal China'.[8]

It might also be noted, however, cutting against these records of success, that much of the Pacific Asia region has an essentially peasant agricultural base. In these parts of the region, in China, Indo-China and Southeast Asia, much of the population remains poor relative to the more affluent inhabitants of the area; indeed, much of the region displays all the familiar traits of under-development: the disruption of relatively settled forms-of-life, rural-urban migration and the proliferation of novel patterns of life as people and groups adjust to the intrusive demands of industrial-capitalism.[9]

Cultural patterns

On the basis of political economic integration it has been argued that Pacific Asian civil society is developing. A series of elements can be cited, including 'the diffusion of information, popular culture, urban consumerism, the proliferation of intra-regional mass tourism'.[10] It is these networks of information, activity and recreation which together facilitate the emergence of a regional sense of identity. It is the mixture of economic networks, institutional structures and cultural identification which together build towards the construction of an 'imagined community', a self-identification as 'Asians'.

An aspect of these changes is the emergence of a new Asian middle class which displays in various ways many of the concerns for consumption familiar in the developed industrial-capitalist countries. A related issue is the way in which these consumption patterns are read into Western debate, where the new rich of Asia have been presented as both the crucial new market for Western exporters and as evidence of an inherent economic dynamism which will provide the locomotive for the global economy in the twenty-first century. Robison and Goodman speak of a 'cargo-cult mentality'[11] in some sections of Western commentary. A measured social scientific analysis reveals a complex pattern of new consumption patterns and equally complex relationships between changing class composition, rising consumption and patterns of political reform.

It has been suggested more particularly that Japanese popular culture is being diffused throughout the region, however it is necessary to look at how local areas are located within regional patterns. There are flows of consumption styles through the region which have Japanese, Chinese and American sources, and in each case the reception of any inherent cultural messages is achieved in terms of the logics of local cultures.

In general terms, a movement towards a common civil society could include: (i) regionalized urban spaces, such that the cities of the region have increasingly common patterns of production and consumption; (ii) regionalized tourism, for example intra-regional travel and the passion for golf amongst newly-affluent elites; and (iii) the networks of Chinese urban bourgeoisie which stretch through much of the region. But all this is tentative and speculative. Bernard[12] suggests that whilst there has been a growth in interconnectedness within the region the prospects for further integration are fraught with difficulties. Yet in debates about the nature of the region a particular cultural claim has been made about 'Asian values', where these are taken to be peculiar to the region.

In the context of scholarly historical work, the territory of theories about civilizations and societies is awkward as it involves making very broad comparisons between cultural spheres and claiming a received cultural coherence for what might in practice be large diverse areas. In the case of Pacific Asia there have been many attempts to distinguish the putatively typically Asian from the typically Western, indeed these attempts date from the nineteenth century when the driving logic of industrial-capitalist expansion first brought significant numbers of European and American traders to Asia.[13] It is, of course, easy to record the differences in the forms-of-life found within the region and to draw broad contrasts with the patterns familiar within the West; this is, after all, the familiar territory of anthropology. However, the next step in the argument, the move to a claim to the natural 'givenness' of recorded differences is rather contentious. The current balance of opinion within the classical tradition of social theorizing would probably want to insist upon the contingent social nature of all forms-of-life.

In the case of contemporary Pacific Asia it is worth noting that there is an indigenous line of resistance to Western political ideas expressed via the notion of Asian values, which reports that the societies of Asia are more naturally consensual than the individualistic societies of the West, and that this finds appropriate expression in disciplined hierarchical polities. This argument has been vigorously advanced in public debate by figures such as Lee Kuan Yew and Dr Mahathir, and they have made these claims on the basis of sometimes sharp criticisms of the West. In the same vein an influential external view of Asia has characterized it as a coherent cultural bloc along with several others, all of which are taken by the author, Huntington, to be potential competitors with the West.

Robison[14] has reviewed this area of debate in a rather different way and considered the ways in which these debates play within domestic Asian and Western intellectual, business and political circles. In other words, Robison pulls back from the substantive claims and considers the material interests of the various participants. The ideological critique suggests that what is at issue here has little to do with any social-scientifically plausible characterization of Asian societies and much more to do with the rhetorical needs of various participants as they pursue quite particular interests. In the case of Asian proponents the rhetoric serves to deflect the criticisms of foreign and domestic critics, and in the case of Western proponents the rhetoric serves selectively to read the Asian experience into Western debates such that the domestic agendas of the business world are advanced. In all these debates, the social scientific substance takes second place to the demands of various rhetorics. In general, on all this, more measured analyses point to the particularity of the historical development experience of Asia,[15] note the utility of the claim for the region's more authoritarian leaderships and record the usefulness of the misreadings of Asia for Western conservatives and market liberals.

Overall, the Pacific Asian region does evidence an increasingly self-conscious integration. However, in looking at the development of the region it is clear that there are also problems: (i) local production fits into a Japan-centred hierarchy and this creates dependence as Japanese keep control; (ii) regional production has required local political and class patterns to be fixed in place and this inevitably creates tensions; (iii) there are ethnic tensions within regional production as some groups are seen to be advantaged relative to others; (iv) in Japan there are the problems of rich country/poor people; (v) there is also the tension created by the region's exports in particular to the USA; and (vi) there is the question of the growing power of China.

The Future of the Region

As the region becomes more integrated a series of questions have been raised and these cluster around a series of interlinked concerns: (i) the problem of integrating the powerful countries within the region including the possible political leadership role of Japan, the role of China and the related diminution of the role of the USA; (ii) the evolution of the position of the USA which is the key trading partner and security guarantor for the region; and (iii) the business of ordering the multiplicity of economic linkages within a large diverse area.

The Japanese core, regional integration and problems of leadership

After the Meiji restoration the Japanese government sought to strengthen the economy as the basis for a strong country able to join the modern world on terms of equality with the West. The objective required both resources from the Asian region and an appropriate framework for securing these resources. In the late nineteenth century these matters were construed in terms of spheres of influence and a Japanese empire in Asia was constructed which survived until 1945. Thereafter, the ongoing concern of the Japanese government for security and equality has found expression in commerce. The schedule of war reparations was dealt with in terms of the export of goods (rather than the transfer of existing machinery or cash) and this assisted the recovery of Japanese industry and helped secure influence within the region. As the Japanese economy was rebuilt, so too were commercial relationships. A new departure for the Japanese government was economic aid to developing countries. The aid was concentrated in Asia and typically tied to Japanese suppliers.[16] Over the years a parallel process of aid-financed infrastructural work and private foreign direct investment developed. The Japanese aid strategy within Asia was criticized, but these activities began the process of laying the basis of an integrated regional economy.[17] This process received further encouragement with the 1985 Plaza Accords which revalued the yen against the US dollar and provoked a wave of Japanese foreign direct investment in the Asian region as manufacturers moved to escape the effects of the revaluation.[18] It has been argued that the Japanese ideal is of an integrated and complementary regional division of labour, which should flow from the revealed comparative advantage held by each country (in other words, Japan is the advanced core and the other countries are variously materials suppliers and providers of lower technology manufactures).[19]

A series of quite particular relationships between Japan and the various countries in the region can be identified.[20] In the first place, Japan's relationship with the four tigers (Singapore, Hong Kong, Korea and Taiwan) is complementary-competitive. They are relatively advanced and have trade surpluses with the USA and deficits with Japan. Singapore and Hong Kong are largely production platforms for exports to third countries and have very high deficits with Japan. Taiwan and Korea have a broader trade exchange with Japan. Then in the second place Japan's relation with Southeast Asia and China is skewed but complementary. Japan traditionally had a trade deficit with Southeast Asia as it imported raw materials but in recent years there has been a surplus as Southeast Asia takes more manufactured goods; some of which are components for products to be exported. Relatedly, in the case of China, Japan has a large trade deficit. However, this exchange is at a relatively early stage given cold war problems over many years. And finally, Japan's relationship with Australasia is complex and multi-faceted; Australisia comprises sophisticated industrial-capitalist countries. Japan takes raw materials from Australia and primary products from New Zealand; thereafter there are a range of exchanges with tourism, real-estate, and manufactures.

It has been argued that Japan can constitute the core of the region but that the region's export-dependency on the USA means that the region cannot become a closed bloc.[21] This claim is misleading because it is unlikely that any bloc within the regionalized global system would pursue rigorously exclusionary policies. It is more useful to think in terms of regional integration and autonomy, the power to identify and pursue a distinctive route to the future, and this requires leadership.

In recent years the possibility of the Japanese assuming a leadership role in Pacific Asia has been considered but the results of debate have proved inconclusive. A series of inhibitions to any leadership role have been identified (historical memories within the region, unclear objectives within the Japanese polity and the continuing foreign policy links with the Americans), yet it remains the case that the Japanese economy is the regional core.

The position of China within the region

The role of a resurgent China is a key issue. The economic power of China is at present slight as they have many poor people in what remains in large measure an agricultural economy, but the economy is growing very quickly. Goodman reports that the economy has grown 'at an average rate of about 9 per cent a year from 1978 to 1991'.[22] It seems likely that the Chinese economy will attain a global significance within a relatively few years.

The Chinese development strategy borrowed heavily from the experience of the Asian NICs in general and Japan in particular.[23] The East Asian strategy of the state sponsored pursuit of economic growth oriented to export markets has provided the general model, a way of realizing the goal of raising the level of living of the Chinese population whilst retaining an authoritarian central political control, whilst the Japanese state's involvement in directing economic activity via MITI has provided an attractive model for the reform of the extant state-socialist pattern of development. The Pacific Asian model of economic growth, social control and political-cultural conservatism has proved congenial to the Chinese state-regime. It has also clearly proved to be extensively successful although there are at the same time significant problems.

At the present time economic activity is concentrated in the coastal cities, and has created growth, inequality, corruption and a heavy rural-urban migration (with attendant social problems of unemployment and crime). Goodman and Segal[24] have argued that the nature of the development experience of China in the years following Deng's reforms is such that the centre is being weakened at the expense of the peripheries. The detail of the argument has been unpacked by Segal[25] who records the process of the devolution of powers from the metropolitan centre to the regional level and adds that it is difficult to see how this shift in patterns of power could be reversed.

There is also a Chinese diaspora in Asia. It might be recalled that the nineteenth century saw large flows of migration from southern China towards the south where they lived and worked within the expanding colonial economies of the region, as labourers, servants, farmers and traders. The flows of

migrants continued until 1940.[26] It is the role of merchant which has proved
to be of greatest contemporary interest. It is possible to bundle together the
overseas Chinese and the affluent mainlanders of the SEZs and identify
thereby a large, prosperous and influential population. The role of the overseas Chinese networks were noted above and in respect of China they serve
to feed in large amounts of foreign direct investment and to provide a strong
commercial network which runs through the region. Taylor[27] has identified
a southern sub-regional area encompassing Taiwan, Hong Kong, the coastal
provinces of southern China, and thereafter Singapore and the overseas
Chinese scattered throughout the ASEAN countries.

Hong Kong is a quite particular case. The city began to develop in the
nineteenth century under British colonial rule. In the late nineteenth and
twentieth centuries it prospered as a colonial trading port, a major European
gateway to China. In the years following the 1949 victory of Mao the city
developed further, receiving a substantial inflow of capital and people. Over
the long post-war period the city has experienced strong economic growth.
It is now a key location within the broad southern China sub-region and a
key nexus within the global industrial-capitalist system. The transfer of power
in 1997 from the departing colonial authorities to China was accomplished
within the general framework of the policy known as 'one country, two
systems'. The official Chinese declarations state that Hong Kong SAR is to
enjoy a large measure of autonomy such that its form of life will be protected
for fifty years. In reality, the future of Hong Kong will be bound up with the
future of southern China, itself dependent upon relations with the centre in
Beijing. At the present time the economy of Hong Kong spills over into
Guandong Province and is a major source of capital for the region's growth,
and there is little reason to suppose that this economic dynamism will either
slacken or loose those unfortunate economic and social side effects which
have become apparent in other areas of China.[28]

In the region, and wider global system, the political influence of China is
growing. In line with the four modernizations specified by Deng Xiao Ping
China is upgrading its military forces. It has claims on Taiwan (and has not
ruled out the use of force to secure them), a series of oil-rich islands in the
South China Sea and has unresolved border disputes with a number of other
neighbours. The Chinese military build-up is causing unease throughout the
region and has met with a twofold response in the countries of ASEAN: first,
an increase in membership of the organization which has brought in Vietnam,
Cambodia, Laos and Burma, such that all the southern Pacific Asian countries
bordering China are now lodged within the one sub-regional organization;
and second, the purchase of significant quantities of new advanced military
equipment. In the northern parts of the region adjoining China, the countries
of Northeast Asia, Taiwan, South Korea and Japan have long had very strong
defence forces and all enjoy defence linkages with the USA.[29]

The position of a resurgent China within the international system has been
grasped in conventional international relations terms as offering regional and

Western governments a dilemma between integration and containment, but it would seem to be clear that the only plausible strategy is one of integration and this is likely to entail some accommodation towards the requirements of the regime in Beijing.

The role of the USA within the region: engagement and distance

In the main tradition of international relations there are available theories which look to the necessary logics of inter-state relations, in particular realist analyses which are influential within the USA and which look to the ways in which states pursue their interests within the unregulated inter-state system. This strategy of analysis generates the view that global or regional stability requires a hegemonic power. In Pacific Asia the security system which was in place over the long years of the cold war did see two major powers confronting each other and USA hegemony within the richer market-oriented sphere. In the cold war period the role of the USA within the region was clear; a matter of security plus an open market. However, the security role is now being reworked in a context where China, the prospective regional opponent, is nonetheless lodged within an integrating economic region where US economic linkages in the present and in the future are important. At the present time the precise manner in which the USA will approach the region is unclear but it can be recalled that the key regional ally and trading partner of the USA is Japan. It is unlikely that this will alter in the immediate future.

In the post-cold war period there has been a shift away from geo-strategy towards geo-economics, and in the case of Pacific Asia it is possible to point to regional organizations, often including the USA, which acknowledge the sphere of economic exchange, however, it would be true to say that the extent of formal regional integration remains slight. The future role of the USA within the region is a key issue. In the post-Second World War period the USA contained China and assisted the economic growth of capitalist Pacific Asia. The USA economy now has some problems – hence tensions about trade – and they cannot and do not want to contain China, but it is not clear how China can be eased into the established international system, and so there are, for example, great tensions around the question of China's involvement in the WTO. At the same time there are tensions about the Japanese trade surplus with the USA.

In general, whilst the US does remain engaged in the region the nature of that involvement is changing.[30] The overall US strategy has been presented as tripartite, with APEC securing an open trading regime in Asia, NAFTA doing the same in Latin America, and NATO/OECD securing the continuing influence of the US in Europe, with the new international body of the WTO securing the whole apparatus. In this optimistic scenario the linking point of the three spheres is Washington.

The present limits of integration

It can be argued that the global industrial-capitalist system is presently reconfiguring in the form of a tripolar regional pattern. It is evident that regional integration has been extensively secured in North America. It is equally evident that the project of the European Union has secured a measure of integration in the economic, social and cultural spheres. However, it is equally clear that there is a much lower level, or extent, of integration within Pacific Asia.

A series of comments might be made: (i) we can note the diversity of the region in terms of received historical structural configurations (there are different mixes of economies, societies and cultures in different parts of the region); (ii) there are relatedly a diversity of particular historical development trajectories in the region, a series of different and continuing routes to the future, and there is no particular guarantee that these routes will converge at some point in the near future; (iii) it is within the context of this received diversity and difference in historical paths that contemporary problems find expression (problems of economic development, problems of inter-racial exchanges where differing communities order their social affairs differently and problems with inter-cultural exchanges); (iv) yet working against received diversity and contemporary problems are structural forces for integration; and (v) these find expression in social practices, institutions and sets of ideas (which once again are not unproblematical as there are diverse ways of articulating a vision for the future of the region).

(i) Diversity of received economic, social and cultural structures
A recent anthropological text on Pacific Asia spoke of the Asian cultural mosaic.[31] It is true that the region embraces a wide diversity of forms-of-life and these fundamental anthropological differences, as they were modified in the long exchange with colonial tutelage, carry over into the present day, along with the residues of the colonial era and the pattern of adjustments to the demands of the present day. The region is thus economically diverse (with patterns of livelihood ranging from peasant farming, through urban petty trade, to fordist manufacturing, high tech and service industries); socially diverse (with a mix of traditional, modern and postmodern social forms); and culturally diverse (as the resources of long established cultural and ethnic groups mix and meld with the secular materialism of the interdependent global industrial-capitalist system). The scope for confusion, conflict and disharmony within the region is clearly very great and these circumstances circumscribe the projects of key agents, including state-regimes looking to associate themselves with a wider notion of Pacific Asia.

(ii) Diversity of historical trajectories
The countries of the region have followed a diversity of historical routes to the modern world and these have lodged, within established practices and

institutions, particular sets of expectations about how the world works and how local territories can plausibly fit within it; in other words, a series of modes of production with associated modes of regulation. These received historical trajectories cannot be altered at will and they do limit the possibilities of political action; for example the inability of Singapore and Malaysia to make their union work in the early sixties owed something to local politics and a lot to structural economic patterns and associated practices and expectations. In Pacific Asia there are a diversity of established historical trajectories and this implies that any integrative process will move slowly.[32]

(iii) Contemporary problems
There has been a growth in interconnectedness within the region but the prospects for further deeper integration are fraught with difficulties and tensions. Problems/contradictions: (i) local production fits into a Japan-centred hierarchy and this creates dependence as the Japanese keep control, and there are related financial problems with debts denominated in yen; (ii) regional production has required that local political and class patterns be fixed in place and this inevitably creates tensions; (iii) there are ethnic tensions within regional production as some groups are seen to be advantaged relative to others; (iv) in Japan there are the problems of rich country/poor people; and (v) there is also the tension created by the region's exports, in particular to the USA.

(iv) Integrative forces
The region is now extensively linked to the global industrial-capitalist system and inevitably a series of structural flows of power run through the region. A structuralist, international political economy argument would read these structural forces as the occasion for regionalization as local agents respond in order to plot new routes to new futures. It is this body of argument which has informed the discussion in this text.

(v) Institutional mechanisms
The structural pressure for integration has found institutional expression in a series of regional bodies. Indeed, the region now boasts a plethora of acronyms, including ASEAN, AFTA, APEC, and EAEC. These bodies have been established by the various countries of the region and represent ordered diplomatic spaces within which the future direction of the region might be discussed and sketched out. It is clear that the future of the region is heavily contested and that there are a series of versions of the future on offer. The US vision is of an open liberal trading area. In contrast the Malaysian state-regime has proposed a more restricted vision, an Asia for Asians. The Japanese are taken to be caught between Asia and the West, and the whole endeavour is complicated by the pace of economic advance in China. It is likely that the institutional mechanisms which are presently being established within the region will in many instances perform a simple consultative function. The

more detailed links are being made in the economic sphere, at a level away from the realm of high politics. It is certainly the case that the Pacific Asia region is not likely in the foreseeable future to attain anything resembling the integration of the European Union, much less that of US-dominated North America.

Conclusion

A series of points can be made: (i) the region is culturally diverse and has recorded a series of routes to the modern world; (ii) the contemporary situation within Pacific Asia remains diverse; (iii) there is strong pressure towards regional integration; and (iv) the end point of any integration is presently unclear. Overall, it is quite clear that the region is economically vigorous and, notwithstanding some doubts as to the explanation of its prosperity, there is no reason to suppose that the dynamism will slacken. It is upon this basis that observers of the region anticipate that it will experience continuing success.

Notes

1   M. Bernard 1996: Regions in the Global Political Economy in *New Political Economy*, p. 340.
2   Ibid., p. 342.
3   Ibid., p. 342–3.
4   K. Yoshihara 1988: *The Rise of Ersatz Capitalism in Southeast Asia*, Oxford University Press.
5   J. Rigg 1997: *Southeast Asia: The Human Landscape of Modernization and Development*, London: Routledge.
6   R. Robison and D. Goodman, eds, 1996: *The New Rich in Asia: Mobile Phones, McDonald's and Middle-Class Revolution*, London: Routledge.
7   Bernard 1996, p. 343.
8   Ibid.
9   The status of the debate about development is also difficult. A critical voice is M. Hobbart, ed., 1993: *An Anthropological Critique of Development*, London: Routledge; and a sanguine celebration of the modernization of the region is offered by Rigg 1997.
10 Bernard 1996, p. 346.
11 Robison and Goodman 1996, p. x.
12 Bernard 1996.
13 E. Wilkinson 1990: *Japan Versus the West*, Harmondsworth: Penguin; J. Goody 1996: *The East in the West*, Cambridge: Cambridge University Press.
14 R. Robison, ed., 1996: *Pathways to Asia: The Politics of Engagement*, St Leonards: Allen and Unwin, see chapter one.
15 In the case of Singapore two such pieces have recently been presented: Robert Bartley et al. 1993: *Democracy and Capitalism: Asian and American Perspectives*, Singapore: Institute of Southeast Asian Studies, chapter one; B. H.

Chua 1995: *Communitarian Ideology and Democracy in Singapore*, London: Routledge.

16   A. Rix 1993: *Japan's Foreign Aid*, London: Routledge.

17   D. Yasutomo 1986: *The Manner of Giving*, Lexington: Heath.

18   P. Phongpaichit 1990: *The New Waves of Japanese Investment in ASEAN*, Singapore: Institute for Southeast Asian Studies.

19   R. P. Cronin 1992: *Japan, the United States and the Prospects for the Asia Pacific Century*, Singapore: Institute for Southeast Asian Studies.

20   Ibid.

21   Ibid.

22   D. Goodman 1996: The People's Republic of China: Party-State, Capitalist Revolution and New Entrepreneurs in R. Robison and D. Goodman, eds, p. 227.

23   Ibid. Also R. Taylor 1996: *Greater China and Japan: Prospects for an Economic Partnership in East Asia*, London: Routledge.

24   D. Goodman and G. Segal, eds, 1994: *China Deconstructs: Politics, Trade and Regionalism*, London: Routledge.

25   G. Segal 1994: *China Changes Shape: Regionalism and Foreign Policy* (Adelphi Paper 287), London: International Institute for Strategic Studies.

26   L. Pan 1990: *Sons of the Yellow Emperor: The Story of the Overseas Chinese*, London: Mandarin.

27   Taylor 1996.

28   A general review is offered by M. Yahuda 1995: *Hong Kong: China's Challenge*, London: Routledge.

29   R. Thompson 1994: *The Pacific Basin since 1945*, London: Longman; M. Yahuda 1996: *The International Politics of the Asia-Pacific, 1945–1995*, London: Routledge.

30   M. Yahuda 1996: *The International Relations of the Asia-Pacific, 1945–1995*.

31   G. Evans ed. 1993: *Asia's Cultural Mosaic: An Anthropological Introduction*, Singapore: Prentice-Hall.

32   The matter of harmonization of divergent historical trajectories has figured before in the general process of the global shift to the modern world. In the case of the USA in the nineteenth century it is generally taken to have precipitated the civil war (B. Moore 1996) and in the present case of the European Union opponents of the process of integration routinely cite the problems associated with differences in economic levels of living.

Part IV

The Development Experience of Pacific Asia

10

The Particularity of the Historical Development Experience of Pacific Asia

The countries of Pacific Asia have been the subject of much recent commentary. The apparent emergence of a coherent Pacific Asian regional economy which matches in broad outline the potency of the European and American economies has occasioned extensive debate. Yet the nature of the economies, societies, cultures and polities of the countries of the region have been considered over a longer period, and the preoccupations of the participants of these older debates find new expression within current debate. In the light of contemporary concerns it can be suggested that a common area of interest has been the historical development experience of these countries, where this would include the reconstruction of Japan, the drive for socialist development in China, the dynamics of the rapid growth of the NICs, and the pursuit of post-colonial national development in Southeast Asia.

In reviewing these debates it is clear that the issue of the nature of the dynamics of complex change in Asia is a highly contested one with participants taking up sharply differing positions. We can take note of the scope of these debates, and note the particular contribution which can be made in terms of the resources of the classical tradition of social theorizing.

The early development theorists considered the records of the sometime colonial territories of the region and spoke of the successful pursuit of effective nation statehood. The work is an instance of a wider body of work concerned with the shift within the Third World from traditional to modern societies, that is modernization theory. It is also true that modernization theory in turn can be slotted into a broader package of ideas influential within the US sphere in the immediate post-Second World War period linking modernization, the convergence of East and West and the anticipated end of ideology to the putative fundamental logic of industrialism. The work retains a residual/continuing influence and has been used to analyse Pacific Asia, where the evolutionary achievment of modernization is recorded.

The more explicitly market-liberal theorists, concerned initially with the rise of the NICs, have read the success of market economies within the region as confirmation of the veracity of neo-classical analyses and policy strategies derived therefrom. The market-liberal work has been hugely influential in Anglo-American public debate over the 1980s and the proponents of the free-market model have perforce been obliged to address the record of Pacific Asia, which it is claimed exemplifies the vigour of minimally regulated capitalism.

However, we can argue against both these two of lines of analysis that an examination of the record of Pacific Asia in terms informed by the classical tradition of social theorizing reveals a much more complex story of global structural changes and local agent responses.

The Early Analyses of the Orthodox Development Theorists

In the post-Second World War period as the European, American and Japanese empires were dismantled social theorists turned to the task of analysing the processes of national development. An elaborate body of theoretical material was assembled and was used to provide advice to those concerned with development within the new nations, international organizations and commercial operations. In the literature of development theory the goal which was imputed to the replacement elites of the new nation states can be characterized as the pursuit of effective nation statehood, which unpacks as the search for cultural coherence, political stability and economic progress. The orthodox theorists of development would read the recent historical experience of the countries of Pacific Asia in terms of their having successfully secured effective nation statehood. However, there are problems and they reside in the spread of assumptions affirmed, the notion of what it is to be 'developed' which lies at the heart of the approach. In the end the orthodoxy produces subtle mis-descriptions.

In the first place the search for cultural coherence has been understood by orthodox development theorists in terms of the construction of nation statehood. Yet it is clear that nation statehood is an historically novel form of socio-political organization. The ideas were formulated in the Enlightenment and given first expression in the republics created in the Americas from territories which had belonged to much broader geographical empires. It is here that notions of territorial sovereignty and a common community of free citizens find their first expression. The model was then shifted back into western Europe and thence, by various means, to the rest of the world.[1] In the post-Second World War period we have witnessed the spread of this socio-political form through the process of decolonization.

In the developed countries the experience of nation statehood is largely taken for granted, however for the countries of Pacific Asia nation states are historically novel. In general terms the pre-colonial polities were not nation states and new elites have faced the task of nation-building. It can be argued that many of these new nation states are best seen as political projects which are yet to be completed. More sceptically one can doubt whether all regional political elites are necessarily concerned with effective nation statehood. And in terms of common experience, whilst the public politics of nationalism might be familiar there is reason to doubt that sentiments of nationality are deeply felt. In the ethnographically complex regions which comprise the Pacific Asia region there are loyalties which are older and run deeper than nation, most obviously those of family, kin networks and wider cultural communities.

The new elites have exerted power and deployed ideology to secure their positions, and orthodox development theorists have read this as an aspect of the process of the pursuit of effective nation statehood, but the reality is much more complex. Orthodox development theory has typically taken political and cultural coherence to be either a spontaneously occurring adjunct to development-in-general, or rather more plausibly, as a matter for the elite to engineer. In this context, long established forms-of-life identified by anthropologists, for example, present themselves as problems for political elites and theorists committed to a national coherence. The elite groups in Pacific Asia have pursued a variety of goals and we can speculate that their prime commitment has been to the maintenance of a variety of status quos which have ensured their positions of power. Thereafter they may act in line with the demands of effective nation statehood, for example the Asian NICs, or almost wholly ignore them, for example the assorted military dictatorships in the Pacific Asia region over the post-war era.

The second task indentified by orthodox theorists of development looked to elites to secure political stability. In new nation states there is much scope for conflict as disparate groups are moulded by a new elite towards the objective of a single community. The search for stability by the replacement elite requires mechanisms to engineer political and social stability. These mechanisms both replace, or refashion, familiar colonial arrangements, with their attached patterns of conflict, and are contested in practice as groups manoeuvre for advantageous positions. The orthodox development goal of liberal democracy with its multi-party competition has not generally been pursued by elites in the Pacific Asia region who have generally preferred more authoritarian political models.

Political and social conflict within Pacific Asian nations has been significant in the post-colonial period, and the authoritarian response of governments has become commonplace. Outside commentators of the orthodox view have seen these conflicts as regrettable disturbances serving only to distract the attention of ruling elites from the problems of the pursuit of development. Yet less sanguine observers have doubted the commitment to development of more than a few of the Pacific Asian region's elites. Overall, of the triune task allotted by the orthodox view to these replacement elites, coherence, stability, and development, it is surely the power aspects of one and two – securing a territory – which have concerned them most.

The third task identified by orthodox theorists centred on the pursuit of economic growth. The first generation nationalist leaders of the new nation states of the Pacific Asian region typically affirmed ideologies of national development which lodged claims to nation statehood as a prerequisite to economic development and social welfare. Indeed many first generation leaders were steeped in European and American political and social philosophy as a result of contacts with the institutions of control and authority maintained by colonial rulers – schools, missions, universities, administrations. However, subsequent commentators have come to doubt not merely the technical efficiency of the replacement elites of the Pacific Asia region but their actual commitment to orthodox development goals.

In the wake of the Pacific War, development was construed in largely technical terms. All this was expressed in Keynesian terms and the key role of capital investment was stressed as was the requirement of state planning. The route to the future for the countries of Pacific Asia involved industrialization as economies based centrally on industrial production for the marketplace were to replace the largely agricultural peasant economies. It is clear that the approach rested upon a quite particular set of culturally specific assumptions.

In the first place economic rationality was assumed to be a common trait of human beings, and it was supposed that all human beings could be construed as egocentric satisfaction maximizers, but in reality patterns of economic activity are hedged about with myriad social rules and cultural assumptions.[2] The ideal of economic rationality affirmed by orthodox market-liberal economics is both culture-specific and ideological. A distinctively Anglo-Saxon notion of economic rationality was taken to be common to all humanity. The early modernization theorists managed to muddy the issue further by talking of irrational traditionalism. Then, similarly, the ethical desire for unlimited consumption was assumed to be universal, whereas it is specific to Western capitalism, as the idea that human beings can with ethical propriety nurse unrestricted consumption desires was first presented in seventeenth-century English political philosophy.[3] European thinkers had earlier supposed that human morality entailed curbing, for a variety of reasons, such greed. And finally, a general cultural impulse to technological innovation was supposed, and in the West economic growth feeds from natural scientific research. However whilst it is true that cultures other than European have contributed to the creation of modern natural science, and whilst all cultures must perforce acknowledge the intellectual and productive potency of that mode of thinking, it is now the case that natural scientific power is concentrated almost entirely in the West.

Overall, the economic, social, intellectual and political circumstances of the post-Second World War period generated the goal of the pursuit of effective nation statehood. The ideal unpacks into three spheres: the search for political and cultural coherence; the search for political and social stability; and finally, the pursuit of development, usually read as growth and welfare. The resultant model of 'development' assimilates to the particular experience of the western countries the diverse historical development experience of the countries of Latin America, Africa and Pacific Asia. It is an unreflexive analytical strategy. Against these simplifications (no matter how detailed their technical elaboration), it is clear that in the post-colonial territories of Pacific Asia the tasks of the replacement elites were particular and specific. The patterns of colonial withdrawal varied and the subsequent development experiences of the countries of the region were similarly varied. If there was a common thread to the experience in the early post-Second World War years it was the dominance by the region of the double core of the USA and Japan. However, against the sanguine expectations of the orthodox theorists in the evolutionary convergence of the societies of the region upon the Western model of a liberal-democratic industrial society, it must be insisted that the reality is much more complex. The activities of replacement elites have only run intermittently with the imputed goals of the orthodox position. The patterns of change within countries have only intermittently rehearsed the simple schemas of the theorists of modernization. Against the intellectual, political and policy inclinations of those working within the orthodox tradition we must insist that the reality of Pacific Asia is of post-colonial adjustment mediated by the continuing and irresistible demands of the world industrial-capitalist system.

The Recent Analyses of Metropolitan Liberalism

The earliest discussions of the rise of the Pacific Asian miracle economies focused on the NICs, the four Asian tigers of Hong Kong, Taiwan, South Korea and Singapore. These debates took place within an ideologically sensitive intellectual environment and tended to be cast in terms of the proof or disproof of the claims of dependency theory as against the market-liberal versions of the development orthodoxy.[4] A little later, the 1980s saw the theories of free markets attain a fashionable status, and again the Asian tigers were advanced as proof of the benefits of open-market capitalism. Of course a series of replies were made which insisted that the records of the countries in question derived significantly from state actions.[5]

The market-liberal theorists offer a stark restatement of nineteenth-century economic liberalism. An overarching theoretical claim is made that free markets maximize human welfare and in turn this unpacks as a series of interlinked claims: (i) economically, the claim is that as free markets act efficiently to distribute knowledge and resources around the economic system, then material welfare will be maximized; (ii) socially, the claim is that as action and responsibility for action reside with the person of the individual, then liberal individualistic social systems will ensure that moral worth is maximized; (iii) politically, the claim is that as liberalism offers a balanced solution to problems of deploying, distributing and controlling power, then liberal polities ensure that political freedom is maximized; and (iv) epistemologically, the claim is that as the whole package is grounded in genuine positive scientific knowledge, then in such systems the effective deployment of positive knowledge is maximized.

The substantive core of the package is made up of the claims in respect of the functioning of the free market. The free market comprises atomistic individuals who know their own autonomously arising needs and wants and who make contracts with other individuals through the mechanism of the marketplace to satisfy these needs and wants. The market is a neutral mechanism for transmitting information about needs and wants, and goods which might satisfy them, around the system. A minimum state machine provides a basic legal and security system to underpin the individual contractual pursuit of private goals. Thereafter, in terms of promulgating the package within the wider public sphere, a series of strategic institutions (IFIs, MNCs and key western governments) and a number of major theorists have been crucial.

The pro-market position of the market liberals has informed the policy of the World Bank, the IMF, the GATT and the American government over the post-Second World War period. The position of the market liberals translates into policy advice around a series of principles: (i) any regulation of the market is to be avoided, save for crises and the removal of malfunctions or inhibitions to full functioning; (ii) any intervention in the market is to be avoided, save to remove causes of price distortions, so subsidies should be abolished, tax rates adjusted to encourage enterprise, tariff barriers removed along with other non-tariff barriers or disguised restrictions; (iii) any government role in the economy should be avoided, as private enterprise can usually do the job better, and when governments do become involved it should be both market-conforming, short-term and involve a minimum of regulations; (iv) any collective intervention in the market should be avoided, so labour unions must be curbed; and (v) international trade should be free trade with goods and currency freely traded.

It might be thought, at this point, that the historical development experience of the countries of the region of Pacific Asia would be resistant to the analytical wiles of the proponents of market liberalism. However, the development experience has been variously embraced by both market liberals and conservatives in the West.[6] It is an elaborate game, where intrinsically implausible theory is conjoined to extensive misdescription in order to produce an anxious rhetoric of emulation.

A key recent figure has been Friedman[7] who argues that laissez-faire capitalism where economic power is widely dispersed, is a necessary condition of political freedom. In a competitive capitalist society individuals freely enter into exchanges in the marketplace and in society. The separation of economic power from political power lets the former act as a check on the concentration tendencies in the latter: the proper role of the latter, the state, is in setting the rules of the social game and arbitrating disputes. This position is taken to rule out not only the historical objective of socialism but also the social-democratic welfare states of post-Second World War Europe.

The theorists of market liberalism insist that the development experience of the countries of Pacific Asia confirms their advocacy of free markets. In respect of the familiar line of reply which points to the interventionist role of regional states, the liberals reply that where such intervention has had effect it has done so by adopting a market-conforming strategy so that the fundamental logic of the marketplace is respected. It is within this intellectual, political and policy-making context that the recent study of the development experience of the countries of Pacific Asia, prepared by the World Bank,[8] attains a modest significance in that the document acknowledges that something different has happened in Pacific Asia, continues to insist on the priority of markets, and signally fails to grasp the fundamental processes shaping the region.[9]

The Classical European Tradition and the Pacific Asian Model

It is possible to read the historical development experience of Pacific Asia in terms of the classical European tradition as a series of routes to the modern world. However, it is clear that the classical European tradition is not a simple set of techniques to be deployed mechanically, rather it is a developing tradition of formal argument-making ordered around a set of substantive preoccupations.

The analyses of the historical development experience of the countries of Pacific Asia made with the resources of the classical tradition lead towards the conclusion that within Pacific Asia a particular and novel form of industrial-capitalism is in the process of formation. This analytical perspective has informed the substantive discussions of this text. In the present context it is the formal aspects of the approach that we need to display, so at this point our discussion becomes formal and schematic. In other words, we will use the strategy of ideal-typical analysis in order to advance matters. We can speak of a model of Pacific Asia and note is central characteristics: (i) the economy is state-directed; (ii) state-direction is policy-pragmatic (not ideological except for an overriding commitment to economic expansion); (iii) state-direction is top-down style; (iv) society is familial and thereafter communitarian; (v) society is non-individualistic; (vi) politics is typically restricted to an elite sphere; (vii) political thinking amongst the population is diffuse and demobilized; (viii) political life is pragmatic and not centred on a public sphere; (ix) culture comprises a mix of officially sanctioned tradition and market sanctioned consumption; and (x) culture stresses consensus and harmony and eschews conflict. In this ideal-typical analysis we can attempt to uncover the key common aspects of the multiple particular forms-of-life lodged within the region of Pacific Asia.

The political economy of the Pacific Asian model

The development orthodoxy would speak of the evolutionary planned achievement of effective nation statehood. In the case of Pacific Asia this would find expression in terms derived from modernization theory. The Pacific Asian countries have successfully achieved 'take-off', and as their economies mature so are their societies being remade in a fashion familiar in other industrial countries, and in time their polities might be expected to shift away from their presently authoritarian style towards the liberal democracy familiar in the West. Thereafter the recently influential market-liberals would offer a rather different version of the orthodox tale, and in place of the stress on planning they would bring to the fore the dynamic logic of the free market. Market-liberals would point to the the prosperous Pacific Asian economies, and would read this as evidence of the successful spontaneous order which minimally regulated capitalistic business enterprise might be expected to produce.

Against these simplifying strategies, there are numerous more plausible replies available. A sophisticated reading of the Japanese variant of the Pacific Asian model calls attention to the active role of the state. In this perspective, to simplify, the development experience of Japan is read in terms of the exchange between an oligarchic ruling class (involving the bureaucracy, business, politicians, and in earlier versions the military), determined to secure the position of a late-developer within the expanding global-system, and the structures of that system, which flowed from the activities of the other major participants/players. In the post-Second World War period this drive to achieve position and security has evidenced itself in a strategic concern for economic expansion. As Johnson[10] has it, Japan has a capitalist developmental state.

Overall, in summary, we can say that the countries of the region have seen the successful pursuit by capitalist developmental states of economic growth and some social and political change. The political-economic aspect of the Pacific Asian model does seem to be distinctive.

The social-institutional order of the Pacific Asian model

It is often argued that the political-economic success of the countries of Pacific Asia is due in no small measure to the particular character of the local societies. In particular, Pacific Asian society is held to be familial and communitarian rather than individualistic on the model of the West (a model dominated by the experience of the USA). And relatedly Pacific Asian society is held to be disciplined and ordered unlike the West which is taken to be riven by the unfortunate consequences of excessive individualism (again with the image of the USA to the fore).[11]

It is clear that in the territory of Pacific Asia there are enormous differences in patterns of life which are found in the area. It is important to recall the detail in order to avoid lapsing into stereotypical thinking. The general nature of the social system of Pacific Asia is said to centre on the family and thereafter on kin networks. Thereafter, the family lodges itself within the wider group, either village or urban area or extended kin network, within which it operates. In other words the focus is on family group and local community. This pattern is taken to be sharply different from the situation obtaining in the West where the position of the individual is much more central to social philosophical thinking. In classical liberal terms there are only individuals and families and the social world is thereafter a realm of contract. The distinction can be made positively (Pacific Asia is lucky to have escaped the trials of Western individualism) or negatively (Pacific Asia is mired in an anti-individualist traditional culture). A related theme in the positive literature which deals with the model of Pacific Asia is the continuance of social discipline and order in contrast with the West. Proponents of the model of Pacific Asia point to traditions of respect for family, for elders and for those set in authority. All this is contrasted with the individualistic, ill-disciplined and declining West.

In general, in terms of a model of Pacific Asian society, it is clear that we do not have the individualistic societies of the West. A greater role is reserved for family and kin groups.

The culture and political culture of the Pacific Asian model

There is much to say with regard to the culture of the Pacific Asian model. Yet Evans comments: 'The use of the term Asia can be extremely misleading if it is used to denote some sort of cultural uniformity throughout the geographical area'.[12] However, the strategy of looking to broad historical-cultural areas points to regions inhabited by peoples who have, over the years, developed cultural traits which can somehow be taken to be typical. This strategy of characterization points to patterns of life, language groups, physiology (race) and common experience. The best we can say in respect of broad historical-cultural areas in Pacific Asia is that there are three main cultural streams: (i) the Indian, flowing into Southeast Asia, (ii) the Southeast Asian, which originates in that area; and (iii) the Chinese, which originates in that area and which has spread throughout the region as a whole. With this in mind we can note that on the standard characterizations there is a familial, communitarian and non-individualistic pattern of life in Pacific Asia.

The political-cultural life of the countries of Pacific Asia has routinely diverged sharply from the model of the West. The state-directed pursuit of economic growth has often simply overridden any discussion amongst the wider population. Indeed, generally the peoples of the region have no historical experience of the open debate within the public sphere which informs at least in principle the core of Western democratic political life. The detail of these processes within the Pacific Asian countries is complex. However, within this general sphere of the political culture of Pacific Asia we can note that local theorists are speaking now of a Pacific Asian model of democracy. It is clearly both an affirmation of local models of political practice and a counter-statement directed at critical outsiders usually from the West.

The notion of democracy can be read in terms of political-social philosophy in which case it comes in several versions, including, in schematic terms, republican democracy, liberal democracy and ideas of communitarian democracy.[13] In terms of institutional vehicles (the ways in which ideas generally affirmed are expressed in concrete and practical institutional machineries) the notion of democracy comes in several varieties including US-style representative democracy (having a written constitution, separation of powers, open debate, interest groups, all theorized typically via notions of liberal political pluralism), and Northwest European social-democracy (having written constitutions, a clearly dispersed pattern of power, open debate, and an active and involved citizenry, all of which may be regarded as coming closest in practice to the model of republican democracy).[14]

In terms of the overall political-economic and cultural package it might be possible to speak, after the style of Macpherson,[15] of models of democracy, including the Northwest European, the North American and a Pacific Asian. On this last, we can note the arguments from Chan[16] where we meet an idea of communitarian democracy, and she suggests tentatively that the Pacific Asian model of democracy involves the following: (i) communitarian rather than individualistic; (ii) deferential rather than competitive; (iii) having a dominant party system; and (iv) a strong state. It seems to be increasingly widely granted that there is something in these arguments, notwithstanding elements of elite excuse-making, and it is certainly the case that democratic polities are ongoing historical achievements.

Overall, the current debate in respect of the existence, character, prospects and implications of the Pacific Asian model of industrial-capitalism can present itself in an intensely ideologically-charged fashion. In schematic terms we can say that amongst American theorists, policy analysts and political actors, the novelty or otherwise of the Pacific Asian model has direct implications for the self-understandings of orthodox US thinkers. If Pacific Asia offers a distinctive variant of industrial-capitalism then many familiar claims to the universality of American models fall, and the pattern of life and thinking within the US becomes merely one amongst many. In brief, the rise of Pacific Asia challenges US hegemony. However, amongst Europeans the issues run differently. Amongst those disposed to affirm Anglo-Saxon notions of free markets the problems recall those of celebrants of US hegemony. Amongst the majority of Europeans the rise of Pacific Asia points both to a tripolar world and thereafter reaffirms the distinctiveness of the European experience.

Of course, these remarks are made from the perspective of an inhabitant of the European classical tradition of social theorizing with its concern to elucidate the dynamics of complex change. The view from China, Japan, the tiger economies or ASEAN would be different, as different cultural resources would be put to use to read different structural circumstances. The business of reading the shift to the modern world (in my terms) can be accomplished in multiple ways. The following sequence of chapters will review some of the scholarly and ideological implications of the Pacific Asian experience for those working within or with reference to the classical European tradition of social theorizing.

Conclusion

The classical tradition of social theorizing with its concern for the critical elucidation of complex change, deployed in the context of dialogue with local scholars, promises a detailed grasp of the processes of change at work in Pacific Asia. The substantive judgement in regard to Pacific Asia is that there is a distinctive type of industrial-capitalism taking form. It is neither the social-market typical of the European Union and nor is it the individualistic market competition exemplified in the case of the USA.

Notes

1   B. Anderson 1983: *Imagined Communities*, London: Verso.
2   See S. Gudeman 1986: *Economics as Culture*, London: Routledge; R. Dilley, ed., 1992: *Contesting Markets*, Edinburgh: Edinburgh University Press.
3   C. B. Macpherson 1973: *Democratic Theory: Essays in Retrieval*, Oxford University Press.
4   P. W. Preston 1987: *Rethinking Development*, London: Routledge; P. W. Preston 1994 *Discourses of Development*, Aldershot: Avebury.
5   G. White ed. 1988: *Developmental States in East Asia*, London: Macmillan; R. Wade 1990: *Governing the Market: Economic Theory and the Role of Governments in East Asian Industrialization*, Princeton, NJ: Princeton University Press.
6   R. Robison ed. 1996: *Pathways to Asia: The Politics of Engagement*, St Leonards: Allen and Unwin.
7   M. Friedman 1962: *Capitalism and Freedom*, University of Chicago Press; M. Friedman and R. Friedman 1980: *Free to Choose*, London: Secker and Warburg.
8   The World Bank 1993: *The East Asian Miracle: Economic Growth and Public Policy*, Oxford University Press.

9 R. Wade 1996: Japan, the World Bank and the Art of Paradigm Maintenance: The East Asian Miracle in Political Perspective in *New Left Review* 217.
10 C. Johnson 1982: *MITI and the Japanese Miracle*, Stanford University Press; see also R. P. Appelbaum and J. Henderson, eds, 1992: *States and Development in the Asian Pacific Rim*, London: Sage.
11 And both of these claims are made also by conservatives and market liberals, as Robison, ed., 1996 has made clear.
12 G. Evans, ed., 1993: *Asia's Cultural Mosaic*, Singapore: Prentice-Hall, p. 6.
13 D. Held 1987: *Models of Democracy*, Cambridge, Polity.
14 P. Anderson 1992: *English Questions*, London, Verso.
15 C. B. Macpherson 1966: *The Real World of Democracy*, Oxford University Press.
16 See R. L. Bartley et al. *Democracy and Capitalism: Asian and American Perspectives*, Singapore: Institute of Southeast Asian Studies.

11

The Pacific Asian Model I: Political-economic and Social-institutional Processes

It is clear that the countries in the Pacific Asian region have developed very rapidly in recent decades. The historical development experience of the countries of the region has attracted considerable scholarly, policy analytical and political interest, both within the region and the wider international community. It is also true to say that these interlocking patterns of reflection remain suffused with controversial argument. In this chapter we will consider the debates surrounding the political-economic and social-institutional processes of the region.

The Political Economy of Pacific Asia

Questions in respect of the particular nature of the Pacific Asian political-economies were submerged within broader cold war concerns over the long period of the post-Second World War era. However, the 1978 reforms in China, the 1985 Plaza Accord and the 1991 end of the cold war ensured that the question of the precise nature of the development experience of the countries of the region came under direct and open scrutiny.

The standard agency data allow the presentation of a broad overview of the political economy of Pacific Asia. However, it should be recalled that the data are inevitably inscribed with the rich spread of ideological preferences which are embodied in institutional practices, the realm of what Galbraith has called 'institutional truths'.[1] The truths of the IMF, World Bank, OECD and the other international financial institutions (IFIs) first established in the Bretton Woods period, revolve around the notion of a liberal rule-governed free trading market system and their data sets reflect these expectations in respect of economic life.

It is possible to point to a spread of institutions and related sets of ideas and characterize them as constituting a coherent discourse in which a package of sometimes explicit but often implicit ideas are presented. In the work of the major Western IFIs a model of the West in general and the USA more particularly is rather taken for granted. The intellectual appropriateness and practical utility of this familiar discourse is one central issue in respect of the analysis of the political economy of Pacific Asia. However, the data can offer us a rough idea of the order of magnitude of the political economy of Pacific Asia.

The standard agency data

In the post-Second World War period the political economies of the countries of Pacific Asia have undergone extensive change. In almost all cases there has been a state-sponsored pursuit of economic growth, a matter of catching up with the developed West. The record is one of extraordinary success.

The USA, the European Union and Pacific Asia are the three major economic groupings within the global industrial-capitalist system. The relative position of the three regions has altered dramatically over the post-Second World War period. Thus in 1960 the USA GNP was US$ 500 billion, with a GNP per capita of US$ 2,500; the EEC GNP was US$ 270 billion, with a GNP per capita of US$ 1,000; and Japan's GNP was US$ 40 billion, with a GNP per capita of US$ 400.[2] At this time the USA had the world's most powerful economy. And subsequently in 1989 the USA GNP was US$ 5.2 trillion, with a GNP per capita of US$ 21,000; the EU GNP was US$ 4.8 trillion, with a GNP per capita of US$ 15,000; and Japan's GNP was US$ 2.8 trillion, with a GNP per capita of US$ 23,100.[3] At this time the USA had the world's single strongest economy but was only one of three more or less similarly powerful economies. However, it should also be noted that the data record only Japan's economy within Pacific Asia. The economies of South Korea, Taiwan, Hong Kong and Singapore fall within the region and are sophisticated industrial-capitalist economies with a combined 1990 population of approximately 55 million and GNP per capita's in the US$ 5,000–11,000 range.[4] The poorer countries of the region – China, Indo-China, Southeast Asia – record a 1990 population of 1577 million, a GNP per capita of US$ 600 and a combined GNP of US$ 939 billion. Overall, an approximate summary of the political economy of the region would point to an early 1990s population of some 1655 million, with a GDP per capita of US$ 2,765 and a combined GDP of US$ 4,603.[5]

A variety of development tracks

The global system is now organized in terms of three major regions, and in each there is a powerful economy with the capital, people and intellectual/scientific resources that can generate autonomous growth. The regions are different from each other and they are internally diverse, especially Pacific Asia. The current pattern of political-economic development in Pacific Asia has developed over a lengthy period of time and on this question one commentator has presented these matters in terms of an inter-linked historical sequence, geographical pattern and contemporary hierarchy: first, Japan; second, the NICs; third, Southeast Asia; and fourth China.

Zysman[6] argues that the region comprises a series of tiers where each was put in place at a particular period in time and now occupies a particular status within the integrating regional pattern. The first country (in all senses) was Japan whose nineteenth-century success established a technologically autonomous economy and ensured its current position. The second countries (in all senses) are Korea and Taiwan whose economies grew in the years following the Korean War using transferred technology such that they now follow the Japanese lead. The third group (in all senses) are the countries of Southeast Asia whose territories have recently received investments from the regional cores in order to process exports directed outside the region. The fourth country (in all senses) is China whose membership is most recent, least developed and noticeably dependent. It is clear that the various development tracks followed by the countries of Pacific Asia do have resemblances, but are nonetheless distinct within what remains a large and politically and economically loosely linked area.

In the first place the Japanese core has developed in a competitive relationship with the West and the territories of Pacific Asia were seen quite early on as falling within the Japanese sphere of interest. The Japanese now aspire to lead the area in a strategy which stresses a regionally beneficial division of labour. Then the countries of the inner periphery of South Korea, Taiwan, Hong Kong and Singapore have various colonial histories and in the post-Second World War period have developed rapidly. Thereafter, the countries of the outer periphery of Southeast Asia have developed much more slowly. In the post-colonial period strategies of ISI slowly gave way to EOI with the arrival of Japanese capital and the area is now growing rapidly. And further, the newly open countries of the old socialist bloc, Cambodia, Laos, Vietnam and China, have developed in recent years. In the 1980s the Chinese economy grew very rapidly, and as the war in Cambodia subsided, the American embargo against Vietnam was lifted and investment flowed into these countries.

A region in formation

It is worth recalling that the history of the region's shift to the modern world had left many western commentators in the years before the Second World War convinced that Asia was moribund and irretrievably backward.[7] Yet the episode of the Pacific War meant that European and American direct colonial rule was ended and a series of Asian state-regimes inherited power. The withdrawal of the Europeans and Americans was largely accomplished in the 1940s and 1950s. The subsequent American presence was very significant for the economies and security of the region but direct involvement in comparison with what had gone before was relatively modest. The Asian state-regimes have held power for only forty years or thereabouts yet it is over this period that Pacific Asia has emerged. It is now clear that a region is in process of formation and Zysman notes that: 'As a fact of economic geography, the economic world consists of three powerful trading groups: Asia, North America and Europe. These three groups together constitute close to 70 per cent of the global GDP'.[8] And it is in the period since the dramatic advances in Pacific Asian regional integration which followed the Plaza Accords of 1985 that many have begun to speak not merely of the emergence of an integrated region but also of the particularity of its form of industrial-capitalism.

The Pacific Asian Model of Political Economy Debated

It can been argued that the development experience of the territories of the region can be aggregated and taken to be a coherent distinctive model, what we can tag as the Pacific Asian model of industrial-capitalism. There are a series of versions of this particular aspect of the story which derive from quite specific intellectual and political sources. The familiar ones begin with the work of the orthodox theorists of Third World development, a little later a wider intellectual constituency began to take note of the success stories of the Asian NICs and it is in recent years that an interdependent region has been discussed.

The development orthodoxy and the subsequent debate about the NICs

The development orthodoxy centred their analyses on the core model of the evolutionary and planned achievement of effective nation statehood. The model was derived from the historical experience of the West and was represented in technical terms so that development within the Third World could be effectively planned. In the case of Pacific Asia this found familiar expression in modernization theory which characterized the traditional societies of the area and then looked for a pattern of evolution converging on the model of the modern. In this perspective the present Pacific Asian countries have achieved take-off and as their economies mature so are their societies being remade in a fashion similar in other industrial countries, and in time their polities might be expected to shift away from their presently authoritarian style towards the liberal democracy familiar in the West.[9]

One aspect of the tale told by modernization theorists related to the development of the economic sphere. The earliest work had been distinctly Keynesian in tone and had looked to the business of planning, that is to the role of the state, however, in the quickly dominant US versions these Keynesian elements gave way to more straightforward free-market neo-classical ideas. Subsequently, in the 1960s and 1970s a sharp debate in respect of the experience of the Asian NICs developed between proponents of then influential dependency theory and overtly market-liberal theorists.

The development experience of the Asian NICs had one paradoxical consequence in that it contributed to an emphatic restatement of the claims of market liberalism. In place of the stress on planning they would bring to the fore the dynamism of the free market. The market-liberals pointed to the dynamic nature of the Pacific Asian economies and read this as evidence of the spontaneous order which minimally regulated industrial-capitalist business enterprise might be expected to produce. In presenting this position they offer a very particular version of the tale which subtly combines mis-understanding, omission and dogma in the three areas of economy, society and polity.

The market-liberals analyse the economy in a fashion which calls attention to the role of businessmen who are characterized as 'wealth creators' (in crude contrast with everyone else involved in the economy who appear as either simple followers or indigent mendicants). It is true that businessmen have a different status in Pacific Asia, as members of an increasingly self-conscious regional elite comprising businessmen, politicians, bureaucrats and academics, but their role is subsumed within a developmental capitalism which revolves around the state. The business elites of Asia cannot be taken to be equated with the mythical figures of liberal economic dogma.

The market-liberals also call attention to the stress on education and the habits of hard work within Pacific Asia. It is true that there is a concern for education and for work but this is bound up with broad commitments to family and community within the ambit of developmental capitalism. The typical Pacific Asian concern for education and work is not an element of an individualistic calculative strategy for personal advancement. Once again the market-liberals misread an element of the Pacific Asian form of life and there-after adduce it in support of their dogmatic beliefs.

The market-liberals also call attention to the presence within the region of disciplined authoritarian polities as contributors to economic success. The clear implication is that Western countries would do well to curb the excesses of those socialistic (or social-liberal) elements whose concerns for the indi-vidual rights of ordinary people militate against the pursuit of economic advance. It is true that Pacific Asian polities are often highly disciplined but again this must be set within the context of the operation of developmental capitalisms which have both claimed obedience and offered high rewards. The obedient workers of the successful countries of Pacific Asia are members of communities they are not the cowed insecure workers which economic liberalism looks to create in order for its automatic market-place to operate efficiently.

It might finally be noted that the expectations of the market-liberals with regard to the future seem to be cast in terms of more of the same, to a global system of free capital movements as business moves to take advantage of an increasingly integrated system, a 'borderless world'.[10] Yet in the light of the substantive analyses of the historical development of the region it is difficult to take the claims of the market-liberals seriously. Indeed one is inclined to think that no-one could be quite that foolish. However, there is an alternative reading available which reduces the materials of market liberalism to the status of a rhetorical adjunct to the demands of US capitalism, in which case we are talking about an essentially political project, what has been called 'predatory liberalism'.[11]

The World Bank and the contemporary debate

It is clear that the World Bank is one of the institutional locations of the influential discourse of marketplace-secured spontaneous order, the intellectual core of the market-liberal project. The intellectual claims of the Bank (and market liberalism) in respect of the development experience of Pacific Asia found recent expression in a major report entitled *The East Asian Miracle*.[12] The Bank's report deals with the four tigers of Hong Kong, Taiwan, South Korea and Singapore, plus Indonesia, Malaysia and Thailand, and Japan. After a review of their performance, the document acknowledges that something different has happened in Pacific Asia whilst continuing to insist on the priority of markets. The Bank's analysis is an interesting example of neo-classical apologetics.

At the outset these countries are taken out of their historical 'real world' context and represented in the technical language of the Bank as members of a descriptive economic category, the high-performing Asian economies (HPAEs). Thereafter a comparative review of the standard agency data in pursuit of general and technical lessons is possible. The descriptive factors mentioned include high growth rates, a measure of equality in growth and sharply improved human welfare. The Bank offers an explanation for this successful record in terms of 'getting the basics right'[13] and this is taken to include: (i) private domestic investment and human capital growth; (ii) sound development policy; and (iii) government intervention.

It is evident that the first two factors cited are anodyne, and it is with the final point that we are introduced to the major unstated (but omnipresent) theme of the report, how to deal with an ideologically unwanted and neoclassically unanticipated record of state-directed success. The Bank makes two moves: (i) methodology is invoked, thus whilst success has occurred it is difficult to be precise about the role of government intervention (maybe success happened for other reasons); (ii) the HPAEs are disaggregated and the role of intervention played down, thus there seems to have been some successful interventions in Northeast Asia, but fewer in Southeast Asia, and the latter may have more lessons outside the region than the former. The policy record of the governments of the HPAEs is summarized in an exercise in theoretical persuasive definition as 'market-friendly'.[14]

Overall, the Bank systematically misreads descriptive material in the light of its a priori commitment to a neo-classical policy stance, and thus the HPAEs become merely a somewhat eccentric and unreplicable variant of the standard free-market model espoused by the Bank. And it is also clear that the Bank systematically disregards the specific actual development experiences of the eight countries in question, matters which require not description informed by a priori commitments, as this just produces low-grade ideological material, but instead analysis informed by the reflexive deployment of the political-economic, social-institutional and culture-critical machineries of the classical tradition, concerned to analyse complex change with a view to ordering subsequent change.

American anxieties

The material of the World Bank can only be treated as political rhetoric, but the contestedness of the lessons of the historical development experience of Pacific Asian countries within the present spread of IFIs should be noted. The assertion of the novelty of the Pacific Asian experience is a matter of interest for the Japanese, a matter of celebration for leaders such as Mahathir and Lee, and it is quite clear that the denial of these claims is a matter of anxious concern for the USA.[15]

The reasons for the anxieties of US commentators and policy analysts are not hard to find. As their economic hegemony within the global system declines, and as this relative decline is underscored by the falling away of the salience of their security role, there is anxiety about the future order of the system. The US government has evidenced a concern to sustain an open liberal trading order. It is here that disquiet is expressed in respect of the Pacific Asian model, and there are two variants: one focused on the problems of business and the other concerned with the broad and sweeping issue of the nature of different civilizations.

The business-centred work is concerned with the economic challenge to the USA of Japan (and the wider group of rapidly growing East Asian economies) and expresses a series of themes: the rise to economic power of Japan; the threat of this power to the position of the USA; the unfair nature of competition from Japan (a mix of export drives and closed home markets are familiar themes); and the urgent necessity for the US to take action to remedy the situation (from reconstructing the US economy to retaliating against the Japanese). This set of concerns takes American theorists, commentators and policy makers into difficult territory as they attempt simultaneously to deny the problems of their own economy (as judged by the economic ideas which they publicly affirm), affirm a continuing role as regional military hegemonists (in the face of domestic and regional doubts), and pressure nominal allies into making political-economic changes (which evidently favour US interests notwithstanding the official position in favour of open rule-governed trade). The upshot has been a series of occasionally ill-tempered and inconclusive debates about reordering trade relations.

Relatedly, the genre of commentary which focuses on Japanese business overlaps with a related line of argument which seems to be a generalization of the argument from an economic focus to a discussion of 'civilizations'. Huntington[16] has suggested that the post-cold war era is likely to be dominated by a 'clash of civilizations' as East and West compete for global domination. A subsidiary element of this analysis seems to be the call for the USA to lead the West. It would seem that Huntington's efforts are little more than the 1960s theory of convergence rewritten in contemporary guise. It is unlikely that the countries of Pacific Asia will acquiesce in these characterizations, and it is clear that Europeans will decline the invitation to order their affairs according to agendas written in Washington.

The state-sponsored pursuit of development

Once we move outside the wide sphere of discourse informed by market liberalism it is clear that there is a thoroughly sophisticated reading of the Pacific Asian model in the process of construction. The classical tradition of social theorizing has been deployed to analyse complex change within the region by a number of scholars. A series of texts have been presented which discuss both particular countries and the growing interdependence of the region.[17] In a similar fashion, over a rather longer period of time, the political economy of the core economy of the region has also been actively pursued.[18] In the structural perspective affirmed by these theorists, the historical development experience of Japan is read in terms of the exchange of structures and agents within the dynamic global system. The analysis looks to a crucial exchange between an oligarchic ruling group, involving the bureaucracy, business, politicians and in earlier phases the military, determined to secure the position of a late-developer within the expanding global system, on the one hand, and on the other, the structures of that system which flowed from the activities of the other major participants/players. In the years running up to the Great War the result was a country concerned to catch-up and participate in the international system essentially on Western terms and the result was that late-industrialization issued in late-colonialism. A little later in the 1930s, as Japanese relations with the West cooled and the military came to hold power, the result was a mobilized, militaristic and expansionist country. In the years following the Pacific War the drive to achieve position and security has evidenced itself in strategic concern for economic expansion. The Japanese political economy is suffused with a complex of political imperatives in respect of material advance and national security within the regional/global systems. The industrial-capitalism of Japan does not advance simply in line with the logic of the unfettered market-place but is subject to the routine direction of a capitalist developmental state.

Overall, in summary, it is clear that the countries of Pacific Asia have successful pursued the goal of economic development over the post-Second World War period. The state has played a key role in these success stories. It is reasonable to speak of the state-sponsored pursuit of development.[19] In brief, we can speak of the successful pursuit of development ordered by developmental states. The upshot is a quite particular variant of industrial-capitalism which we can characterize as 'developmental capitalism'. It is clear that the particular experience of these countries raises quite profound questions for extant classical European and also American traditions of social science.

The General Social Scientific Debate on Political Economy

Johnson's[20] notion of the developmental state is focused on Japan; however, the idea has also been applied to Asian NICs. A number of issues are raised which centre on the relationship of state and market, and the possible role of the state in ordering development. There are a number of ways of addressing these issues and theorists have spoken of the following: (i) the particularity of the historical development experience of the countries of Pacific Asia; (ii) the varieties of industrial-capitalism; and (iii) drawing on the foregoing, the process of the rectification of the misunderstandings of orthodox economics and political science (in order to grasp the particular variant of industrial-capitalism evidenced in the region).

The particularity of the development experience of the region

The particularity of the development experience of the countries of the region has been widely canvassed. Shibusawa et al.[21] speak of developmentalism and note the role of strong government, a relationship between public and private sectors which acknowledges national development, the role of foreign direct investment, the habit of deferred gratification and the utility of the American security umbrella.

It is both clear that this analysis does usefully call attention to relevant detail, but it does not directly address the issue of strategies of analysis. In very brief terms it can be said that sophisticated description is not enough.

In simple terms, it can be argued that if the region does have a particular historical development experience, then it will necessarily fall outside the bounds of received western social science – simply because that tradition grew up alongside the historical development of the West. On the other hand, if the experience can be grasped by western social science then the experience cannot be wholly other, in which case it is not wholly particular. In order to settle this matter it is necessary to shift into the realm of the philosophy of social science and ask about the extent to which Western social scientists can grasp the internal logics of the patterns of life of Pacific Asia.

It is clear that the forms-of-life within Pacific Asia are not wholly different from those in Europe or the USA, so the question can be remade in terms of commonalties, differences, and the possibilities of interpretive exchanges between scholars lodged within the various regions and traditions.

The idea of varieties of industrial-capitalism

It has been argued that the crucial issues flowing from the recent experience of the countries of the region is that they have evidenced a specific version of industrial-capitalism. There is an important intellectual debate here which centres on the extent to which Western scholarship can plausibly claim universal application. Those theorists disposed to affirm the universality of the results of their social scientific enquiries are not disposed to grant that there are varieties of industrial-capitalism. They hold the view that industrial-capitalism has one fundamental logic and the variations in forms-of-life are either superficial, hangovers from the past, or inhibitions to market functioning sponsored by particular groups looking to protect sectional advantage. This argument finds particular emphatic presentation in the work of mainstream market-liberal neo-classical economists. On the other hand, there is a wealth of social theoretical material centred on the classical tradition which grants the global diversity of forms-of-life, and insists upon the limited, tentative and culture-bound nature of all claims to knowledge. In this perspective the development of a novel Pacific Asian form of industrial-capitalism it is not overwhelmingly surprising, and thereafter the task is the elucidation of its particular logics.

In more substantive terms, it has been proposed that the countries of North America affirm a rule-governed contractual liberal market capitalism, that the countries of the European Union affirm a social market capitalism and that the countries of Pacific Asia affirm a community and state-centred capitalism. This debate confronts directly the business of making characterizations of the regions of the global system.

In the context of these general debates one rather more focused question has been addressed which looks to the character of the role of the state within the countries of the region. In place of the single rule-setting model affirmed by market-liberals a series of possibilities may be identified. Appelbaum and Henderson[22] review the overall policy orientations of the state-regimes in power and speak of 'market-ideological' (USA, UK), 'plan ideological' (former socialist countries), 'market rational' (countries in mainland Europe), and 'plan rational' (countries in Pacific Asia).

The position which has been adopted in this text is that there are a diversity of forms-of-life which embody different economic, social and political logics, and these may be interpretively grasped in concert with local scholars. It is certainly the case that the exchange between these varieties of capitalism will be of considerable interest in the next few years. In this context two arguments may be noted: (i) it has been argued that the largest economic bloc will set the global trading rules, and Thurow[23] has pointed out that the European Union is becoming the largest economic bloc and will write the rules for the twenty-first century; and (ii) it has been argued that the exchange between the blocs in respect of trade will move beyond any simple liberal rule-making towards the difficult territory of grasping the different ways in which economies work (and these debates pick up on the points in respect of economies being lodged in societies being lodged in cultures) and ordering their exchanges equitably.[24]

The rectification of confusions

The concern with the rectification of confusions begins with a claim that orthodox Western social scientists have typically systematically misread the situation of the countries of Pacific Asia. The confusions of orthodox economics and mainstream political science are frequently cited. A step towards the creation of plausible analyses is therefore the removal of confusions.

The Pacific Asian model cannot be grasped by orthodox neo-classical economics. A wide debate has ensued. Again, the precise nature of the neo-classical orthodoxy is opened-up, and the reaction of the celebrants of the orthodoxy in organizations like the Bank and the Fund, leads to the view that the approach is primarily an exercise in delimited-formal ideology making with only a tenuous linkage to the concerns of the classical tradition of social science. However, against conventional economics the strategies of economic sociology and economic anthropology have been widely used to analyse Pacific Asian patterns of economic life – as with, for example, the role of networks/connections amongst Chinese business or the notion of relational contracting advanced by Dore.[25]

The Pacific Asian model has direct implications for mainstream political science. The commitment to liberal-democratic goals and pluralist analyses which are inscribed in the work of the mainstream, take issue in the diagnosis of Pacific Asian polities as variously deficient. However, it is clear that these polities are stable and successful. Against the expectations of conventional political science there are clear implications for familiar Western affirmations of free-market vehicled liberal democracy as the Pacific Asian model escapes the scope of these familiar official western ideologies.[26]

An interim conclusion

The Pacific Asian region has experienced extensive economic change in recent years and the scale of economic advance is a matter of record. The position of the region's political economy within the general global system has also undergone extensive change, and Pacific Asia is now one of three major regions within the global system. However, the ways in which all this might be understood is not so clear. In terms of the classical tradition the countries of Pacific Asia have experienced a phase of rapid complex change as the demands of the global system have worked to reconfigure established relationships within a new regional pattern. Against this view, orthodox theorists would speak merely of the immutable logic of the marketplace. It does seem to be clear that the celebrants of the free market are wrong; however, the extent to which the former group has grasped the truth remains unclear. Moreover, it is necessary to acknowledge the point that local social theorists have begun to offer their own views as to the nature of the development experience of Pacific Asia, which draw on indigenous intellectual and cultural resources. It is perhaps in the context of dialogic exchanges with Asian scholars that a plausible set of statements might be made.

The Society of Pacific Asia

As with debates on the nature of the Pacific Asian political economy, the issue of the particular nature of the social-institutional structures of the countries of the region has become suffused with the ideological concerns of the various disputants. Here, as before, we will seek to review the main elements of these debates before venturing a tentative conclusion.

It is often argued by commentators considering Pacific Asian patterns of economic growth that the political economies of the territories have been successful because the character of the local societies is particularly appropriate to the pursuit of economic advance. Pacific Asian society is presented as familial, communitarian and disciplined. These arguments are available within the general literature of social science and are advanced by European, American and Pacific Asian scholars. The ways in which the arguments are made are various but there is an underlying distinction drawn between the communitarian East and the individualistic West.

The standard agency data offered us a starting point. They point to a diverse region where the more affluent countries enjoy levels of living similar to those of the USA or Europe, whilst the poorer follow patterns of life more associated with the Third World.

The standard agency data

The United Nations Development Programme (UNDP) has constructed an index which combines economic and social measures relating to human material and social achievement.[27] The 'human development index' aggregates data in respect of economic activity, life expectancy and educational attainment such that a figure of 1.00 represents a maximum and 0.00 a minimum. The index records the following data: Japan 0.981; Hong Kong 0.913; South Korea 0.871; Singapore 0.848; Brunei 0.848; Malaysia 0.798; Thailand 0.685; North Korea 0.654; China 0.612; Philippines 0.600; Indonesia 0.491; Vietnam 0.464; Burma 0.385; Papua New Guinea 0.321; Laos 0.240; and Cambodia 0.178.

The UNDP categorized countries above 0.800 as having high human development; between 0.799 and 0.500 as medium; and 0.499 and below as low human development. The data for Pacific Asia record a diverse region. The core economy of the region, Japan, records an index figure second only to Canada and ahead of the USA and European Union countries. The countries of the inner periphery record developed country figures. The figures for countries in the outer periphery and socialist bloc are weaker. The six countries in Indo-China and Southeast Asia record low levels of human development. Nonetheless it is clear that, with the exception of Papua New Guinea and the war damaged countries of Indo-China, the Pacific Asian region has shifted decisively away from the status of underdeveloped Third World.

It should be recalled that in the territory of Pacific Asia there are enormous differences in patterns of life to be found in the area. It is important to be able to grasp the detail and a series of strategies can be identified: (i) one could focus on the relationship of culture and society and look at the ways in which particular sets of ideas contribute to given patterns of social life, for example one could accomplish the comparative task in terms of the great religious traditions of Confucianism, Buddhism, Hinduism and Islam, or one could characterize a series of broad ethno-cultural groups, thus Chinese, Malay, and Indian; (ii) one could also consider the demands of the business of earning a livelihood and one could accomplish the comparative task by characterizing a series of broad forms of economic life with maritime traders, wet/dry rice farming, petty production, urban-dwellers, denizens of the modern economy and the informal sectors; or (iii) one could focus on patterns of development and look at how countries have dealt with the processes of modernization, and here one could accomplish this comparative task in terms of the position of various territories on an evolutionary continuum between traditional and modern.

Place, region and global system

A somewhat different strategy of grasping the diversity of the region would use the resources of the classical tradition in order to focus on the current exchange between place, region and global system. As territories shift to the modern world the dynamics of structural change will transmit particular demands to local peoples, and their actions will generate a spread of particular social forms. One could accomplish the task of making a comparative summary statement in respect of the social forms of the region by detailing the characteristics of the discrete spheres surrounding the core country of Japan: Japan; the inner periphery; the outer periphery; the socialist group; and Australasia.

(i) The nature of Japanese society

Japanese society can be characterized as centred upon family, work and community. It is routinely said that Japanese society is characterized by the numerous groups to which individuals typically belong. The shift to the modern world established a particular mobilized variant of the family on the basis of existing Tokugawa practices. The locus of the exchange between individual and collectivity was the continuing family. The reforms of the US occupation authorities, and the subsequent economic growth, have ushered in a series of modestly secured but wide-ranging reforms and changes.

Hunter[28] argues that in the shift to the modern world two key events have shaped modern Japan – the Meiji restoration and the US occupation – yet the starting point is Tokugawa. It was a period of stability. The ruling groups sought to control the social-institutional structure by specifying in great detail the nature of an hierarchy and the duties of inhabitants at each level in the hierarchy. Hunter comments that society 'as a whole was subdivided into various strata whose existence was the result not of any process of economic or social change, but of government decree'.[29] It is clear that the government extended its control throughout the social-institutional structure and secured detailed control. Hunter notes that throughout 'the Tokugawa period the lifestyles, customs, work practices and privileges of each caste were minutely regulated by a host of detailed sumptuary laws and other provisions'.[30] The individual was born into a specific class or sub-class and the pattern of their life was thereafter established. It is clear that there was relatively little scope for social mobility.

Over the later years of Tokugawa the economic successes of the period began to undermine the caste system, and the manner in which Japan was opened to the West after Perry's visits called further attention to the need for reform. The Meiji Restoration began a period of far-reaching changes including social-institutional reform. However, the Meiji oligarchy was concerned to control change and the resources of tradition were called upon to help secure this objective. Hunter records that 'the new regime attempted to manipulate selected facets of Tokugawa society to impose a uniform social structure'.[31] The social ethic of Tokugawa derived from Confucianism and stressed loyalty, filial piety and obedience. The Japanese historical experience of military rule issued in a stress on obedience/loyalty. The upshot was what Nakane calls a 'vertical society'.[32]

In the social-institutional structure the continuing family was the key organization, translating ideals into routine practice, and the model was copied to other social organizations such as the state and private firms. The social-institutional structure tightly circumscribed the actions of the individual Japanese. Hunter notes: 'The combination of vertical and group ties was such that individuals tended to be viewed by others not as individuals, but as group members, and a network of reciprocal obligations and feelings between group members was the key to the maintenance of social order. The categorization of individuals by position in the hierarchy and group membership made it impossible for an individual to divorce himself from his social role . . . the dividing line between the private and public domain was blurred. This was the basis upon which later propaganda of community of interests between the individual and the state could usefully be constructed'.[33]

It is here that we find the modern root of the Japanese trait of 'groupism'. The family was the first group which the individual encountered in the process of socialization and it was merely the first of a continuing sequence of such groups. The individual would participate with an informally assigned rank in similar social units in school, neighbourhood and workplace. Hunter notes that 'the most important and all embracing of these groups was the "family state", which figured prominently in the official political ideology',[34] and it is clear that it was the culture of the village community which remained central to the imagery of the official ideology. Hunter remarks that 'the village came to be represented as the source of all the traditional virtues, the head of the Japanese tradition'.[35]

In the 1930s, as the military came to dominate political life, the state involved itself ever more closely in patterns of social life. As the country became embroiled in wars, social regimentation increased. After the Pacific War the occupation policy of SCAP had two key objectives. In the first place was the concern for demilitarization. In the second place there was a self-conscious drive to create a liberal-democratic free-market Japan, and a crucial element was the reconstruction of the old social-institutional patterns. However, even with the abolition in 1945 of the continuing family, and the promulgation of a new civil code formally enshrining social rights, the social ethos of belonging continued (albeit declining slowly in the face of material advance).

The impact of rising material levels of living has meant an increasingly urban lifestyle, smaller families, rather fewer multiple generation households and greater role divisions between the sexes as women operate within the domestic sphere whilst the men look to their workplaces. However, the extent of social change should not be overstressed. The Japanese have a strong sense of themselves and their unique traditions. Hunter notes that most Japanese 'are quite satisfied with the roles which society expects them to play. Their major concerns remain their nation, their families, their work and their friendship groups'.[36]

(ii) The nature of society in the inner periphery
The countries of the inner periphery of South Korea, Taiwan, Singapore and Hong Kong have populations which are predominantly ethnic Chinese, or which have been lodged within the broad Chinese cultural sphere for many centuries. The social-institutional structures centre therefore on family and kin networks. However the current patterns of social life can be characterized in terms of the surviving legacies of those traditions, and demands of recent rapid economic growth. The historical experience of Hong Kong and Singapore as trading cities has meant that, in the colonial period, the social structure of the societies was unusual in that both territories received inward migration from China which was preponderantly male and of relatively short duration, as migrants either moved on to other destinations or returned to home areas. In Taiwan the pattern of life was more settled and agricultural, with rural life centring upon the peasant household and village, and the same held in the long-term Chinese tributary state of Korea.

In the years following the Pacific War these four countries experienced significant internal upheaval, including war, mass immigration and ethnic conflict. In these countries the populations have been mobilized in pursuit of material advance. In these countries there has been a long experience of economic success and they are now prosperous. In these countries a new middle class is forming with the material, and perhaps political tastes, familiar in the West.[37]

(iii) The nature of society in ASEAN
In the outer periphery of ASEAN social patterns are more dispersed. These territories are home to a diversity of ethnic groups within countries which have only relatively recently emerged from colonial rule. In a sense these countries are rather more traditional than Japan and the NICs. The traditions reach back to local readings of Hinduism, Buddhism and Islam. Hardacre comments that each country 'has within it local cultures of ethnic, religious and tribal groups, yielding a great mosaic of patterns'.[38] The fundamental traditional social-institutional pattern was provided by peasant agriculture. However, in the long period of colonial rule there were significant changes. The area's involvement in the global industrial-capitalist system issued in the extensive development of plantation agriculture (which draws people away from traditional peasant farming or draws in migrants and makes them rural labourers), mining industries (which draws in labourers), and the growth of new colonial cities (which receive flows of rural–urban migrants who operate in the informal sectors of the city economies). In all these cases long established social-institutional patterns are more or less radically remade.

In the post-colonial period there has been extensive economic growth and this has occasioned a further series of changes to familiar social-institutional patterns. In Thailand and Indonesia there is rapid social change as land short-ages in rural areas occasion new social practices locally and migration to urban areas. One novel form of activity revolves around MNCs which have set up assembly plants in the region. Hardacre notes: 'The industries involved in Southeast Asia, particularly microelectronics and garment work, are labour intensive and depend primarily upon young, unmarried women workers'.[39] In Malaysia, Indonesia and the Philippines these workers are drawn from rural areas into low-skilled jobs which offer no particular possibility of advance and the migrant workers remit money and upon marriage typically discontinue working. Women workers also figure in the extensive sex industries of the region.[40]

In these countries the social changes underway are those typically associ-ated with development. There is a movement of population from rural to urban areas, and long established rural social relationships are reworked in both areas. There are new patterns of family life, economic activity and patterns of consumption. The process of development is haphazard and uneven, and the patterns of change in any one area will be quite particular.

(iv) The nature of society in the socialist countries

In the countries of the socialist bloc, the social-institutional patterns fuse the legacies of established traditions and the post-1949 influence of state ideolo-gies of social reform. The pattern has been further complicated by warfare and in recent years a measure of economic liberalization. In China and Vietnam there have been many changes in the course of development. On the other hand, in Cambodia, the particular nightmare of the Pol Pot regime has devastated the country, and in Laos there has also been wartime dis-location to a similarly largely peasant agricultural economy.

The key social institution was the patrilineal family and within the family unit the key relationship was father/son. The family would arrange marriages for children and the new wife had a low status. The society was hierarchical and unequal, with wealth and gentry on the one hand, and very poor peasants on the other. Yet the class hierarchy was not immutable. In pre-contact China society was stratified according to four classes, the scholar-gentry, peasants, artisans and merchants, and it was possible to move upwards (and to sink downwards). It was the bureaucracy, recruited by examination, which offered the one major opportunity for male class mobility.

The late nineteenth century and early twentieth century saw the begin-nings of change as China belatedly began to shift into the modern world. A series of coastal cities came into routine contact with the traders of the West and as links developed these cities became more prosperous and a more outward-looking urban culture developed. It was amongst the urban intelli-gentsia that the drive for republican revolution was fostered.

The 1911 revolution in China generated a mixture of social reform as Western ideas were adopted within the burgeoning cities, and collapse took place as an intermittent civil war developed which eventually spread to encompass many of the most populous regions of the country. The 1949 revolution in China ushered in great changes in social life with the equality of women enshrined in law in 1950 and demands for greater equality figuring in the years of the Cultural Revolution. Mackerras[41] points out that these changes were more immediately acknowledged in urban areas whilst rural areas adopted them only slowly. In rural areas the commune system was substituted for the old family and clan networks. In the wake of the 1978 reforms the commune system has collapsed, and in rural areas there are signs of a renewal of pre-revolutionary patriarchal families. At the same time in 1979 the 'one child' policy was introduced and this has had a dramatic effect upon family life. Also as economic growth continues in the coastal areas of China there is a process of internal migration as peasant workers from poorer provinces move towards the towns.

In Vietnam the years of war have radically disrupted pre-war social patterns. Hardacre notes: 'The recent history of Vietnamese society has been dominated by war, producing an uneven demographic pattern in which women outnumber men . . . and children under fifteen . . . comprise about half the total population'.[42] Hardacre adds: 'The nation as a whole idealizes a classless society, but while much progress towards that goal has been made, many inequalities between women and men remain'.[43] In the war years women moved from farm and household into industry. At the present time 'women form about two-thirds of the workforce across all sectors of the economy, with the exception of heavy industry'.[44] And finally, we note that a similar story of disruption might be told for the essentially peasant societies of Cambodia and Laos.

(v) Australia and New Zealand
In Australia and New Zealand patterns of family, work and community are similar to those of the West. One recent set of changes in both countries has entailed a greater openness to the Pacific Asian region – a mixture of economic liberalism which has opened local markets to Pacific Asian investors and producers, and a sharp change in policies relating to immigration such that both countries now have very significant and growing populations of Asian immigrants. However, overall, one might want to suggest that these recent changes are merely slight variations on established Western patterns and do not resemble in scale the social changes experienced in the post-Second World War period in other parts of the Pacific Asian region.

The Pacific Asian Model of Society Debated

The debates about the nature of society in the broad Pacific Asian region centre upon a number of commonly cited characterizations. It is claimed that Pacific Asian society is familial, communitarian, ordered, disciplined and anti-individualist. In recent Western commentary these putative traits are routinely cited as key contributory factors in the economic success of the region.

Family, kin and community in Pacific Asia

In the literature of colonial analysis and post-colonial development theorizing, the societies of Southeast Asia were grasped in terms of the ideas of dual, plural and loosely structured societies[45] whilst the societies falling within the Chinese cultural sphere were characterized in terms of peasant forms-of-life lodged within strict social hierarchies. The wealth of social forms in the region is very large. However, the available characterizations have a series of recurrent themes. In all cases, to simplify, it is suggested that the general nature of the social-institutional system of Pacific Asia centres upon family and kin networks. The focus of the personal life of an individual is the family group, kin network and local community. It is within the family household that the routines of life are pursued, with kin networks as an additional sphere of activity and the community forming the routinely present sphere of collective order. The anthropologist Scott[46] has spoken of the moral resources of peasant-centred 'little tradition' as a way of gesturing to the self-contained nature of peasant life. Thereafter, the moral schedules of wider authorities – religion or state – present themselves in the materials of 'great tradition'. It would seem that the pre-contact form of life of the majority of people in the Pacific Asia region was some variant or other on the model of household-centred peasant life, with more distant authorities making varying claims upon the people, relatively slight in Southeast Asia, more extensive in the Chinese cultural sphere, and thoroughly intrusive in later Japanese feudalism.

It is equally evident that these pre-contact patterns of social relationships have been radically remade over the long period of the shift to the modern world. The demands of an expansive industrial-capitalism have drawn people into plantations, mines, colonial cities and more recently into the growing internationalized sphere of economic life via the operations of MNCs. In the more highly developed areas within the region the pattern of life is shifting to resemble that of the developed West with increasing materialism and a diminution of received social forms and beliefs. Nonetheless, it would be wrong to anticipate a convergence upon an atomistic, materialistic individualism, the dystopia of an easily recognizable version of a possible Western future; rather, the development of the countries of Pacific Asia will continue to entail the subtle reworking of received social patterns as the countries continue their shift into the modern world.

A non-individualist form of life

The Pacific Asian model claims that family, kin networks and community are central social-institutional structures in the Pacific Asia region. One consequence of this characterization of social life is that the collectivity is prioritized over the individual. The way in which the matter has been dealt with so far makes this merely a practical report on the nature of the Pacific Asian pattern of life. However, we can add two related lines of possible commentary: social theoretic, in particular the ontology of social life, where the resources of the sociological stream within the classical tradition would point to the social nature of humankind; and ethical, where the resources of the democratic philosophical stream within the classical tradition would point to the appropriateness of lodging practical moral reasoning/activity within the context of the relevant collectivity. In other words, it is possible to argue that the non-individualist form of life affirmed in the Pacific Asian model is appropriate to the fundamental character of human social life.

In contrast, in classical liberal terms there are only individuals and families (a sort of individual writ large) and the social world is thereafter a realm of contract. It is possible to review classical liberalism in favourable terms as the set of ideas which informed/legitimated the actions of the early English mercantile bourgeoisie in their struggles with feudal absolutism. However, the subsequent development of liberal societies has generated an atomistic expressive individualism which many regard as unsatisfactory, and the liberal tradition itself has come to be regarded as fundamentally misconceived.[47]

The distinction between Pacific Asia and the West (with the USA as the crucial comparator) can be made positively, in which case Pacific Asia is lucky to have escaped the trials of Western individualism, or negatively in which case Pacific Asia is unfortunate to be mired in an anti-individualist traditional culture. It is also clear that this distinction can be read into a series of particular debates ranging from the style of political life, through to forms of workplace organization and down to patterns of children's behaviour and school performance.

Discipline and social order in Pacific Asia

A related theme in the literature which deals with the model of Pacific Asia is the putative continuance of social discipline and order in contrast to the West (again with the image of the USA central). The proponents of the model of Pacific Asia point to traditions of respect for family, for elders and for those set in authority. All this is contrasted often quite explicitly with the individualistic, ill-disciplined, and, by implication, declining West. Robison[48] has noted how Western conservatives and neo-liberals affirm this image in order to propose the adoption of the schedule of practices in the West, a disciplined obedient and deferential population providing an equally obedient workforce. It is clear that these appeals to the Asian model are exercises in ideological rhetoric, designed to advance domestic political agendas. However, it is clear that the historical development experience of these territories has generated a different way of construing and ordering the relationship of the individual and broader society, one that does, in general, place more weight on the collectivity.

An ordered society

It is clear that the debates about the nature of society in the Pacific Asian region invoke a number of specific features and characterize society as familial, communitarian, ordered and disciplined. The distinction between the Pacific Asian sense of community and the Western preference for expressive individualism serves as the axis around which a spread of debates and judgements revolve. In recent Western commentary these putative traits are routinely cited as key contributory factors in the economic success of the region. In recent Pacific Asian commentary these putative traits are routinely cited as key contributory factors in the decline of the West. It is clear that the debate carries a heavy ideological/rhetorical load but nonetheless we can grant that the claims to the particularity of the Pacific Asian model do carry a significant measure of truth.

The General Social Scientific Debates on Society

A more general question drawn from this material is the extent to which we can make comparative or cross-cultural analyses.

Culture and comparative analysis

In the literature of development theory there is an area of debate which looks to the relationship of culture and society with respect to economic progress. The work of the German social theorist Max Weber is invoked.[49] Weber argued against those who looked to economic determinism to explain change, suggesting that there was a role for willed action in the general process of development. The argument was addressed to the somewhat politically passive German bourgeoisie whom Weber wished to encourage in order to secure liberal democracy within the country. In its particular context, Weber's work is cogent and persuasive. However, the material has been routinely taken out of context and used by modernization theorists to argue a variety of incompatible positions in respect of the relationship of Pacific Asian culture and society to the chances of the region advancing economically. In the immediate post-Second World War period, the argument suggested that Pacific Asian culture and society offered no analogue to the disciplined, socially-progressive protestantism which Weber is widely taken to have argued was the key to capitalist development. If there was no Pacific Asian equivalent of mobilized protestantism then there could be no Pacific Asian capitalism, and the region was condemned, in the absence of outside assistance, to remain traditional and backward. However, as the Pacific Asian region has become ever more evidently economically dynamic, the argument has shifted. It is often argued now that the reason for Pacific Asia's success is precisely the particular mixture of Pacific Asian culture and society.

It is clear that the received debate on the 'Weber thesis' has been confused. It is perhaps best set on one side. However, the debate does raise the issue of the basis of comparative analysis. In simple terms it is a matter of the extent to which there is a single global industrial-capitalist form of life: (i) if there is a global industrial-capitalist system (no matter how fragmented) then we can do some cross-cultural work; (ii) if there is no global industrial-capitalist system then we cannot do cross-cultural work as we would have no basis upon which to make the comparisons. The latter alternative seems deeply implausible. The expansion of the industrial-capitalist system over the centuries from its original European heartlands has drawn most, if not all, non-capitalist cultures into its ambit. This is the argument of Worsley[50] and Gellner[51] whom we met earlier when discussing social theory. However, again, it seems equally clear that the global system is not a unitary system. The claims of economic liberals and postmodernists seem implausible. We are left therefore with an idea of an evolving diverse global system which presently exhibits a pronounced regional pattern. We are forced back to the provisional conclusion of the preceding chapter dealing with political economy – there is a global industrial-capitalist system but it has developed in such a way as to produce discrete versions of the form of life in question.

Overall, it would seem that we have several conclusions to make: (i) that the Max Weber of modernization theory and lately business-economic celebrations of the Asian success story has little to do with the turn of the century theorist who addressed the situation of Germany and the responsibilities of the local bourgeoisie; (ii) that it is evident that culture and society do make a difference to development tracks but the process of analysing complex change is awkward and difficult and offering a deterministic cultural reductionism is no better than familiar deterministic economic reductionism; (iii) that one cannot advance enquiry by endeavouring to read the detail of one society in terms of a simple model or generalization of the historical experience of another; and (iv) if one wants to grasp the nature of the contribution of sets of ideas and social institutions then one has to attend to the detail of actual cases – hence the reflexive, sceptical and interpretive analysis of particular patterns of structural circumstances and agent-group responses.

The individual and the collectivity

There is an available debate which posits a Western individualism and a Pacific Asian concern for community. The general issue raised is that of the relationship between the individual and the collective. It seems clear that the ways in which particular individuals can construe their relationship to the collectivity of which they are members can vary from obedient submission through to idiosyncratic self-assertion. It is also clear that the issue admits of a variety of social theoretical answers. It also seems to be clear that the post-Second World Anglo-American liberal individualist social scientific common sense is no longer dominant. The rise of Pacific Asia has created a practical real world alternative to the schemes of the Western orthodoxy. It is quite clear that the intellectual debates will continue with some vigour in future years.

An interim conclusion

Evans[52] makes clear that the Pacific Asian region is ethnographically very diverse. A series of very broad cultural sub-regions can be identified – East Asia, Southeast Asia – and the question with regard to the particularity (or otherwise) of the social-institutional structures of the region is thoroughly awkward. Yet on balance it does seem to be the case that a series of significant differences can be pointed to between the social-institutional forms of Pacific Asia and the other major areas of the emergent tripolar global industrial-capitalist system.

Conclusion

In recent years the recent historical development experience of the countries of Pacific Asia has drawn considerable attention from a variety of commentators within the region and the wider international community. In Japan, China and parts of ASEAN, the record of success has been the basis for a reassertion of the autonomy, vigour and likely future prosperity of the peoples of Asia. It would be true to say that both the record and the new Asian assertiveness have captured the attention of the USA which has on occasion responded in a similarly assertive fashion. The countries of the European Union have responded rather differently on the basis of a different historical experience and a recent period of eclipse within the post-war sphere of the USA. However, it would also be true to say that these vigorous debates have not generated any intellectual consensus amongst scholars. The debate about the particularity of the historical development experience of the countries of Pacific Asia is likely to continue and whilst the outcome is unclear it is difficult to imagine how the various proponents of the presently influential market-liberal orthodoxy could secure broad agreement. One might anticipate a series of explanations, each cast in the broad terms of one of the three key regions within the tripolar global system, and thereafter, the key to effective analysis will lie in scholarly, policy analytical, and political dialogue.

Notes

1 J. K. Galbraith in *The Guardian*, London, 28 July 1989.
2 E. Wilkinson 1990: *Japan versus the West*, Harmondsworth: Penguin, p. 8.
3 Ibid.
4 World Bank 1992: *World Development Report 1992*, Oxford University Press.
5 J. C. Abegglen 1994: *Sea Change*, New York: Free Press, p. 4.
6 J. Zysman 1996: The Myth of a Global Economy in *New Political Economy* 12, p. 162.
7 G. Barraclough 1964: *An Introduction to Contemporary History*, Harmondsworth: Penguin, p. 160.
8 Zysman 1996, p. 159.
9 P. W. Preston 1986: *Making Sense of Development*, London: Routledge; P. W. Preston 1996: *Development Theory*, Oxford: Blackwell.
10 K. Ohmae 1990: *A Borderless World*, Tokyo: Kodansha.
11 An expression I take from Richard Higgot, see R. Higgot Ideas and Identity in the International Political Economy of Regionalism: The Asia Pacific and Europe Compared in *ISA-JAIR Joint Convention*, Makuhari: Japan.
12 World Bank 1993: *The East Asian Miracle: Economic Growth and Public Policy*, Oxford University Press.
13 Ibid., p. 5.
14 Ibid., p. 10.
15 R. Wade 1996: Japan, the World Bank and the Art of Paradigm Maintenance: The East Asian Miracle in Political Perspective in *New Left Review* 217.
16 S. P. Huntington 1993: The Clash of Civilizations in *Foreign Affairs*.
17 R. Higgot and R. Robison eds 1985: *Southeast Asia: Essays in the Political Economy of Structural Change*, London: Routledge; R. P. Appelbaum and J. Henderson, eds, 1992: *States and Development in the Asian Pacific Rim*, London: Sage; K. Hewison, R. Robison and G. Rodan, eds, 1993: *Southeast Asia in the 1990s*, St Leonards: Allen and Unwin; R. Higgot, R. Leaver and J. Ravenhill, eds, 1993: *Pacific Economic Relations in the 1990s*, St Leonards: Allen and Unwin.
18 B. Moore 1966: *Social Origins of Dictatorship and Democracy*, Boston: Beacon; R. Dore 1986: *Flexible Rigidities*, Stanford University Press; K. van Wolferen 1989: *The Enigma of Japanese Power*, London: Macmillan; C. Johnson 1995: *Japan Who Governs?*, New York: Norton.
19 M. Shibusawa et al. 1992: *Pacific Asia in the 1990s*, London: Routledge.
20 C. Johnson 1982: *MITI and the Japanese Miracle*, Stanford University Press.
21 Shibusawa 1992, p. 54.
22 Appelbaum and Henderson 1992, p. 21.
23 L. Thurow 1994: *Head to Head: The Coming Economic Battle Among Japan, Europe and America*, New York: Morrow.
24 Zysman 1996.
25 R. Dore 1986: *Learning From Japan*, Stanford University Press.
26 See Johnson 1995; D. Williams 1996: *Japan and the Enemies of Open Political Science*, London: Routledge; J. Fallows 1995: *Looking at the Sun: The Rise of the New East Asian Economic and Political System*, New York: Vintage.
27 United Nations Development Programme 1992: *Human Development Report 1992*, Oxford University Press.

28   J. Hunter 1989: *The Emergence of Modern Japan*, London: Longman.
29   Ibid., p. 64.
30   Ibid., p. 65.
31   Ibid., p. 66.
32   Chie Nakane cited in ibid., p. 68.
33   Ibid., p. 68.
34   Ibid., p. 71.
35   Ibid.
36   Ibid., p. 78.
37   Robison and Goodman 1996.
38   H. Hardacre 1995: Class, Status and Gender in C. Mackerras, ed., *Eastern Asia*, London: Longman, p. 497.
39   Ibid., p. 499.
40   N. Heyzer 1986: *Working Women in Southeast Asia: Development, Subordination and Emancipation*, Milton Keynes: Open University Press.
41   Mackerras, ed., 1995.
42   Hardacre 1995, p. 500.
43   Ibid.
44   Ibid., p. 501.
45   H. D. Evers 1980: *The Sociology of Southeast Asia*, Kuala Lumpur: Oxford University Press.
46   J. C. Scott 1976: *The Moral Economy of the Peasant*, New Haven, CT: Yale University Press.
47   C. B. Macpherson 1973: *Democratic Theory: Essays in Retrieval*, Oxford University Press; A. MacIntyre 1981: *After Virtue*, London: Duckworth.
48   Robison 1996.
49   Preston 1996.
50   P. Worsley 1984: *The Three Worlds: Culture and World Development*, London: Weidenfeld.
51   E. Gellner 1964: *Thought and Change*, London: Weidenfeld.
52   Evans, ed., 1996.

12

The Pacific Asian Model II: Cultural and Political-cultural Processes

The success of the countries of Pacific Asia in political-economic terms has often been explained with reference to social-institutional factors, as we have seen, but the recorded success has also routinely been ascribed to the particular cultural resources of the region. Many commentators have called attention to what are perceived to be deferential and obedient people working within hierarchical systems which appear to acknowledge the notion of the community more directly than familiar Western market-liberal systems. It might be noted that there is a long tradition of invoking cultural explanations within the social sciences and in the past they have sometimes been treated as somehow less satisfactory than the arguments citing matters economic or social, but this is unreasonable. The notions of culture and political culture are simply further concepts available within the lexicon of the social sciences and when properly deployed they can be put to good use.[1]

The Idea of Culture

In recent years a series of arguments have been presented which claim that the sets of ideas present within Pacific Asian cultures are particularly favourable to the process of rapid economic advance, and putative traits of deference, obedience and commonality have been identified. Against the enthusiasts, it has been pointed out that this is all rather ironic, because in the early post-Second World War years, when little success was anticipated, the cultures of the region were described in familiar nineteenth-century

European terms as fatalistic, conservative and steeped in irrational religious tradition. We can begin with the idea of culture and note the business of the invention of Asia, before going on to look at contemporary Pacific Asian culture.

The idea of culture typically points to the realm of ideas, rather than practice, and pulls towards the particular rather than the general, however when the idea is unpacked it becomes clear that there is a range of meanings attached to the term. It is important to take note of this spread of ideas, and to locate the term in the context of the classical tradition of social theorizing.

Multiplicity of meanings of the term 'culture'

Jenks[2] reviews the multiplicity of meanings of the term 'culture' as it appears over the years within the European and American traditions of philosophy, literature and social science. A series of strands of reflection are identified: (i) the nineteenth-century reaction to industrialism which stressed culture; (ii) the classical notion of culture as civilization in opposition to barbarism; (iii) the sociological and anthropological notions of culture as sets of ideas or more broadly social practices; (iv) the German philosophical notion of culture as acquired learning/sensibility; and (v) a contemporary Anglo-American usage within social sciences which looks to the diversity of social practices of groups and sub-groups. All of these can be distilled into three very broad areas of meanings: firstly, culture as a cognitive category, a state of mind, with an ideal goal implied (the realm of the arts and ethics); secondly, culture as a level of collective social development, which is the realm of talk about culture and society (the realm of the humanities); and thirdly, culture as the way of life of a people, which is the realm of talk about routine practical activity, praxis, (the realm of the social sciences).

The idea of culture-as-praxis derives from the humanist tradition of Marxism and designates the dense sphere of meanings carried in language which flow from and inform ordinary social life.[3] In the work of Marx, historical materialism made culture an emergent property of economic structures; thereafter the work was developed in a positivistic fashion which led into Marxism-Leninism (the official ideology of the USSR) where ideas were seen as a simple reflection of economic structures; and finally humanist Marxism, including Lukács, Gramsci, Goldman, and the Frankfurt School, was concerned one way or another with the sets of ideas embedded in the ordinary routines of industrial-capitalist society, understood most centrally in terms of ideology. So far as their practical politics were concerned they tended to argue that a necessary condition of radical change was a broad social appreciation of the manipulative nature of civil society in advanced industrial-capitalism. It was the business of social critics to fracture received common sense so as to open the possibility of wider progressive debate. The humanist Marxist tradition lets us attend to the detail of ordinary life and allows that agents can marshal the cognitive resources of a culture in order to read the circumstances of that culture as the basis for urging subsequent particular courses of action.

The idea of Asia

Said[4] has discussed the creation of a Western image of the East in the process of the pursuit of scholarship and the practical goals of empire. Evans remarks that 'Asia or the Orient is an artefact of the European imagination'.[5] The notion of Asia slowly took form amongst Europeans as the early trading voyages of the fifteenth century reached the Pacific Asian region. In the eighteenth century the idea of the orient began to take shape and became the dominant motif in European analyses and commentaries in the nineteenth century as the drive to colonize the area reached its most energetic phase. The result is a construct which characterizes the East as radically different from the West. The East is taken to be irrational, mystical and wreathed in impenetrable tradition, the antithesis of Enlightenment rationalism.[6]

Evans[7] sketches the process of the construction of the notion of the East, and notes how it was both naturalized with reductive arguments pointing to 'race' and adopted by the peoples of the region, and thereafter turned back against the colonizers in the form of a reactive nationalism. It is in this way that the present cultures of the Pacific Asian region – as they are expressed in routine practice and established institutions – represent the outcome of a complex exchange with the expanding industrial-capitalist system. It is clear that sets of ideas (philosophies and social scientific theories) and social practices (institutional practices such as modern schools, universities, newspapers, political parties and so on) have been taken from the West and reworked in a Pacific Asian context in order that local agents could read and react to the patterns of structural changes which enfolded their lives.

It is clear that this sort of dynamic is general,[8] however, we might note that one consequence of these reflections is that the claims of Pacific Asian nationalists – to a long national history cruelly disturbed by Western expansion – is untenably oversimplified. The route to the modern world in Pacific Asia generates both a series of cultural residues, thus the collective memories and practices from the various stages in the process, and establishes a series of presently central cultural resources, in particular, the ideas of nations, states and nation states. Further, as the shift to the modern world generated ideas of particular nationalisms it also generated a general idea of Asianness which has found expression in political and cultural programmes of a pan-Asian nature. At the present time the contemporary concern for a Pacific Asian region can be taken to be the inheritor of these lines of political and cultural reflection.

Overall, it is clear that the notion of culture is one that must be approached rather more carefully than some of the other ideas within the lexicon of social science. And with these provisos in mind we can turn to the issue of the culture of Pacific Asia.

The Cultures of Pacific Asia

In Pacific Asia there are great differences in existing patterns of life. A series of overlapping and cross-cutting strategies for grasping this diversity can be identified. There are two lines of reductive argument which can be noted: (i) evolutionary arguments; and (ii) linguistic deterministic arguments. Thereafter there are a series of more familiar social scientific lines of argument: (i) those which look to broad historical-cultural areas, the Indian world, Chinese world and the Malay world; (ii) those which look to language groups; (iii) those which look to the great tradition religions of Buddhism, Confucianism, Islam and Hinduism; and (iv) those which look to the shifting dynamics of place, region and global system.

Evolutionary and linguistic-determinist arguments

The emergence of humankind and its subsequent pattern of distribution is a topic which concerns archaeology, palaeontology, biologists and anthropology (where evidence of culture separates humans from animal forebears). These disciplines have contributed to the attempt to reconstruct the history of humankind as a species, detailing origins, major stages in development and patterns of distribution.

Bowdler summarizes current specialist opinion by noting that our early human ancestors, *Homo habilis* and *Homo erectus*, are likely to have 'appeared in Africa 2.5 to 2.0 million years ago'.[9] The first humans, *Homo sapiens*, have been dated at between 200,000 and 100,000 years ago. It would seem that expert opinion is agreed that *Homo habilis* and *Homo erectus* emerged in Africa. However, Bowdler[10] reports that there are two main models which attempt to explain how *Homo sapiens* subsequently spread around the planet: (i) the regional continuity model, which posits an early movement out from the African source of *Homo erectus* and thereafter evolutionary changes to generate four main version of *Homo sapiens* (caucasoids, negroids, mongoloids and australoids); and (ii) the replacement model, which posits a movement from the African source of *Homo sapiens* and the replacement of already existing early-human forms.

The lines of argument presented here all treat humankind as one more animal species whose physical characteristics allow their categorization and thereafter their patterns of evolution and distributions to be described in scientific terms. All humans are taken to belong to one species, and thereafter the subspecies identify what are popularly known as races. However, the issue of race in human affairs is fraught and experts find that scientific debate, already difficult, is made more awkward by politics. The matter of differences between humans remains contested; but cast in these terms, Pacific Asia is populated by two varieties of humans, mongoloids and australoids.

A rather more precise strategy of classification looks to linguistic groups. Prasithrathsint[11] reviews the arguments derived from the work of

Sapir-Whorf which point to linguistic determinism and considers them in the case of Pacific Asia.

The Sapir-Whorf hypothesis posits a deterministic relationship between language and practical human activity. It is argued that a language offers a way of constituting the world of lived experience and thereby determining what may and may not be thought and done. Whorf presented empirical evidence from American Indian languages which he showed diverged significantly from standard American/European languages. Prasithrathsint summarizes the hypothesis in terms of two assertions, first that our 'thought and perception of the environment depend on the language we speak' and, second, the 'larger the discrepancy between any two languages, the more different the world views of the speakers of these languages'.[12] It should be noted that cast in these terms the issue has been highly controversial, although the nature of language and the implications of an assertion of the centrality of language for human experience for the social sciences have been widely debated.[13]

The Whorfian scheme of linguistic determinism can be applied to Pacific Asia: (i) Indian language is rich in abstract terms and construes personality subjectively, which linguistic traits feed into discourse favouring subjective interpretation; (ii) Chinese language avoids the abstract in favour of the concrete, itself presented in multiple varieties, which linguistic traits feed into discourse favouring the detailed specification of particulars; and (iii) Japanese downplays the personal pronoun and uses elaborate formal greetings, which linguistic traits feed into a discourse which is group-centred and concerned with schemes of polite good manners.[14]

Any simple version of the Sapir–Whorf argument is rather implausible but a softened scheme which looks to explicate the relationship of language and social practice in terms of the notion of culture, the sets of cognitive resources carried in language and available to agents, looks more useful – for example, in elucidating the workings of complex religious, ethnic or political idea systems.

In Pacific Asia there are numerous languages, and linguists would identify seven major language groups with maybe in excess of one thousand natural languages. It is worth noting that one crucial issue in the broad process of the shift to the modern world has been the choice of languages for national use.

Historical-cultural areas and Great Traditions

Evans comments: 'The use of the term Asia can be extremely misleading if it is used to denote some sort of cultural uniformity throughout the geographical area'.[15] However, the strategy of looking to broad historical-cultural areas points to broad regions inhabited by peoples who have, over the years, developed cultural traits which can somehow be taken to be typical. This strategy of characterization points to patterns of life, language groups, physiology (race) and common experience.

In the Pacific Asian region we can point to the pattern of life of the Chinese, or the Malays, or the Indians. In each case we can point to a long established forms of life with elaborate social-institutional forms and associated cultural schemes. They may be called civilizations. Evans comments that 'These broad Culture Areas have some intellectual attractions . . . But . . . these are large generalizations whose value for understanding the details of individual societies and cultures are limited'.[16] It is also true that if one looks to the detail of any particular country within the region that further divisions and sub-divisions will be found.

The best we can say in respect of broad historical-cultural areas in Pacific Asia is that there are three main cultural streams: the Indian, originating in South Asia and flowing into Southeast Asia; the Southeast Asian, which originates in that area; and the Chinese, which originates in Northeast Asia and which has spread southwards throughout the region as a whole.

The closely related strategy of looking at great traditions focuses on the cultural construct of religion. The argument is made that religious beliefs and their associated institutional practices have decisively shaped the patterns of life of people within broad regions. We can speak of the influence of Hinduism flowing into Pacific Asia from India. We can speak of the influence of Buddhism flowing into Pacific Asia from India, and we can also speak of the diverse tradition of Confucianism originating in China and dispersing through the region. And we can speak of the influence of Islam flowing into the region from Arabia. The great tradition religions have established institutional structures, regular patterns of worship and accumulated bodies of sacred texts. It is on the basis of these characteristics that it is argued that they have a wider and continuing cultural influence.

Schak[17] has summarized the broad character of the religions of the area as follows: China is 97 per cent atheist/eclectic; Japan is 84 per cent Shinto/Buddhist; Indonesia is 88 per cent Muslim; Malaysia is 58 per cent Muslim and 30 per cent Buddhist; Thailand is 95 per cent Buddhist; South Korea is 72 per cent Buddhist/Confucian; Taiwan is 93 per cent Buddhist/Confucianist/Daoist; Vietnam is 60 per cent Buddhist; Hong Kong is 90 per cent traditional; and the Philippines is 83 per cent Roman Catholic. The key religious traditions are thus Buddhism, Islam and Chinese traditional religion (assuming that the present reports for China reflect official socialist ideology), and the only significant presence of Christianity is in the Philippines.

It is worth noting that the pattern of religious belief has been a matter of concern for many commentators who have looked to the wellsprings of human motivation in religious doctrines, drawing a broad distinction between traditions encouraging action in the light of prescribed ethical schemes or doctrines and those stressing the acceptance of circumstances. The distinction recalls the work of Max Weber who argued that it was the practical secular implications of their doctrinal asceticism which in part triggered the development of capitalism in Europe. The work of Weber has inspired a series of further reflections upon the relationship of systems of religious belief and patterns of development.[18]

Place, region and global system

However, against these approaches and in line with the preference of this text for the resources of the classical tradition of social theorizing, we can look to the shifting nature of the resources of culture in the process of the shift to a modern world. The present patterns of culture within Pacific Asia can be treated as a mixture of those presently effective residues of earlier phases in the development of the region and their present creative reworking, as agents draw upon them in order to read and respond to structural patterns in order to fashion various routes to the future. It is the idea of culture-as-praxis which offers assistance in this task. It is clear that the shift to the modern world has been variously accomplished within the region.

In the first place, there are a group of long established industrial-capitalist countries: Japan, Australia and New Zealand. The practical form-of-life of the Japanese is modern in that they inhabit an industrial-capitalist society, yet differs from the West because the pattern of life of Japanese people entails overlapping group memberships, what has been called 'groupism'. The more self-conscious self-understanding of the Japanese can be elucidated with reference to the literature of *nihonjinron* which celebrates the particularity of the Japanese.[19] Overall, the key to the form of life of the Japanese people lies in their mobilized pursuit of national security via material advance. And in a similar way in Australia and New Zealand the form-of-life is that of a long established, mature industrial-capitalism. However, there have been two major political-cultural shifts in recent years: firstly, there has been a movement towards policy making cast in business-economic terms which favours international capital (thereby opening local economies to Pacific Asian exports and direct investment); and secondly, there has been a movement towards an immigration policy which looks to draw in certain categories of Pacific Asian migrants.

In the second place, there is a more recently developed group, the NICs. The practical form-of-life of these countries is similarly modern, in that they inhabit industrial-capitalist forms-of-life. However, they do so in the company of powerful neighbours in China and Japan. Sum[20] identifies American, Japanese and Chinese versions of the future of the region and the NICs within it, and adds that these readings run into internal debates about the future which often imply multiple identities as participants draw upon diverse backgrounds and specify various routes to the future.

Finally, matters are more fluid in the more recently developing areas of Southeast Asia and the reforming socialist bloc. The practical form-of-life of the outer periphery of ASEAN is lodged within the process of rapid complex change as the shift to the modern world of the sub-region accelerates with the post-colonial drive to independent effective nation statehood both continuing and simultaneously being re-presented or re-expressed in terms of the opportunities/constraints of the increasingly integrated Pacific Asian region. In conventional terms these cultures are experiencing rapid modernization. Relatedly, the practical form-of-life of the old socialist bloc is experiencing extensive change as the post-war pursuit of a socialist model of development is set aside in favour of marketization and nationalism in the context of rapidly growing linkages with the Pacific Asian region. The government of China is asserting its place in the region. Again, in conventional terms these sub-regional cultures are experiencing rapid modernization.

The Pacific Asian Model Debated

It has been argued that in the aggregate the cultures of Pacific Asia are suffused with the demands of traditional religious ideas. The religious belief systems of the region are various but can be characterized as stressing either resignation in the face of enduring natural and spiritual forces, or obedience to a system of authoritatively prescribed rules of social behaviour, or adherence to systems of sacred revelation. The bodies of religious belief offer no clear basis for active human concern for material advance. At the same time the secular practices of the region have looked to reconcile individuals with hierarchical power structures and have stressed deference, obedience and supplication. All these are contrasted with an equivalent stereotypical characterization of the West as individualistic, rational and progressive.

It is clear that there is an available Western notion which stresses the priority of individuals. In its liberal version the individual is the key to understanding human life and the sphere of the social is merely an aggregate of contractual relationships between individuals. It is easy to see how liberal individualism can read the patterns of life of Pacific Asia as non-individualistic. It is also easy to see how the commitments of liberalism imply that non-individualistic social arrangements are either irrational or despotic. It is, finally, worth noting that the last forty years or so have seen a strong American influence upon European social theorizing with a concomitant process of reading liberalism into social theorizing (as with for example convergence theory). Overall, it is clear that there is an available Western stereotype of the East which presents the people of the region as subordinate to the demands of their societies.

However, we can assert that it is possible to conceive the relationship of individual and collectivity in a wide variety of ways. We are not forced to the opposition of rational individualism and irrational/despotic social subordination. This being the case, it is possible to characterize the cultures of Pacific Asia in terms of the particular ways in which the relation of individuals and collectivities are construed. In terms taken from the classical tradition it is clear that in Japan and the inner periphery, the cultures are variants of established global industrial-capitalist forms-of-life. In the other areas the nature of the shift to the modern world thus far accomplished varies; however, in all cases the resultant culture is particular to the locale and region, and in very general terms can be grasped in terms of the ideas of obedience, conformity and communality.

In the Western rational scientific Enlightenment tradition there is an expectation that the shift to the modern world involves, amongst other things, a falling away of the relevance and influence of religious ideas. The argument is available in a variety of forms but the two most directly influential are those which point to economics and look to material advance undermining religious ideas and those which look to culture and look to the natural science-based expansion of rationality. The familiar Western social scientific discussions tend to be centred on an ideal of instrumental rationality, the conscious measurement of alternatives in the process of making decisions. In this context there is an available historically received disposition to regard the West as the repository of reason whilst the East is the realm of continuing unreason.

Again, a sharp divide is being posited – reason versus unreason – and it is supposed that the route to the modern world involves shifting from the unreason of traditional society to the reason of modern society. And so far as Western stereotypes are concerned, Asia is suffused with the demands of unreason in the form of religious traditions and local superstitions. In this way the cultural resources of Pacific Asia are seen to be coloured by the residues of historically traditional irrationalisms.

However, once again, we can suggest that matters are perhaps more complex. The distinction between reason and unreason may be too sharp. It is certainly the case that the idea of 'reason' has been subject to extensive recent investigation and the possibility that reason is to some extent shaped by context can be entertained. It is possible thereafter to critically deconstruct the familiar Western liberal equation of instrumental rationality with reason per se. It is further possible to look at the patterns of life of other cultures as evidencing situational-logics which work in their own ways.

The sacred organization of the cultures of Pacific Asia does seem to be more prominent than is the case in the West and it also seems to be less distant from the routines of ordinary life. In Pacific Asia many people would have family altars in their homes and would look to these (and other gods) for assistance in ordinary practical matters. In other worlds, the sacred realm threads through ordinary life in a way different from the situation in the West.

The exchange between the resources of Western social science and the cultures of the peoples of the Pacific Asian region have generated a series of particular areas of debate and we have noted some of these. However, we can pull back from these particular issues and ask whether the experience of trying to grasp the cultures of the region offers any lessons for Western social science in general and the classical tradition more particularly.

Identifying regions and making generalizations

In this text we have identified a Pacific Asian region. A series of lines of argument have been presented which indicate systematic patterns of activity within the territory and a commonality in forms-of-life has been tentatively identified. It is on the basis of these lines of argument, and a set of broad strategic comparisons with other areas within the global system, that the Pacific Asia region is identified. It is clear that Pacific Asia is an intellectual construct, it is one way in which diffuse patterns of structural change can be read and action thereafter ordered, and the way in which this construct is established is a matter of concern.

It is clear that a region is not simply given. A region has no essence waiting to be discovered and described thus it will not do to report on the cultural essence of a region. A region has no clear simple boundary, so the temptation to run geographical reductionist arguments must also be resisted. The classical tradition informed approach of structural international political economy looks to the exchange of structures and agents within the ongoing development of the global system. The approach posits a complex pattern of structures which enfold/penetrate agent groups, including states, whose actions, informed by their intentions and by their shifting partial grasp of their circumstances, thereafter reconstitutes those structures in a dialectical process of historical change. A region takes shape as a mixture of shifting structural configurations, agent recognition and thereafter action in pursuit of particular projects. The constitution of a region is thus a matter of re-cognition and action in respect of slowly changing configurations of structural power.

If we ask how a participant/observer can grasp the extent and logic of any particular region then it is clear that there are a variety of strategies available: geographical, economic, social, cultural and political. These social scientific strategies of analysis are deployed in line with the contemporary concerns of the community of enquiry to which we belong. It is clear, for example, that the regions which European scholars have identified have changed over the years: Cathay, the Orient, the Far East, Asia and now Pacific Asia. It is clear that the relationship of scholarship to wider sets of circumstances and the extent to which the scholarly identification of a region can be grounded remain awkward and open questions. There is no simple positivistic answer rather it is necessary to locate scholarship within the social world as one variant of a generic human concern to make sense of shifting historical circumstances. Over the years the concerns of Europeans with Pacific Asia have shifted and the focus of scholarship has similarly changed.

A related question can be raised by recalling the anthropological distinction between emic and etic descriptions, the view of insiders and that of outsiders. It is clear that the analysis of Pacific Asia made in this text, which is explicitly grounded in the classical tradition, is an etic one. We might ask therefore about the extent to which the form of life of Pacific Asian peoples was accessible to Europeans. It seems likely that we construct our model of the other in our terms. It is therefore a limited understanding of the other. However, the extent to which we can reliably grasp the logics of other cultures remains open. In practical terms it is at this point we run into the problems of stereotyping.

It can be argued that the notion of 'Asia' is a social construct which was first contrived by Westerners in the period of high colonialism and which has subsequently been unhelpfully assimilated, reproduced and disseminated by elites. The manner in which the putative construct impacts upon general contemporary processes of economic, social and cultural reproduction is a matter of current investigation.

It is clear that there are acute problems in making generalizations about other patterns of life. We can generate the ethnographies and prepare the data sets but beyond that we are shifting to generalizations and these can only be shaped by particular intellectual agendas. We depend upon both a common humanity (the base for anthropological ethnography) and as has been argued here a common pragmatic social root in the ongoing historical development of the global industrial-capitalist system.

Cognitive and moral relativism

A series of philosophers have argued that reason and ethics are context dependent. In its recent form the work traces back to the philosopher of language Wittgenstein who offered an extended dispersed reflection upon the nature of human language and social life and concluded that they were two sides of the same coin, so to say, and that they came in a wide variety of discrete forms. Wittgenstein expressed this insight in terms of the idea of particular forms-of-life being carried in particular language games. On this view patterns of human life and thought are always particular to a time and place. They might well be regarded as variations on the theme of being human but there is no overarching form of life and there is no overarching language game. On this view it is important to look to dialogue and to be modest in ones expectations as to the extent to which the ideas and meanings carried in one form of life or language game can be translated into the terms of another. A corollary of this philosophical position points to a strategic problem with orthodox positivistic social science in that it wrongly seeks to promote one form of life or language game to a privileged position, namely natural science, and thereafter wrongly construes the nature of the work within its own field.

An interim conclusion

Once again, it seems clear that the peoples of the region of Pacific Asia inherit patterns of life which are both internally diverse and quite distinct from other regions within the tripolar system. There is a wealth of historical, sociological and anthropological material which attests this point. However, although it is fairly clear that the patterns of life of the peoples of the region are different from those of other regions within the global system, and different from each other, it is not easy to specify in general terms just what the cultures of the region have in common. It is certainly easy to make broad generalizations but what must remain in question is the value of such generalizations. It seems that they must be used very carefully. Nonetheless, it seems safe to assert that historical legacies and contemporary exchanges do permit a characterization to be advanced of the culture of the Pacific Asia model as hierarchical, obedient and disposed to communality.[21]

Political Culture, Identity and Change

It can be argued that political-cultural identities are ways of reading enfolding structural circumstances. The nature of political-cultural identity will be shaped by the exchange of powerful groups, established institutions and the informal resources of ordinary life. In the modern period a key agent in identity formation has been the state. It is the state which has fostered projects of building national identities. The recent emergence of regional structural patterns suggests that new post-national identities could develop.

A political-cultural identity expresses the individuals relationship to the community considered as an ordered body and may be elucidated in terms of the ideas of locale, network and memory. In terms of the notion of locale, the focus is on how an individual construes their relationship to the community they inhabit, and how thereafter the person considers that their community relates to the wider world. The accumulation of these personal views will constitute the folk knowledges of local communities. In terms of the notion of network we are looking at how individuals lodge themselves in dispersed groups, and thereafter how the individual considers that the grouping of persons construe their relationship to other groups within the wider collectivity. This the sphere of operation of ideologies, both delimited-formal, as the group propounds its position, and pervasive-informal, as the general cultural sphere is suffused with the competing positions of many groups. And in terms of the notion of memory we are looking at the ways in which individuals, groups and collectivities secure their understandings of the power aspects of patterns of social relationships in the material of folk traditions, institutional truths and the official histories of states.

If we approach these matters from a structural direction and look at how the collectivity embraces the person we can begin to speak of ideologies and the extent of the development of the democratic public sphere. The formal positions of parties, governments and states represent the ways in which groups read and react to structural circumstances and as these alter so too do political-cultural identities.

In the modern world states have routinely sought to control spontaneous popular sentiments through the promulgation of ideas of nationalism. The response of elites to shifting structural circumstances will involve amongst other things the promulgation of political projects which will seek to mobilize populations by offering an image of a developing identity. There have been a series of such identities on offer within the region as indigenous forms-of-life were subsumed within colonial projects which in turn modulated into a variety of projects of post-colonial nation building. The present structural pattern within the area can be grasped in terms of the notion of the Pacific Asian region.

It seems clear that familiar patterns of political-cultural identity are likely to change in the future as the global structures which such constructs grasp become more complexly ordered. Overall, it is clear that we need to consider: (i) the patterns of understanding lodged in ordinary life; (ii) the projects of state-regimes; (iii) the phases of change as the global system reconfigures; and (iv) the present situation of Pacific Asia.

Pacific Asian Routes to the Modern World

The modern history of Pacific Asia centres on the shift to the modern world. In schematic terms this can be taken to include the pre-contact period, absorption within the colonial system, the post-colonial pursuit of effective nation statehood and the rise of Pacific Asia.

The pre-contact forms-of-life of the peoples of Pacific Asia can be seen to have taken two broad forms: first, the East Asian sphere, with the closed hier-archical, bureaucratic, feudal, agrarian society of imperial China and the similar society of Japan; and second, the Southeast Asian sphere with the fluid and shifting riverine, agrarian, personalized empires of Indo-China and the similarly fluid maritime trading empires of Southeast Asia. It should also be noted that Asia's third major cultural area, South Asia, centred on India, has exerted considerable influence on the other two areas (as with, for example, Islam, Hinduism and Buddhism). It provided, for example, the literary and dramatic Hindu epics of the gods which fed into Southeast Asian notions of secular princely empire. It was this spread of long-established civilizations and the simpler peasant forms-of-life lodged within their bounds which the carriers of the expanding global capitalist system first encountered in the sixteenth century.

As European and American-based capitalism expanded the territories of the region were slowly remade in political-economic, social-institutional and cultural form, in line with the schedule of needs of the metropolitan centres. The upshot was the pre-1941 situation of colonial Asia where the Dutch and British controlled Southeast Asia, the French ruled in Indo-China, the Americans occupied the Philippines, the Japanese occupied Korea and Taiwan, and all these powers competed for advantage in China. The political life of colonial territories had a common pattern in foreign elite rule and local subordination, where colonial cities linked local patterns of life to metropolitan and global economic, social and cultural flows. At this point the entire sphere of Asia had been drawn one way or another into the Western-centred industrial-capitalist system.

The military victories of the Imperial Japanese armed forces in 1941–2 destroyed the European and American colonial structures and through the chaos of the period laid the basis for post-war independence throughout the region. The disruption of familiar economic, social and political patterns left a space open for indigenous nationalist movements. These nationalist movements turned Western ideas – nation, state and sovereignty – against their colonial past and affirmed ideals of independence. In the post-Second World War period the withdrawal of the European and American colonial powers was accomplished, in the main, relatively quickly. One significant aspect of the post-war situation was the victory of the Chinese communists in 1949 and the consequent pursuit by the USA of a policy of containment in Asia. The result was the division of Pacific Asia into two spheres: an autarchic socialist bloc; and an outward-looking group subject to the hegemony of the USA.

Contemporary Political-cultural Identities in Pacific Asia

The Pacific region over the post-Second World War period has been divided by cold war institutions and rhetoric. The Western-focused group has been subject to the economic, political and cultural hegemony of the USA, whilst the countries of the socialist bloc spent decades following autarchic development trajectories. However, over the post-war period the region's economies have prospered and the new prosperity is encouraging change. The Western-focused group in Pacific Asia is experiencing the beginnings of a political-economic and cultural emancipation from the hegemony of the USA, and the socialist bloc in Pacific Asia is opening up to the wider world industrial-capitalist system. A new regional pattern has been in the process of creation.

In the absence of the rhetoric of the cold war which insisted upon regional division, it is possible to see a developing Pacific Asian region and the issue of identity can be raised. In particular, it can be asked whether the ideal of a Pacific Asia region could offer the disparate countries of the area an overarching theme around which more local identities could be ordered and with reference to which they could locate themselves within the tripolar global system.

The legacies of war, present relationships and questions of leadership

The historical presence of Japan within Pacific Asia involves both pre-eminence as the first developed modern nation state within the region and obloquy as key precipitant of a disastrous war. The present relationships of Japan and the countries of Pacific Asia are coloured by memories of Japanese expansion and war but are increasingly focused on the pragmatics of mutual material advance.

One theme which runs through the available discussions of Japan's role in Pacific Asia is the matter of leadership. Commentators ask whether Japan wishes to exercise leadership, and whether it is able. It is often suggested that an overt leadership role would require significant prior internal reform. On this point, a general diagnosis of the problems of Japanese politics is given by Buckley[22] who notes that there are problems with: (i) political and business corruption; (ii) a pork-barrel style of local politics; (iii) a secretive and powerful bureaucracy; and (iv) a general inability of the political system to effectively articulate and thereafter deal with a spread of domestic and international policy problems.

The schedule of reforms canvassed in respect of polity and economy is large, and their interactions various, and the proposals all have widespread implications for the nature of Japanese society. The practical problems which are routinely cited include: (i) poor housing; (ii) poor public facilities; (iii) long hours of work (and commuting); (iv) inequality between genders; (v) excessive examination-centred schooling; (vi) lack of leisure time for families; (vii) habits of conformity are overstressed; and (viii) the problems of an aged population. In all, the Japanese people are presented as the unwitting victims of the successful corporatist system which they have created and from which they restrictedly benefit. Yet Sheridan[23] notes that 'there still has been surprisingly little popular public debate in Japan about the future directions of economic development and national purpose'.

It is clear that the present-day relationship of Japan and Pacific Asia is bound up with economic linkages. The present relationships had their occasion in post-war reparations agreements. The patterns of official development aid run alongside patterns of foreign direct investment and both bolster trade within the region. Yasutomo[24] deals with the diplomatic rationale of Japanese aid and notes that its role is lodged within a concept of comprehensive national security, which urges that national security depends upon regional security and this in turn is helped by economic growth in the area. It seems safe to conclude that Japan will assert no overt leadership role within Pacific Asia in the near future.

The inner periphery of East Asia

The expansion of the Japanese state into the area of East Asia began in the late nineteenth century and came to involve large holdings in Manchuria, colonies in Korea and Taiwan, and extensive interests in China. The war against China precipitated the Pacific War and in the early period of successful expansion the Japanese government looked to the formation of a Great East Asia Co-prosperity Sphere, which was conceived as a sphere of mutually beneficial economic activity. However the rhetoric was never matched in reality and the initiative was swept away in the chaos of war and defeat. In the post-Second World War period the colonies of South Korea and Taiwan were taken from Japanese control and taken under American protection. In both countries severely authoritarian regimes received US backing and prospered economically. Halliday[25] characterizes their extensive economic links with Japan in terms of their constituting an inner periphery. Nonetheless the relationship at both popular and governmental levels is somewhat fraught as ever present historical memory continues to haunt otherwise successful economic exchanges.

In Korea the Japanese colonial era saw harsh treatment of the indigenous population. It would seem that there is a legacy of bitterness down to the present day and whilst it is difficult to see any broad positive legacy the colonial period did see some industrialization. However, at the present time pragmatism and geographical proximity underpin economic linkages. South Korea constitutes, according to Shibusawa et al., a 'near-perfect example of a developmental state'.[26] The circumstances of independence plus the dominant role of the military fed into an authoritarian pattern of development. Yet after some thirty years of post-war success the political economy, society and culture advanced to the point of rejecting the authoritarian aspects of the system. A series of distinct groups can be identified within society, and each has its own interests, and these include the world of business, an educated middle class and an energetic working class. In recent years there has been extensive political liberalization. At the same time South Korea has attempted to shift the focus of its development away from Japan and the USA in order to embrace a wider spread of Pacific Asian and OECD partners. The relationship with the USA which was forged in the post-Second World War period of aggressive anti-communism has been crucial to South Korea. It has always been viewed with doubt by sections of the population in Korea and it must be expected that it will change in the wake of the end of the cold war. In contrast the relationship with Japan is both historically long established, close in practical terms and difficult.

A broadly similar situation holds in Taiwan, the economic record of which is if anything even more remarkable than that of South Korea. In Taiwan the colonial episode was similar to that of Korea but is, perhaps, recalled more positively. The episode of decolonization was lost, so to say, within the confusions of the Chinese civil war and the retreat of the KMT forces to the island in 1949. A severely authoritarian regime suppressed local opposition and ruled with US backing throughout the years of the cold war. The present linkages with Japan are extensive. In the late 1980s a process of reform-from-above was begun in the political sphere and in recent years attempts have been made to redirect the linkages of the economy with the global system. In this case it is a matter of winding back dependence on the USA and Japan in order to look to the region and the countries of the OECD. However, in the case of Taiwan a major economic linkage is developing with mainland China. In terms of patterns of identity it would seem that as Pacific Asia changes it is the link to China which will dominate Taiwanese thinking for the foreseeable future.

Overall, at the present time in respect of the East Asian view of the role of Japan within the growing Pacific Asian region we can point to a mixture of historical memory, post-Second World War economic success, and a regional situation which is slowly changing in the post-cold war period with the relative eclipse of the USA, the economic pre-eminence of Japan and the recent rise of China. As the USA slowly reconfigures its relationship with the countries of the region in the wake of the ending of the cold war, the countries of the inner periphery face the task of maintaining a continuing relationship with Japan, where the burgeoning economy and political instability of China constitute a further and developing relevant context.

The outer periphery of Southeast Asia

The relationship of Japan with the other Pacific Asian countries is often characterized with reference to the metaphor of flying geese where Japan is the leader with the other countries following. The ideal relationship implied by this metaphor is one of a regionally complementary division of labour centred on Japan. The countries of Southeast Asia had their most direct exchange with Japan in the Pacific War and thereafter the economic role of Japan has increased and is now very significant.

In the outer periphery the legacies of war are complex. In the Dutch East Indies the early phase of exertion of Japanese control gave way to a measure of cooperation. An army of indigenous people was formed as was an organization of political representation led by Sukarno. In this sense the Japanese had a role to play in fostering an eventually successful nationalist movement. And in Burma a similar situation held with Aung San's army and political organization which modulated into an independence movement which secured its goal. Relatedly, in Malaysia, where the Japanese encouraged Malay nationalism whilst harshly treating the Chinese, the Japanese interregnum has had a lasting impact in the form of communalist politics, whose occasion may in part be traced to the wartime period. And in Singapore the wartime episode was harsh and is remembered as such by the largely Chinese population, however as with other areas of Pacific Asia there is a pragmatic focus on economic cooperation. Finally, in the Philippines a similar pattern is visible in that the Filipino elite cooperated with the Japanese and ideas of independence were floated, however the return of the USA saw the reestablishment of the status quo ante, leading to a pattern of American-dependent crony capitalism that culminated in the era of Marcos. It is difficult to identify a positive legacy of Japanese rule and current determinants of the relationship are the pragmatics of economic growth coupled to geographical proximity. And it should also be noted, finally, that if the political impact of the period of Japanese colonial rule for the outer periphery was ambiguous, then it must be said that the economic impact was severe but of short duration, as these territories were absorbed as materials supplying elements of a war economy that in turn quickly collapsed.

Cronin[27] points out that the contemporary linkages which Japan has with Southeast Asia express a 'complementary cooperation' skewed in Japan's favour. Overall, Japanese involvement contributes to economic growth and regional integration, and Dobson[28] points out in respect of the ASEAN case that it is clear that in recent years host governments have welcomed inward investment. Phongpaichit[29] suggests that we can distinguish between domestic capital, state capital and foreign capital and thereafter we can plot the shifting patterns of interest and how these are expressed in response to incoming foreign direct investment. In ASEAN, broadly, there was an early resistance to foreign investment as state and domestic capital prospered. Then in the depression of the early 1980s state capital ran into trouble and began to run up significant debt. At this point foreign investment became attractive to ASEAN governments and with the incoming investment the phase of export-oriented industrialization took off. It is clear that each country has had a particular experience of foreign investment assisted export oriented industrialization, but in each case the acceptance of foreign investment must be seen as an expression not of passive acceptance but of agency. In these terms, the actions of Southeast Asian state-regimes over the late 1980s can only be read as a knowing acquiescence in the dominance of the region by Japan.

In Malaysia the government instituted an explicit 'look east' policy in the early 1980s which took Japan as the model for Malaysian development. Khoo[30] argues that this was the policy of a group of modernising technocrats surrounding the Prime Minister Dr Mahathir and that the drive for development has overridden other more traditional groups within Malaysian society. It has been a policy conducive not merely to economic growth but also to extensive social conflict which found partial expression in politically charged debates about the nature of 'Malayness'.[31] And in a similar fashion the increasing prominence of the Japanese sphere within the global economy has been noted in Singapore, where Japan is a major trading partner. The government have recently promulgated a policy which acknowledges Singapore's dual role as partner to the Japanese and as a long-established nexus in the global system in terms of the goal of the status of regional hub economy. Thereafter, relatedly, in the resource-rich areas of Southeast Asia, that is Thailand and Indonesia, MacIntyre[32] comments that there is 'little doubt that their economies have been profoundly influenced by Japan and the four NICs' and that both countries have benefited from being located in a rapidly growing region. In the future it is likely that the key problems will not be economic, rather they will be political and social as the broader impacts of the recent phase of outward directed growth work themselves through the societies of Indonesia and Thailand. And, finally, in the Philippines the situation continues to be rather special in that the Spanish and American legacies (religious, economic and political-cultural), coupled to internal tensions (class and ethnic) and an absence of thoroughgoing post-Marcos reform mean that Japanese economic interest has not been fully expressed, leaving the Philippines rather following behind events.

China and Indo-China

The reforms of the early 1980s in China have led to increasing Japanese involvement in that country's economy. Against an historical backdrop which included both centuries of exchange, where Japan was the cultural borrower, and a post-Meiji series of antagonism culminating in the war of 1937–45, the linkages of the recent decade have been dominated by the pragmatics of economic expansion. At the present time contemporary economic links are well established. It would seem that a mix of historical/cultural similarities plus delicacy over the Second World War provide the base for pragmatic links whereby the Chinese secure a source of capital and the Japanese markets plus regional stability.

Shibusawa et al.[33] report that the 1978 reforms initiated by Deng Xiao Ping looked to secure the 'four modernizations' (agriculture, industry, science and defence). The story thereafter is one of burgeoning success coupled to internal social and political stress. It is clear that the reform process inaugurated by Deng Xiao Ping has led to significant economic advance; however in recent years there have been three key problems: (i) the unequal nature of economic change with coastal regions experiencing rapid growth whilst the inner agricultural regions are left behind; (ii) the enhanced powers of regional centres at the expense of Beijing in the light of the increasing linkages of the coastal areas of China with the Pacific Asian region; and (iii) the avoidance of political reform to the party/state machinery can be taken to have led to the political tensions which culminated in the demonstrations and repression now familiarly associated with Tiananmen Square. In the future, commentators anticipate that the outward directed development of China will continue and that social and political change are inevitable.

In Indo-China a similar story can be sketched. After the wartime occupation the drive for independence in Vietnam began and an attempt to recreate the status quo ante by the French failed, as did the subsequent attempts of the USA. There were similar post-war conflicts in Cambodia and Laos. The eventually successful nationalist resistance movements involved the Vietminh, Khmer Rouge and Pathet Lao. It is difficult to identify a positive legacy of either the Japanese wartime occupation or the subsequent years of cold war proxy conflict. At the present time, once again, we note the over-riding influence of economic power. The key aspect was the resolution of the Cambodian problem and relatedly the removal of the American veto on multi-lateral development agency assistance to Vietnam. The region is now rapidly reorienting itself to the global capitalist system in general and the Japanese regional core in particular.

Australasia joins Pacific Asia

In the case of Australia we find a long-running concern with the issue of identity, and indeed many of the terms of debate pre-date the rise of Pacific Asia. The invention of a 'British Australia' was accomplished only around the turn of the twentieth century where before there had been colonies looking to the UK. These ideas of Australia were informed by notions of 'British stock' making up an immigrant community who had, given their pattern of economic life, a particular affinity with 'the bush'. The invention of this tradition can be traced to particular groups of intellectuals and journalists. The native people of the continent, the aboriginals, were simply written out of the story. However, in the post-Second World War period the story itself is revised and a notion of the 'Australian way of life' emerges in the context of a general Western anti-communism, and this view of Australia has been implicitly anti-immigrant in line with ideas of 'White Australia'. Overall, this general record forms the background to the deliberate 1980s turn towards Asia which has seen an explicit 'multiculturalism' in the domestic sphere linked to a concern to locate Australia in its wider geographical context of Asia. Many of the arguments which have been adduced to support this reorientation point to the country's economic linkages to Pacific Asia, yet against this it has been argued that the economic policies of the 1980s were deeply flawed and that the economic linkages to Asia have been oversold.[34]

In the case of New Zealand the accession of the UK to the EEC caused great damage to the local economy and a process or reorientation began. In the 1980s a series of New Right governments continued the marketization and regionalization of the New Zealand political economy and with it a shift to an Asia-sensitive multiculturalism with regard to identity.

The Pacific Asian political model

In terms of a simple review of the politics of the countries of the Pacific Asian region, and beginning with the more industrially developed, we can say that Japan is nominally a liberal democracy; however, it is a thoroughly odd democracy, where on van Wolferen's analysis an absent state permits the rule of a group centred on the elites of bureaucracy, business and politics with the mass of ordinary Japanese as their victims. Relatedly, the inner periphery has for many years been characterized as authoritarian in one form or another, and recent debate has tended to revolve around the pace of a political liberalization which might be taken to flow from recently acquired economic prosperity. On the other hand, the outer periphery of somewhat less developed countries combines countries which can be characterized as restricted

democracies (Singapore, Malaysia, Thailand, some which can be characterized as authoritarian (Indonesia, Burma), plus one absolute monarchy
(Brunei), and one country which is often characterized as anarchically *sui
generis* (the Philippines). And, finally, the old socialist bloc is now taken to
be emerging from many years of authoritarian political stasis, however the
emergent patterns are not clear. Thereafter there are a few cases of states in
significant disarray (Cambodia and North Korea) or rather remote from
current changes (Laos, Papua New Guinea). If we abstract from the overall
record of the region we can distil a series of key elements of the Pacific Asian
model: (i) the developmental state; (ii) routine authoritarianism; and (iii) the
rise of Asian Values.

General Social Scientific Issues Arising

The political life of the countries of Pacific Asia has routinely diverged from
the model of the West. In the available literature of social science this has
been seen as problematical, however local theorists are speaking of a Pacific
Asian model of democracy. It is clearly both an affirmation of local models
of political practice and a counterstatement directed to critical outsiders,
usually from the West.

Ways of construing self and ordered political collectivity

The classical tradition of social theorizing has been routinely concerned with
the sphere of political life, which has typically been analysed in terms of the
shifting patterns of groups within the developing division of labour in
the process of the shift to the modern world. The rise of nations, states
and the familiar present conceptual lexicon of political discourse have all been
topics for intensive debate.

In the classical tradition of social theorizing the core conception of the
proper relationship of political actor to ordered collectivity has been cast in
terms of the notion of democracy. The tradition is sceptical, diverse and
tolerant, whilst remaining firmly committed to an expectation of material
and moral progress rooted in the fundamental rational character of
humankind. In this tradition political democracy is both an ongoing
historical achievement and a continually refined and restated goal.

However, in the post-Second World War period the hegemony of the USA
has seen these intellectual resources set aside in favour of an emphatic statement of the related tradition of liberalism. The claims of liberalism are bolder
and a disposition to claim that the rules of the liberal game have been
satisfactorily identified and that they are universally applicable is evident. In
the post-Second World War period these resources found bold expression in
the official ideology of the free world and in recent years the claims have been
restated in the absurdities of the theorems of the end of history.

The tradition of liberalism has a very clear view of the relationship of individual to ordered collectivity and construes this matter in terms of the idea of contract. The liberal world view begins with autonomous rational individuals whose multiplicity of contracts generate the agreed social world leaving those not so integrated to the status of potentially threatening mass. The role of the state is to secure and protect the making of contracts, that is 'law and order', and political life is a matter of recruiting office holders to secure these functional objectives. The clarity of vision of liberalism in this matter, coupled to the disposition to claim universality and the accidents of US hegemony, have combined to generate an emphatic assertion of the givenness of the model of liberal democracy. However, it is clear that the assertion is untenable.

The matter of the relationship of self and ordered collectivity admits of a spread of treatments. In Pacific Asia the developmental state plays a key role in ordering an hierarchical society and an obedient political culture. The needs of the collectivity come to the fore and the particular idiosyncratic desires of the individual are placed firmly in the background.

Evolving patterns of political life

It is clear that democracy is an historical real-world achievement. It is neither generated spontaneously by systemic evolution nor is it a recipe to be authoritatively applied by an enlightened elite; rather it is a laboriously achieved set of ideas, institutions and routine social practices.

The first country to make the shift to the modern world was England. The Civil War broke the power of the absolute monarchy and a liberal mercantile capitalism developed. In the USA the War of Independence established a democratic republic (of distinctly liberal character) and this model was exported back to Europe. In France a revolution established a republican democratic tradition which has endured through the vagaries of the nineteenth and twentieth centuries. It can also be noted that their have been failures of political development, most clearly in the case of the 1930s rise of fascism in Europe.

A similar line of enquiry can be pursued in respect of the historical political-cultural achievements of Pacific Asia. The starting point would be the rich variety of pre-contact political forms, ranging from rational bureaucratic states through to the personal rule of traditional sultanates. There is no history of democracy in pre-contact Pacific Asia. It is also true that there is very little democracy in the subsequent period of Western colonial rule. However, in the post-colonial period the pursuit of effective nation statehood did entail an affirmation of the goal of democracy. In the socialist sphere the notion of democracy was integral in theory but not routinely evident in practice. At the present time the Pacific Asian region offers a variety of political forms, and it would be true to say that popular involvement is increasing; nonetheless the forms of political life remain particular to the region.

The Pacific Asian model of democracy

The effective role of political ideas can be grasped in terms of ideas, institutions and historical practice. Thus, firstly, the notion of democracy can be read in terms of classical European political philosophy. The equivalent Pacific Asian ideas will be located in the great traditions, little traditions and the imported schemes of the first generation of nationalists. Then, secondly, in terms of institutional vehicles, the ways in which ideas generally affirmed are expressed in concrete and practical institutional machineries, it is quite clear that the notion of democracy comes in varieties with American-style representative democracy (having a written constitution, separation of powers, open debate and conflicting interest groups – all theorized typically via notions of political-liberal pluralism) and European social-democracy (with its written constitutions, a clearly dispersed pattern of power, open debate and an active and involved citizenry – all of which come close to the model of republican democracy). In a similar way, Pacific Asian institutional vehicles typically revolve around elite-ordered developmental states oriented to the pragmatic pursuit of material advance. Then, thirdly, the developmental achievement of political advance can be elucidated in terms of the ways in which various groups have read enfolding structural circumstances in the long process of the shift to the modern world. The pattern of development in Pacific Asia is an historically specific experience and involves colonial rule, world war, the pursuit of independence and the emergence of an integrated region.

In sum, overall, it does make sense to speak of Pacific Asian models of democracy but at the same time scholarly commentary needs to be sensitive both to the real world diversity of political experience in the region and to the element of elite excuse making in those countries where the governments are simply authoritarian.

Conclusion

The cultural resources of Pacific Asia are diverse yet one can point to a series of traits around the notions of hierarchy, consensus and communality, which allow an ideal-typical differentiation of the region from the social democratic traditions of Europe and the liberalism of the USA. It is also clear that the patterns of life of the peoples of the region are experiencing a measure of convergence as regional economic integration continues and begins to generate social-institutional and political-cultural structures. It is certainly the case that a measure of regional elite self-identification as Asians is taking place. In this relatively simple sense there is a Pacific Asian model of industrial-capitalism. Thereafter, more practically, we can note that the form-of-life of the peoples of the region will continue to change in the course of the ongoing shift to the modern world. The resources of tradition feed into the continuing distinctive historical development trajectories of the countries of the region.

In the region the elite-level response to the withdrawal of long familiar cold war ways of understanding the world has been an interest in the idea of Pacific Asia. The structural occasion for the elite discourse resides in changing patterns of economic power within the global system. A broad commonality in political economy, society and culture will be further deepened around the energetic expansion of the regional core economy of Japan. As elite groups respond to these slowly changing structural circumstances by advancing an idea of Pacific Asia one might expect the emergent new identities to find both institutional and popular expression in new patterns of political linkages, new patterns of economic activity and new patterns of political-cultural understanding.

Notes

1 On this see P. W. Preston 1997: *Political-Cultural Identity: Citizens and Nations in a Global Era*, London: Sage, where the argument of the present chapter is presented at greater length.
2 C. Jenks 1993: *Culture*, London: Routledge.
3 Z. Bauman 1976: *Culture as Praxis*, London.
4 E. Said 1978: *Orientalism*, London: Routledge.
5 G. Evans ed. 1993: *Asia's Cultural Mosaic: An Anthropological Introduction*, Singapore: Prentice-Hall, p. 1.
6 J. Goody 1996: *The East in the West*, Cambridge: Cambridge University Press.
7 Evans 1993, p. 19.
8 See B. Anderson 1983: *Imagined Communities*, London: Verso.
9 S. Bowdler 1993: Asian Origins: Archaeology and Anthropology in Evans, ed., pp. 38–40.
10 Ibid., p. 40.
11 A. Prasithrathsint 1993: The Linguistic Mosaic in Evans, ed.
12 Ibid., p. 70.
13 See R. Bernstein 1976: *The Restructuring of Social and Political Theory*, London: Methuen; S. Pinker 1994: *The Language Instinct: The New Science of Language and Mind*, London: Allen Lane.
14 Prasithrathsint 1993, p. 76.
15 Evans 1993, p. 6.
16 Ibid., p. 6.
17 D. Schak 1995: The Role of Religions in Modernizing Asia in C. Mackerras, ed., *Eastern Asia*, Melbourne: Longman, p. 509.
18 P. W. Preston 1996: *Development Theory: An Introduction*, Oxford: Blackwell Publishers.
19 P. Dale 1986: *The Myth of Japanese Uniqueness*, London: Routledge; K. Yoshino 1993: *Cultural Nationalism in Contemporary Japan*, London: Routledge. A discussion of postmodernist analyses is presented by J. Clammer 1995: *Difference and Modernity: Social Theory and Contemporary Japanese Society*, London: Kegan Paul International.

20   N. L. Sum 1996: The NICs and Competing Strategies of East Asian Regionalism in A. Gamble and T. Payne eds: *Regionalism and World Order*, London: Macmillan.

21   The idea of a model lets us sharpen our focus on contemporary debate, and there has been a fraught debate on this topic, see R. Robison, ed., 1996: *Pathways to Asia: The Politics of Engagement*, St Leonards: Allen and Unwin.

22   R. Buckley 1990: *Japan Today*, Cambridge: Cambridge University Press.

23   K. Sheridan 1993: *Governing the Japanese Economy*, Cambridge: Polity, p. 3.

24   D. Yasutomo 1986: *The Manner of Giving: Strategic Aid and Japanese Foreign Policy*, Lexington: Heath.

25   J. Halliday 1980: Capitalism and Socialism in East Asia in *New Left Review* 124.

26   M. Shibusawa et al. 1992: *Pacific Asia in the 1990s*, London: Routledge, p. 69.

27   R. P. Cronin 1992: *Japan, the United States, and the Prospects for the Asia Pacific Century: Three Scenarios for the Future*, Singapore: Institute of Southeast Asian Studies, p. 33.

28   W. Dobson 1993: *Japan in East Asia: Trading and Investment Strategies*, Singapore: Institute of Southeast Asian Studies.

29   P. Phongpaichit 1990: *The New Wave of Japanese Investment in ASEAN*, Singapore: Institute of Southeast Asian Studies.

30   K. J. Khoo 1992: The Grand Vision: Mahathir and Modernization in J. S. Kahn and K. W. Loh, eds, *Fragmented Vision: Culture and Politics in Contemporary Malaysia*, Sydney: Allen and Unwin.

31   A. B. Shamsul 1994: Nations of Intent in Malaysia in S. Tonneson and H. Antlov, eds, *Asian Forms of the Nation*, London: Curzon.

32   A. J. MacIntyre 1993: Indonesia, Thailand and the Northeast Asia Connection in R. Higgot et al., eds, *Pacific Economic Relations in the 1990s: Cooperation or Conflict*, St Leonards: Allen and Unwin, p. 261.

33   Shibusawa et al. 1992.

34   See G. Whitlock and D. Carter, eds, 1992: *Images of Australia*, Queensland: University of Queensland Press; M. Byrnes 1994: *Australia and the Asia Game*, St Leonards: Allen and Unwin.

Part V

Pacific Asia in the New Global System

13

Pacific Asia in the Twenty-first Century Global System

The routes to the modern world taken by the countries of the region of Pacific Asia have been diverse in their detail but have it in common that the driving force has been the relentless expansion of the industrial-capitalist system. The overall historical development experience of the countries of Pacific Asia encompasses the movement of a diversity of extant forms-of-life through a series of phases towards a present-day pattern of loose regional integration. However, the extent of the integration of the countries of the region, their future and the implications of their established success are all issues which remain controversial and open.

In this concluding chapter we will recall the ideas of a global system, tripolarity and regionalization, as it is within this context that it makes sense to speak of a Pacific Asian region. Thereafter we will rehearse the broad scholarly, policy-analytical and political implications of the current patterns of complex change in Pacific Asia.

The Shift From Bipolarity to Tripolarity within the Global System

In the post-Second World War period the political-cultural thinking of many people was dominated in its public aspect by the rhetoric of the cold war which posited a bifurcated global system pitting the free world against communism. On the basis of the vantage point of the late 1990s it is clear that this rhetoric blinded the generality of American and European scholars, policy analysts and political actors to the reality of the structural changes running through the global system in general and Pacific Asia in particular. It was the coincidence of a sequence of events (including the 1971 collapse of Bretton Woods; the 1978 reforms in China and the 1985 Plaza Accords) coupled to the shock of the 1989–91 dissolution of the USSR which finally set the obfuscatory rhetoric of cold war aside and allowed the direct recognition of patterns of structural change which had been in process for many years.

The collapse of the received certainties of the cold war left many commentators in Europe and American confused as to the nature of their new situation. The intellectual resources deployed to theorize the bipolar cold war global system were inadequate to the new situation and a confused period ensued when theorists cast around for new materials with which to work. A series of responses were made including the affirmation of the centrality of the victory of the West, the announcement of the ethico-political end of history, the declaration of a new global order, and more familiarly, various people began looking for new enemies in either other cultures or the threat of asteroids hitting the earth.[1] However, in time a useful distinction was made between geo-strategy and geo-economics and we might speculate that it was at this point that one discourse fell away and its replacement began to take shape.

In the wake of the end of the short twentieth century and the related collapse of the received certainties of the cold war which had shaped the understandings of European and American thinkers it has become clear that a new integrated global industrial-capitalist system is taking shape. Hobsbawm[2] argues this is an unstable system which recalls the equally unstable global system of the latter years of the long nineteenth century. A series of tendencies within the global system can be identified as patterns and styles of production change. First, in the developed economies of the G7 group, the intermingled upgrading and hollowing out of the metropolitan core economies (flexible-specialization and the new international division of labour). Second, the collapse of the state-socialist bloc and its confused shift towards market-based political economies (a mixture of political collapse and thereafter general reconstruction in the USSR and Eastern Europe, and authoritarian market reforms in China and Indo-China). And third, the further partial dependent integration of certain areas of the developing world in Asia, Latin America and the oil-rich Middle East, and the slow shift of other areas of the underdeveloped world into a situation of apparent semi-detachment from the global system (much of Africa south of the Sahara). It is also clear that within the broad sphere of the developed countries the US-sponsored Bretton Woods system has broken down and a new tripolar system is visible with core groupings in the Americas, Europe and Pacific Asia.

At the present time the global industrial-capitalist system shows a number of cross-cutting tendencies: (i) to integration on a global scale including financial, commercial and manufacturing operations; (ii) to regionalization within the global system with three key areas emerging where intra-regional linkages are deepening; and (iii) to division on a global scale with areas of the world apparently falling behind the regionalized global system.

Globalization, Tripolarity and the Regions

The end of the received certainties of the cold war left many commentators in Europe and American confused as to the nature of the new situation. A confused period ensued as theorists cast around for new materials with which to work. In time a useful distinction was made between geo-strategy and geo-economics and a new discourse emerged. The new discourse revolves around the dynamics of globalization, regionalization and local political-cultural projects. It is at this point that commentators were able to speak of the sphere of the USA, the development of the European Union and the emergence of Pacific Asia. This new view of the tripolar global system has proved to be very influential, and now guides new research agendas.

The USA in the Emergent Global System

The Second World War saw the emergence of the USA as the premier economic and military power within the global system. The power of the USA was used to establish and underpin the Bretton Woods system within the sphere of the West. The economic and military power of the USA was central to the military/diplomatic confrontation with the socialist bloc. There was a period of US hegemony in the 1950s and 1960s. However in the 1970s the system came under great pressure. The following factors have contributed to the decline: (i) the financial implications for the USA of the war in Vietnam and the end of the Bretton Woods system in 1971; (ii) the oil price shocks of 1973; (iii) the rise of the EU and the Japanese sphere in East Asia; and (iv) the partial and uneven globalization of the industrial-capitalist system. It is clear that the position of the USA was unchallenged until the mid 1970s. However, the late 1970s saw economic dislocation within the Western sphere. In the 1980s the military build up inaugurated by Reagan led to the USA becoming a debtor nation. In addition the USA was the major sponsor of the doctrines of economic liberalization which have further undermined the order of the global system. The upshot of all these changes over the period 1973-91 has been a movement into an unstable, insecure and novel tripolar global industrial-capitalist system.

The end of the cold war has seen the USA continuing to press for an open global trading system but these arguments are now made within the context of a tripolar system. The influence of the Washington-based IMF and World Bank is extensive in promoting liberal free trade, and recent expressions of these concerns have led to establishment of NAFTA and APEC which link the USA to Latin American and the Asia-Pacific respectively. A link to the Europeans is secured via the security mechanism of NATO and the routine conversations of the G7 economic group. A key element of US policy is the objective of a series of multilateral open trading areas whose institutional structures have a common locus in the USA.

In the context of an increasingly regionalized global system the key elements of the American economy, society and culture might be taken to include: (i) commitment to an open market economy; (ii) a strong preference for individualism and a tradition which celebrates the achievements of ordinary people; and (iii) a cultural tradition of liberal individualism along with a public commitment to republican democracy. It is on the basis of these established cultural resources that the USA will seek to deal with the peoples of the other regions.

Patterns of change in the European Union

In the post-Second World War period the peoples, organizations and government machines of Europe understood themselves within the overall framework of cold war bipolarity. In Eastern Europe matters were cast in terms of the achievement of a socialist polity and in Western Europe they were understood in terms of the notion of the free world. The East was ordered according to the tenets of Soviet state socialism and became an autarchic region within the global system. On the other hand the West was ordered at the macro-structural level in terms of the ideas, institutions and power relationships established by the Bretton Woods agreement which made the USA the core economy of an open liberal trading region. The West experienced a long period of unprecedented economic prosperity.

However, as the post-Second World War settlement began to weaken following the confusions of the early 1970s, the countries of Europe moved to adjust to the new circumstances. The countries of Western Europe slowly moved towards a closer union. The countries found an available mechanism in the guise of the European Community (EC), itself a development of the European Economic Community (EEC) which had been founded back in the early 1950s. These ideas and institutional mechanisms were in place when the extent of structural change finally became unequivocally clear with the 1989–91 collapse of the USSR. At Maastricht the idea of the European Union (EU) moved to the fore and it is now the overarching political project around which European political life revolves.

The core of the European Union lies in northwestern Europe. In Germany the end of the cold war meant the end of the division of the country and it meant an unexpected movement to the centre of Europe as the most populous nation with the strongest economy. The commitment of the core countries of the European Union was affirmed in the Maastricht Treaty and Germany, the Netherlands, Belgium and France maintain a pro-union stance, as does Italy. In recent years the Scandinavian countries, with the exception of oil-rich Norway, have joined the Union, as has Austria. In Spain, Portugal and Greece the European Union has been the institutional space within which post-military liberal-democratic regimes have developed. In a similar way the newly-independent countries of Central Europe have announced their intentions of joining, a matter of a return to Europe. Overall, the project of European unification begun in the wake of the Second World War shows no sign of faltering and, notwithstanding tensions and confusions, the established institutional machineries look set to provide the vehicle for a distinctive European region.

In this context, the key elements of the European economy, society and culture could be said to include: (i) a political economy in which state and market interact, with the state having a directive role; (ii) a social-institutional structure which affirms an idea of the importance of community, and sees economy and polity acknowledging the important role of the community; and (iii) a cultural tradition which acknowledges established institutions, a broad humanist social philosophy, and a tradition of social-democratic or Christian-democratic welfare politics.

Structural change and agent response in Pacific Asia

The key exchange in the Pacific Asian area in the post-Second World War period has been that of the Japanese and the Americans. It is this link which has provided the context of Japanese recovery and prosperity. The countries of the inner periphery of East Asia have prospered over a long period of economic development in the political and military shadow of the USA and the economic shadow of Japan. Thereafter the countries of the outer periphery of Southeast Asia have recently reoriented themselves towards the economic model of Japan. Relatedly we can note the turn of the countries of Australasia towards the Pacific Asian economies. Finally we have the ongoing process of the reorientation of China and Indo-China in the wake of Deng Xiao Ping's reforms and the 1985 Plaza Accords which generated a flood of yen for foreign investment. Overall, the region has been undergoing considerable structural change since the late 1970s and there is now a significant measure of regional trade, integration and acknowledged cultural commonality.

One key contemporary public issue concerns the arguments to the effect that the pattern of change in Pacific Asia is such that we can talk about an 'Pacific Asian model of development' where this is taken to be a particular variety of industrial capitalism distinct from the American or European models. It is true that the Pacific Asian region is more accurately grasped as a series of complex economic, social and cultural processes, but the simplification of the notion of a model does allow a clear perception of the particularity of the ongoing historical development experience of the region. A speculative illustration of the economy, society and culture of Pacific Asia would include the following: (i) the economy is state-directed and oriented to the pragmatic pursuit of economic growth; (ii) state-direction is top-down style and pervasive in its reach; (iii) society is familial and thereafter communitarian; (iv) social order is secured by pervasive control machineries and a related hegemonic common culture; (v) political debate and power is typically reserved to an elite sphere and debate and action amongst the masses is diffuse and demobilized; and (vi) the culture stresses consensus, acquiescence and harmony, and eschews open conflict.

Pacific Asia in the New Tripolar Global System

The 1990s saw the emergence of a tripolar global system as the post-Second World War global system with its two great powers, a divided Europe and a marginalized Third World, was finally superseded in the period 1989–91. The ways in which a series of agent-groups understand themselves and their place in the global system is presently undergoing significant change. In the case of Pacific Asia the pace of development since the late 1970s has been so rapid that the region is becoming an economically powerful unit within the ever more integrated global system. The Pacific Asian countries trade amongst themselves, invest in each others countries and they have established a set of international forums where they can meet and order their interactions. It is clear that political, business and intellectual elites within the region increasingly cast themselves as Asians.

Scholarly implications

The social scientific movement away from received enlightenment claims to the universality of the European experience which has been in progress for several years finds new practical impetus in the development experience of Pacific Asia. A series of key fundamental issues are represented, including the nature of the modernist project, the role of intellectuals and the ways in which economies, societies and cultures are construed/ordered and action thereby proposed/undertaken.

Within the context of these key revisions a series of more local debates are implied including the nature of the pursuit of people's livelihoods, the relationship of society and self, and implications of the variety of styles of self-conscious reflection upon patterns of life carried within culture.

The economic development experience of Pacific Asia has occasioned a series of hotly debated issues including: (i) the nature of the role of the state, where debate revolves around the costs/benefits of such interventions; (ii) the nature of the role of social networks in economic activity to supplement or replace the marketplace (for example, in Japan and amongst Chinese businessmen); (iii) the role of political elites in the pursuit of economic growth; and (iv) the role of politicians, bureaucrats and other strategic groups in the process of economic growth. It should be noted that these enquiries routinely call into question the plausibility of orthodox market-based economics.

The social development experience of Pacific Asia generates a series of issues that are hotly debated and include: (i) the nature of social discipline, how it is secured and thereafter legitimated; (ii) the relationship of the individual self to key social institutions (family, community, local town and state/country); and (iii) the extent to which the state can self-consciously and legitimately order the structure and dynamics of society. It should be noted that these enquiries routinely call into question the liberal individualism of Europe and the USA.

The cultural development experience of Pacific Asia generates a series of issues that are again hotly debated and include: (i) the nature of Asian great traditions and the extent to which there can be said to be a discrete package of Pacific Asian values; (ii) the nature of Pacific Asian little traditions and the extent to which these might be subsumed within developing national cultures; (iii) the extent to which Pacific Asian cultural resources are being in turn subsumed within a global postmodernist culture; (iv) relatedly, the value of culturalist explanations of the success of Pacific Asia; (v) the nature of political legitimacy in Pacific Asia; and (iv) the extent to which the notion of democracy has (and might be expected to have) purchase within Pacific Asian polities. It should be noted that these enquiries call into question the routine disposition to ethico-political universalism evident in Western discourse.

Policy-analytical implications

The historical development experience of Pacific Asia presents three areas of particular concern for European and American policy makers: first, in respect of economic policymaking; second in regard to security; and finally, in the specific matter of trade relations.

In respect of economic policymaking it is clear that the claims to universality of the Western experience are now in question. The tales told by expert social scientists working within or with reference to the core Western traditions will have to adjust to the lessons of the development experience of Pacific Asia. In European, American and Third World countries this implies that the 'learning from Japan' literature needs to be continued and supplemented with a 'learning from Pacific Asia' literature.

Pacific Asia offers a working specimen of a quite particular version of industrial-capitalism. In the standard market liberal account, the industrial-capitalist system is ordered by the marketplace and it is through this mechanism that general social benefits are maximized. However, it is clear that, in the case of Pacific Asia, the economic system is subject to the routine and extensive control of state-regimes and intra-regional socio-cultural networks (in particular the circuits of Japanese and Overseas Chinese capital). It makes no sense whatsoever to speak of 'disembedded' markets in the Pacific Asia region. The experience of Pacific Asia offers lessons for policy-making in the areas of economic, social and political management.

A key practical area of concern will be with security networks and alliances as the apparatus of cold war winds down. There is now a regional arms race and concern to fill the vacuum left by the partial disengagement of the USA.

The area is in the process of reconfiguring around an economically strong Japan and an assertive China. The Japanese armed forces are powerful and technologically advanced. The Korean peninsula is heavily militarized as is the island of Taiwan and the countries of ASEAN are rapidly upgrading and moving to position themselves with regard to China.

The most immediate area of policy concern focuses on trade linkages, as the region develops and further develops its links with America and Europe. This is potentially a thoroughly awkward area. If it is true that the three regions evidence different versions of industrial-capitalism then managing their relations becomes much more than applying a simple set of agreed rules. Zysman comments: 'One implication of this analysis, with its theoretical emphasis on the institutional foundations of distinct national market dynamics, is that, increasingly, in the years to come, the politics of trade, defined broadly, will be about reconciling differently structured political economies that express different values'.[3]

It is clear that trade relationships will have to deal with the ways in which economies are lodged within societies which in turn are lodged in cultures. If there is no simple liberal market-inspired set of rules able to govern economic exchanges between various agents then policy analysts will have to fashion ways of dealing with the substantive differences between versions of industrial-capitalism. Zysman comments that debate will come to revolve around 'deep market access'.[4] It is clear that: 'The notion of competing capitalisms implies at once a rivalry between economic systems, conflicts between governments, and competition between companies from different countries advantaged or handicapped by the market logic of their home bases . . . In any case, disturbing or congenial, the interplay of these several national market logics will define much of the trade politics in the years to come'.[5]

Political implications

The key implication is that political elites acknowledge the requirement of managing the emergent tripolar system in the new post-Bretton Woods era. This implies work in the areas of economics and security. Thereafter, the issues of regionalism and the intersection of regions with the global system will be central to political activity.

As the tripolar system develops a whole set of multilateral and bilateral exchanges at the state/state-level are underway. American theorists are aware of the need to adjust and the stress on geo-economics is evidence of a new position. The organizations NAFTA and APEC are ways of ordering the emergent system to US advantage. Relatedly, the European Union is both pursuing its own programme of integration and re-engaging with Pacific Asia after the gradual disengagement of the period of American hegemony.

Conclusion: Pacific Asia in the Tripolar Global System

The routes to the modern world taken by the countries of the region of Pacific Asia have been diverse in their detail but have it in common that the driving force has been the relentless expansion of the industrial-capitalist system. The overall historical development experience of the countries of Pacific Asia encompasses the movement of a diversity of extant forms-of-life through a series of phases towards a present-day pattern of loose integration within the region. The extent of integration of the countries of the region, their future and the implications of their established success are all issues which remain controversial and open. The extent to which it is possible to offer firm conclusions in respect of the character, lessons and implications of the established record is restricted. Yet in brief, it seems clear that the global industrial-capitalist system is slowly forming into the three distinct blocs of the Americas, the European Union and Pacific Asia. The success of Pacific Asia is likely to continue and this will offer scholars, policy analysts and political actors much to consider in the years to come.

Notes

1 Arguments presented in mid-1997 by US defence and space industry spokesmen.
2 E. Hobsbawm 1994: *The Age of Extremes: The Short Twentieth Century*, London: Michael Joseph.
3 J. Zysman 1996: The Myth of a Global Economy in *New Political Economy* 12, p. 180.
4 Ibid.
5 Ibid., p. 181.

Bibliography

Abegglen, J. C. 1994: *Sea Change*, New York: Free Press.

Aglietta, M. 1979: *A Theory of Capitalist Regulation*, London: Verso.

Albrow, M. 1996: *The Global Age*, Cambridge: Polity.

Allen, J. and Massey, D. (eds) 1989: *The Economy in Question*, London: Sage.

Anderson, B. 1983: *Imagined Communities*, London: Verso.

Anderson, P. 1992: *English Questions*, London: Verso.

Appelbaum, R. P. and Henderson, J. (eds) 1992: *States and Development in the Asian Pacific Rim*, London: Sage.

Ariff, M. 1991: *The Malaysian Economy: Pacific Connections*, Oxford University Press.

Aron, R. 1973: *The Imperial Republic: The USA and the World 1945–1973*, London: Weidenfeld.

Barraclough, G. 1964: *An Introduction to Contemporary History*, Harmondsworth: Penguin.

Bartley, R. L. (ed.) *Democracy and Capitalism: Asian and American Perspectives*, Singapore: Institute of Southeast Asian Studies.

Bauman, Z. 1976: *Socialism the Active Utopia*, London: Allen and Unwin.

—— 1976: *Culture as Praxis*, London.

—— 1976: *Towards a Critical Sociology*, London: Routledge.

—— 1987: *Legislators and Interpreters*, Cambridge: Polity.

—— 1988: *Freedom*, Milton Keynes: Open University Press.

—— 1991: *Modernity and Ambivalence*, Cambridge: Polity.

—— 1992: *Intimations of Postmodernity*, London: Routledge.

Beasley, W. G. 1990: *The Rise of Modern Japan*, Tokyo: Tuttle.

Bedlington, S. S. 1978: *Malaysia and Singapore: The Building of New Nation States*, Ithaca, NY: Cornell University Press.

Bello, W. and Rosenfeld, S. 1990: *Dragons in Distress: Asia's Miracle Economies in Crisis*, Harmondsworth: Penguin.

Bennington, G. 1989: *Lyotard Writing the Event*, Manchester: Manchester University Press.

Berlin, I. 1989: *Four Essays on Liberty*, Oxford University Press.

Bernard, M. 1996: Regions in the Global Political Economy in *New Political Economy* 1(3).

Bernstein, R. 1976: *The Restructuring of Social and Political Theory*, London: Methuen.

Borthwick, M. 1992: *Pacific Century: The Emergence of Modern Pacific Asia*, Boulder, CO: Westview.

Bowring, R. and Kornicki, P. (eds) 1993: *The Cambridge Encyclopedia of Japan*, Cambridge University Press.

Boxer, C. R. 1990: *The Dutch Seaborne Empire 1600–1800*, Harmondsworth: Penguin.

Brenner, R. 1977: The Origins of Capitalist Development: A Critique of Neo-Smithian Marxism in *New Left Review* 104.

Breslin, S. 1996: China in East Asia: The Process and Implications of Regionalisation in *The Pacific Review* 9(4).

Brett, E. A. 1985: *The World Economy Since The War: The Politics of Uneven Development*, London: Macmillan.

Brookfield, H. C. 1972: *Colonialism, Development and Independence: The Case of the Melanesian Islands in the South Pacific*, Cambridge University Press.

Buckley, R. 1990: *Japan Today*, Cambridge University Press.

Buruma, I. 1994: *Wages of Guilt*, London: Cape.

Byrnes, M. 1994: *Australia and the Asia Game*, St Leonards: Allen and Unwin.

Caute, D. 1978: *The Great Fear: The Anti-Communist Purges Under Truman and Eisenhower*, London: Secker.

Chan, S. 1990: *East Asian Dynamism*, Boulder, CO: Westview.

Chen, P. (ed.) 1983: *Singapore: Development Policies and Trends*, Oxford University Press.

Chua, B. H. 1995: *Communitarian Ideology and Democracy in Singapore*, London: Routledge.

Clammer, J. 1995: *Difference and Modernity: Social Theory and Contemporary Japanese Society*, London: Kegan Paul International.

Croll, E. 1994: *From Heaven to Earth: Images and Experiences of Development in China*, London: Routledge.

Cronin, R. P. 1992: *Japan, the United States, and Prospects for the Asia Pacific Century: Three Scenarios for the Future*, Singapore: Institute of Southeast Asian Studies.

Cummings, B. 1997: *Korea's Place in the Sun: A Modern History*.

—— 1981: *The Origins of the Korean War*, Princeton, NJ: Princeton University Press.

Dale, P. 1986: *The Myth of Japanese Uniqueness*, London: Routledge.

Devan, J. ed. 1994: *Southeast Asia Challenges of the Twenty-First Century*, Singapore: Institute of Southeast Asian Studies.

Dilley, R. ed. 1992: *Contesting Markets*, Edinburgh: Edinburgh University Press.

Dobbs-Higginson, M. S. 1995: *Pacific Asia: Its Role in the New World Disorder*, London: Mandarin.

Dobson, W. 1993: *Japan in East Asia: Trading and Investment Strategies*, Singapore: Institute of Southeast Asian Studies.

Dore, R. 1987: *Taking Japan Seriously*, Stanford, CA: Stanford University Press.

—— 1986: *Flexible Rigidities*, Stanford, CA: Stanford University Press.

Duiker, W. J. 1995: *Vietnam: Revolution in Transition*, Boulder, CO: Westview.

Eccleston, B. 1989: *State and Society in Post-War Japan*, Cambridge: Polity.

Evans, G. ed. 1993: *Asia's Cultural Mosaic: An Anthropological Introduction*, Singapore: Prentice-Hall.

Evers, H. D. and Schrader, H. (eds) 1994: *The Moral Economy of Trade*, London: Routledge.

Far Eastern Economic Review, Hong Kong: Review Press .

Featherstone, M. 1991: *Consumer Culture and Postmodernism*, London: Sage.

Friedman, M. 1962: *Capitalism and Freedom*, Chicago, IL: University of Chicago Press.

—— and Friedman, R. 1980: *Free to Choose*, London: Secker and Warburg.

Frobel, F. and Heinrichs, J. 1980: *The New International Division of Labour*, Cambridge: Cambridge University Press.

Fukuyama, F. 1992: *The End of History and the Last Man*, London: Hamish Hamilton.

Furber, H. 1976: *Rival Empires of Trade in the Orient 1600–1800*, University of Minnesota Press.

Furnivall, J. S. 1939: *Netherlands India: A Study of Plural Economy*, Cambridge.

Gamble, A. and Payne, T. 1996: *Regionalism and World Order*, London: Macmillan.

Gellner, E. 1964: *Thought and Change*, London: Weidenfeld.

—— 1983: *Nations and Nationalism*, Cambridge: Cambridge University Press.

Gibney, F. 1992: *The Pacific Century*, Tokyo: Kodansha.

Giddens, A. 1971: *Capitalism and Modern Social Theory*, Cambridge: Cambridge University Press.

Gipoloux, F. (ed.) 1994: *Regional Economic Strategies in East Asia: A Comparative Perspective*, Tokyo: Maison Franco-Japonaise.

Girling, J. L. S. 1981: *Thailand: Society and Politics*, Ithaca: Cornell University Press.

Godement, F. 1997: *The New Asian Renaissance*, London: Routledge.

Goodman, D. and Segal, G. (eds) 1994: *China Deconstructs*, London: Routledge.

Goody, J. 1996: *The East in the West*, Cambridge: Cambridge University Press.

Gudeman, S. 1986: *Economics as Culture*, London: Routledge.

Halliday, F. 1989: *Cold War Third World*, London: Radius.

Halliday, J. 1980: Capitalism and Socialism in East Asia in *New Left Review* 124.

—— and McCormack, G. 1973: *Japanese Imperialism Today: Co-Prosperity in Greater East Asia*, Harmondsworth: Penguin.

Hamilton, C. 1983: Capitalist Industrialization in East Asia's Four Little Tigers in *Journal of Contemporary Asia* 13.

Harvey, D. 1989: *The Condition of Postmodernity*, Oxford: Blackwell.

Held, D. 1987: *Models of Democracy*, Cambridge: Polity.

Hettne, B. (ed.) 1995: *International Political Economy: Understanding Global Disorder*, London: Zed.

Higgot, R. 1996: Ideas and Identity in the International Political Economy of Regionalism: The Asia Pacific and Europe Compared in *ISA-JAIR Joint Convention*, Makuhari: Japan.

—— et al. (eds) 1993: *Pacific Economic Relations in the 1990s*, St Leonards: Allen and Unwin.

Hirst, P. and Thompson, G. 1996: *Globalization in Question*, Cambridge: Polity.

Hobbart, M. (ed.) 1993: *An Anthropological Critique of Development*, London: Routledge.

Hobsbawm, E. 1994: *The Age of Extremes: The Short Twentieth Century*, London: Michael Joseph.

Honda, K. 1993: *The Impoverished Spirit of Contemporary Japan*, New York: Monthly Review Press.

Howell, J. 1993: *China Opens Its Doors*, Hemel Hempstead: Harvester.

Hughes, R. 1988: *The Fatal Shore*, London: Pan.

Hunter, J. 1989: *The Emergence of Modern Japan*, London: Longman.

Huntington, S. P. 1993: The clash of civilizations in *Foreign Affairs*.

Ienaga, S. 1978: *The Pacific War: World War Two and the Japanese, 1931–1945*, New York: Pantheon.

Inglis, B. 1979: *The Opium War*, London: Coronet.

Jackson, R. H. 1990: *Quasi-States: Sovereignty, International Relations and the Third World*, Cambridge: Cambridge University Press.

Jameson, F. 1991: *Postmodernism: Or the Cultural Logic of Late Capitalism* London: Verso.

Jeffrey, R. (ed.) 1981: *Asia: The Winning of Independence*, London: Macmillan.

Jenks, C. 1993: *Culture*, London: Routledge.

Johnson, C. 1982: *MITI and the Japanese Miracle*, Stanford, CA: Stanford University Press.

—— 1995: *Japan: Who Governs?*, New York: Norton.

Kahn, J. S. and Loh, K. W. (eds) 1992: *Fragmented Vision: Culture and Politics in Contemporary Malaysia*, Sydney: Allen and Unwin.

Kerkvliet, B. 1977: *The Huk Rebellion: A Study of Peasant Revolt in the Philippines*, University of California Press.

Keyes, C. F. et al. (eds) 1994: *Asian Visions of Authority: Religion and the Modern States of East and Southeast Asia*, University of Hawaii Press.

King, A. D. 1990: *Urbanism, Colonialism and the World Economy*, London: Routledge.

Kolko, G. 1968: *The Politics of War: US Foreign Policy 1943-45*, New York: Vintage.

—— 1997 *Vietnam: Anatomy of a Peace*, London: Routledge.

Koppel, B. M. and Orr, R. J. (eds) 1993: *Japan's Foreign Aid: Power and Policy in a New Era*, Boulder, CO: Westview.

Lawson, P. 1993: *The East India Company: A History*, London: Longman.

Lee, P. P. 1978: *Chinese Society in Nineteenth-Century Singapore*, Kuala Lumpur: Oxford University Press.

Lee, L. T. 1995: ASEAN and the South China Sea Conflict in *The Pacific Review* 8(3).

Long, N. ed. 1992: *Battlefields of Knowledge*, London: Routledge.

Lyotard, J.-F. 1979: *The Postmodern Condition*, Manchester: Manchester University Press.

Macdonald, P. 1994: *Giap: The Victor in Vietnam*, London: Warner.

MacIntyre, A. 1981: *After Virtue*, London: Duckworth.

Mackerras, C. ed. 1995: *Eastern Asia*, London: Longman.

Maclear, M. 1982: *Vietnam: Ten Thousand Day War*, London: Thames/Methuen.

Macpherson, C. B. 1966: *The Real World of Democracy*, Oxford University Press.

—— 1973: *Democratic Theory: Essays in Retrieval*, Oxford University Press.

Mak, J. N. 1995: The ASEAN Naval Build-Up: Implications for Regional Order in *The Pacific Review* 8(2).

McCord, W. 1991: *The Dawn of the Pacific Century: Implications for Three Worlds of Development*, New Brunswick: Transaction.

Miliband, R. 1982: *Capitalist Democracy in Britain*, Oxford University Press.

Moise, E. 1994: *Modern China*, London: Longman.

Moore, B. 1966: *The Social Origins of Dictatorship and Democracy*, Boston: Beacon.

Myrdal, G. 1958: *Value in Social Theory*, London: Routledge.

Nairn, T. 1977: *The Break-Up of Britain*, London: New Left Books.

—— 1988: *Enchanted Glass*, London: Radius.

Nester, W. R. 1990: *Japan's Growing Power over East Asia and the World Economy: Ends and Means*, London: Macmillan.

—— 1992: *Japan and the Third World*, New York: St. Martin's.

Ohmae, K. 1990: *A Borderless World*, Tokyo: Kodansha.

Ormerod, P. 1994: *The Death of Economics*, London: Faber.

Orr, R. M. 1990: *The Emergence of Japan's Foreign Aid Power*, New York: Columbia University Press.

Osborne, M. 1995: *Southeast Asia: An Introductory History*, St Leonards: Allen and Unwin.

Pan, L. 1990: *Sons of the Yellow Emperor: The Story of the Overseas Chinese*, London: Mandarin.

Pandy, B. N. 1980: *South and Southeast Asia 1945–1979: Problems and Policies*, London: Macmillan.

Pang, K. F. 1984: The Malay Royals of Singapore, unpublished dissertation, Department of Sociology, National University of Singapore.

Phongpaichit, P. 1990: *The New Waves of Japanese Investment in ASEAN*, Singapore: Institute for Southeast Asian Studies.

Pinker, S. 1994: *The Language Instinct: The New Science of Language and Mind*, London: Allen Lane.

Piore, M. and Sabel, C. 1984: *The Second Industrial Divide*, New York: Basic Books.

Piriyarangsan, S. 1983: *Thai Bureaucratic Capitalism 1932–1960*, Bangkok: Chulalongkorn University Social Research Centre.

Pluvier, J. M. 1977: *Southeast Asia From Colonialism to Independence*, Oxford University Press.

Pollard, S. 1968: *The Idea of Progress*, Harmondsworth: Penguin .

—— 1983: *The Development of the British Economy 1914–1980*, London: Arnold.

Preston, P. W. 1982: *Theories of Development*, London: Routledge.

—— 1985: *New Trends in Development Theory*, London: Routledge.

—— 1987: *Rethinking Development*, London: Routledge.

—— 1994: *Discourses of Development: State, Market and Polity in the Analysis of Complex Change*, Aldershot: Avebury.

—— 1995: Domestic Inhibitions to a Leadership Role for Japan in Pacific Asia in *Contemporary Southeast Asia* 16(4).

—— 1996: *Development Theory: An Introduction*, Oxford: Blackwell.

—— 1997: *Political-Cultural Identity: Citizens and Nations in a Global Era*, London: Sage.

Reading, B. 1992: *Japan: the Coming Collapse*, London: Orion.

Regnier, P. 1987: *Singapore City State in Southeast Asia*, London: Hurst.

Reynolds, H. 1982: *The Other Side of the Frontier*, Ringwood: Penguin.

Rigg, J. 1997: *Southeast Asia: The Human Landscape of Modernization and Development*, London: Routledge.

Rix, A. 1993: *Japan's Foreign Aid*, London: Routledge.

Robertson, R. 1992: *Globalization: Social Theory and Global Culture*, London: Sage.

Robison, R. and Goodman, D. (eds) 1996: *The New Rich in Asia: Mobile Phones, McDonald's and Middle-Class Revolution*, London: Routledge.

Robison, R. ed. 1996: *Pathways to Asia: The Politics of Engagement*, St Leonards: Allen and Unwin.

Rodan, G. 1989: *The Political Economy of Singapore's Industrialization*, London: Macmillan.

—— (ed.) 1993: *Singapore Changes Guard*, Melbourne: Longman.

Rostow, W. W. 1960: *The Stages of Economic Growth: A Non-Communist Manifesto*, Cambridge: Cambridge University Press.

Said, E. 1978: *Orientalism*, London: Routledge.

Sandhu, K. S. and Wheatley, K. 1989: *The Management of Success*, Singapore: Institute of Southeast Asian Studies.

Scott, J. 1971: Protest and Profanation: Revolt and the Little Tradition in *Theory and Society*.

Scott, J. C. 1985: *Weapons of the Weak*, New Haven, CT: Yale University Press.

Segal, G. 1991: *Rethinking the Pacific*, Oxford: Clarendon.

—— 1993: *The Fate of Hong Kong*, London: Simon and Schuster.

—— 1994: *China Changes Shape: Regionalism and Foreign Policy* (Adelphi Paper 287), London: International Institute for Strategic Studies.

Sheridan, K. 1993: *Governing the Japanese Economy*, Cambridge: Polity.

Shibusawa, M. et al. 1992: *Pacific Asia in the 1990s*, London: Routledge.

Sinha, R. 1982: Japan and ASEAN: A Special Relationship? in *The World Today* 38.

Sklair, L. 1991: *The Sociology of the Global System*, London: Harvester.

Smart, B. 1993: *Postmodernity*, London: Routledge.

Steven, R. 1990: *Japan's New Imperialism*, London: Macmillan.

Strange, S. 1988: *States and Markets*, London: Pinter.

Streeten, P. 1972: *The Frontiers of Development Studies*, London: Macmillan.

—— 1994: The Role of Direct Foreign Investment in Developing Countries, in Sophia University, Tokyo, ADMP Series.

Tarling, N. 1962: *Anglo-Dutch Rivalry in the Malay World 1780–1824*, Cambridge: Cambridge University Press.

—— 1975: *Imperial Britain in Southeast Asia*, Kuala Lumpur: Oxford University Press.

Tate, D. J. M. 1971/9: *The Making of Southeast Asia*, Oxford University Press.

Taylor, R. 1996: *Greater China and Japan: Prospects for an Economic Partnership in East Asia*, London: Routledge.

Thompson, R. C. 1994: *The Pacific Basin since 1945*, London: Longman.

Thorne, C. 1978: *Allies of a Kind*, Oxford University Press.

—— 1980: Racial Aspects of the Far Eastern War of 1941–45 from *Proceedings of the British Academy*, Oxford University Press.

—— 1986 *The Far Eastern War: States and Societies 1941–45*, London: Counterpoint.

Thurow, L. 1994: *Head to Head: The Coming Economic Battle Among Japan, Europe and America*, New York: Morrow.

Tonneson, S. and Antlov, H. (eds) 1996: *Asian Forms of the Nation*, London: Curzon.

Tregonning, K. C. 1965: *The British in Malaya: The First Forty Years 1786–1826*, University of Arizona Press.

Trocki, C. 1979: *Prince of Pirates: The Temmenggongs and the Development of Johor and Singapore 1784–1885*, Singapore University Press.

—— 1990: *Opium and Empire: Chinese Society in Colonial Singapore, 1800–1910*, Ithaca, NY: Cornell University Press.

Tsurumi, S. 1987: *A Cultural History of Postwar Japan 1945–80*, London: Kegan Paul International.

Turnbull, M. 1977: *A History of Singapore 1819–1975*, Oxford University Press.

van Wolferen, K. 1989: *The Enigma of Japanese Power*, London: Macmillan.

Vogel, E. 1980: *Japan as Number One*, Tokyo: Tuttle.

Wade, R. 1990: *Governing the Market: Economic Theory and the Role of Government in East Asian Industrialization*, Princeton, NJ: Princeton University Press.

—— 1996: Japan, the World Bank, and the Art of Paradigm Maintenance: The East Asian Miracle in Political Perspective in *New Left Review* 217.

Wake, C. H. 1975: Raffles and the Rajas in *Journal of the Malalysian Branch of the Royal Asiatic Society*.

Warren, J. 1984: Living on the Razor's Edge in *Bulletin of Concerned Asian Scholars* 16(4).

Waswo, A. 1996: *Modern Japanese Society 1968–1994*, Oxford University Press.

Watson-Andaya, B. and Andaya, L. Y. 1982: *A History of Malaysia*, Oxford University Press.

Watts, D. 1993: *The Times Guide to Japan: Understanding the World's Newest Superpower*.

White, G. (ed.) 1988: Developmental States in East Asia, London: Macmillan.

Whitlock, G. and Carter, D. (eds) 1992: *Images of Australia*, University of Queensland Press.

Wilkinson, E. 1990: *Japan Versus the West*, Harmondsworth: Penguin.

Wong, L. K. 1980: Review Article: The Chinese in Nineteenth Century Singapore in *Journal of Southeast Asian Studies*.

Wong, J. 1979: *ASEAN Economies in Perspective*, London: Macmillan.

—— 1995: China in the Dynamic Pacific Asia Region in *The Pacific Review* 8(4).

Woodcock, G. 1969: *The British in the Far East*, London: Weidenfeld and Nicholson.

World Bank, 1993: *The East Asian Miracle: Economic Growth and Public Policy*, Oxford University Press.

Worsley, P. 1984: *The Three Worlds: Culture and World Development*, London: Weidenfeld.

Yahuda, M. 1995: *Hong Kong: China's Challenge*, London: Routledge.

—— 1996 *The International Politics of the Asia Pacific, 1945–1995*, London: Routledge.

Yasutomo, D. 1986: *The Manner of Giving: Strategic Aid and Japanese Foreign Policy*, Lexington: Heath.

Yoshihara, K. 1988: *The Rise of Ersatz Capitalism in Southeast Asia*, Oxford University Press.

Yoshino, K. 1993 *Cultural Nationalism in Contemporary Japan*, London: Routledge.

Zysman, J. 1996: The Myth of a Global Economy in *New Political Economy* 1(2).

Index

Abbeglen, J. C., 148
Aborigines, 50, 76, 124
Acheh, 49, 58
Africa, 8, 113, 191, 227, 252
AFTA, 116, 138, 181
agents
    and changing structures, 3, 7, 141, 233
    in historical development experience, 22–3
    see also elites; international organizations; multi-national corporations; regional institutions; states
agriculture, 8
    China, 25, 32, 35–6, 125–6, 164
    Indo-China, 26, 32, 46
    Japan, 25, 32, 42, 44–5
    Korea, 65
    Southeast Asia, 26, 68–9
    Taiwan, 66
    Thailand, 48
    Vietnam, 26, 32
Americas *see* Latin America; North America
Amsterdam Company, 57
Angkor, 47, 48
Annam, 47
APEC, 24, 116, 138, 148, 164, 179, 181, 253, 258
Appelbaum, R.P., 208–9
archipelago islands *see* Asia, Southeast
Aron, Raymond, 88
ASEAN, 23, 24, 148, 181
    assertiveness, 221

Buddhism, 214
Chinese military build-up, 178
development strategies, 103–4
expansion of, 128, 166, 178
investment in, 30, 122–4, 132, 157, 158–9, 241
modernization of armed forces, 164, 258
nature of society, 214–15, 230–1
Pacific Asia phase, 146, 170
    see also Burma; Cambodia; Indonesia; Laos; Malay peninsula; Malaysia; Philippines; Thailand; Vietnam
Asia, notion of, 226, 234
Asia, Southeast
    agriculture, 26, 68–9
    cultural stream, 229
    development experience, 201
    economic patterns, 171, 173
    GNP per capita, 200
    human development index, 211
    industrialization, 122, 171
    Islam, 26, 34, 48, 72, 214
    and Japan, 147–8, 156, 176, 240–2, 255
    nation-building/cold war phase, 29, 146, 170
    nature of society, 217, 230–1
    Pacific Asia phase, 122–4
    as part of Dutch empire sphere, 27–8, 54, 58, 68–9, 236
    pre-contact phase, 26, 34, 48–9, 146, 170, 217, 236
    regional structures, 145

Asia, Southeast (*contd*)
  trade expansion of the West, 49,
    68–9
  see also Indonesia; Malay peninsula;
    Malaysia; Philippines; Thailand
Asian Development Bank, 148
Atsumi, R., 36, 44–5
Aung San, U., 83, 240
Australia
  empire phase, 54, 76–7
  and Japan, 148, 156, 176
  nature of society, 216, 230
  Pacific Asia phase, 30, 124–5, 132,
    170, 243, 255
  pre-contact phase, 50
Austria, 254
authoritarianism, 189–90, 203–4,
    243–4
Ayuthya Dynasty, 48

Bali, 49, 58
Banjarmassin, 58
Bantam, 49, 57, 58
bargains, 7
Barraclough, G., 58, 82–3
Batavia, 58
Bauman, Z., 10, 11
Beasley, W. G., 44, 68
Belgium, 8, 254
Bello, W., 118
Berlin, Congress of, 56
Bernard, M., 143, 144, 145, 169, 174
Borneo, 27
Borthwick, M., 40, 42, 43, 65, 66, 67
Bose, Chandra, 83
Bowdler, S., 227
Boxer Rebellion, 59
Brenner, R., 20
Bretton Woods system
  collapse of, 11, 12, 107, 162, 251,
    252, 253
  establishment of, 13, 112, 141, 161,
    253
Brunei
  human development index, 211
  nation-building/cold war phase, 29

as part of British empire sphere, 27,
    49
political system, 244
Buckley, R., 94, 129, 238
Buddhism, 211, 229, 236
  ASEAN, 214
  Burma, 37
  China, 25, 37
  Indo-China, 26, 47
  Japan, 25, 43, 62
  Thailand, 37, 47
Bugis peoples, 49
Burma
  Buddhism, 37
  conflict with Sukhothai
    kingdom, 48
  human development index, 211
  independence, 88
  Japanese occupation, 83, 240
  membership of ASEAN, 166, 178
  nationalism, 83, 240
  as part of British empire system, 48,
    88
  political system, 244
  pre-contact phase, 26, 32, 48

Cambodia
  development experience, 201
  human development index, 211
  membership of ASEAN, 166, 178
  nation-building/cold war phase, 30,
    108
  nature of society, 215, 216
  Pacific Asia phase, 127, 128, 242
  as part of French empire sphere, 27,
    48, 74, 107
  political system, 244
  pre-contact phase, 26, 32, 47
Canada, 211
Canton, 58, 148
capitalism *see* industrial-capitalism;
    mercantile-capitalism
Caute, D., 104
Celebes, 49
Ceram, 49
chaebol, 118, 171
Chakri Dynasty, 48
Champa Dynasty, 47

Chan, S., 196
change
    and classical social theories of, 3–8
    contemporary social theories, 8–13
    episodic theories of, 6, 21
    evolutionary theories of, 6
    Gellner's neo-episodic theory of, 4–6
    international political economy
        strategies, 6–7, 19–24, 141,
        194
    interpretation of patterns, 4, 17–21
    Moore's routes to the modern
        world, 6
    reflexive analysis of, 18–19
    structural, 112–14, 255–6
    substantive characterizations of, 7–8
    see also historical development
        experiences
Chiang Ching-kuo, 120
Chiang Kai-shek, 60, 105, 120, 161
China
    absorption as quasi-colony, 21, 26,
        28, 39, 54, 59–61, 146, 160,
        170, 236
    agriculture, 25, 32, 35–6, 125–6,
        164
    assertiveness, 221, 231, 258
    British traders, 27, 39, 58
    Buddhism, 25, 37
    civil war, 60, 82, 90–1, 104–5, 161,
        215–16
    collectivization, 106
    Cultural Revolution, 106, 125, 216
    cultural stream, 229
    development experience, 201
    as dominant force in socialist bloc,
        154
    Dutch trading concessions, 27, 58
    economic growth, 113, 126–7, 177
    economic patterns, 173
    economic reforms, 29, 30, 108, 113,
        125–7, 132, 139, 146, 164–6,
        199, 251, 255
    elites, 21, 34, 105, 166
    family, 25, 36, 215, 216
    French trading concessions, 27, 74
    GNP per capita, 200

    Great Leap Forward, 106
    and Hong Kong, 120, 165, 178
    human development index, 211
    industrialization, 126, 127, 165
    influence in Korea, 25, 40–1, 63–5
    investment in, 113
    and Japan, 28, 42, 59, 60, 63, 64,
        65, 67–8, 79–81, 105, 117,
        148, 156, 166, 176, 239, 242
    Korean War, 107
    modernization of armed forces, 164,
        165, 178
    modernization reforms during
    Qing Dynasty, 60
    nation-building/cold war phase, 29,
        30, 104–6, 108, 146, 170
    nature of society, 215–16, 217, 231
    Pacific Asia phase, 30, 122, 125–7
    political influence, 178
    pre-contact phase, 25, 26, 32, 34–9,
        146, 170, 215, 217, 236
    regional structures, 145
    regionalism, 24, 177–9
    religion, 229
    and Srivijaya, 49
    and Taiwan, 120, 165, 178, 240
    Tiananmen Square incident, 126–7,
        165, 242
    trade expansion of the West, 21, 25,
        26, 39, 46, 57, 58, 59
    treaty ports, 39, 46, 58
    and United States, 23–4, 82, 90–1,
        104, 105, 160, 161, 179
    US trading concessions, 28
    and Vietnam, 47, 73
Chinese Communist Party (CCP), 60,
    90–1, 104–6, 125–6
Chinese diaspora, 171, 173, 177–8,
    214
Chinese language, 228
Choi Kyu-Hah, 118
Christianity, 229
Chulalongkorn, King, 48, 73, 103
Chun Doo-Hwan, 118
civilizations, theories about, 143, 144,
    174
civilizations phase see pre-contact phase
class patterns, 172, 173

Clinton, Bill, 30
cold war, 7, 112, 237, 251–2
  end of, 23–4, 139, 199
  in Europe, 254
  significance of, 137–8
  see also nation-building/cold war
    phase
colonial phase, 19–20, 26–9, 54–83,
    146, 170
  Australia, 54, 76–7
  Cambodia, 27, 48, 74, 107
  France, 26, 27, 47, 48, 54, 73–4,
    107, 146, 170, 236
  Indo-China, 27, 48, 54, 73–4, 236
  Japan, 26, 28, 39, 41, 54, 63, 64–8,
    79, 96, 97–8, 117, 146, 147,
    155, 170, 176, 236, 238–9,
    240–1
  Korea, 28, 39, 41, 63, 64–6, 96,
    117, 236, 239
  Laos, 27, 47, 48, 74, 107
  Malay peninsula, 27, 48, 54, 58,
    69–73, 88
  New Zealand, 54, 77
  Philippines, 28, 54, 74–6, 102, 160,
    236, 240
  Singapore, 27, 58, 70–2, 88, 100
  Southeast Asia, 21, 27–8, 54, 58,
    68–9, 236
  Taiwan, 28, 39, 41, 63, 64, 65,
    66–7, 96, 97–8, 117, 236, 239
  United Kingdom, 26, 27, 48, 49,
    54, 57–9, 69–73, 76–7, 146,
    170, 236
  United States, 26, 28, 54, 74–6,
    146, 160, 170, 236
  Vietnam, 27, 47, 48, 73–4, 107
colonialism, 8, 18, 22, 236–7, 245
Committee for the Preparation of
    Korean Independence, 96, 97
communitarian democracy, 196
community, 141, 195, 217, 220–1
competition, 149–51
conflict, 23
Confucianism, 25, 37, 47, 211, 212,
    229
Confucius, 37
contract, idea of, 245

Cox, R., 140–1
Crisman, L., 41
critique, 10, 11
Cronin, R.P., 122, 148, 149–51, 156,
    157, 241
cultural coherence, 188–9, 191
cultural diversity, 11
cultural patterns, 173–5, 195–6
cultural processes, 143, 144, 224–35
culture
  analysis of, 219–20
  idea of, 224–6
  see also traditions
Cummings, B., 96

Daoism, 37
de-industrialization, 12
decolonization, 29, 87–108, 189
democracy, 196, 244, 245–6
  see also liberal democracy
Deng Xiao Ping
  assumes power, 106, 164
  death of, 166
  economic reforms, 30, 108, 113,
    125–7, 146, 154, 164, 255
  four modernizations, 178, 242
deregulation, 12
development experiences see historical
    development experiences
dialogue, 10, 11, 234
discipline, 218–19
diversity, 11, 141, 180–1, 208, 209
Dobbs-Higginson, M.S., 119
Dobson, W., 122, 157, 159–60, 241
Dore, R., 121, 209
Doumer, Paul, 74
Duiker, W. J., 74
Durkheim, Emile, 7
Dutch East Indies Company, 57–8

EAEC, 116, 138, 148, 181
The East Asian Miracle, 204
East India Company, 57–8
Eccleston, B., 130
Eckert, C. J., 96
economic determinism, 219
economic diversity, 180

economic growth, pursuit of, 190–1,
    203
economic liberalism *see* market-liberal
    theory
economic patterns, 170–3, 181
economic policy making, 257
economic rationality, 190
economic systems, theories about, 143
Edo Period, 44
education, stress on, 203
elites, 20, 22–3, 113–14, 172, 247
    businessmen, 203
    in China, 21, 34, 105, 166
    commitment to development, 190,
        191
    in Indonesia, 102
    in Japan, 21–2, 46, 54, 79, 93, 116
    in Korea, 40–1
    in Malay peninsula, 73
    and nation statehood, 18, 189
    in Philippines, 28, 75, 76, 90, 102,
        240
    political stability, 189–90
    regional integration, 141
    in South Korea, 118
    in Thailand, 48, 103
empires *see* colonial phase; colonialism
England, 245
Enlightenment, 8, 10, 188
ethics, 234
Euro-centrism, 17–18
Eurodollar market, 12
Europe/European Union
    Asian assertiveness, 221
    cold war phase, 254
    colonial withdrawal, 202
    GNP per capita 153*n*, 200
    influence on future global trading,
        209
    key elements of, 255
    Marshall Plan, 161
    nation-building/cold war phase,
        87–92
    as part of tripolar global
        system, 12, 13, 30, 110, 138, 142,
        148–9, 202, 258
    patterns of change, 254–5
    regional integration, 141, 142, 180

shift to the modern world, 8, 17
    unemployment, 12
    variety of industrial capitalism, 208
    see also France; Netherlands; United
        Kingdom; West
European Community (EC), 254
European Economic Community
    (EEC), 254
European monetary system (EMS), 12
Evans, G., 195, 221, 226, 228, 229
evolution, 227
exchange controls, 12

family, 195, 217
    China, 25, 36, 215, 216
    Indo-China, 26, 215
    Japan, 25, 44–5, 62, 212, 213
feudalism, 8
financial markets, internationalization
    of, 12, 13, 116, 140, 143
financial structure, 7
flexible production, 12
Flores, 58
foreign direct investment (FDI), 116
    in ASEAN, 30, 122–4, 132, 157,
        158–9, 241
    by Japanese, 30, 117, 122–4, 146,
        147, 155, 157–9, 176, 238,
        255
    in China, 113
    concentration in advanced
    economies, 11
    and multi-national corporations,
        157–8
    in newly industrialized countries
        (NICs), 122, 158
    in Singapore, 122, 158
    in Vietnam, 128
France
    Chinese trading concessions, 27, 74
    democracy, 245
    empire phase, 26, 27, 47, 48, 54,
        73–4, 107, 146, 170, 236
    EU membership, 254
    expansion of industrial-capitalism, 8
    military defeat in Europe, 57–8
    nation-building/cold war phase, 90,
        91, 107–8

France (*contd*)
  trade expansion, 57
  Triple Intervention against Japan,
    65, 68
  Vietnam War, 90, 91
Frankfurt School, 225
Friedman, M., 193
Fujian Province, 119, 126, 148
Fujiwara family, 42
Fukuyama, F., 9
Funan, 47

G7 group, 252, 253
Galbraith, J. K., 199
Gamble, A., 140, 141
GATT, 112, 116, 192
Gellner, E., 4–6, 220
Germany, 54, 65, 68, 79, 81, 254
Giap, Vo Nguyen, 127
Girling, J. L. S., 73
globalization, 9, 11–13, 116, 137–52,
    253–6
  of Japan, 149–50
  linkages to regional and local
    activities, 142–3
  tendencies within, 252
  versus internationalization, 139–40
gold standard, 13
Goldmann, Lucien, 225
Goodman, D., 173, 177
Gramsci, Antonio, 225
Greater East Asian Co-Prosperity
Sphere, 23, 117, 239
Greece, 254
Guandong Province, 120, 126, 178

Halliday, J., 99, 117, 239
Hamilton, C., 65, 67, 121, 123, 158
Han Chinese, 35
Han Dynasty, 38, 40
Hardacre, H., 214, 215, 216
Hatta, Muhammad, 90, 101, 102
Heian period, 42–3
Henderson, J., 208–9
Hinduism, 26, 34, 48, 211, 214, 229,
    236
Hirst, P., 11–13, 140

historical development experiences
  agent's projects in, 22–3
  breaks in, 20–2
  classical social theory, 3–14, 17–19,
    193–7, 206, 210
  cultural processes, 143, 144, 224–35
  debates about, 256
  diversity of, 180–1
  market-liberal theory, 121, 188,
    190, 191–3, 194, 203–5, 210
  orthodox theorists, 187–91, 194,
    202–4, 210
  particularity of, 187–97, 207, 255
  phases in, 19–20, 24–31, 141,
    145–7, 169–70
  political culture, 129, 196, 235–47
  political-economic processes, 19–24,
    141, 194, 199–210
  shifts in patterns of, 22
  social-institutional processes, 194–5,
    210–21
  state interventionism, 121, 193,
    203, 204–5, 206–7, 208–9
  variety of tracks, 201
historical-cultural areas, 228–9
history
  end of, 9
  multiple nature of, 18–19
Ho Chi Minh, 107
Hobsbawm, E., 146, 252
Hodge, General, 96
Hong Kong
  ceded to British, 39, 58
  and China, 120, 165, 178
  development experience, 201
  economic patterns, 171, 173
  GNP per capita, 200
  human development index, 211
  and Japan, 147, 156, 176
  market-liberal theory, 191
  nation-building/cold war phase, 95,
    98
  nature of society, 214
  Pacific Asia phase, 117, 118, 120
  regionalism, 145, 148
  religion, 229
  World Bank report, 204
Howell, J., 36

Hughes, R., 50
Huks, 102
human development index, 211
humanist Marxism, 225–6
Hunter, J., 77, 79, 212, 213–14
Huntington, S. P., 163, 206

Ibrahim, 70
idealism, 10
identity formation, 235–6, 237–44
IFIs, 199, 200
Ikeda, Hayato, 115
IMF, 13, 112, 116, 138, 192, 199, 253
imperialism *see* colonialism
India, 57, 88, 229, 236
Indian language, 228
individualism, 195, 217–18, 219, 220–1, 231, 254, 257
Indo-China
   agriculture, 26, 32, 46
   Buddhism, 26, 47
   economic patterns, 173
   family, 26, 215
   GNP per capita, 200
   human development index, 211
   and Japan, 107, 242–3
   nation-building/cold war phase, 29, 30, 88–90, 107–8, 146, 170
   Pacific Asia phase, 127–8, 242–3
   as part of French empire sphere, 27, 48, 54, 73–4, 236
   pre-contact phase, 25–6, 32, 46–8, 146, 170, 236
   see also Cambodia; Laos; Vietnam
Indonesia
   elites, 102
   human development index, 211
   influence on Malays, 72
   and Japan, 123, 241–2
   Japanese occupation, 83, 88, 101, 240
   nationalist movement, 69, 83, 88, 101–2
   nation-building/cold war phase, 29, 88–9, 101–2
   nature of society, 215
   Pacific Asia phase, 123

   political system, 244
   religion, 229
   World Bank report, 204
industrial-capitalism
   cross-cutting tendencies of, 252
   demands of, 56
   development in Europe, 8
   geographical expansion of, 8, 18–20, 21, 26–9, 51–2, 54–7, 59, 137, 220
   idea of varieties of, 208–9
   Moore's routes to the modern world, 6
   nineteenth century analysis of, 6
   original historical occasion of, 20
   and postmodernity, 9–10
   present dominance of, 18
   reconfiguration of, 142
   strategy of international political economy, 6–7
   tripolar global system, 12, 13, 30–1, 110–32, 138, 142, 148–9, 202, 253–9
industrialism, Gellner's neo-episodic theory of, 4–6
industrialization
   ASEAN, 122, 241
   China, 126, 127, 165
   Japan, 21–2, 28, 62–3, 114–15
   as route to development, 190
   Singapore, 120–1
   South Korea, 118
   Southeast Asia, 122, 171
   Taiwan, 66, 119
   see also newly industrialized countries (NICs)
inflation, 12
international financial institutions (IFIs), 199, 200
international organizations, 22, 23
   see also G7 group; GATT; IMF; NATO; OECD; regional institutions; World Bank; WTO
internationalization, 11–13, 24, 30, 110, 139–40
interpretation, 10, 11
investment *see* foreign direct investment (FDI)

irrational traditionalism, 190
Islam, 211, 229, 236
    China, 25
    Indo-China, 26
    Southeast Asia, 26, 34, 48, 72, 214
Italy, 8, 254

Jakarta, 57
Japan
    active role of state, 121, 194
    agriculture, 25, 32, 42, 44–5
    aid programmes, 117, 147, 155,
        159–60, 176, 238
    assertiveness, 221
    and Australia, 148, 156, 176
    British trading rights, 59
    Buddhism, 25, 43, 62
    and China, 28, 42, 59, 60, 63, 64,
        65, 67–8, 79–81, 105, 117,
        148, 156, 166, 176, 239, 242
    clash with the West, 79–83
    as core economy, 7, 22, 24, 29, 30,
        114, 129, 132, 145, 147–8,
        154, 155–60, 162–3, 170,
        175–7, 191
    culture, 231–2
    development experience, 194, 201,
        206–7
    diffusion of popular culture, 144,
        174
    diplomatic presence, 160
    drift towards military rule, 67–8
    'Dutch learning', 46, 77
    Dutch trading rights, 46, 58, 77
    economic challenge to USA, 162–3,
        205–6
    elites, 21–2, 46, 54, 79, 93, 116
    empire phase, 26, 28, 39, 41, 54,
        63, 64–8, 79, 96, 97–8, 117,
        146, 147, 155, 170, 176, 236,
        238–9, 240–1
    family, 25, 44–5, 62, 212, 213
    globalization, 149–50
    GNP per capita 153n, 200
    groupism, 212, 213, 230
    and Hong Kong, 147, 156, 176
    human development index, 211
    and Indo-China, 107, 242–3

    and Indonesia, 83, 88, 101, 123,
        240, 241–2
    industrialization of, 21–2, 28, 62–3,
        114–15
    investment by, 30, 117, 122–4, 146,
        147, 155, 157–9, 176, 238,
        255
    leadership role, 129–31, 149–51,
        177, 201, 238
    military forces, 160, 164, 166, 178,
        258
    military influence (1930s), 80–1
    modernization reforms, 62–3
    nationalism, 77, 80
    nation-building/cold war phase, 29,
        91, 92–5, 108, 146, 170
    nature of society, 130, 212–14, 230,
        238
    and New Zealand, 148, 156, 176
    occupation of Burma, 83, 240
    occupation of Malay peninsula, 73,
        88, 100, 101, 240
    occupation of Philippines, 28, 240
    Pacific Asia phase, 30, 113, 114–17,
        121, 122–3, 129–31, 132, 170
    as part of tripolar global system, 12
    political system, 129–30, 238, 243
    pre-contact phase, 25, 32, 41–6,
        146, 170, 217, 236
    regionalism, 116–17, 145, 147–8,
        156–60, 175–7
    religion, 229
    and Singapore, 147, 156, 176, 240,
        241
    and South Korea, 97, 119, 147,
        156, 176
    and Southeast Asia, 147–8, 156,
        176, 240–2, 255
    Taisho democracy, 79–80
    and Taiwan, 120, 147, 156, 176,
        239–40
    and Thailand, 123, 241–2
    trade expansion of the West, 25, 46,
        62, 77–9
    and United Kingdom, 65, 79, 82
    US occupation, 83, 92–4, 114, 161,
        212

US post-war relations, 114–15, 150, 162–3, 164, 166, 178, 179, 255
US pre-war relations, 82
and Vietnam, 242–3
war reparations, 117, 147, 155, 160, 176, 238
wars with Russia, 28, 63, 64, 65, 67, 82–3
World Bank report, 204
see also Meiji Restoration; Plaza Accords; Tokugawa Shogunate
Japanese language, 228
Java, 48, 49, 58, 70
Jenks, C., 225
Jogjakarta, 58
Johnson, C., 121, 194, 207
Johor-Riau, 49, 70, 72, 100
Jomon period, 42

Kabo reform movement, 65
Kamakura period, 42, 43
Keynesianism, 9, 190, 203
Khmer kingdom, 47, 48
Khmer Rouge, 128, 242
Khoo, K. J., 123, 241
Kim Il Sung, 97, 107
Kim Yong Sam, 119
kin networks, 195, 217
knowledge structure, 7
Koguryo, 40
Korea
  agriculture, 65
  Chinese influence, 25, 40–1, 63–5
  elites, 40–1
  Japanese influence, 42
  military forces, 258
  nation-building/cold war phase, 91, 96–7, 107
  as part of Japanese empire sphere, 28, 39, 41, 63, 64–6, 96, 117, 236, 239
  pre-contact phase, 25, 39–41, 64
Korea, North, 97, 107
  human development index, 211
  political system, 244
Korea, South
  defence linkage to USA, 178
  development experience, 201
  economic patterns, 171
  elites, 118
  GNP per capita, 200
  human development index, 211
  and Japan, 97, 119, 147, 156, 176
  market-liberal theory, 191
  military forces, 178
  nation-building/cold war phase, 95, 96–7, 107
  nature of society, 214
  Pacific Asia phase, 117, 118–19
  political-cultural identities, 239
  religion, 229
  and United States, 118, 119, 166, 178, 239
  World Bank report, 204
Korean War, 91, 94, 96–7, 107, 115, 161
Koryo Dynasty, 40, 64
Kowloon Peninsula, 58
Krawang, 58
Kublai Khan, 38
Kuomintang (KMT), 60, 104–5
  Malay peninsula, 72
  US support for, 82, 90, 98, 105, 161
  withdrawal to Taiwan, 90, 96, 98, 120, 161, 239
Kurile Islands, 28

language games, 234
Laos
  conflict with Sukhothai kingdom, 48
  development experience, 201
  human development index, 211
  membership of ASEAN, 166, 178
  nation-building/cold war phase, 108
  nature of society, 215, 216
  as part of French empire sphere, 27, 47, 48, 74, 107
  political system, 244
  post-war conflicts, 242
  pre-contact phase, 47, 48
Latin America, 8, 113, 191, 252
League of Nations, 79, 81
Lee, K. H., 72–3

Lee Kuan Yew, 174, 205
Lee Teng-Hui, 120
Legalism, 37
legislation, 10, 17
Liaotung, 68
liberal democracy, 9, 140, 189, 245
liberalism, 218, 231, 244–5
Light, Francis, 72
Lin Zexu, 39
linguistic determinism, 227–8
linkages, economic
    Australia and Pacific Asia, 125, 132
    between the two blocs, 154
    China and Taiwan, 120, 240
    Japan and Taiwan, 239–40
    Japanese influence, 117, 122,
        147–51, 155–60, 175–7, 238
    pre-contact phase, 26, 146
    regional, 110, 145–7, 170
    South Korea, 239
    to developing global system, 110,
        132, 137–52
    see also relationships
locale, notion of, 235
Long, N., 18
Louvre accords, 12
Low Countries, 8
Lukács, György, 225
Lyotard, J.-F., 10

Maastricht Treaty, 254
MacArthur, Douglas, 92, 94, 97
Macassar, 58
Macau, 165
McCoy, A.W., 75
MacIntyre, A., 123, 241
Mackerras, C., 37, 216
Macpherson, C.B., 196
Majapahit, 49
Mahathir bin Muhammad, 123, 174,
    205, 241
Malacca Empire, 49, 57, 58, 72
Malay peninsula
    elites, 73
    Japanese occupation, 73, 88, 100,
        101, 240
    nationalism, 72–3, 88, 100

as part of British empire sphere, 27,
    48, 54, 58, 69–73, 88
pre-contact phase, 34, 49, 69–70
Malaysia
    human development index, 211
    and Japan, 123, 241
    nation-building/cold war phase, 29,
        99–100
    nature of society, 215
    Pacific Asia phase, 123
    political system, 244
    religion, 229
    union with Singapore, 101, 181
    World Bank report, 204
Manchu Dynasty, 41, 64, 67
Manchuko, 67, 81
Manchuria, 35
    Japanese sphere of influence, 65, 67,
        81, 117, 238
    Russo-Japanese conflict, 63, 64
Mao Tse-tung
    becomes leader, 28, 94, 164
    civil war, 105
    Cultural Revolution, 125
    Great Leap Forward, 106
    utopian socialism, 154
March First Movement, 66
Marcos, Ferdinand, 103, 123, 240
market-liberal theory, 139–40, 190,
    194, 210
    newly-industrialized countries, 121,
        188, 191–3, 203–5
    varieties of industrial capitalism, 208
market-place, central role of, 9–10,
    139–40, 192, 257
Marshall Plan, 161
Marx, Karl, 7, 225
mass consumption, 8
mass production, 8, 12
Mataram, 49
Meiji Restoration, 28, 41, 46, 54,
    62–3, 79–80, 118, 212
Melanesia, 50–1
memory, notion of, 235
Menangkabau peoples, 49
Mencius, 37
mercantile-capitalism, 8, 51, 57–9
metal trade, 8

metanarratives, 10
Micronesia, 50–1
Middle East, 252
Minamoto faction, 43
Minamoto Yoritomo, 43
Ming Dynasty, 38, 40, 41, 64, 67
minority groups, 21
modernity, 3, 8, 10–11, 56
modernization theory, 187–8, 190,
    194, 202–3
Moise, E., 34, 37–9, 59, 105, 106,
    126–7
monetarism, 12
Mongkut, King, 73, 103
Mongolia, 35
Mongols, 38, 40, 41, 43, 64
Moore, B., 6, 14, 35, 60, 61
Morris-Suzuki, T., 77
multi-national corporations (MNCs),
    11, 12, 13, 22, 23, 140, 217
  in ASEAN, 215
  and direct investment, 157–8
  influence on economic patterns, 171
  order of global system, 116, 138
Muromachi period, 42, 43

NAFTA, 179, 253, 258
Nagasaki, 46, 58, 77
Nakane, Chie, 213
Nanjing, Treaty of, 58
Nara period, 42
nationalism, 82–3, 189, 226, 236, 237
  Burma, 83, 240
  Indonesia, 69, 83, 88, 101–2
  Japan, 77, 80
  Malay, 72–3, 88, 100
  Philippines, 75, 83
nation-building/cold war phase,
    29–30, 87–108, 146, 170
  Cambodia, 30, 108
  China, 29, 30, 104–6, 108, 146,
    170
  France, 90, 91, 107–8
  Hong Kong, 95, 98
  Indo-China, 29, 30, 88–90, 107–8,
    146, 170
  Indonesia, 29, 88–9, 101–2
  Japan, 29, 91, 92–5, 108, 146, 170

Korea, 91, 96–7, 107
Laos, 108
Malaysia, 29, 99–100
Netherlands, 88–90, 101–2
newly industrialized countries
    (NICs), 29, 146, 170
Philippines, 29, 88, 90, 91, 102–3
Singapore, 29, 100–1
Southeast Asia, 29, 146, 170
Taiwan, 95, 96, 97–8
Thailand, 103
United Kingdom, 88, 98, 99–101
United States, 17, 29, 30, 87–92,
    96–7, 98, 102–3, 108, 112,
    160–1
Vietnam, 90, 91, 107
nation statehood
  democracy, 245
  orthodox development theory, 187,
    188–91
  post-colonial pursuit of, 7, 18, 20,
    194
NATO, 179, 253
Netherlands
  Chinese trading concessions, 27, 58
  empire phase, 26, 27–8, 49, 54,
    57–8, 68–9, 146, 170, 236
  EU membership, 254
  expansion of industrial-capitalism, 8
  Japanese trading rights, 46, 58, 77
  nation-building/cold war phase,
    88–90, 101–2
  in Taiwan, 41, 66
  trade expansion, 57–8
network, notion of, 235
New Guinea, 58
New Zealand
  empire phase, 54, 77
  and Japan, 148, 156, 176
  nature of society, 216, 230
  Pacific Asia phase, 124, 170, 255
newly industrialized countries (NICs),
    12, 24
  development experience, 203, 207
  economic patterns, 171
  elite pursuit of
  nation statehood, 189
  investment in, 122, 158

newly industrialized countries (*contd*)
market-liberal theory, 121, 188, 191–3, 203–5
modernization of armed forces, 164
nation-building/cold war phase, 29, 146, 170
nature of society, 214, 230
Pacific Asia phase, 30, 117–22, 123, 132, 146, 170
see also Hong Kong; Korea, South; Singapore; Taiwan
Nixon, Richard, 95, 112
North America
colonisation of, 8
as part of tripolar global system, 12, 13, 30, 110, 138, 142, 148–9, 202, 258
regional integration, 141, 142, 180
variety of industrial capitalism, 208
see also United States
Norway, 254

OECD, 179
oil crises, 12, 95, 113, 115, 159, 253
opium tax farms, 71–2
Opium Wars, 39, 58, 59
Orr, R. M., 159
Osborne, M., 75, 99

Pacific Asia phase, 110–32
Australia, 30, 124–5, 132, 170, 243, 255
Cambodia, 127, 128, 242
China, 30, 122, 125–7
Hong Kong, 117, 118, 120
Indo-China, 127–8, 242–3
Indonesia, 123
Japan, 30, 113, 114–17, 121, 122–3, 129–31, 132, 170
Malaysia, 123
New Zealand, 124, 170, 255
newly industrialized countries (NICs), 30, 117–22, 123, 132, 146, 170
Philippines, 123
Singapore, 117, 118, 120–1, 122
Southeast Asia, 122–4
Taiwan, 117, 119–20

Thailand, 123
United States, 122, 131–2, 162–4
Vietnam, 127–8, 242–3
Pacific Islands
colonial phase, 27, 28, 54, 74, 77, 160
pre-contact phase, 50–1
Pacific War, 23, 28, 29, 81–3
US involvement, 82, 90, 161
Paeckche, 40, 42
Palembang, 58
Pangkor Engagement, 71, 72
Papua New Guinea
human development index, 211
nation-building/cold war phase, 29
political system, 244
Paracel Islands, 166
Park Chun Hee, 97, 118
Payne, T., 140, 141
Penang, 58, 72
Perry, Commodore Matthew Calbraith, 46, 59, 77
Philippines
elites, 28, 75, 76, 90, 102, 240
human development index, 211
and Japan, 242
Japanese occupation, 28, 240
nationalism, 75, 83
nation-building/cold war phase, 29, 88, 90, 91, 102–3
nature of society, 215
Pacific Asia phase, 123
as part of US empire sphere, 28, 54, 74–6, 102, 160, 236, 240
political system, 244
religion, 229
Phongpaichit, P., 122, 123–4, 157, 158–9, 241
Plaza Accords, 12, 113, 115, 132, 139, 199, 202, 251
and Japanese investment, 30, 122–3, 146, 147, 157, 158, 176, 255
regional production patterns, 172
Pluvier, J., 69, 74, 75–6, 103
Pol Pot, 128, 215
political coherence, 188–9, 191
political culture, 129, 196, 235–47

political economy
    Pacific Asia model, 199–210
    strategies of, 6–7, 19–24, 141, 194
political stability, 189–90, 191
Polynesia, 50–1
Port Arthur, 68
Portsmouth, Treaty of, 65
Portugal, 8, 49, 68, 254
post-Fordism, 12
postmodernity, 9–11, 139
power structures, 7, 20–1, 22, 181,
    233
Prasithrathsint, A., 227–8
pre-contact phase, 24–6, 32–52, 146,
    170, 217, 236
    Australia, 50
    Burma, 26, 32, 48
    Cambodia, 26, 32, 47
    China, 25, 26, 32, 34–9, 146, 170,
        215, 217, 236
    democracy, 245
    Indo-China, 25–6, 32, 46–8, 146,
        170, 236
    Japan, 25, 32, 41–6, 146, 170, 217,
        236
    Korea, 25, 39–41, 64
    Laos, 47, 48
    Malay peninsula, 34, 49, 69–70
    Pacific Islands, 50–1
    Southeast Asia, 26, 34, 48–9, 146,
        170, 217, 236
    Taiwan, 25, 39, 41
    Thailand, 26, 32, 47–8
    Vietnam, 25, 32, 47, 48
Priangan, 58
productive structure, 7
progress
    and culture and society, 219–20
    metanarratives of, 10
    uneven nature of, 22
Pu-yi, Henry, 81

Qing Dynasty
    bureaucratic system, 37
    collapse of, 38–9, 41, 59, 61, 64, 67
    modernization programme, 60
    and Taiwan, 41, 66

Raffles, Sir Thomas Stamford, 70
Reagan, Ronald, 253
reason, 10, 232, 234
reflexive criticism, 18–19
regional institutions, 181–2
    see also AFTA; APEC; ASEAN;
        EAEC; international
        organizations; NAFTA
regionalization, 11–13, 20–1, 24, 30,
    110, 202
    and competition, 150–1
    contemporary dynamics, 170–5
    future of, 175–82
    and the global system, 137–52
    identification of, 233–4
    and the Japanese core, 116–17, 145,
        147–8, 156–60, 175–7
    and Japanese leadership, 129–31,
        149–51
    limits of integration, 180–2
    linkages to global and local activities,
        142–3
    logic of, 143–5
    phases of, 145–7, 169–70
    tripolar global system, 12, 13, 30–1,
        110–32, 138, 142, 148–9, 202,
        253–9
Reid, A., 69, 101
relational power, 7
relationships
    change in post-war patterns,
        154–67, 170–5
    inter-state, 143–4
    Pacific Asia and the wider
    global system, 137–52
    patterns of, 143–8
    see also linkages, economic
religion, 19, 229–30, 231, 232
    China, 25, 36–7
    Indo-China, 26, 47
    Japan, 25, 43, 62
    Southeast Asia, 26, 34, 48, 72, 214
Revolutionary Alliance, 60
Reynolds, H., 76
Rhee, Syngman, 97, 107, 118
Riau Sultanate, 70
Rix, A., 117, 160
Robison, R., 173, 175, 218

Roh Tae Woo, 118
Russia
    early overtures to Japan, 46, 77
    expansion of industrial-capitalism, 8
    Triple Intervention against Japan,
        65, 68
    wars with Japan, 28, 63, 64, 65, 67,
        82–3
    see also Soviet Union
Ryujuku Islands, 28

Said, E., 226
Sakhalin Island, 65
samurai, 45
Sapir, Edward, 228
Scandinavia, 254
SCAP (Supreme Commander for the
    Allied Powers), 92–4, 114, 161,
    213
Schak, D., 229
Scott, J. C., 217
security networks, 257–8
security structure, 7
Segal, G., 177
Sekigahara, Battle of, 43
Serekat Islam, 69, 72
Sheridan, K., 45, 115, 131, 238
Shibusawa, M., 116, 207
    China's economic reforms, 125,
        127, 164–5, 242
    South Korea, 119, 239
Shimonoseki, Treaty of, 65, 68
Shintoism, 25, 62
Silla, 40, 42, 64
Singapore
    development experience, 201
    economic patterns, 171
    GNP per capita, 200
    human development index, 211
    investment in, 122, 158
    and Japan, 147, 156, 176, 240, 241
    market-liberal theory, 191
    nation-building/cold war phase, 29,
        100–1
    nature of society, 214
    Pacific Asia phase, 117, 118, 120–1,
        122

as part of British empire sphere, 27,
    58, 70–2, 88, 100
political system, 244
union with Malaysia, 101, 181
World Bank report, 204
Sinkiang, 35
Sino-centrism, 23
Smith, Adam, 7
social discontinuity, 23
social diversity, 180
social order, 218–19
social stability, 189–90, 191
social theory, classical, 3–14, 17–19,
    193–7, 206, 210
    formal elements of, 4–7
    political life, 244
    substantive elements of, 7–8
    varieties of industrial capitalism, 208
social theory, contemporary, 8–13
social-institutional order, 194–5,
    210–21
    see also family; kin networks
societies, theories about, 143, 144, 174
Song Chin-U, 96
Song Dynasty, 38
South Manchurian Railway Company,
    67, 81
Soviet Union, 161
    dissolution of, 139, 252, 254
    establishment of communes, 35
    and Korea, 96, 97
    and Vietnam, 128
    see also Russia
Spain, 8, 75, 254
spice trade, 8
Spratley Islands, 166
Sri Lanka, 37, 57
Srivijaya, 49, 70
states, 22, 23, 103–4, 142
    identity formation, 235–6
    interventionism, 121, 193, 203,
        204–5, 206–7, 208–9
stereotyping, 234
Strange, S., 7
Streeten, P., 157–8
structural analysis, 143, 144–5, 169–70
structural power, 7, 20–1, 22, 181, 233
Suharto, 102

Sui Dynasty, 38
Sukarno, 83, 90, 101, 102, 240
Sukhothai kingdom, 47–8
Sum, N.L., 230
Sumatra, 49
Sun Yat Sen, 60, 104, 105
Surakarta, 58

Taika reform, 42
Taiping Rebellion, 39
Taisho Code, 42
Taisho democracy, 79–80
Taiwan
    agriculture, 66
    and China, 120, 165, 178, 240
    Chinese nationalists, 90, 96, 98,
        120, 161, 239
    development experience, 201
    economic patterns, 171, 173
    GNP per capita, 200
    and Japan, 120, 147, 156, 176,
        239–40
    market-liberal theory, 191
    military forces, 178, 258
    nation-building/cold war phase, 95,
        96, 97–8
    nature of society, 214
    Pacific Asia phase, 117, 119–20
    as part of Japanese empire
    sphere, 28, 39, 41, 63, 64, 65, 66–7,
        96, 97–8, 117, 236, 239
    political-cultural identities, 239–40
    pre-contact phase, 25, 39, 41
    regionalism, 145, 148
    religion, 229
    and United States, 98, 119, 120,
        166, 178, 239
    World Bank report, 204
Tang Dynasty, 37, 38, 40
Tankoon, 40
Taoism, 37
Tate, D. J. M., 49
Taylor, R., 178
technology, 116, 190–1
Temmengong, 70, 71, 72
Ternate, 49, 58, 70
Thailand
    agriculture, 48

British influence, 48, 73
Buddhism, 37, 47
    elites, 48, 103
    human development index, 211
    and Japan, 123, 241–2
    nation-building/cold war phase, 103
    nature of society, 215
    Pacific Asia phase, 123
    political system, 244
    pre-contact phase, 26, 32, 47–8
    religion, 229
    World Bank report, 204
Thompson, G., 11–13, 140
Thorne, C., 81–2, 83
Thurow, L., 209
Tiananmen Square incident, 126–7,
    165, 242
Tibet, 35
Tidore, 49, 58, 70
tiger economies see newly industrialized
    countries (NICs)
Timor, 49
Tokugawa Ieyasu, 43, 44
Tokugawa Shogunate, 25, 41–2, 44–5,
    62, 79, 212
Tonkin, 47
trade, 13
    change in Western demands, 49, 51,
        56–7
    historical expansion of, 8, 57–9
    internal linkages pre-contact
    phase, 26, 146
    linkages in tripolar system, 258
    Malay maritime trading
    empires, 34, 69–70
    Philippines, 75
    present day Japan, 147–8, 156, 176
    Western traders expansion into
        China, 21, 25, 26, 39, 46, 57,
        58, 59
    Western traders expansion into
        Japan, 25, 46, 62, 77–9
    Western traders expansion into
        Southeast Asia, 49, 68–9
traditions, 10, 19, 229, 231, 232
trans-national companies (TNCs), 11,
    13, 140
treaties, 116, 138

Trocki, C., 70, 71, 72
Truman, Harry S., 97
Turnbull, M., 101

unemployment, 12
United Kingdom
  de-industrialization, 12
  empire phase, 26, 27, 48, 49, 54,
    57–9, 69–73, 76–7, 146, 170,
    236
  expansion of industrial-capitalism, 8
  influence on Thailand, 48, 73
  and Japan, 65, 79, 82
  Japanese trading rights, 59
  liberal international system, 13
  nation-building/cold war phase, 88,
    98, 99–101
  and New Zealand, 124
  Opium Wars with China, 39
  Pacific War, 82
  role in modern world order, 141
  trade expansion, 57–9
  in Vietnam, 90
United Nations, 107
United Nations Development
  Programme (UNDP), 211
United States
  anxieties about Pacific Asia, 24,
    205–6
  Asian assertiveness, 221
  challenge of Pacific Asian
  model, 196–7
  and China, 23–4, 104, 160, 179
  Chinese civil war, 82, 90–1, 105,
    161
  Chinese trading concessions, 28
  colonial withdrawal, 202
  de-industrialization, 12
  democracy, 245
  dollar flotation, 95, 112, 139
  in emergent global system, 253–4
  empire phase, 26, 28, 54, 74–6,
    102, 146, 160, 170, 236
  expansion of industrial-
  capitalism, 8
  future role in Pacific Asia, 179, 258
  global institutions, 138
  globalization drive, 141

GNP per capita 153n, 200
  hegemony in post-war Pacific Asia,
    7, 23, 138, 144, 154, 162,
    163–4, 170, 179, 191, 237,
    253
  individualism, 195
  and Indonesian independence, 90
  Japanese economic challenge,
    162–3, 205–6
  key elements of, 254
  Korean War, 91, 96–7, 107, 161
  as major export market, 129, 145,
    151, 170
  market-liberal theory, 192
  mediation in Manchuria, 65
  nation-building/cold war phase, 17,
    29, 30, 87–92, 96–7, 98,
    102–3, 108, 112, 160–1, 179
  occupation of Japan, 83, 92–4, 114,
    161, 212
  Pacific Asia phase, 122, 131–2,
    162–4
  Pacific War, 82, 90, 161
  and Philippines, 28, 54, 74–6, 102,
    123, 160, 236, 240
  relations with post-war Japan,
    114–15, 150, 162–3, 164, 166,
    178, 179, 255
  relations with pre-war Japan, 82
  role in modern world order, 141
  and South Korea, 118, 119, 166,
    178, 239
  and Taiwan, 98, 119, 120, 166,
    178, 239
  and Thailand, 103
  Vietnam embargo, 201
  Vietnam War, 12, 91, 107, 127–8,
    162, 253
  see also Bretton Woods system;
    North America; West
USSR see Soviet Union

van Wolferen, K., 129–30, 243
Vietnam
  agriculture, 26, 32
  and China, 47, 73
  conflict with Sukhothai kingdom, 48
  development experience, 201

human development index, 211
investment in, 128
and Japan, 242–3
membership of ASEAN, 128, 166,
    178
nation-building/cold war phase, 90,
    91, 107
nature of society, 215, 216
Pacific Asia phase, 127–8, 242–3
as part of French empire sphere, 27,
    47, 48, 73–4, 107
pre-contact phase, 25, 32, 47, 48
religion, 229
Vietnam War, 12, 90, 91, 107, 127–8,
    162, 253
Vogel, E., 121

Wade, R., 121
Walter, J., 76, 124
Waswo, A., 94, 95, 114
Weber, Max, 7, 219, 220, 229–30
welfarism, 8
West
    Asian resistance to political ideas of,
        144, 174
    clash with Japan, 79–83
    discipline and social order, 218
    geographical expansion of
    industrial-capitalism, 8, 18–20, 21,
        26–9, 51–2, 54–7, 59
    individualism, 195, 218, 219,
        220–1, 231, 254, 257
    Japanese colonialism, 59–60, 67, 68

trade expansion into China, 21, 25,
    26, 39, 46, 57, 58, 59
trade expansion into Japan, 25, 46,
    62, 77–9
trade expansion into
    Southeast Asia, 49, 68–9
    see also Europe; France; Netherlands;
        United Kingdom; United States
White Lotus Buddhist sect, 39
Whorf, Benjamin Lee, 228
Wilkinson, E., 148, 163
Wilson, Thomas Woodrow, 79
Wittgenstein, Ludwig, 234
work, stress on, 203
World Bank, 112, 116, 138
    institutional truths, 199
    market-liberal theory, 121, 192, 193,
        204–5
    promotion of free trade, 253
Worsley, P., 22, 35, 56, 220
WTO, 116, 138, 179

Yamato state, 42, 43
Yao Chia-wen, 120
Yasutomo, D., 117, 238
Yaun Dynasty, 38
Yayoi period, 42
Yi Dynasty, 40–1, 64, 65
Yi Sung-Kae, 40, 64
Yo Un-Hyong, 96
Yuan Shih-K'ai, 60, 104

Zysman, J., 138, 142, 143, 148–9,
    201, 202, 258